THE PAUL'S CROSS SERMONS

UNIVERSITY OF TORONTO DEPARTMENT OF ENGLISH

Studies and Texts, No. 6

A SERMON AT PAUL'S CROSS
Reproduced by permission of the Society of Antiquaries of London

The
Paul's Cross Sermons
1534-1642

MILLAR
MACLURE

—

UNIVERSITY OF TORONTO PRESS

COPYRIGHT ©, CANADA, 1958, BY
UNIVERSITY OF TORONTO PRESS
PRINTED IN CANADA
LONDON: OXFORD UNIVERSITY PRESS
Reprinted in 2018
ISBN 978-1-4875-7726-1 (paper)

Preface

THIS STUDY was originally undertaken as a special inquiry into the Elizabethan background comparable in method and supplementary to G. B. Harrison's *Elizabethan Journals*. Professor Harrison advised me in its first stages, and the Register of Sermons which serves as a semi-autonomous supplement to the text of this volume owes its form to his suggestions. Some of the materials collected were embodied in a doctor's thesis presented at the University of Toronto in 1949; since then the amount of source-material laid under contribution has been at least doubled, the whole study rewritten, and the original conclusions sharply revised.

The outdoor sermon, addressed to all estates in a place of public assembly, is a medieval institution of great historical importance. In this book I have set out to describe how that institution was transformed by political devices and theological conflict during and after the English Reformation. The Paul's Cross pulpit was as familiar and intimate a monument of pre-Cromwellian London as Nelson's column in the London of these days. The most serious issues affecting the destiny of England as she gradually separated herself from purely European relationships to assume a new existence as an Atlantic Protestant power were proclaimed and argued from that pulpit. There the pastors rebuked worldliness and proclaimed the acceptable day of the Lord; there they exercised their best powers of persuasion according to the traditional rules of rhetoric, and thundered their way into literary history. I have sought to describe and co-ordinate these various aspects of the Paul's Cross sermons.

I can claim no more for the result than that it is an adequate survey of the subject. It is not, indeed could not be, exhaustive. Given the facilities of travel to great libraries and of microfilm, it is not too difficult to lay one's hands on a representative if incomplete collection of printed sermons. But one has to depend for notices of sermons, and those often of greater historical interest than the printed effusions, upon the whims of diarists, fugitive allusions or abstracts in state papers and ecclesiastical documents, the intense but unscientific industry of the early church historians. I have not collected all these references, or nearly all; and some of those I have collected lack a context, or have perhaps been placed in a wrong context through ignorance or inaccessibility of source-material.

In order to avoid swamping the text in footnotes, and attaching a bibliography of works consulted which would prove no more than that I have like Robert Burton (though with much less imagination) "confusedly tumbled over the books in our libraries," I have set up, at the cost of considerable repetition, the Register of Sermons to serve three purposes: (1) to provide a journal of occasions at Paul's Cross over a century, which may be read independently or used as a reference work in chronology; (2) to serve as a substitute for many otherwise necessary footnotes; (3) in conjunction with the index of names, to fill the place of a short-title bibliography of published sermons.

Besides the debt to G. B. Harrison, already mentioned, I must here gratefully acknowledge the advice, encouragement, and practical assistance which I have received from various persons and institutions.

I owe most gratitude to A. S. P. Woodhouse, both for his careful and illuminating comments on my manuscript and for his long-continued interest in and support of this project. Among other colleagues in the University of Toronto who have helped me in various ways, I wish to thank especially H. S. Wilson and N. J. Endicott for many valuable suggestions and much friendly interest, and D. J. McDougall, for his contribution to my knowledge of Tudor and Stuart history.

I wish to acknowledge also the help given me at various times by the staffs of the University of Toronto Library, the Houghton Library at Harvard, Guildhall Library, and especially the Librarian of St. Paul's Cathedral.

In 1952 I had a travel grant from the Board of Regents of United College, Winnipeg, and I have had assistance also from the fund for research in the Humanities of the University of Toronto; a large number of sermons on microfilm was provided for me by the University of Toronto Library on the Department of English appropriation. The Humanities Research Council of Canada has assisted me with two grants in aid of research, in 1951 and 1952, and the publication of this book has been made possible partly by a generous grant in aid of publication from the same source. I should like to acknowledge also assistance from the Publications Fund of the University of Toronto Press.

In the preparation of the manuscript for the press, I have had the benefit of the expert and painstaking assistance of the Editorial Department of the University of Toronto Press.

M. M.

Victoria College in the
University of Toronto
October 4, 1957

NOTE ON QUOTATIONS

Quotations are given in the original spelling and punctuation, with the following exceptions: normalization of i, j and u, v; expansion of contractions with m, n; elimination of italics to conform with modern usage.

Contents

	PREFACE	v
I	ANTIQUARIAN	3
II	HISTORICAL	20
	1. Winds of Doctrine	20
	2. The Establishment and its Enemies	54
	3. Jacobean Interlude	88
	4. The Gathering Storm	107
III	SOCIOLOGICAL	116
IV	HOMILETIC	142
V	CONCLUSION	167
	NOTES	175
	A REGISTER OF SERMONS PREACHED AT PAUL'S CROSS, 1534–1642	184
	INDEX OF NAMES	257

THE PAUL'S CROSS SERMONS

Paul's Cross was a kind of Stone Tent, with leaden roof, at the N.E. corner of Paul's Cathedral, where sermons were . . . preached in the open air; crowded devout congregations gathering there, with forms to sit on, if you came early. . . . Paul's Cross, a kind of *Times Newspaper*, but edited partly by Heaven itself, was then a most important entity.

THOMAS CARLYLE
Letters and Speeches of Oliver Cromwell

"Paules Crosse, and the Crosse in Cheape"

Aurea cur Petro posita est crux, plumbea Paullo?
Paulinam decorant Aurea verba crucem.

JOHN OWEN

From this pulpit the human mind has been viewed in every possible variety. Unlike others, appropriated solely to the honours of the Divinity and support of Morality, it has been the stage for the essays of intrigue, politicks, defamation, curses, and confession of crimes; the support of preachers whose doctrines hanged some and burnt others.

J. P. MALCOLM
Londinium Redivivum

Paul's Cross, the Broadcasting House of that age.

DOM DAVID KNOWLES

It is a great and publique taske for the Lords Voices to cry unto a Citie.

FRANCIS WHITE
Londons Warning by Jerusalem

I ANTIQUARIAN

THE MOST FAMILIAR PICTURE of the preaching cross in St. Paul's churchyard (see Frontispiece) was originally executed, probably about 1616, for one Henry Farley, "a pious, disinterested and zealous person," who published more than one appeal for the repair of the Cathedral. In the caption usually attached to the engraving made for Wilkinson's *Londina Illustrata* (1811), the picture is described as

> an accurate delineation, the only Correct Vestige that remains of this Ancient and Curious Object, as it appeared on Sunday the 26th. of March, 1620; at which time it was visited by King James, the I; His Queen, and Charles, Prince of Wales; attended by the Archbishop of Canterbury, Bishops, Officers of State, Nobility, Ladies, &c. &c.; Who were received with great Magnificence by Sir William Cockaine, Lord Mayor of London; assisted by the Court of Aldermen, Recorder &c.; When a most excellent Sermon was preached from a text purposely selected by his Majesty, (Psalm CII, Verses 13:14) by Dr. John King; Bishop of London; recommending the speedy reparation of the Venerable Cathedral of St. Paul, which, with its unsteepled Tower, and incumberances of Houses &c. appear on the back, and side grounds.

But Queen Anne died in 1619, and it seems clear that the picture represents an ideal rather than an actual occasion.[1] It is indeed in some respects more icon than sketch, but nevertheless a treasury of significant details.

The Cross itself is an octagonal structure of wood, mounted on a stone base, with stone steps leading up to it, surmounted by an ogee-shaped roof, on which is set an ornamental cross. The whole structure is of a fourteenth-century memorial type. The preacher stands between two of the supporting pillars; to his right, prominently placed, is an hour-glass; on the wall beneath him is a coat of arms, which may be that of Thomas Kempe, fifteenth-century Bishop of London, under whose direction this cross was built. The cross is enclosed by a low wall of brick, within which sit a number of privileged persons.

The walls of the transept and choir, facing the cross, are built up with covered galleries, the "houses" as they were called, in which the dignitaries are seated: King, Queen, Prince of Wales, members of the Privy Council, the Lord Mayor and aldermen. The main body of the audience, unrealistically small, is seated on forms in something like a "garland or ring," as Bishop King termed it during his sermon of 1620. There is a solid group of what are presumably meant to be the crafts in their liveries, with a sprinkling of fine gentlemen and citizens' wives. To the left, two grooms hold the horses of gentlemen in the audience, and a mounting-block is placed there for their greater convenience. The men wear their hats, except for one personage who stands at the rear, his eye devoutly fixed on the preacher, and another in sweet converse with a lady. A noisy dog is being lashed by the verger; beyond him a Christianly charitable person drops a coin into a large poor box.

Above them all towers the ancient church of St. Paul, mute witness to the need for the Bishop's exhortation, with its tower lacking a steeple since the fire of 1561, stumpy and flat in contrast with the lift and surge of the windows. Beneath them, in the yard, lie the dead, layer upon layer. Beneath slept the memories of plague, above the prophecy of fire.

If we look at the scene as a whole, it reminds us of the Elizabethan theatre: groundlings and notables, pit and galleries, and, in the midst, the pulpit as stage. Indeed it was a theatre; to borrow a title from the young Spenser, "a Theatre, wherein be represented as wel the miseries and calamities that follow the voluptuous worldlings as also the greate joyes and pleasures which the faithfull do enjoy." Sermons, proclamations, processions, and penances were all theatrical, and many a preacher of the Puritan persuasion acknowledged and fulminated against the competition from the Bankside.

In what follows, by a survey of certain antiquities, I shall account for some of the details in the picture, and others not there included.

How long a cross stood upon this spot is unknown.[2] The cross probably antedates the erection of a church, and was perhaps set up at the entrance of an ancient burial ground, to remind the passers-by to pray for the dead there interred. In pre-Norman times, crosses were sometimes erected as memorials of a "preaching station" where the populace had been won to Christ, for example, by St. Kentigern (*fl.* 600). There is some quiet disagreement as to the form of the cross at St. Paul's in medieval times. It may have been a pillar raised upon a flight of steps, like the "Mercat" cross in Edinburgh, where officials might stand *super crucem*, as the documents put it, to make proclamations, or a proper preaching cross elevated *in cimiterio*, like those which survived in the churchyard of Hereford Cathedral and St. Frideswide's Priory, Oxford. Although some historians find evidence of assemblies at Paul's Cross from the twelfth century, the earliest documentary evidence of its use dates from 1241, when Henry III met the citizens of London there to consult with them about a projected visit to Gascony in connection with the French war. Paul's churchyard was anciently a place of popular assembly. From a writ *quo warranto* of 1287, dealing with a dispute between the King and the City authorities, it is evident that the citizens had been wont to hold folk-moot there, and the assembly of 1241 was probably a folk-moot, that is, a hundred court. Traditionally these gatherings were held at some marked place, such as a ford, a stone, a bridge, or a burial cross. In any case, when the Cross is first mentioned in surviving documents, it is rather a place of assembly for the hearing of proclamations than a preaching place.

Yet the use of the Cross for ecclesiastical purposes came about naturally through the proclamation there of bulls and other ecclesiastical instruments. A bull was published there in 1261, another in 1270. In 1299 the Dean of St. Paul's, *super crucem*, solemnly cursed a number of persons who had been excavating in the church of St. Martin's-in-the-Fields for hidden treasure. The earliest recorded instance of a sermon at Paul's Cross is of 1330, when William de Renham, Chancellor of St. Paul's, preached and rehearsed the sentence of excommunication upon Lewis of Bavaria, whose Italian adventure had sharpened the divisions within both Church and Empire. In 1356–7 a notable series of sermons against the mendicant orders was preached there by Richard Fitzralph, Archbishop of Armagh. By 1361 sermons at the Cross were apparently an institution; in that year Michael de Northburgh, Bishop of London, provided in his will one thousand marks for small loans, and the preacher at St. Paul's Cross was to announce the disposition of the pledge if any loan was not paid within a year.

The history of Paul's Cross comes down to us in the irregular way beloved of the diarist and contemned by the scientific historian. Crises and dramatic occurrences are recorded, with silences between the notable events. One such event is recorded from 1382, when the Cross was severely damaged by "a tempest of lightning"; in 1387 Archbishop Courtenay issued letters inviting contributions for restoration of the Cross, offering an indulgence of forty days. In the preamble of this appeal the Cross is referred to as "the High Cross in the greater churchyard of the church in London, where the word of God is habitually preached, both to Clergy and Laity, being a place very public and well known."[3] The Cross was repaired in consequence of this appeal, for there are notices of sermons there two years later; it may have been damaged in the "grete tempeste" of 1443; at any rate the structure of wood and stone which survived, with repairs and alterations, till 1643, was erected about 1449 through the efforts of Thomas Kempe, Bishop of London, who also provided a fund for the maintenance of sermons at that place.

The outdoor sermon, preached in a cemetery, is perhaps unattractive as well as unfamiliar to most of us. Some of the drawbacks were apparent even in the sixteenth century. In a characteristic reproof, at once personal and practical, Latimer noted the unsanitary condition of the place:

I do much marvel that London, being so rich a city, hath not a burying-place without; for, no doubt, it is an unwholesome thing to bury within the city, specially at such time when there is great sickness, so that many die together. I think, verily, that many a man taketh his death in Paul's churchyard, for I myself, when I have been there in some mornings to hear the sermons, have felt such an ill-favored, unwholesome savour, that I was the worse for it a great while after.[4]

But I have found no evidence of cessation of burial there, nor indeed any other reference to inconvenience suffered in those surroundings. The only reference to arrangements for the accommodation of the rank and file of the audience is a fugitive notice that in the earlier seventeenth century forms were rented at 1*d.*; on the other hand the London Corporation and other records[5] supply much information about provision for the comfort and convenience of dignitaries. In 1567 the gutter "whereby the rayne water falleth upon the offycers of the Cytie" was diverted, and their benches enlarged. In 1569, Sir Thomas Roe, the Lord Mayor, had built "at his own charges" a "house for the ladie mayres and other Ladies and Aldermans wives to heare the sermon"; at the same time the pulpit was moved one yard eastward. The brick wall of the 1620 picture was built in 1595. The pulpit was kept locked during such times as it was not in weekly use. There was a caretaker; at least in 1629 there was an old man "that belongs to the Cross."

Arrangements for the audience and for the upkeep of the Cross were not the only problems. The weather might be unseasonable, and the sermon cut short by a sudden squall. If the aspect of the heavens was ominous at sermon time, the sermon was preached in the Shrouds, that is, the crypt, though on at least one occasion in the Grey Friars.

One may suppose that the audience was small on a wet morning. It seems to have been exceedingly large on some occasions. The diarist Henry Machyn mentions, under 1553, "grett bars" placed at "evere gatt" of Paul's churchyard, for "grett throng of pepull." It is difficult to believe that as many as six thousand persons were sometimes present,[6] though Bishop King speaks of "many thousands of soules" at his sermon of thanksgiving for King James's recovery from sickness in 1619, and on various occasions the audience is described as "huge," notably to hear Bishop Gardiner defend himself against the Lord Protector Somerset in June 1548. Even that dour Puritan John Stockwood, while complaining that church-going was decayed, was forced to report that one would usually find "a reasonable company" at Paul's Cross. There is little doubt that Londoners went there who did not attend their own parish churches, and during the crucial early days of the Reformation attendance was mandatory, or at least strongly urged. Witness this item from the reminiscences of John Louthe:

A commandement was gyven that all curattes . . . should not be at sermones nor servyce longer than ix of the clocke, that then the curattes with the paryshes myght come to Poles crosse and heare the prechers. To this sayd this good curatt, I wyll . . . make an ende of service at the proscribed howr gladly, seing I muste needes so doo, But so longe as any of these heretykes preche at the Crosse as nowe adayes thei do, I wyll never here them, for I wyll not come there. I wyll rather hange.[7]

(The pious Louthe adds that "he did hange." The period was rich in such manifestations of special providence.)

The audience was not of Londoners only, since the Cross was an obvious place to visit for persons up from the country, and during Parliament and term times the auditory must have been all England in a little room. Not only Englishmen but foreigners found there spectacle and instruction, and Robert Sibthorpe said that it was the resort "of every nation under heaven."

In those days, when amplifiers were happily unknown, a preacher needed a big voice to reach all parts of such a large audience assembled in the open air. John Hales of Eton, a modest man of no great lung-power, confessed: "Seen I may be of many, but to be heard with any latitude and compass, my natural imperfection doth quite cut off." George Montaigne, Bishop of London, that "canary-sucking prelate," though famed as a wit, was inaudible to two-thirds of his audience when he preached there in 1622; but since part of his sermon was a lame defence of benevolences, it is perhaps not surprising that he mumbled.

Nor was the audience always quiet and attentive. There were some violent scenes at the Cross, when men's passions ran high upon matters of religion; of these the most notorious, recorded in every Protestant martyrology, was the riot of August 13, 1553, when Gilbert Bourne, Queen Mary's chaplain, was saved from an angry crowd by John Bradford and others. Not to speak of such scenes, there is evidence that many of the crowd walked about and talked during the sermon, with the manners of Paul's Walk, as Francis Marbury observed caustically in his sermon of June 1602, and there were those who came upon their own business. In *The Testament of Lawrence Lucifer* (1604), for instance, Benedick Bottomless, "most deep cutpurse," is licensed to ply his office "at Paul's Cross in the sermon time."

Often the audience must have grown restive under a long sermon. Many preachers were conscious that they might be, or had been, tedious, and apologized accordingly. Yet the patience of the sermon-goers, and their appetite for sermons, upon which modern historians never fail to comment, were truly remarkable. The customary length of a Paul's Cross sermon during the Tudor and Stuart period was two hours; the preacher usually turned the hour-glass twice. John Dove was witty upon the time, speaking of his "two hours discourse of this one and laste houre," and from a number of references it is clear that although one hour was permissible, more than two was not. George Benson, for instance, called to the Cross from his Worcestershire parish, wrote out a long sermon—"we country fellows cannot digest our matters by the clocke"—and because of the time limit had to cut off much and mangle the rest in delivery. Often the preacher, one eye on the hour-glass, had to scamp the latter parts of an elaborate "division" of his text.

As for the other elements in the service, an opening prayer was customary, and of course a closing prayer. After the return of the Marian exiles the fashion of congregational psalm-singing began at those assemblies. How long this singing "Genevay ways" continued I do not know.

The institution of "Spital" and Rehearsal sermons is best described in Stow's words:

A part of the large churchyard pertaining to [St. Mary's] hospital [without Bishopsgate] yet remaineth as of old time, with a pulpit cross therein. . . . And here is to be noted, that, time out of mind, it hath been a laudable custom, that on Good Friday, in the afternoon, some especial learned man, by appointment of the prelates, hath preached a sermon at Paules Crosse, treating of Christ's Passion; and upon the three next Easter holidays, Monday, Tuesday, and Wednesday, the like learned men, by the like appointment, have used to preach on the forenoons at the said Spittle, to persuade the article of Christ's resurrection; and then on Low Sunday, one other learned man at Paules cross, to make rehearsal of these four former sermons, either commending or reproving them. . . . And that done, he was to make a sermon of his own study, which in all were five sermons in one. At these sermons . . . the mayor, with his brethren the aldermen, were accustomed to be present in their violets at Paules on Good Friday, and their scarlets at the Spittle in the holidays, except Wednesday in violet, and the mayor with his brethren on Low Sunday in scarlet, at Paules Cross, continued until this day.[8]

The Rehearsal sermons for 1559, 1560, and 1562 were preached by Thomas Sampson, "in regard of his excellent elocution and memory." The Rehearsal sermon for 1614, by John Hoskins, is extant, and illustrates the preacher's procedure on these occasions. First he summarized the "Spittle" sermons, in what he called "my harsh abridgments of those delightful treatises," and continued that it was high time "to blesse you with a dismission, or to dismisse you with a blessing, did not custome rather . . . heere command mee only to mention . . . some passage of holy Scripture for conclusion." He lighted on a proper text for the purpose, Isaiah 62:6, concerning the Lord's "remembrancers," and expatiated at considerable length.[9]

In addition to these Eastertime sermons, there were special sermons in Whitsun week, on Monday, Tuesday, and sometimes Wednesday, for which it was ordered that "not only my Lord Mayor and Aldermen to be there in scarlet for Whitsun Sunday and Monday, and in violet of Tuesdays, but their wives to be there . . . in such apparel as they like."[10]

From these records emerges a glimpse of that great age, at once intimate and strange, of a fat alderman struggling into his scarlet, angrily asking his wife where she has mislaid his points, while she decked herself in such apparel as she liked—

> It is ful fair to been ycleped "madame."

The colour and grace and form of the scene was not for show alone. The idea of each man in his place, properly attired, had not died by any means; the solid burgher, fat with gains from wool and wine, dreaming perhaps of land and a great house, was still a member of a stable body politic which was also in its way a work of art, and as such appeared in his hallowed place upon the great festivals of the Church.

There were other occasions for procession, pageantry, and formal assemblage at Paul's Cross. Such were the anniversaries of the sovereign's accession: of Elizabeth, November 17; of James I, March 24; of Charles I, March 27. The anniversary of the Powder Plot was a "holy day" with a special sermon opening the horrors of the Papists; in the reign of James, August 5, the day of the Gowrie conspiracy, was commemorated at the Cross, and in those sermons the adulation of the "English Solomon" was especially fulsome. A visit from the monarch was above all to be remembered. Philip II was there on December 2, 1554, to hear Gardiner proclaim the re-admission of the realm into Catholic Christendom; Elizabeth appeared in state on November 24, 1588, the occasion of the last of a series of thanksgiving sermons for the defeat of the Armada; James graced the scene in 1620.

It has been noted how from the beginning Paul's Cross was a place for the reading of proclamations. In the Tudor period proclamation became propaganda, and the process is most instructive; but simple proclamations and indeed news reports were still delivered there. The sermon of thanksgiving for the rout of the French at St. Quentin was also a news "broadcast," since the preacher "declared how many wher taken, and what nobullmen they were." News and propaganda were nicely combined in William Barlow's announcement, on March 1, 1601, of the sayings of Essex before his execution. One kind of announcement from this pulpit deserves special notice; this is the appeal for the poor, or for discharged soldiers and prisoners of war. In 1538, for instance, it is recorded that two persons stood at every gate of the churchyard to collect money for the relief of the poor of London, and that a register was kept of the disbursements. Collections were taken in 1582 for the relief of English captives of the Turks, and in 1586 the preachers were ordered by the Bishop of London to recommend to the audience the distressed estate of maimed begging soldiers who had lost their limbs in the Low Countries. In 1590, a collection was taken for the relief of John Battaie, Michael Hornat, and Matthias Petrus, Hungarian prisoners of the Turks unable to pay their ransoms. About Easter 1601, a collection was taken there for the redemption of captives in Barbary.[11] Christendom was still united against the infidel.

Some escaped both sermon and collection, as a Marian pamphleteer sharply observed: "If there be a sermon at Paules crosse, after they have taried there a while, to here some newes, and the preacher at the prayers, lorde how they vanishe away in clusters, repairing into Paules, and either by and sell some bargaine in the body of the churche, or els telle some tale of an Asses Shadowes."[12]

Who, under ordinary circumstances, were the preachers? How were they escoted?

Newcourt is the main authority on this point:

The Persons that are to preach these Sermons, are from time to time appointed by the Bishop of London, and are chosen out of such as either have been or are of either of our Universities, by turns: They have usually about a Months notice before; and had each of them 45s. as a Reward, and Four days Diet and Lodging, at the House of such Person as the Bishop did appoint, who is commonly called the Shunamite, who, for the same was allow'd 15s. per Week. But the Preachers' Reward is now [1700] reduced to 35s. paid by the City, and 5s. by the Church [of St. Paul's].[13]

The title-pages and dedicatory epistles of many published Paul's Cross sermons show that the preachers were often young men down from the universities to make their mark; these sermons provide a remarkable collection of juvenilia.

There had always been a fund out of which the preachers were paid, but whether it had been discontinued, or had shrunk in real value, by about 1581 it needed to be re-established. John Aylmer, Bishop of London, was foremost in this worthy effort; the City fathers, however, showed no spirit of co-operation. Laurence Dyos, preaching at the

Cross in September 1581, attacked them for failing to respond to the Bishop's appeal for funds, asserting "that if the appointment of preachers were committed to them, they would appoint such as would defend usury, the family of love, and puritanism" (the court of aldermen did dispute with the Bishop of London the right to appoint the "Spittle" preachers). Other appeals for the preachers' maintenance were made in the years following. William Fisher, in October 1591, broke off the ordinary course of his sermon to call for "a necessary Benevolence, and a Christian subsidy, to be supplyed in respect of the Godly preachers, called . . . from both the universities," who had to come when summoned "at their owne great cost and charge." And A. W., in the next year, told the City authorities that "they that come from far to this place, with great labour and to their cost, are little regarded or thought upon." Finally, about 1594, the fund was established from which the customary payments were afterwards made. Bishop Aylmer left £300, plus £1,000 committed to his charge by Elizabeth, Countess of Shrewsbury; Stephen Forster, then Mayor of London, contributed £40. Other bequests were added in later years, for example, £200 in 1615 by "Dr. Ratcliffe de Grayes Inn." The total endowment seems to have been about £1,770, besides rent charges annually of £44. 6s. 8d.[14] After 1594, there were few complaints from the preachers; indeed it became the custom for them to pay tribute in their sermons to the three outstanding contributors to the endowment: Aylmer, Bess of Hardwick, and Thomas Russell, Citizen of London: "All these . . . had this care . . . , that the feet of the Saints should not be unwashed . . . that the fighters of the Lords battels, should be refreshed with a competencie of bread and wine . . . , that the Prophets should not want a chamber and more than so, a table; and more yet, a candlestick."[15]

Of all the arrangements for the stipend and lodging of Paul's Cross preachers, the house of the Shunamite is alone well known, and that justly, for it has been immortalized by a good man and a fine stylist. The mistakes Walton unwittingly made about the character of Mrs. Churchman, who nursed "Mr. Hooker" through a cold so that he could preach at the Cross, and then cursed him with her daughter, have been corrected by Professor Sisson,[16] but it is from Walton that we get the unforgettable picture of the student summoned from his college, where he had been pursuing his studies "with all quietness," arriving in London wet and miserable, but ready to dare Calvin with quiet logic.

The preachers were, however, by no means always fresh from the universities. Many of them were rectors or curates of City churches; some were officials in the various dioceses or in the universities; the Lady Margaret lecturers in divinity were required by their statute to preach at Paul's Cross every two years; preaching there was the duty and privilege of the canons and prebendaries of the cathedral. These were routine appointments. At certain seasons, and for special occasions, more distinguished talent was called up. Bishops always preached in "the Parliament time." They were present for the session, and could be used to declare the mind of the government in matters ecclesiastical, as they did during the critical sessions of 1534 and 1571. The Bishop of London preached there more than any other prelate, at ordinary and special times, since Paul's Cross was the most important pulpit in his diocese; Bishop Aylmer called it "my chaire." Lenten sermons were important, and prominent ecclesiastics preached there every Lent.

The appointment of preachers was ordinarily within the power of the Bishop of London, and theoretically he acted in this matter on his own discretion. There is extant one of Laud's letters of appointment, for November 29, 1629, which illustrates the procedure:

You shall understand that you are appointed to preach at St. Paul's Crosse on Sunday the 29 of November next ensuinge. . . . These are therefore to require and charge you not to faile of your day appointed, and to send your answer of acceptance hereof in writing to my Chaplaine . . . and to bring a Coppie of your Sermon with you, and not to exceede an houre and a halfe in both Sermon and Praier. As also to certifie your presence some time on Thursday before your day appointed to John Fleming Draper in Watling street at whose House your entertainment is provided.[17]

It is probable that Laud, while Bishop of London, shortened the time of the sermons; he was not given to lengthy sermons himself; he distrusted the extravagant use of the pulpit: the shorter the time the less chance of sedition. The order to produce a copy of the sermon in advance is also rather an indication of Laud's tight discipline than of general practice in the past. At this time Laud was busy reforming the diocese after the slack administration of Bishop Montaigne, and he feared lest a Puritan lecturer should steal upon him in sheep's clothing. The preacher is required to be on hand well in advance, presumably to receive last-minute instructions from the ordinary. The peremptory tone of the letter is not, however, purely Laudian. A summons to the Cross was always mandatory, and many preachers could doubtless echo the complaint of Miles Mosse, author of the *Arraignment of Usury*, who, unable to get a substitute and fearful of the consequences of refusal, came up to preach in the midst of a painful sickness.

The Bishop of London might be approached by some influential person on behalf of a protégé (the Earl of Hertford, for example, secured for his chaplain John Pelling a morning at the Cross in 1607). In times of crisis he never made his appointments without the advice and direction of the Council. Paul's Cross was always potentially and often in fact the mouthpiece of the administration. During the critical years after 1533 Cromwell and Cranmer personally directed much of the propaganda for the Henrician Reformation which was disseminated from that pulpit; in 1551 the Bishop of London was instructed by the Council to send the preacher appointed for October 25 to receive his instructions directly from them. During the vestiarian controversy in 1565–6, Cecil sent Archbishop Parker a "bill" of preachers for the Cross. It is well known that the preachers were briefed very carefully at the time of the Essex rebellion and the executions which followed, and in another emergency, the Sunday after the discovery of the Powder Plot, William Barlow, who had served so manfully as mouthpiece in 1601, was again pressed into service, preaching upon direct instructions from the Council, and relying for his facts upon "divers circumstances sensibly conceived and imparted . . . over night by the Earle of Salisbury."

No matter how tight the control of appointments, there was still the possibility that the preacher, once on his feet before the multitude, would grossly disappoint those who had called him to that place. Consider, for example, the difficulties of Bishop Sandys with Mr. Crick and Mr. Wake in 1573. The former was chaplain to the Bishop of Norwich (who did, it is true, encourage nonconformity in his diocese), the latter had "made a good sermon" the previous year; and in addition both had been warned in person by Sandys, and seemed to assent to his wishes, though somewhat non-committal. Yet to Sandys' disgust they both preached pure Cartwright. Even under the firm hand of Bishop Bancroft, assisted by Cecil, there were troubles in 1599 with Cambridge men who favoured the Earl of Essex, touching on matters of state not their concern, and excusing their behaviour, legally, as Bancroft was forced to admit, by contending that they were supposed to pray for their Chancellor when they came to the Cross. Other embarrassments occurred in the reign of James. John Drope of Magdalen, preaching in 1617, complained of the King's unjust impositions, and was "called in question" for it. About June 1619 Isaac Singleton was committed for railing in his sermon against the Lord Chancellor Bacon's court, and touching somewhat scandalously on the Lord Chancellor's private life. Although James had ordered that the clergy should not meddle with state matters, a "young fellow" spoke, on December 17, 1620, "very freely in general" against the negotiations with Spain; a Mr. Wilson did likewise in 1623. There were daring and intemperate spirits among the clergy, and these were not necessarily Puritans. One such was happily forestalled in 1620. The Council discovered that William Clough, vicar of Bramham, had said that "The King was a fool, and fit for nothing but catching dotterels; the Lord President was a fool, only fit for gaming; the north was governed by an old doting bishop, &c; also that he would get leave to preach at Paul's Cross, and would expose the evils of government."[18] He was likely in his cups, and would not have gone through with it anyway, but the remark illustrates the importance of the Paul's Cross pulpit.

The continuance of the ritual of public penance or recantation at Paul's Cross is one of the most interesting aspects of the history of the Cross between the Reformation and the Long Parliament, for it indicates a conception of the body politic little emphasized—indeed often entirely overlooked—in social histories of the age; it goes to make up the immense complexity of a highly active and revolutionary society which nevertheless in many important respects never broke with the past. The appearance before a public pulpit of penitents in white sheets, bearing tapers or faggots as they were execrated by the preacher, is the sort of phenomenon which one loosely calls "medieval." Is this the age of Shakespeare and Bacon, of Harvey and Milton? It is. One historian of sermons[19] assumes that these spectacles, which were no doubt one of the "sights" of Elizabethan and Jacobean London, were very funny at the time. "Profane persons" (Fuller's phrase) were probably amused, but it is certain that the ecclesiastical authorities would not have continued to order these performances if the effect had not been, in general, salutary. Public penance was an expression of the continuing ideal of the Christian society, in which the commons are directed by wise and righteous governors for the weal of the body politic. The heretic and the malefactor must be rooted out, and by such example made of them the diseases of the body politic are exposed and in a manner exorcised. It is indeed a "medieval" idea, and it is visibly expressed in the very symbolism of apparel and action which informs the moralities. I have spoken of the preaching place as a kind of theatre. A sermon at Paul's Cross, accompanied by the speech and act of the penitent, was a morality play, or rather life exhibited as morality.

There are several variations in the ritual prescribed. The penitent heretic stood "in the verie eye of the multitude," before the preacher, wearing a white sheet, carrying faggots and a taper, signifying the death by burning which he deserved and often suffered. If pardoned he wore thereafter a badge representing a faggot in flames. Archbishop Grindal's directions for public penance in churches prescribe a sermon or homily (usually though not necessarily on the sin of the penitent), the position of the offender "directly over against the pulpit," and public interrogation of the penitent by the preacher. I find no example of this interrogation at Paul's Cross, but the penitent either repeated his form of penance after the preacher or delivered it himself from a prepared text. Sometimes the preacher struck the penitents as he "showed their oppynyons," and in these cases the penitent appeared with the rod of correction in his hand. The sermon itself was often a recantation, and writers of heretical and "naughty" books were required to cut them in pieces before the audience.[20]

For a century after the Reformation heretics, schismatics, and "mechanic preachers" published their errors at Paul's Cross. In 1544 Robert Warde of Thapstead confessed:

Good people ye shall understand that wanting . . . bothe experience wytte and learnynge I have dyverse tymes in alehouses and uncomelie and unmeate places taken upon me to bable talke and rangle of the Scripture whiche I understode not yea and to expounde it after my folyshe fantasie chieflie these tymes when I have not ben myne owne man but over come with Ale.

He besought the people to take example by him "tavoyde and not to fall into the lyke sayenges and doynges." In 1627 John Hetherington of Putney, a boxmaker, confessed to attendance at prohibited conventicles, to expounding Scripture at those assemblies, and to belief in certain Familist doctrines. The preacher, Stephen Denison, improved the occasion by making a survey of "the severall kinds of Mysticall Wolves breeding in ENGLAND." Penance at the Cross was an accepted punishment for seditious utterances. Sir Richard Wynne, who was in the entourage of Prince Charles when he visited Spain in 1623, hearing a Jesuit preaching against Queen Elizabeth, observed "that it made our ears glow to hear him, wishing he had stood at Paul's Cross."

Penance was enjoined for a wide variety of offences. It was a powerful weapon against scandal, which is best silenced by humiliating its authors. In November 1561 the diarist Henry Machyn was forced to do penance, "for alle ys fryndes that he had worshiphulle," for spreading the story that the Calvinist preacher John Veron had been "taken with a wenche." At some time between 1561 and 1580 John Cooke, registrar of the diocese of Winchester, instructed the boys of Winchester school to say that, being in a tree, they should see the Bishop of Winchester (Horne) commit adultery under the tree (some confused reminiscence of the *Canterbury Tales* is embalmed in this record). He was adjudged to "stande at Poles crosse, and to declare and preche there hys owne shame; but with owt blushyng, for hys . . . Croydon complexyone wolde not suffer hym to blushe, moe then the black dogge of Bungey."[21] Penance was enjoined for pretence of demonic possession, and especially for offences against the marriage laws. In 1541 two priests did penance for performing an illegal marriage; there was another such penance in 1559. A man did penance for bigamy in 1560. On March 13, 1586, there stood before the preacher "a most heinous malefactor in a white sheet," whose mistress had been executed for the murder of their misbegotten children. He made open confession of his fault, and the preacher "tooke occasion to aggravat the dangerous sinne of fornication and adulterie," and spoke "verie honourable of the dignitie of marriage, and against the frequented vice of usury." Usury forsooth. Penances imposed by the ecclesiastical courts for indecency and immorality continued to be performed at the Cross until the 1630's. Moll Cutpurse, sentenced in 1612 in the Court of Arches to do penance for wearing indecent and manly apparel, made a farce of the proceedings, "beeing discovered to have tipled of three quarts of sacke before she came to do her penaunce." In November 1618 Lady Markham did penance in a sheet for going through a form of marriage with a servant, her husband being still alive; in 1625 Sir Robert Howard was publicly excommunicated at the Cross for contempt of the Court of High Commission, then engaged upon proceedings against Lady Purbeck, with whom he was living in adultery; in 1631 Sir Giles Alington did penance for marriage within the table of kindred and affinity. One suspects the influence of Laud in this reinvigoration of the ancient custom.[22]

Heretical and seditious books were burned at Paul's Cross from time to time. Sometimes, as when Thomas Becon recanted his heresies in 1543, the penitent tore up his own books upon the fire; or the burning might be accompanied with a profitable exhortation, such as that of Bishop Montaigne at the burning of Paraeus' dangerous works upon limitation of sovereignty in 1622.

"Paul's Cross sermons" continued after the Restoration, but they were preached in the Cathedral. (After the burning of old St. Paul's in 1666, the sermons were removed temporarily to St. Katherine Cree church, the Guildhall Chapel, and St. Mary le Bow.) "Bills" of Paul's Cross preachers exist in eighteenth-century ecclesiastical documents; later the endowment was assimilated into the fund for the Sunday morning preachers in St. Paul's.[23]

Sermons were not preached in the churchyard after 1633. In 1635 the vergers of St. Paul's petitioned the Dean of the Arches that the sum of 12*d.* weekly, bequeathed by Mr. Thomas Chapman, to be paid to "some fitt person to keepe sweete cleane and decent the preaching place of Paules Crosse," should be paid to those who performed similar services within the church. There is also an entry in the charge books of St. Paul's for June 1635 which records payments to labourers to carry away "the Lead, Timber, &c. that were pull'd downe of the Roomes where the Prebends of the Church, the Doctors of the Law, and the Parishioners of St. ffaith's did sett to heare Sermons at St. Paul's Crosse."[24] On July 17 of that year, Thomas Drant of Shaston preached in the church on the Paul's Cross foundation, and other title-pages of the time confirm this arrangement. The last episcopally appointed royalist sermon "preached at Pauls Crosse" which I have found is the accession day sermon of 1642 (March 27), by Richard Gardiner, canon of Christ Church. On September 16, 1642, the House of Commons set up a committee to prepare an order for appointing preachers "at Paul's Cross," and in the following May an ordinance was passed enabling the Lord Mayor to appoint the preachers. The preaching place is spoken of at that time as not "prepared & fitted," and presumably the preachers were to speak in the Cathedral or elsewhere.[25]

Until 1643 the Cross itself, silent now after so many centuries, still stood. It was demolished in that year, presumably under the general authority of an "Ordinance for removing Images, Altars, &c., out of Churches."[26] The foundations of the Cross were uncovered by F. C. Penrose in 1879; the north wall of Wren's church is practically on the line of the south side of the Cross.[27] In the northeast triangle of the churchyard, a few yards from where the Cross stood, the visitor now finds a memorial cross of some dignity, erected about forty years ago under the will of H. C. Richards, M.P. The inscription reads, in part:

On this plot of ground stood of old "Paul's Cross" whereat amid such scenes of good and evil as make up human affairs the conscience of church and nation through five centuries found public utterance.

II HISTORICAL

1. *Winds of Doctrine*

THE PULPIT in Paul's churchyard was the most important vehicle of persuasion used by the government during the period 1534–1554. What we now call the "official line" in matters ecclesiastical was promulgated at the Cross; if there were changes and inconsistencies in the policies, there was a corresponding access of vehemence and sometimes subtlety in the presentation. With that nice sense of continuity, real or feigned, which animates the statutes of the Reformation Parliament, Henry VIII and his servants availed themselves of the ancient tradition of that pulpit as a place for the exhibition of error and the proclamation of the royal will. Scattered fifteenth-century references show that Paul's Cross had been a powerful instrument for the suppression of Lollard doctrines: Wycliffe's works were burned there in 1413; the library of Sir John Oldcastle, in which the heads and names of saints had been obliterated, was exhibited there in 1417; in 1495 "iiij Lollers" did penance "wt the bookes of their lore hangyng abowte them." The claims of Edward IV and of Richard III to the crown of England were, in scambling and unquiet times, set forth there.[1] Yet through all vicissitudes one doctrine only, the faith of Catholic Christendom, had been preached in that churchyard. Now, from 1533 onward, the Cross became a veritable chamber of Aeolus, from which proceeded violent winds of doctrine, Catholic, Lutheran, "Anglican," Calvinist. It is no wonder that by 1559 the nation was ready for the Elizabethan settlement, that triumph of expediency over all forms and conditions of zeal.

What the constitutional historians have decided concerning the nature of the English Reformation and its place in the traditions of the common and civil law, the theories of kingship adumbrated in the statutes of the Reformation Parliament and their relation to the theories of Marsilius of Padua or Luther, is for the most part irrelevant to the material here considered. For the revolution which Henry VIII sponsored and directed with such Machiavellian skill was not manifest, at the time, in any such terms. Even the lawyers who drafted, with such profuse and canny verbiage, the preambles to the statutes worked with only that deceptive consistency which is the product of expediency. The preachers, like Cuthbert Tunstall, who in the 1520's spoke from Paul's Cross against heresy upon the ancient assumptions of the Catholic faith, and found themselves defending the King's courses in the 1530's, were servants and not masters of their theories. Theory was, like all else, invalid before the royal will, whose dictates, brutal or subtle, swept now one party, now the other, into prominence or into the shadows. Moreover the issues, as they were set forth from a popular pulpit, could be delivered, either before or after the separation from Rome, only in the familiar terms of heresy or the still more familiar terms of slander. Neither as they were presented, nor in any summation or analysis of them, can these events be divorced from the personalities or particular events in the lineaments of which they appeared.

Yet though one cannot with any confidence find in every incident the evidence for a simple and consistent pattern, even the dullest member of the auditory at Paul's Cross, as he listened to fulminations against the two great dangers of the time, heresy and treason, must have perceived, between say 1526 and 1536, a fundamental change in view, proceeding from the basic change in the relations of church and state. The nature of this change, often misunderstood, is best defined, not by reference to the theories of medieval canonists or even to *The Obedience of a Christian Man*, but by consideration of feudal "rights." The very essence of feudalism was the fusion of public and private rights; wrongs against individuals and corporations possessed of certain "liberties" were not distinguished from crimes. The early Tudors engaged to release England from these "liberties," whether secular of the magnates, or ecclesiastical of the church, and in this process the sweeping acts of Henry VIII in Parliament which we call the English

Reformation were episodes in a larger process of making the Crown in Parliament omnicompetent in the realm.² The medieval church in England was not a "national" church in the modern sense; it became a national church when England became a national state. Now as this applied to heresy, it meant that the determination of heresy rested with a national church, in which, even if its Supreme Head did not (so it appeared) claim *potestas ordinis*, he exercised absolute legal control, either in his own person or in Parliament (here authorities differed) over those who did claim it. As for slander, slander became treason, either directly as it was slander of the supremacy or its ministers, or indirectly as it disturbed, or could be shown to have disturbed, the peace of the whole realm. This citizen in the Paul's Cross audience found that his own loyalties were ultimately owing to one authority, not two or three, that definitions were at once clearer—hence more useful for propaganda purposes—and at the same time more dangerous. He was not, as Foxe would have had his readers believe, bathed in the light of the Gospel, and persecuted by reactionary churchmen for taking advantage of his rights under a system of reformed belief and practice, but rather carried about upon every wind of doctrine, as the national policy in its various practical expedients to ensure the survival of the national experiment veered now one way and now the other.

A survey of some notices of sermons at Paul's Cross in the decade before 1533 discloses that the two main worries of the ecclesiastical authorities were the spread of the Lutheran heresy and the activities of translators of the Scriptures. It is instructive to note how uncomplicated the issues appeared in comparison with their ambiguity during the first years of the "English Schism." The campaign against Luther was officially opened on May 12, 1521, when, with Wolsey present in great state, John Fisher, Bishop of Rochester, condemned the doctrines of Luther as heretical and pernicious, declaring that in burning the Pope's bull, Luther had clearly shown that he would have burned the Pope too had he been able.³ This saying was not forgotten when, a few years later, Tyndale's New Testament was similarly attacked, and Tyndale observed that the bishops, in burning Christ's Word, had shown that they would willingly have burned also its divine author.⁴ (The extreme reformers were given to such exasperating exhibitions of analogy *quae non sequitur*.) Some Lutheran books were burned in the churchyard during the sermon. In February 1526 Fisher again preached against Luther at Paul's Cross; on this occasion five persons did penance for Lutheran heresy, four "Easterlings" and Dr. Robert Barnes, prior of the Augustinian friars at Cambridge, whose troubles in that churchyard were just beginning.[5] In that same year, through the efforts of London merchants of Protestant sympathies and with continental business connections, began the circulation of Tyndale's New Testament, that translation in which the text itself became a vehicle for controversy. In October, Tunstall preached at Paul's Cross against the book as "naughtily translated." Some copies were burned publicly there in 1530, having been bought up by Tunstall for confiscation.[6]

The New Testament was not the only heretical book current in England in those years. In 1531, the first Sunday in Advent, the preacher at the Cross, on the authority of John Stokesley, then Bishop of London, forbade the reading of some thirty heretical books in English, some of which, though with the colophons of continental printers, were probably printed in London. Besides Tyndale's book, this group of prohibited and dangerous works included a Psalter, Simon Fish's *Supplication of the Beggars* (one of the most radical works of the period, since it virtually recommended the dissolution of the whole church establishment), a book called the Burying of the Mass, the "Books of Moses" (apparently Coverdale's translation of the Pentateuch), the "ABC against the Clergy," a book against St. Thomas of Canterbury, a Disputation of Purgatory, and the "Practice of Prelates."[7] How wide a circulation these pamphlets had it is hard to say. Nor is it possible to guess with any assurance the extent to which the King already had assessed the true outcome of his negotiations with the Pope, and expecting failure was encouraging the spread of such works to prepare the minds of some at least of his subjects for the changes to come. It has been said that he kept Fish's inflammatory book in his desk, and the record shows that he studied it to some purpose. The pardon of the clergy of both provinces for being in a *praemunire,* which cost them £118,840, was ominous; but the first Act of Annates, of 1532, was held in abeyance in the expressed hope of a full agreement with the Pope. In 1533, however, came the notable Statute of Appeals (24 Hen. VIII, c. 12), which repudiated the papal jurisdiction and asserted that England was an "empire," alleging historical precedent for that term and its implications.

The need for the most virile exercise of persuasion now became clear. At Easter, when Dr. George Browne, prior of the Austin friars, prayed for Queen Anne at the Cross, nearly all the congregation left the place in protest. The "night-crow" was detested by the people at large.[8] On July 4 the Pope excommunicated Henry, and towards the end of the year the Council ordered that none should preach at Paul's Cross without declaring that the authority of the Bishop of Rome was no greater than that of any other foreign bishop.

Before turning to the methods used in preaching the supremacy, it is necessary to make some mention at least of the *cause célèbre* of 1533, the case of the so-called Holy Maid of Kent, Elizabeth Barton, who had long had a reputation for sanctity. While still a serving-maid at Aldington, she had had trances in which, she asserted, she had visions and revelations from the Virgin. She was installed by Dr. Edward Bocking, a monk of Canterbury, in the convent of St. Sepulchre's in that town, and in her fits of prophecy she said that she had seen the place in hell prepared for the King should he proceed in his courses. She was apparently becoming the dupe of certain persons who were using her for political ends, though Warham and Fisher were, it would seem, persuaded of the validity of her visions. She did public penance, with nine of her associates, at the Cross on November 23, 1533, when the sermon was preached by John Salcot [Capon], Bishop-elect of Bangor. "The object of this comedy," wrote Chapuys, the Imperial ambassador, "was to blot out of people's minds the impression they have that the Nun is a saint and a prophet."[9] A conspiracy had been contrived, said the preacher,

not only to put our most noble sovereign in danger of his realm and crown, and the nobles and commons of this realm in continual strife, dissension, and mutual effusion of blood, but also to distain his Grace's renown and fame in time to come, as though his Grace had been the most wicked and detestable prince that ever reigned in this world hitherto.

This was putting it rather strong, to say the least. Having so prepared his audience for disclosures of horrible enormities, he reviewed the case, insinuating that the Nun was incontinent, and a dupe; he advanced the astounding contention that "under this manner, by false visions and relevations of the nun, hath grown the great sticking, staying, and delaying of this the King's Grace's marriage." This seems a crude performance, illogical, full of wild statements and proceeding by faulty inference and unjustified innuendo, but it should be remembered that when officialdom makes the most of a good thing for propaganda purposes the result is likely to be something like this, in any age. The Nun was a focus of disaffection until her execution the next April; apparently a sermon casting doubts on the official view of the case was preached at the Cross early in 1534.[10]

Once committed to the policy of establishing the absolute supremacy of the Crown in matters spiritual in the realm, the government found it necessary to instruct the people in the new doctrine. The two chief means used were the press and the pulpit, and although the possibilities of the former were exploited to a degree unequalled until the Puritan revolution, the pulpit was all-important, and especially in London, where the chief preaching place in the city became the most important weapon of the reformers. Preachers at Paul's Cross were ordered to declare, Sunday after Sunday,

that he that now called himself Pope, and any of his predecessors, is and were only Bishops of Rome, and have no more authority or jurisdiction, by God's laws, within this realm, than any other bishop had, which is nothing at all; and that such authority as he has claimed heretofore has been only by usurpation and sufferance of the Princes of this realm.[11]

To these asseverations was sometimes added the "proof" that the Pope is Antichrist, or the statement that the power of the civil magistrate in causes ecclesiastical has from the beginning been of God's ordinance.

These were the doctrines set forth by the bishops of the Henrician church in 1534 and 1536, at Paul's Cross; they were the doctrines of the treatise *De vera differentia* (1534) and of the *Necessary Doctrine and Erudition for any Christian Man* (1543). From them emerged a new definition of *ecclesia,* with profound effects upon English theology and English politics. But at the time those long-range results were for the most part hidden, not only from the laity who stood in Paul's churchyard and elsewhere under the apologists of the new dispensation, but from the clergy themselves. For though what the King had secured was clear enough in the light of jurisdiction, it was by no means clear in the light of Catholic doctrine, and the preachers spoke accordingly from the midst of a dangerous confusion. As early as Easter 1534 Cranmer was forced to inhibit preaching which tended to the slander of Catholic doctrine, and on April 26 of that year John Stokesley, Bishop of London, preached at the Cross on the virtue of masses. Some clerics were willing to go far, to see the spirit of Protestantism in the letter of the statutes (as a matter of fact, there was, beyond some pious persiflage, no religious spirit of any kind in those statutes). Among these was John Hilsey,

> which sometyme was a blacke fryer [Dominican], and came from Bristowe, and was [in 1533] Pryor of the Blacke Fryers in London [sic], and was one of them that was a great setter forth of the syncerity of Scripture.

He was appointed in April 1534 the provincial of his order, and commissioner with Dr. George Browne to visit the friaries. Their visitation was unpopular, and was denounced by the Pilgrims of Grace. He succeeded to the see of Rochester on the execution of Fisher in 1535. The chronicler continues:

> [Hilsey] occupied preachinge most at Pawles Crosse of any bishopp, and in all the seditious tyme, when any abuse should be shewed to the people eyther of idolatrye or of the Bishop of Rome, he had the doeynge thereof by the Lord Vicegerentes [Cromwell's] commaundement from the Kinge, and allso had the admission of the preachers at Pawles Crosse theise 3 yeares and more.[12]

These simple phrases conceal the muddled story of the contention between Hilsey and Stokesley, Bishop of London, for the command of the Cross preachers, a contention sharpened by Hilsey's radical reforming tendencies and Stokesley's orthodoxy.

By 1536 the official line for preachers to follow was set down with some coherence, more, one suspects, from motives of *realpolitik* than from "the syncerity of Scripture." The smaller religious foundations were to be suppressed, and the Imperial ambassador shrewdly suspected that the purpose of the course of important sermons at the Cross in Lent was to persuade the people there was no purgatory, for these foundations were endowed to say masses for the dead. A fairly full if occasionally ambiguous report of one of these sermons survives, preached by Latimer on March 12. It is most interesting as an indication of how far the more radical of the reformers were permitted to go. Shaxton presumably went so far, but certainly not Tunstall. The opening illustrates how Latimer, the yeoman's son, was, as often, carried away by the theme of injustice:

> He saide that byshopis, abbatis, prioris, parsonis, canonis resident, pristis, and all, were stronge thevis, ye dukis, lordis, and all; the kyng, quod he, made a marvelles good acte of parliament that certayne men sholde sowe every of them ij acres of

hempe, but it were all to litle, were it so moche more, to hange the thevis that be in England. Byshopis, abbatis, with soche other, shold not have so many servauntes, nor so many dysshes, but to god their first foundacion, and kepe hospitalytie to fede the nedye people, not jolye felowis with goldyn chaynes and velvet gownes, ne let theym not onis come to the howsis of religion for repaste; let theym call knave byshope, knave abbat, knave prior, yet fede non of theym all, nor their horses nor their dogges, nor yet sett men at lybertye [?]; also eat fleshe and whit mete in Lent, so that it be don without hurtyng of weke consciences, and without sedition, and lykewise on Frydays and all dayes. . . . The byshope of Canterbury seythe that the kingis grace is at a full poynte for fryers and chauntry pristis, that they shall awaye all that, savyng tho that can preche.[13]

Latimer speaks as if the ground had been well prepared for the vigorous invective against the religious. It had indeed been prepared, if somewhat diffidently, by the "book of articles" prepared in this spring and signed by Cromwell and the bishops, in which transubstantiation was upheld, but only three sacraments (baptism, penance, and the Eucharist) admitted, and the doctrine of purgatory discredited. But these articles were not published at this time, and on July 12 the king forbade all preaching except by bishops until Michaelmas. The inference is obvious: the first major dissolution was to be carried out with as little use of theological argument as possible, but with a vigorous appeal to the ancient prejudices of the people. It was a sound procedure, if one somewhat disconcerting to the pious historian.

Two very different sources of opposition to the new order illustrate the distinction between the supremacy issue itself and the theological implications of it explored by some of Cromwell's preachers. The chief centres of resistance in 1534 were the monks of the Charterhouse (an order of special sanctity), the Brigittine brethren and nuns of Sion, and the Observants of Greenwich. The curious or the devout may read their sad story in the standard histories of the period; here I consider only some aspects of their resistance, early made known at Paul's Cross. In 1534, probably before the opening of the Parliament in November, one of the preachers proclaiming the royal supremacy at the Cross was interrupted by one of the Greenwich friars, who offered to dispute with him; in the next year the Carthusians were required to attend the Paul's Cross sermons every Sunday, to receive instruction and also as a kind of penance; on February 27, 1536, four of these monks did public penance for refusing to acknowledge the supremacy, Tunstall preaching the sermon. It is likely that they were supporters of the important group arrested under an order issued in April 1535, which included John Houghton, prior of the Charterhouse, and a priest named Robert Feron, who saved himself by accusing one of the others. The Observant Friar Forest, who had been confessor to Queen Katherine, was likewise the victim of a brother. Cromwell had an agent in the house at Greenwich, a lay brother named Richard Lyst, who pursued the unfortunate Forest with all the energy of a spiteful nature stimulated by greed and ambition. In a letter to Cromwell, written while Anne Boleyn was still Marchioness of Pembroke, Lyst reported that Forest was attempting to expel a brother who was on the King's side, that he affirmed that Cromwell would have him removed for fear of what he might reveal, and that he had made a sermon at Paul's Cross, "more lyker barkynge and raylynge than prechinge," speaking of the decay of the realm and slandering Dr. Rowland Lee. His authority in the friary undermined by Lyst and others, Forest was subjected to a long imprisonment, with repeated examinations. He was kept till 1538, but in that year, having refused to recant publicly at Paul's Cross on May 12, was burned ten days later, in the flames of the Welsh image called Darvell Gadarn, one of the images and relics destroyed in that year.[14]

Two years before the end of Friar Forest's case, however, a far more serious opposition to the new order had become active over a large part of the realm. The resistance from the Carthusians and Observants had been, after all, dangerous merely for the example set to other less intransigent if not less devout persons. But in 1536 Henry and his Council were faced with widespread insurrection against the religious changes. The series of abortive uprisings dating from September 1536 to June 1537 is known as the Pilgrimage of Grace. The steps taken towards the dissolution of the smaller monasteries, coming after the ambiguously Protestant articles of the convocation, and the Injunctions, which commanded the clergy to preach the articles, to urge the people not to observe superstitious holy days, to discourage pilgrimages and to condemn images and relics, were too much for the north to bear. The supremacy itself, with restraint of annates and appeals, though it established a national church, did not by itself make for any great change in the ordinary habits of the people. But these orders entered into the everyday lives of all men, put an end to a hundred long-established customs, sounded the death knell of the antique time. In the little villages scattered upon the lonely moors the men of the north rose in wrath, and gathered under market crosses bearing the banner of the five wounds of Christ.

Two days after Norfolk was forced to make a truce with Aske and his followers, on October 29, 1536, Latimer, whose removal the rebels demanded, loudly condemning him as one of the chief heretics, preached at the Cross against them:

> I hear say they wear the cross and the wounds before and behind, and they pretend much truth to the king's grace and to the commonwealth, when they intend nothing less; and deceive the poor ignorant people, and bring them to fight against both the king, the church, and the commonwealth.

If one sees the Pilgrimage of Grace as a spontaneous rising to defend the customs of a traditional piety, one must find this disingenuous, to say the least. Yet Latimer was sincere enough. In what other terms, after all, could the reformer conceive of this disaffection? His thinking was determined by two assumptions of the new order which made his view of the rebellion inevitable. He moved at once to a definition of the "church" and of obedience:

> They rise with the church, and fight against the church, which is the congregation of faithful men. . . . Lo, what manner of battle this warrior St. Paul teacheth us, "to be shod on our feet," that we may go readily and prepare way for the gospel; yea, the gospel of peace, not of rebellion, nor of insurrection: no, it teacheth obedience, humility, and quietness.

The Church, then, is "the congregation of faithful men." But who is to determine whether they are faithful? Why, the king's vicegerent in causes ecclesiastical. The Gospel teaches obedience. To whom? Why, to God surely, but after him to the prince, who is to determine what is a true or a false quarrel. These are doctrines of great import, and Latimer realized their revolutionary character, for he went on:

> But ye say, it is new learning. Now I tell you it is the old learning. Yea, ye say it is old heresy new scoured. Nay, I tell you it is the old truth, long rusted with your canker, and now made bright and scoured.[15]

The day was saved; the crisis of Henry's experiment was weathered successfully. By July 1537 Archbishop Lee was able to report to the Paul's Cross audience the just executions upon the northern rebels.

The crusade against images and relics, which was in full swing with official sanction in 1538, was instituted in the so-called "Second Royal

Injunctions of Henry VIII" drawn up by Cromwell in 1537 or early in 1538, in which the clergy were informed that "the king's highness, graciously tendering the weal of his subjects' souls, has in part already, and more will hereafter travail for the abolishing of such images, as might be occasion of so great offence to God, and so great a danger to the souls of his loving subjects."[16] It is indeed possible, though many have denied it, that Henry did tender the weal of his subjects' souls in this and other matters of religion; certain it is that he tendered the royal purse. Some of the images were themselves costly in materials and workmanship; many of them were heaped about with offerings of gold and silver and precious stones. The shrines were accordingly looted, and the King wore the greatest jewel of the shrine of Becket in a ring.

The manner of proceeding against images was politic. Such simple foolish things as those listed, on the eve of another wave of iconoclasm, by Herbert of Cherbury—"our Lady's Girdle, shew'd in eleven several places, and her Milk in eight, . . . the Pen-knife and boots of St. Thomas of Canterbury, and a piece of his Shirt, much reverenc'd by Great-belly'd Women, two or three Heads of St. Ursuline"[17]—were taken down with sanctimonious zeal, and their removal served as the pretext for a general destruction of images, upon the safe assumption that abuse of images is all too easy for the simple Christian. As part of this programme Hilsey preached at Paul's Cross on two occasions in 1538. On February 24 he exposed the abuse of the Rood of Grace, from Boxley, near Maidstone, "so holy a place, where so many miracles are shewed." So Warham wrote once to Wolsey. Times had changed: in 1510 Henry VIII had offered 6s. 8d. to the Rood. It was a remarkable mechanism, a "bearded crucifix" made of wood, wires, and paste, supposed to have been the handiwork of a French carpenter taken prisoner in the Hundred Years' War. By manipulation from the rear the eyes and lips of the image could be made to move, and Hilsey exhibited this superstition during his sermon, one eyewitness reporting dramatically that while he preached, "it turned its head, rolled its eyes, foamed at the mouth, and shed tears." "The abusion" being so divulged, Hilsey broke the image, which was rotten with age, and threw it among the audience, who completed the work of destruction. On November 24 he did duty once more, with the Blood of Hailes this time, from a Cistercian monastery in Gloucestershire, reputed to be the blood of Our Lord, and much visited; they came "by flocks" to see it. Lord Herbert told a malicious tale of the manner of showing the Blood:

> It was said to have this Property. That if a Man were in mortal Sin, and not absolved, he could not see it; otherwise, very well: Therefore every Man that came to behold this Miracle ... was directed to a Chapel ... the Priest ... putting forth upon the Altar a Cabinet or Tabernacle of Crystal which being thick on one side ... but on the other thin and transparent, they used diversly: For if a rich and devout Man enter'd, they would show him the thick side, till he had paid for as many Masses, and given as large Alms, as they thought fit; after which ... they permitted him to see the thin side, and the Blood.[18]

Such (if we believe the story) were the means of extorting charitable donations from the rich in the good old days of popery. Perhaps a small regret troubled many a reformer in the worldly days of the new dispensation, as he sought to open the parvenu's purse by the word of exhortation alone. Be that as it may, the zeal of the Protestants and the greed of the government admitted at this time no images, and the Blood of Hailes was declared to be that of a duck. The commissioners who examined the relic and appropriated the £30 of offerings on balance in the shrine found it to be "hony clarified and coloured with saffron."

The first wave of iconoclasm in the English Reformation, then, was justified at Paul's Cross; the second also, as appears below; the third took the Cross itself.

The episodes so far described were the results of a religious policy desperately unsettled and determined largely by the exigencies of the moment, more especially by fluctuations in popular and parliamentary sentiment and the amount of the balance in the royal treasury. But after 1539, the spoil of the monasteries safely secured, the necessity or indeed even the possibility of alliance with the German Protestants receding in his mind before the immediate threat of combination from the Emperor and Francis I, Henry determined to publish his essential orthodoxy before all Europe. The decision was taken as a means of self-protection and also perhaps from Catholic convictions never seriously shaken at any time in the last six years. This decision resulted in the Act of Six Articles, the "whip with six strings" which cost the conscientious Latimer and the simple Shaxton their bishoprics, but which scored the backs of remarkably few of the faithful. It was, as

Gairdner has put it, the old religion with the pope left out. Urged by Henry himself, who "confounded them with God's learning," the bishops assented to an act the avowed purpose of which was to abolish "diversity in opinions." The cold wind was beginning to blow on Cromwell, who had now only an earldom, frustration, and death before him. It blew too upon those who had begun to flourish under his protection, the convinced Lutherans like Robert Barnes.

Barnes seems to have been a violent, resourceful, and bigoted man. He was chief of the Lutherans in England, and with others of the same persuasion owed his safety and what licence he had to disseminate his opinions to Cromwell, who supported heresy in a typical blend of faith in politics and cynicism in religion. It proved a fatal course; the balance of power swung to Gardiner, and on February 15, 1540, Gardiner struck, at Paul's Cross. His own report of what he said is worth reproducing at some length:

I sayde now a dayes the devill teacheth, come back from fastynge, come back from confession, come back from wepinge for thy sinnes, and all is backwarde, in so muche as he must lerne to say his Pater Noster backward. . . . And, amonges other thinges, noted the devilles craft, what shift he useth to deceyve man whose felicitie he envieth, and therfore coveteth to have man idle and void of good workes, and to be ledde in that idleness, with a wan hope to lyve merely [merrily] and at his pleasure here, and yet have heaven at the last; and for that purpose procured out pardons from Rome, wherin heaven was sold for a little money, and for to retayle that marchaundise the devyll used freres for his ministers. Nowe they be gone with all their tromperye, but the devyll is not yet gonne. And nowe he perceyveth it can no lenger be borne to buy and sell heaven . . . the devyll hath excogitate to offre heaven without workes for it, so frelye that men shall not nede for heaven to worke at all. . . . And to set forth this the devils craft, there were . . . ministers, but no mo fryers. Fye on the name and the garment! But nowe they be called by an Englyshe name, brethrene, and go apparelled like other men, amonges which be some of those that were freres, and served the devyll in retaylinge of heaven in pardons, for they can skyll of the devylls service. . . . But if the Kynges Majestie, as he hath banyshed freres by the Frenche name, wolde also banyshe these that call them selfe brethren in Englyshe, the devyll shulde be greatly discomforted in his enterprise.[19]

There are two lines of argument here, drawn into one, both of considerable importance, both often misunderstood or deliberately misinterpreted by some ecclesiastical historians. The first is the popular attack upon the doctrine of justification by faith alone, that "men shall not nede for heaven to worke at all." The Catholic apologists were not in England defending the contemplative ideal; they argued with the Reformers on their own ground. Both sought the ideal of the *active* Christian life, and for a century the Protestant divines defended themselves with all the resources at their command—and Calvin offered more resources than Luther—against this very aspersion of Gardiner. It must be emphasized that their adept and vigorous statements of the doctrine that true works are the fruits of faith, which only justifies, were directed not only against formal and learned expositions of Catholic theology, but also (and indeed chiefly) against such simple, colloquial, and therefore dangerous statements as this of Gardiner. This most astute man knew well the value, in an appeal to popular sentiment, of the unequivocal statement of equivocal truths. In the second place, Gardiner here voices the ancient protest of the secular clergy against the friars, that they circumvented the ordinary powers of mediation possessed by the church, in selling easy salvation. But the worst is that they have been succeeded by ministers, some of whom (like Barnes) were friars before, and now continue with a new technique the same campaign against the Church which is the guardian and repository of the faith. With his usual perspicacity Gardiner had noted a fact of the deepest import for the ecclesiastical history of England in the century to follow. A century later Selden was to say that the Puritan lecturers were the descendants of the friars and stood in the same relation as they did to the Establishment. This continuity of opposition between the established Church and a corps of guerilla soldiers of God, "plesaunt" in absolution or expert in the Scriptures as the case might be, is a fact which the followers of Foxe and Neal always fail to see. To see it is to admit the force of what by a fitting anachronism we may call the Tory point of view.

Gardiner had in this case taken the first round. But Barnes with great self-confidence secured permission to preach at the Cross two weeks later. Gardiner's account, which does not differ substantially from that of Foxe, shows pretty clearly what sort of man Barnes was:

There he beganne to call for me to come forth to aunser him; he termed me to be a fightynge cocke, and he was another, and one of the game; he sayde I had no spoores, and that he wold shewe. And after he had pleased himselfe in thallegorie of a cockefight, then, upon a foolysh conclusion, he cast me openly his glove ... and raged in such a sort as the lyke hath not ben herde doone in a pulpete.[2c]

Nor was this the end of the troubles that Lent. On the following Sunday, March 7, an adherent of Barnes, William Jerome, vicar of Stepney, "confirmed Barnes' doctrine" at the Cross; the substance of his argument was "that men's constitutions bind not the conscience." On the following Sunday another of the "brethren" spoke from that pulpit, a certain Thomas Garret or Gerrard, a distributor of Lutheran books in Oxford as early as 1526. He too preached seditious doctrine.

Chiefly to blot out from the popular mind these grave errors, the three culprits were commanded to recant in the Spital sermons during Easter week, and though their performances were not entirely satisfactory, Dr. Wilson, vicar of St. Martin's Bishopsgate, rehearsed them at Paul's Cross on Low Sunday, according to the custom. The offenders were committed to the Tower, and on July 30, two days after the death of Cromwell, they were burned at Smithfield. We are told that in May Cranmer preached at the Cross the "contrary" to what Gardiner had preached in Lent. It seems incredible that Henry would have continued to protect his Archbishop if Cranmer had espoused Barnes's cause and opinions outright in a public pulpit. The King stuck to Cranmer through thick and thin, however. What Cranmer actually said must remain conjecture.

There was trouble in 1541, too, with another Lutheran brother, Alexander Seton, a Scot, a "lecturer" at St. Antholine's, who quarrelled with the doctrine of Dr. Richard Smith, first regius professor of divinity at Oxford, preached at Paul's Cross on November 13. He and William Tolwyn, the rector of St. Antholine's, were forced to do penance at the Cross on December 18 for their erroneous and heretical opinions. Tolwyn's library included works by Frith and Zwingli, and a mysterious Lollard pamphlet.

The incidents just reviewed, though they illustrate some of the means taken to consolidate the so-called Catholic reaction in the last eight years of Henry's reign, do not bring to our attention the major problem confronting the Henrician church: the diversity of opinions concerning the mass. The doctrine of the sacrament of the altar was of course the most important issue in English theology until the accession of Elizabeth, and the changes in popular and official opinion concerning it present a complicated if rather depressing subject of study. Officially the government had done nothing to stimulate the discussion of the mass or to bring its efficacy into disrepute, but the validity of masses for the dead had been pragmatically repudiated, and indeed the very act of the schism had given a strong impetus to discussion of religious dogmas. All that had been long accepted was disturbed, debated in the most important forums of the realm—and in the meanest alehouses. The King seems to have encouraged or at least permitted heretical opinions to bring pressure to bear on the conservatives; when the need for pressure was past the heresies could not be entirely wiped out. Nourished by ancient grievances, by the study of the works of continental Protestants, by freer access to the Scriptures, revolutionary theological opinions continued to flourish like tender plants in a dry ground, springing up and dying, waiting for the blessed rain of official sanction, and that was to come.

All sorts of fantasies were apparently being aired in those years. In 1536 a "tyler" did penance at Paul's Cross for maintaining that the passion of Christ was of benefit only to those who died before the Incarnation; four foreign Anabaptists did penance there while Hilsey was exhibiting the Blood of Hailes in 1538. On December 22, 1538, the first of the self-appointed interpreters of Scripture made his appearance as a penitent. His name was John Harrydaunce, and he was a bricklayer in Whitechapel; he had been giving extempore expositions of the Word from a tub in his garden. One wonders what he had found in the sacred text; the thunders of apocalypse no doubt, or the dawn of the new dispensation. Another eccentric, a priest named George, appeared for having execrated holy water; Robert Ward, who may have been at one time a friar, confessed in 1544 that he had spoken of the mass "folyshlie and unreverentlie." One result of foolish and irreverent talk of the mass seems to have been that ignorant priests, faced with unbelief among their parishioners, attempted to inculcate it by empirical evidence. There are dark hints of abuses in the service of the mass in Foxe and Bale, abuses beyond what they of course considered the blasphemy of the orthodox rubrics. One such instance has come to my attention. On February 8, 1545, a priest from Kent did penance at the Cross for having sought to counterfeit the blood of Christ at mass, by cutting his finger and letting it bleed upon the Host. This was a curious case, and there were no others exactly like it.

Penance for promulgating heretical opinions was not, however, confined to such small fry as these. On Relic Sunday, 1543, three erring ministers proclaimed their errors before that audience. These were Robert Wisdom, at this time curate to Dr. Edward Crome of St. Mary Aldermary, the distinguished Protestant pamphleteer Thomas

Becon, and Robert Singleton. Wisdom declared his errors in denying man's free will, in preaching against veneration of saints, in affirming that persecution is the mark of the true church, and that Barnes, Garret, and Jerome had proclaimed the true church. (It may be noted here that the Protestants were already compiling an informal martyrology, a typical expedient of disgruntled minorities.) Becon, when it came to his turn, acknowledged that he had preached false doctrine in Norfolk and Suffolk, and that in taking the pseudonym Theodore Basil he had acted vaingloriously, for "Basil"means a king. Further, he continued: "In my booke called the Newes oute of hevyn I have so playnely and so evydentlye set forth and avaunced my folye and pryde as I have mervayled that yt hathe not dyscouraged men, to gyve credyte or rede eny other of my books here." The authorities were determined to humiliate him, and did so by the shrewd device of attacking that very powerful vanity, the vanity of an author. He confessed further that he had spoken so of the sacrament of the altar that "men were offended with me." With his own hands he then cut up before the multitude his dangerous books.

After these elaborate recantations, there was little for poor Singleton to add. He was brief:

Worshypfull Audyence my Companyons here presente have spoken unto you many woordes for declaration of them self. I shall conclude in a fewe whiche be theese. I am an unlearned fantastycall foole. Suche hathe been my preachinge and suche hathe been my wrytinge, whiche I heare before you all teare in pieces.

This public humiliation of three prominent gospellers was as nothing compared with the troubles of Dr. Edward Crome, rector of St. Mary Aldermary. He had been infected with Lutheranism as early as 1529, for he was forced to recant a sermon preached in his church in that year. James Bainham affirmed during his interrogation in 1532 that in his opinion Crome and Latimer were the only preachers who ever preached the Word of God sincerely, though he would not believe even Crome when he preached the validity of the doctrine of purgatory. Crome's opinions were like Latimer's, but he was a brittle man and not so highly placed and therefore could be made an example. He was in no trouble till 1539, for in those years there was some tolerance of variety in opinions, but in July of that year he made a sermon in Allhallows Bread Street for which he was reported to the Council. He was convented under the Act of Six Articles, and forced to recant at Paul's Cross on February 13, 1541, being commanded to say that there had been "vanity of opinions and contentions among the people of London" about his sermons, and that he would declare his errors. He affirmed the royal supremacy, but he could not away with the mass. In 1546 he once more ventured upon dangerous ground, asserting in a sermon in the Mercers' Chapel that the mass is unprofitable, and exhibiting the problem of belief posed by the Henrician Catholic reaction:

Among other reasons and persuasions, to rouse the people from the vaine opinion of purgatory, [he] inferred this, grounding upon the said act [for dissolution of chantries]: that if trentals and chanterie masses could availe the souls in purgatorie, then did the parlement not well in giving awaie monasteries, colleges, & chanteries, which served principallie to that purpose. But if the parlement did well (as no man could denie) in dissolving them & bestowing the same upon the king, then is it a plaine case, that such chanteries and privat masses doo nothing conferre to releeve them in purgatorie.

"This dilemma of Dr. Crome," continues the chronicler with perhaps unconscious irony, "no doubt, was insoluble." It was indeed a hard case, to reconcile the omnicompetence of the King in Parliament with the authority of the Church, and both with Scripture. It gravelled more subtle men than Dr. Crome.

He was required to publish his recantation at the Cross on May 9. In the meantime a campaign of preaching against his errors was instituted in the Easter week sermons at the Spital and Paul's Cross. One Richard Wilmot, an apprentice in Bow-lane, who approved Crome's doctrine and said that he should be sorry to hear him recant it, was whipped. On the day appointed Crome preached an outright attack upon the Six Articles; he was commanded by the Council to make a true recantation on June 27, when he finally submitted, acknowledging that the mass used in England was agreeable to the institution of Christ. This sermon "had a very good effect upon the common people, who were greatly affected." In this sermon he confessed that certain "perverse mynded persons" had encouraged him in his resistance; these, including the vicar of St. Bride's, were pursued and punished.[21]

Even before the case of Dr. Crome was cleared up to the Council's satisfaction, the annoying Anne Askew [Ascough] had again to be dealt with. In the preceding year she had been committed to the

Counter for asserting doctrines contrary to the received Catholic position on the sacrament of the altar, but after she had thoroughly annoyed Bonner, who thought he had converted her to the true view, she was released. The mildness of the authorities in her case was truly remarkable. She became offensive again, and in May 1546 she was examined by the Council, notably by Gardiner, who, exasperated by her insistence on the bare letter of Scripture, called her a parrot. On June 18 she was arraigned at the Guildhall for heresy, with Nicholas Shaxton, late Bishop of Salisbury, and two others. Shaxton was persuaded to recant, but she would not, and when Shaxton preached at her burning on July 16 (a shrewd move by the Council) she criticized his exposition of the text.[22] Two further steps were now taken to stamp out this upsurge of heretical opinions. Shaxton recanted abjectly at the Cross in August, and in September a great bonfire of heretical books was made there.

The reign of Henry VIII was nearly over, and all seemed quiet. Without much persecution the country had accepted the Catholic reaction; what dissent there had been was put down. But behind the scenes, in the corridors outside the King's sick-chamber, in scattered papers in Cranmer's desk at Lambeth, were latent the forces which should make a real religious revolution. One very shrewd and competent man, John Feckenham, then chaplain to the Bishop of London, preaching at Paul's Cross a few days before the death of the King, lamented the growth of heresy among the younger generation. "Sanctimony of life is put away," he complained, "with fastings on Wednesdays and Saturdays, and beads. And therefore good men dare not now use them for fear they should be laughed to scorn. What a world shall it be when they shall have the rule, for if they have the swing it will be treason shortly to worship God."

It is clear, then, that the use of the Paul's Cross pulpit as an organ of public persuasion during the post-Reformation years of Henry VIII had more than one result. That the people were told what they should think, how, and above all when they should think it, is evident. There are even signs that the art of provoking "spontaneous demonstrations" was not unknown. But the position of the preacher in whom "syncerity of Scripture" overrode time-serving was indeed ambiguous. Such a one might be privately encouraged or merely left alone so long as he served his limited purpose as a spearhead of innovation, but when his reading of texts led him to potentially seditious conclusions or when the current was set against innovation and "newfangglenes," then he had to be corrected, sometimes upon the very stage where he had won his little hour of applause from the faithful. Not all such preachers were "unlearned fantastycall fooles." Dr. Crome, for instance, was not unlearned, nor fantastical, nor a fool; he simply had the habit of mind which follows steadily from evidence to a conclusion. Such a mind, which one associates with the Puritan apologists of a later day, may be broken, as his was, but not bent. It is significant that when Cromwell sought for preachers to spread an atmosphere of calm reasonableness after the Pilgrimage of Grace he sent for two able academics, Dr. Sandwich and Matthew Parker, to preach at Paul's Cross. They could be counted upon to regard the situation in a clear and reasonable light, to take the long view, and generally to exercise "incorrupte jugement." But the use of guileless and indeed fanatical Protestants created among the auditory, and especially in London, a sort of standard by which other preachers more useful to the government were adversely judged. In 1537, for example, a bishop (not identified but probably Rowland Lee) was ill received. The contemporary Protestant comment is interesting: "He deceived the people with his crafty bowling wit, more fit for the chattering Arches than for the true sincere Christian preaching place." When Dr. Crome failed to recant his opinions of the mass in May 1546 he asserted that the ears of the continental brethren were tuned to his performance. A tradition and a martyrology was being created, and the foundations for it were laid at this pulpit as much as at Tyburn and Smithfield.

The reformers had their hour. In his famous sermon of the Plough, preached at St. Paul's in the Shrouds in January 1548, Latimer, not restored to his episcopal function but preacher extraordinary to the King and all England, set forth admirably the ideal of "reformation without tarrying for any" which men of his persuasion believed to be at hand:

The king's majesty is so brought up in knowledge, virtue, and godliness, but it is not to be mistrusted but that we shall have all things well, and that the glory of God shall be spread abroad throughout all parts of the realm, if the prelates will diligently apply their plough, and be preachers rather than lords.

There are two elements in the spreading of this glory which no historian of the Church of England ignores. The first, the complete control of ecclesiastical change by the secular power, the sympathetic orthodox, whether of the seventeenth or the twentieth century, might wish to deprecate. The second, the Book of Common Prayer, he may justly extol, whatever his persuasion. In this survey of certain aspects of the Edwardian Reformation, however, I can give no more than passing notice to constitutions and liturgies; I am more concerned with the methods used to sweep away the hindrances to the spread of God's glory, and the sometimes melancholy results of those methods in the popular mind. The evidence adduced points rather to a revolution feverishly impermanent than to the first flowering of a great and noble institution. Furthermore it was in the reign of Edward VI that the church was subjected to a process of spoliation and impropriation which effectually weakened it and left it ill equipped for the troubles of the next century. Here it is enough to say that the noblest productions of the Edwardian pulpit are Latimer's and Lever's attacks upon the rapacity of the gentry.

The campaign against images and superstitious observances had proceeded considerably before Latimer, in the sermon just cited, condemned "the maintenance of idolatry done to the brazen serpent." Feckenham's gloomy warning seems to have been not just an outpouring of passion and prejudice, for the significant thing about this campaign was that the iconoclasts were ahead of the administration, radical in potential though the administration was. Those zealous persons, the incumbent and wardens of St. Martin's, Ironmonger Lane, set an example by taking down the images in the church, setting up the royal arms instead of the crucifix, and painting the walls with texts of Scripture "perversely translated."[23] In Lent 1547 Barlow, Bishop of St. David's, preached at Paul's Cross against veneration of images, and was followed by Ridley upon the same theme, while later in Lent Hugh Glasier, Cranmer's commissary for Calais, declared at the same place that Lent was not of God's ordinance, and that the fast might be kept or not at the pleasure of men. Not until July were the Injunctions issued, commanding the destruction of images which had been abused by superstition and other objects of blind devotion. Two such were exhibited by Barlow at the Cross in November. One of them was an image of the Virgin which "they of Paul's had lapped in cerecloth" and hidden in a corner of the cathedral, the other a picture of the Resurrection of a mechanical kind, like the Rood of Boxley. After the sermon, "the boys broke the idols in pieces." That has an unpleasant sound; the icons of one generation are the playthings of the next. The distinction between images abused and images properly used was probably never intended to be maintained, and the fiction was cast off in February 1548 with an Order in Council for the general destruction of images. Whereupon, as is well known, the gentry enriched themselves with the spoil of the churches, manuscripts with idolatrous illuminations were shipped to the continent to be used by bookbinders, or stayed at home in cupboards and jakes, and while the interior of many a country house shone with plundered cloth of gold the Lord was worshipped in the due nakedness of a whitewashed chapel. Even here the Crown was behind-hand: in 1551 and 1552 the Council belatedly took order for the seizure of all church plate and vestments still remaining, and appointed commissions to inquire how much had been already embezzled.

The fanaticism of some of the clergy who stimulated these disgraceful courses was almost incredible. Consider, for example, the curate of St. Katherine Cree, as Stow records his activities in the year 1549:

At the North west corner of this warde [Aldgate] standeth the faire and beautiful parish Church of S. Andrew the Apostle, with an addition, to be known from other churches of that name, of the Knape or Undershaft, and so called S. Andrew Undershaft, because that of old time . . . an high or long shaft, or May-pole, was set up there. . . . The said shaft was laide along over the doores and under the Pentises of one rowe of houses . . . hanged on Iron hookes many yeares, till the third of King Edward the sixt, that one Sir Stephen, curat of S. Katherine Christs Church, preaching at Paules Crosse, said there, that this shaft was made an Idoll. . . . He persuaded therefore that the names of Churches might bee altered: also that the names of dayes in the weeke might be changed, the fishdayes to be kept any dayes. except Friday and Saturday, and the Lent any time, save only betwixt Shrovetide and Easter: I have oft times seene this man, forsaking the Pulpit . . . preach out of an high Elme tree in the middest of the Church yarde, and then entering the Church, to have sung his high Masse in English upon a Tombe of the deade towardes the north. I heard his Sermon at Paules Crosse, and I saw the effect that followed, for in the afternoone of that present Sunday the neighbours, and Tenants . . . over whose doores the saide shaft had laine, after they had dined to make themselves strong, gathered more helpe, and with great labour raysing the Shaft from the hooks . . . they sawed it in pieces, everie man taking for his share so much as had laine over his doore and stall.[24]

For fanatics like this the fear of idolatry was an obsession. In others it was tempered by the instincts of the hoodlum. Witness the story told by an approving zealot of the jape of William Ford, usher in Winchester School:

> Ther was many golden images in Wykam's colleage by Wynton. The churche dore was directly over agaynste the usher's chamber. Mr. Forde tyed a longe coorde to the images, lynkyng them all in one coorde, and, being in his chamber after midnight, he plucked the cordes ende, and at one pulle all the golden godes came downe with *heyho Rombelo*. Yt wakened all men with the rushe.[25]

Of all "idols" the Host was chief. Released from the fear of swift punishment for heresy concerning the sacrament of the altar, numbers of persons debated wildly concerning the nature of the Eucharist, and of the sense in which Christ might be said to be present in it. There seems to have been in the first year of Edward VI an orgy of dispute on this point, as if energies of disputation were released from the confinement of the Henrician reaction. That old criterion of judgment, "the secret motyon of the holy ghost," had found in the new learning an intellectual training, muscularly freeing itself from the bonds of scholastic categories. To wrestle with the sacred Scriptures unimpeded by oversubtlety of technique was the means; the end was the *Verbum Dei*, the genuine, soul-shaking, wonder-working *verbum*, the very hearing of which was in a sense a partaking of Christ. There is in this citation of the WORD something primitive; it is like incantation. If the radical Reformers eschewed the mass because it could not satisfy them empirically, that does not mean that they were empiricists. It means that they had found a new talisman. "By faith!" cried Luther, "by faith!" and rose from the Book a new man. In like manner the preacher shouted his text until its phrases were burned into his and his hearers' brains. With such an attitude it was possible to believe that one could arrive at the truth about the Eucharist by repeating the crucial texts. What was unfortunate and dangerous was that in the preacher's mind, mingled with this naïve and straightforward surrender to the Word, still existed the rag-tag and bobtail of scholastic terminology from his course in divinity, which he often desperately and sincerely or no doubt sometimes lewdly and viciously attempted either to harmonize with or to oppose to the warrant of Scripture. The result, as Cranmer complained, was chaos, "subverting the order of all godliness."

The first statute of the reign was an act concerning the sacrament, ordaining that henceforth the communion should be administered in both kinds; the act contained provision of fines and imprisonment for irreverent disputation concerning the scarament.[26] This was in November 1547. In the same month Ridley preached on the subject at Paul's Cross; at his examination in 1555 he explained how he came to preach:

> You shall understand that there were at Paul's, and divers other places, fixed railing bills against the sacrament, terming it "Jack of the box, the sacrament of the halter, round Robin," with such like unseemly terms; for the which causes, I, to rebuke the unreverend behaviour of certain evil disposed persons, preached as reverendly of that matter as I might . . . , affirming in that sacrament to be truly and verily the body and blood of Christ, effectuously by grace and spirit: which words the unlearned, understanding not, supposed that I had meant of the gross and carnal being which the Romish decrees set forth, that a body, having life and motion, should be indeed under the shapes of bread and wine.

It would seem that Ridley at this stage held to a doctrine existing uncertainly between the Zwinglian position that the rite is purely commemorative, and the orthodox position of the real and substantial Presence.[27] It was not a doctrine easily apprehended by the vulgar. A more uncompromisingly Zwinglian position was taken by Dr. Kyrkham in 1550, when he asserted at the Cross that in the sacrament of the altar "was no substance but brede and wynne."

If some of the Henrician Catholics, like Gardiner, had hoped for some measure of continuity in ecclesiastical policy, they were early deceived. In the first months of the new reign, in May 1547, Dr. Richard Smith, first regius professor of divinity in Oxford, and "the greatest pillar of the Roman catholic cause in his time" (Anthony Wood), was forced to recant at the Cross his book of "unwritten verities," and another book of the mass. He later recanted his recantation at Oxford, was relieved of his preferments, and succeeded as regius professor by Peter Martyr. Pillar of the faith he may have been, but a greater one stood in the see of Winchester. Imprisoned in 1547, then released, stiff in his resistance to Ridley's attempts to bring him around, Gardiner was allowed in Lent 1548 to retire to his diocese, whence he was soon summoned by the Council on the charge that he was secretly arming his servants, and upholding abolished ceremonies. To clear himself of these and other charges he offered to preach at Paul's Cross. While preparing for the sermon, which was to be preached on June 29, he received a warning from Somerset, expressly forbidding him to speak of the sacrament of the altar.

The night before he was to preach he neither ate nor slept. The audience was the greatest ever seen there; there was naturally a burning curiosity to know what he might say, since both his sympathizers and his enemies knew his stubbornness and subtlety. They were not disappointed in the display of either of those qualities. He acknowledged the royal supremacy, grounding his submission on little more than a simple statement with a double edge: "we must obey the rulers." Then, bravely, he affirmed the very presence of Christ's body and blood in the sacrament. The next day he was committed to the Tower, and preachers, including Dr. Richard Cox, the scourge of the libraries, were put up at the Cross to speak against him and his opinions.

Gardiner was put away, but greater dangers awaited the administration. Another turbulent spirit was silenced in March 1549, when the Lord Admiral Seymour was executed for sedition and treason; Latimer's sermon excusing this action was ill received. Then followed the risings in Norfolk and Devonshire, set afoot by the evils of enclosures and other injustices suffered at the hands of the land-hungry parvenus who followed Somerset's star. The sixteen articles which the rebels demanded involved the restoration of the Henrician church, and incidentally raised the question of how far the Protector could go in the King's minority. Cranmer at least was convinced of the validity of his powers, and after celebrating Common Prayer in the cathedral according to the King's Book in July 1549, preached there on the evils of sedition as displayed by the rebels; the sermon was rehearsed afterwards by his chaplain before a larger multitude at the Cross. In the autumn Bonner, still Bishop of London, was accorded the same treatment as Gardiner; he preached at the Cross, as Foxe bitterly reported, much of "the gross, carnal, and papistical presence of Christ's body and blood in the sacrament," and deliberately left out what he was commanded to preach in justification of the acts done in the King's minority. He was committed to the Marshalsea, and the fantastic John Hooper, not yet garbed in what he termed the filthy vestments of a bishop, rehearsed his evil courses three weeks later before the multitude.

The radical minority happened to sit in the seat of power; the only way in which these innovations could be justified was by reiteration of the doctrine of obedience. Never was it more eloquently proclaimed than by Thomas Lever, at the Cross in February 1550. Lever was a man of "much natural probity and blunt native honesty," fresh from St. John's, Cambridge, and, as his second great effort in December was to show, much exercised over the decay of learning and good morals which accompanied rapid religious change under unprincipled administration. England, he said, is full of covetousness, and he fearlessly attacked the misuse of the religious lands by their new possessors, who had "brought a comen wealth into a comen miserye."

> Then some wyll ask thys questyon: Seynge there is no evyll of God, howe can evyll rulers or officers be of God? You honeste men that be here, and dwell in the countrey, heare this lesson, and marke it, and take it home wyth you, for your selves, and your neyghbour.... It is God that maketh these evyl men to be gentlemen rulers, and officers in the countrey; it is the sinnes of the people that causeth God to make these men youre rulers. The man is sometymes evyll, but the authoritie from God is always good, and God geveth good authoritye unto evyll men, to punyshe the synnes of the evyll people. It is not therefore repynyng, rebellyng, or resistyng gods ordinance, that wyll amende evyll rulers.

Let us then, he went on, "patientlye suffer for a tyme, not doubtynge but that that reliefe, comforte and wealth, whyche God hath promysed unto Englande by hys word . . . shal be broughte unto passe, by hys wysdome and myghte."

Such pronouncements as this were commonplaces of popular persuasion in the century to follow. But there are varying shades of emphasis in the presentation of the doctrine of passive obedience. Here it is a crisis manifesto; in less trying times it would be a platitude, the classic text (Romans 13:1–7) invoked against the pope's "usurped authority" or against the feckless minorites and sectaries who dreamed of a millenial transformation of the commonwealth. For Lever in 1550 there was no obvious dichotomy between the theory of obedience and the law of the land; for his Puritan successors, as the royal prerogative encroached upon the sphere of the common law, there was a conflict which put the Inns of Court men and the Puritan theorists into the same ranks, and contributed in no small degree to the great divisions of the 1640's. There is some irony in the fact that the protests against the alleged illegality of the Edwardian acts of uniformity came from Catholic conservatives like Gardiner, while Lever, twenty years later, was to be convented for breaches of church discipline before a court constituted by the royal supremacy.

There was one person in the realm to whom the doctrine of passive obedience might be said to apply very imperfectly, and this was Mary Tudor. Her opinions, tested by zealots who tried to convert her, were well known and unchangeable. No argument from any cleric or politician could shake from the popular mind the simple conviction of her legitimacy, or take the shadow of the crown imperial from her round and stubborn brow. Yet with the folly of zeal and the blindness of ambition it was attempted. On August 31, 1550, one Stephen Caston alluded obliquely in his Paul's Cross sermon to "a great woman," a great supporter of popery, and spoke opprobriously of Henry VIII, which the chronicler thought "herde." That sort of thing did not go down very well. Even less support could be expected for the supporters of Northumberland in 1553, though Ridley, in the phantom reign of "Queen Jane," asserted the illegitimacy of Mary and Elizabeth, and said that the accession of Mary would mean the end of true religion.

What a fantastic adventure was that of Northumberland, undertaken against all the overwhelming evidence of general support for the Tudor and no other, against the very considerable evidence that the realm, even in the south, was still Catholic! If the people were not good Catholics, at least they were more addicted to the comfortable usages of tradition than to the innovations of the last six years. Only one change had passed beyond reversion into the national life: the secularization of church properties. Englishmen wished to pursue their comfortable and bustling worldly ways, to which the new religion was not yet accommodated. That it would some day be so accommodated was then only a burgeoning idea in the brain of William Cecil, or perhaps the young Elizabeth, tested by adversity and worldly-wise beyond her years. At the time the new faith was little more than a passing fanaticism; there was a crude but powerful undercurrent of opposition to it, the opposition which had been waked unwisely by Henry VIII in 1536 and by Somerset in 1549. It comes to the surface in such small ways as in "A Popish Rhyme fastned upon a Pulpit in K. Edwards reigne," a revealing bit of doggerel:

> This pulpit was not here set,
> For knaves to prate in and rayl.
> But if no man may them let,
> Mischef wil come of them, no fail.
>
> If God do permit them for a tyme
> To brabble and ly at their wyl,
> Yet I trust or that be prime
> At their fal to laugh my fill.

> Two of the knaves already we had,
> Thei thrid is comyng as I understand,
> In all the yerth there is none so bad,
> I pray God soon ryd them out of this land. . . .
>
> Al christen men at us now laugh and scorne
> To se how they be taking of hie and lowe,
> But the child that is yet unborn
> Shal curse al on a rowe.
>
> Now God sped thee wel,
> And I wil no more mell.[28]

The people were bored and outraged by the preachers' disputatiousness and insistence. Too much was happening too quickly; they ate the air promise-crammed, and they wished to get back to their capons. Pamphlets and sermons alike exacerbated the mind, not then made numb by mechanically amplified voices. Witness the Capper's outburst in John Hales's "Discourse of the Common Weal" [1549]:

> The devell a whit the good doe ye with youre studies, but set men together by the eares. Some with this opinion and some with that, some holdinge this way and some that waye, and some an other, and that so stiffly as thoughe the truthe must be as they saye that have the upper hande in contention. And this contention is not the least of theise uprors of the people: some holdinge of the one learninge and some holdinge of the other. In my minde it made no matter yf there were no learned men at all.[29]

To this survey of the Paul's Cross sermons during the reign must be added some notice of the penances of Anabaptists there in 1549. Such penances are recorded for 1538, 1549, and 1575. The 1538 group were foreigners, and an example was made of them at that time presumably because of the Munster episode three years before, when the radicals for the first time employed force, which they had hitherto abhorred, seized the town, organized it upon communist principles, permitted such enormities as polygamy, and in effect founded a New Jerusalem according to their dispensation. It was this affair, more than their theology, which caused the odium in which they were thereafter held: "They had struck at the social and political susceptibilities of the time at their most sensitive point, the fear of anarchy."[30] The government, in 1538, proclaimed by putting such persons to penance that it recognized the danger in the sect, and that it was watchful to see that it did not find a foothold in England. Such were also the victims and such the penances of the first of the groups dealt with in 1575. Continued references to Anabaptists in sermons down to 1640 indicate rather the continuance of the tradition than their emergence as a positive threat to the constituted order. They became a bogey. They constituted a horrible example by which to enforce the doctrine of passive obedience. As for the Family of Love, which owed its origin to Anabaptist zealots, it appears in the lists of seditious groups rehearsed by orthodox preachers, a half-ridiculed repository of Anabaptist opinions—and in fact any other unusual opinions otherwise difficult to classify.

But the Anabaptists of 1549, harmless though they appear in their intrusion into the history of Paul's Cross, are worth a little more consideration. Three persons did penance: John Champneys of Stratford on the Bow, Putto a farmer of Colchester, and a butcher dwelling in Old Fish Street. Putto did penance twice, having offended the audience by wearing his cap the first time. These are small fry, no doubt, but they were likely representative of a larger number. How many of these persons were there in England about this time? Such a sudden sequence of penances points to the discovery of a conventicle, and also to the admirably politic habit of Tudor administrations of repeating a good occasion to make the lesson stick. Latimer, preaching before the King on March 29, 1549, said that there was a town in England with above five hundred heretics of this persuasion in it. He seems to have been speaking of Colchester, a centre of radical Protestant activities in the reign of Mary. Putto came from Colchester. The fantastic Christopher Vittels was there in 1555, and in the years 1575-80 the town was a Familist centre. Colchester was for Anabaptists what Lancashire was later for Puritanism.[31]

John Champneys had dangerous notions. He confessed that he had taught and written that a man, after he is regenerate in Christ, cannot sin; that the outward man might sin, but the inward man could not, that the ecclesiastics keep men from this truth for their own purposes, that God permits to all his elect their bodily necessities of all earthly things. The last of these corollaries from the Anabaptist special version of the doctrine of election was the subversive one. By holding to the former a man might fail of salvation, but if too many men held to the latter the magnates would suffer. And if there were probably not very many Anabaptists by count of heads, there were doubtless many who dabbled in speculations not far removed from their subversive doctrines. No state, said Cecil, can live in safety where there is toleration of two religions; one suspects that in the England of Edward and Mary there were not two religions but two hundred.

Events at Paul's Cross during the reign of Mary are disappointing; where one had hoped to find some contemporary justification of the use of the act *de haeretico comburendo*, for instance, which should throw light on that difficult question, one finds only the reiteration of conventional Catholic principles and some evidence for the active though usually ill-organized opposition of certain Protestant minorities. The truth is that Mary did not "tune her pulpits," did not use the forum at Paul's Cross with her father's cleverness or the intemperance of her brother's Council. The Paul's Cross pulpit was used, as before, for proclamations, spectacles, and instruction in officially inspired doctrines, but the important sermons of the reign (when there were any) were preached at Oxford and Smithfield, where the rituals of disputation and burning could support the preacher's arguments. It is not accidental that during this reign the important occasions at the Cross were pageantry—whether the spectacle went always as arranged or not.

Every chronicler, almost every historian, has had his say about the first Paul's Cross sermon of the reign, when Gilbert Bourne, after Bishop of Bath and Wells, preaching on August 13 and condemning the imprisonment of Bonner, had a dagger thrown at him from the crowd and narrowly escaped manhandling by elements in the audience. It is instructive to set side by side a contemporary account and one shaped by Protestant martyrology, to see what partisanship can do to a good story. First, the fullest contemporary version:

In the sermon tyme, because he prayed for the soules departed, and allso in declaringe the wrongfull imprisonment of Doctor Bonner . . . certaine leude and ille disposed persons made a hollowinge and such a cryinge thou lyest, that the audyence was so disturbed, that the preacher was so affrayd by the commotion of the people, that one Bradford, a preacher, pulled him backe, and spake to the people, desyring them in Christes name . . . to pacifie themselves . . . , but one lewde person drewe a dagger and caste yt at the preacher, which as God would, hitt against one of the posts of the pulpit. . . . And so, with great payne and feare the sayd Borne was conveyed from the pulpit to the scholehouse in Powles Churchyard. The Lord Courtney and the Lady Marques of Execeter stoode above my Lord Mayor, with Doctor Bonner . . . , which were sore astonyed to se the rumour [humour?] of the people, and had as much adoe by their meanes to see the sayd Bishop conveyed in safetye through the church, the people were so rude.[32]

In the traditional *Life* of Bradford, the incident has a different slant:

> Bourn, Bishop of Bath made a seditious sermon at Paul's-Crosse, which so moved the people to indignation, that they were ready to pull him out of the pulpit, and one threw a dagger at him: Where upon Bourn requested Master Bradford, who was behind him to stand in his place, and to quiet the people, which accordingly he did; whom when the people saw, they cried, Bradford, Bradford, God save thy life Bradford.... One said to him, Ah Bradford, Bradford, Thou savest him that will help to burn thee.[33]

That last pious clairvoyant ejaculation from the crowd is of course apocryphal. Foxe and Fuller are chiefly responsible for the Protestant account, Fuller contributing a typical phrase, "the people joyfully ingeminated with a loud voice, Bradford, Bradford." The Grey Friars' *Chronicle*, in a brief notice of the episode, differs from all the other accounts; it records that Bourne "there was pullyd owte of the pulpyt by vacabonddes." Henry Machyn says that there was a great uproar, "lyke mad pepull, watt yonge pepell and woman [as] ever was hard, as herble-borle, and castyng up of capes; [if] my lord mer and my lord Cortenay as not ben ther, ther had bene grett myscheff done." Two of the three eye-witness accounts mention Courtenay, and none of them mention Bradford. One wonders if he actually did rescue Bourne almost single-handed. London may have been more Protestant than other parts of the realm, but the same people who had acclaimed Mary two days before were not surely moved to kill her chaplain, as by a general infusion of the Gospel. However, it does not take many to start a riot, and a riot there surely was. The government took immediate steps to keep order, proceeding, as authority always does in such cases, against the most obvious scapegoat. The Council threatened the liberties of the City, and the City fathers promised to keep the apprentices in order, and managed to arrest two or three persons, likely not the real culprits. On the next Sunday the inculcation of right doctrine was formally instituted, under rather forbidding conditions. Dr. Watson, chaplain to Gardiner, preached at the Cross surrounded by two hundred of the royal guard "with ther halberttes." He sneered at the diversity of opinions among the Reformers, and exhorted the people to re-edify the old temple of the faith.

A course of instructive sermons, designed to establish once more, by degrees, the old usages and doctrines, was continued throughout the autumn. Weston, Dean of Westminster, referred memorably to the Protestant communion-table as an oyster-board. James Brooks, Master of Balliol, whose *Sermon very notable, fruictefull, and Godlie* was published, deplored the state of the Church in England in the reign of Edward, likening it to the daughter of Jairus, dead in schism. Now, he proclaimed, a "godly governesse" will restore it to its ancient righteousness.

The men who might have contended with the official preachers were in prison, and what opposition there was to the establishment of the old faith and the projected Spanish marriage was channelled into such abortive risings as Wyatt's in 1554, or issued in strange fashion, in deeds in which zeal and charlatanism, wrath and mischief were blended. Early Sunday morning, April 8, 1554, there was discovered hanging on the cross in Cheapside a dead cat, with shaven crown and a wafer-like object in its mouth, made like a priest celebrating the mass. The thing was at once taken down, and exhibited during the sermon preached that morning at the Cross by Dr. Henry Pendleton, canon of St. Paul's and chaplain to Bonner, who was once more bishop of the diocese. This sort of enormity might be thought peculiar to those times, but the spirit of it did not die from controversy; in a Paul's Cross sermon in 1571 Dr. John Bridges asserted that a priest at mass is like a cat with a mouse, eating Christ, an interesting transformation of medieval grotesquerie into controversial blasphemy.

Pendleton preached at the Cross again on June 10, and then went in danger of his life, for someone fired at him either from the crowd or from one of the houses by the churchyard. The would-be assassin remained undiscovered. Pendleton may have commended the Queen's marriage with Philip; it is clear that disaffected persons were prepared at this time to use any means to stir up popular antagonism to it. Perhaps following the fruitful precedent of the Nun of Kent, "diverse lewd persons" promoted a pious fraud, using as agent a girl named Elizabeth Croft, who was called "the whyte byrde, or the byrde that spake in the wall." In a house near Aldgate "shee had laine whistling in a strange whistle made for that purpose, which was given her by one Drakes," while "diverse companions confederat with her" interpreted her utterances. She spoke seditiously against the mass and the prince of Spain. On July 15, 1554, weeping and pitifully confessing her fault she did penance at the Cross, admitting that she had participated in the fraud in the hope of "many good things given her." The sermon was preached by John Wymmesley, Archdeacon of London, who was reputedly one of the natural children of "old parson Savage," and brother to Bonner.

From the same religious underworld came three other outbreaks in the next year. Two women did penance at the Cross for affirming that a new-born child had spoken miraculously, prophesying the apocalypse, and two men were punished for railing and slander, performed about the preaching place.

Mary's marriage with Philip, the political sanction for the reconciliation with Rome, was performed in July 1554. Promptly the preachers at Paul's Cross were set to proclaim its advantages to the populace. On July 29 Nicholas Harpsfield prayed there for the King and Queen, and on September 30 Gardiner set clearly before the people the meaning of the new political and ecclesiastical dispensation:

> Speaking very much of love and charity, at last he had occasion . . . to speak of the true teachers, and of the false teachers; saying, that all the preachers almost in King Edward's time, preached nothing but voluptuousness, and filthy and blasphemous lies. . . . And when he spake of the sacrament, he said, that all the church from the beginning have confessed Christ's natural body to be in heaven, and here to be in the sacrament, and so concluded that matter. . . . Then he declared what a noble king and queen we have, saying, that if he should go about to show that the king came hither for no necessity or need, and what he had brought with him, it should be superfluous, seeing it is evidently known, that he hath ten times as much as we are in hope and possession of; affirming him to be as wise, sober, gentle, and temperate a prince, as ever was in England.

"Wily Winchester," as Foxe delighted to call him, had lost none of his cunning, though now damaged by illness, and full of honours. Shrewd indeed was the praise of Philip, because for the most part so negative. Gardiner sought to reassure Englishmen that the rapacious followers of a "temperate" prince would not bother to pick up what small spoil England afforded.

Yet another official act waited to be published at Paul's Cross. Cardinal Pole, who as papal legate was to bear the news to England of the reconciliation with the Holy See, had been delayed by Charles V until the Emperor was assured of the consummation of the marriage. He finally arrived in November 1554, and delivered his message to Queen and Parliament. On December 2 the good news was proclaimed at the Cross, with a spectacular procession and a sermon by Gardiner.

Cardinal Poole came from Lambeth by water, and landed at Paules Wharfe, and went from thence to Paules Church, with a crosse, 2 pillars, and 2 pollaxes of sylver borne before him. He was there receaved by the Lord Chauncellor with procession; where he taried tyll the king came from Westminstre by land, at xi of the clock.

One wonders what Philip must have thought if he remembered this occasion thirty-five years later. He was not apt to perceive ironies.

And so the Kinges majesty and my lord cardinall, wyth all the lordes of the privy counsell, beinge presente, with suche an audience of people as was never seene in that place before, my lorde chauncellor entered Poles Crosse. And after that the people ceased, that so muche as a whispering could not be hearde amongst them . . . , he tooke to hys theam these wordes of the epystle of that daye, wrytten by saynte Paule, the holye apostle in the xiii. chapter to the Romaynes, *Fratres, scientes quia hora est iam nos de somno surgere*, whyche parcell of scripture was so godlye and so clearkelye handeled by him, as no manne alyve . . . was able to meande it.

He declared the calamities of the preceding reign; including, for even amid the silence and the silver pollaxes and all the splendour Gardiner remained the realist, the debasing of the coinage and inflation. "A great nombre of the audience" were moved "with sorrowfull syghes and wepynge teares to chaunge theyr cheere" by his recital of the abominable heresies from which the realm was but lately rescued. He also revealed that Henry VIII was prepared to surrender the supremacy at the time of the Pilgrimage of Grace, and that even in Edward's reign the Council was once minded to restore the Pope to the supremacy. These state secrets were nicely turned to the purpose, the first of them illustrating Henry's insecurity and also his capacity for bluff, the second the influence of Wriothsley in the Council about the time of Somerset's fall, and both, so Gardiner meant his audience to see, the uncertainty of English Protestantism. He then published Pole's commission from the Pope to bless England, and gave thanks for the alliance with Philip.

After this, England was officially part of Catholic Christendom, and a partner in the fortunes of the Hapsburgs. On May 26, 1555, Dr. Chedsey proclaimed from the Cross the procession and prayer for peace with France, and in the same month another sermon was preached on the same theme; in September the bull of plenary remission of England's sins, the last papal bull ever to be published there, was set forth; early in 1557 Pole's instruction for confession and fasting were there proclaimed. On August 15, 1557, Londoners took part in a Paul's Cross ceremony celebrating the victory of the imperial forces at St. Quentin. Thus in a few fugitive notations in diaries and chronicles persists the memory of an unhappy and unsuccessful marriage and an unrealistic and uneasy alliance.

2. *The Establishment and its Enemies*

IT HAS BEEN AGREED that the Elizabethan Church was within certain limitations a settled and solid institution. The church historians have understandably emphasized this aspect of events by contrast with the uneasy times preceding and the disaster to follow. Surveyed in the proper perspective the Elizabethan Establishment is conspicuous neither for holiness nor efficiency, but for endurance and a remarkable stability. It remains a monument of stubborn yet valuable imperfection, a slowly developing, sluggish but dependable organism, easy and broad in its comprehensiveness, successful by its very anomalies, typically English (we think) in all these characteristics.

These impressions are true. The claws of crisis were pared, zeal was diluted, fanaticism cooled, violence atrophied. Sunday after Sunday the parsons read the prayers from Cranmer's great Book; the dignified yet supple phrases sank into the popular consciousness to form an ineffaceable pattern of sober grace. Little by little the ancient religious traditions of the parish, drawing their strength as always from tombs and chancels, growing in the shadows of a thousand little spires, became settled after the interlude of violence and dispute, and, tolerated by the comprehensive discipline, provided that continuity with the good old days without which no institution can hope to flourish. The drone of the homilies replaced the mutter of the mass. Babies were christened, women churched, even the recusants turned out betimes, a generation was committed to the ground in the sombre simplicity of the English service. Son succeeded father in the responsibilities of the churchwarden, and men grew old and full of tales as sextons and bell-ringers. A generation arose nurtured upon the "ABC," a generation of men who fingered their Bibles instead of their beads. In all places the preacher's voice was heard, in season and out of season, enforcing the doctrines of the *via media*.

These are the benign images which transmit to us the Elizabethan

Establishment as a work of art, a finished and tranquil parcel of England's heritage. They are the fruits of meditation in the common rooms of many an ancient and noble foundation, of evening walks in many a cathedral close. The historian of Paul's Cross must regretfully forsake these certainties, he is on the firing line, he surveys the bulwarks of the fortress which the historians, with a kind of scholarly primitivism, have described for posterity At Paul's Cross the preachers peer out from the hardly won bastion, and, blessing their gracious Queen, look out over the desolation waste and wild of the papist world, casting by times an uneasy glance at the zealots boring within, shuddering at the worldliness of the age, and calling down the wrath of an angry God upon all who would overturn the righteous order established. The fulminations of these champions of Anglicanism militant present at first no consistent pattern, situations are dealt with as they arise, incoherencies flourish, there are bewildering varieties of opinion and degrees of zeal. Yet as the years pass the preachers are easier to classify, a standard emerges by which they may be judged. The Establishment begins to claim her own, and the preachers begin to speak from a distinctive platform, and to insist upon the fruitfulness of a church blessed by long-continued peace and piety In the fullness of time the Elizabethan church brought forth Richard Hooker

Amid the general rejoicing and confusion which attended the accession of Elizabeth, Dr William Bill, chaplain to the Queen, preached at Paul's Cross, on November 20. Neither his sermon nor the instructions from Cecil upon which it was based have survived, but since John Christopherson, Marian Bishop of Chichester, attacked him as a heretic in the same place the next Sunday, it may be presumed that he celebrated the hope of a return to the reformed religion under the new Queen, although Elizabeth had as yet given no hint of the course she intended to pursue Bill was a moderate, having effaced himself under Mary without going into exile, but competent men of his stamp, if Matthew Parker be excepted, were not numerous among the possibilities for a new bench of bishops or any other important positions in the new order There was danger, amid the general disorder concerning religion, that men's minds might be dangerously stirred up by the preaching of contrary doctrines. The Catholic party, still hopeful of maintaining something at least of what they had gained, spoke out boldly How Christopherson got to the

Cross is a mystery, considering Cecil's care in such matters, but the funeral sermon for the late queen could not easily be interfered with, and on that occasion Bishop White of Winchester spoke very sharply against "the wolves coming out of Geneva." The exiles, at least those who had gone no further than the Low Countries, were beginning to return, and "some Ministers of the Word, impatient of Delay, whilest they chose rather to fore-run then expect Laws, began to sow abroad the Doctrine of the Gospell more freely; first in private houses, and then in Churches; and the People, greedy of Novelties, began to flock unto them in great number."[34] One party feared that the Queen would not reform religion, the other that she would. Because of the dangers inherent in such undisciplined and uninformed wrangling, an order was issued on December 27 inhibiting preaching, and it seems fairly certain that there were no more sermons at Paul's Cross till Thomas Sampson preached the Rehearsal sermon there the following April.

Meanwhile the Marian exiles had returned in numbers, Parliament had met and passed the Act of Uniformity. Worldly policy had triumphed.[35] No diffuse and vulnerable statements of policy or belief were made; the materials at hand, including the returning clergy fresh from the seminars of Geneva, Zurich, or Strassburg, were used; a supple and usable instrument was created which could be adjusted to circumstances. At first all was well. For the publication of a really important issue Dr. Bill was again requisitioned; he justified the imprisonment of the Marian bishops Watson and White on April 9, 1559. Grindal, newly appointed Bishop of London, was required to display the revolution (so far as it was revolution) involved in the restoration of "King Edward's Book." In the next month the new bishops appeared at the Cross, full of their continental sojourn and the nice theology of the foreign churches; even the radical wing of the Protestant cohorts found a voice there. One "Makebray" a Scottish preacher, perhaps a disciple of Knox, preached in September, and Jean Veron, a French preacher, who had been involved in the Bourne riot of 1553 and had languished in jail during Mary's reign, made his appearance there two weeks later. Robert Crowley, the satirist and publisher, preached in October. In fact, although the extremists were not rewarded with bishoprics, the roll of Paul's Cross preachers during the first four years of the reign, which we owe to the indefatigable diarist and undertaker Henry Machyn, includes the names of most of the exiles who desired reformation without tarrying for any. Continental usages were initiated in the services; psalms were sung after the sermon, "Genevay ways." There must have been considerable hostility to these preachers among both those who deplored the loss of the old faith and those who simply felt disturbed at the incursion of the strangers. Veron in particular was the target of some loose talk and casual slander. In November 1561, a young man did penance at the Cross for slandering him; three weeks later the diarist Machyn, who had apparently called the Frenchman "White-hair" and accused him of incontinency, was forced, in spite of his excellent connections, to do likewise. Machyn's enthusiasm for sermons was undiminished by this unpleasant episode.

While the people were getting accustomed to the Marian exiles and the exiles to the policies of Elizabeth's government, the apologists of the Church of England were forced to undertake the defence of the Establishment against Rome. In this first stage of hostilities the issues remained doctrinal rather than political; the English controversialists were engaged to defend Cranmer's Book. Not until the bull *Regnans in excelsis* of 1570 was the burden of political equivocation laid firmly on the consciences of English Catholics. Before that time, the stalwarts of the Anglican cause, hampered by the indifference of the administration, by the high incidence of the old faith in their cures, by want of books and even perhaps by scruples of conscience, conducted a remarkably sustained attack upon the doctrines, rites, and ceremonies of the Roman Church.

Of these stalwarts the chief was John Jewel, Bishop of Salisbury. It was at Paul's Cross that he began his campaign against the adversary, on November 26, 1559, challenging the learned of the Catholic Church to prove their doctrines; this challenge he repeated at the Cross in the following March. His main attack was upon the mass, and his criteria of judgment were the Scriptures and the primitive church. Thus began a long-continued controversy of immense complexity, which, though it exercised the intelligence, patience, and diligence of many divines, had but one enduring good; it produced Jewel's *Apologia Ecclesiae Anglicanae*, a monument not unworthy to stand as a milepost between Cranmer and Hooker. Some chapters of the controversy were rehearsed at Paul's Cross, by Jewel and by Alexander Nowell, Dean of St. Paul's. However enlivened by vigorous phrases and scurrilous personalities, such "replies" to the arguments of Harding and other expatriate Catholics must have been dull fare for the auditory. Of more immediate interest was a passage of arms arising from the destruction of Paul's steeple in a thunderstorm in the summer of 1561. Preaching at the Cross on June 8, Pilkington, Bishop of Durham, exhorted the auditory to a general repentance, and to "humble obedience of the lawes and superior powers," for the burning of the steeple was to be taken as a warning to the whole realm, that the lives of men should be amended. Such disasters occurred, he said, in times of superstition and ignorance and profanation of the sanctuary. In the climate of controversy then prevailing, this interpretation of an "act of God" was too provocative to pass unanswered. John Morwen, formerly chaplain to Bonner, answered Pilkington with *An Addicion, with an Appologie to the causes of the brinninge of Paules Church*; return to the old faith, he insisted, or a greater plague will fall upon you. To this Pilkington was forced to reply with *A Confutacion* (1563). The exchange mercifully ended at that.

The subtle and devious policies by which Elizabeth and her advisers managed to maintain an alliance with Spain and at the same time aid the Huguenots were not known to the Paul's Cross preachers. If they had been known, they would not have been comprehended. For those still fresh from intimate contact with the problems and terrors of continental Protestants, the issues were uncomplicated by statecraft. Grindal was ready in 1562 to point the lesson of God's judgments upon the King of Navarre, since he naturally had no conception of the desperate intrigue necessary to gain control over that most unreliable instrument, the mind of Charles IX. There was at least one sermon pleading the cause of the Huguenots preached at the Spital and rehearsed at the Cross in Easter week, 1563. Whether or not such sermons were a source of embarrassment to the administration there is no means of knowing. At least no one could object to a public thanksgiving for the Peace of Troyes.

In the real crisis of Elizabeth's reign, the period from 1568 to 1571, when the imprisonment of Mary, the rebellion of the northern earls, and the bull *Regnans in excelsis* combined to create a situation of the utmost gravity, the attacks upon Rome at Paul's Cross contain only oblique references to the dangers of the time. What survives is a triad of fulminations against the Whore of Babylon from Jewel, Foxe, and

Bridges. Jewel preached upon the anniversary of the Queen's accession in 1569. The fall of Jericho, he said, is a type of the fall of the power of darkness which is Rome. The Queen is a new Joshua. Foxe, who was at this time engaged upon the preparation of the second edition of the *Acts and Monuments*, consented to preach at the Cross, though after much hesitation, on Good Friday, 1570. He made no specific reference to the political crisis then brewing, his main purpose being to attack the mass. Dr. John Bridges, later famous as the author of *The Defence of the Government Established*, preached after the dissolution of the Parliament of 1571, in which action was taken to inflict the penalties of high treason upon anyone who should by any means attempt to deprive Elizabeth of her crown, or introduce bulls from Rome to absolve any of the Queen's subjects from their allegiance. Like Foxe, Bridges launched a barrage of scurrilous invective against the Catholic religion, and instructed his hearers in justification by faith. He did observe that allegiance to the Pope made a devout Catholic into a traitor. In all these sermons one notes the emergence of a formula of controversy and invective; not until the Spanish menace later in the reign would the anti-Catholic campaign display more flexibility than this.

Meanwhile the palisades had to be raised on the left. Of the first two crises in the development of Elizabethan Puritanism, the vestiarian controversy made little stir at Paul's Cross. By its very nature this issue had to be fought out in the parish churches, in quarrels over injunctions, and in convocation. Poor Parker struggled with a recalcitrant minority of scrupulous ministers, and with an alternately indifferent and querulous Queen. The Puritans, if one may call them that, had raised up unto them two distinguished champions, Laurence Humphrey, President of Magdalen, and Thomas Sampson, Dean of Christ Church. These two stalwarts had engaged in a disputation upon the vestments at Oxford in 1564, and in March of the next year were summoned to Lambeth, where Parker sought to win them to conformity by persuasion. They did not conform, and while under what was virtually open arrest they both appeared in the Cross pulpit, perhaps appointed on the instigation of Leicester. Edmund Guest, Bishop of Rochester, who had opposed them at Oxford, preached at the Cross in the Easter season, and it is probable that he rehearsed against them the arguments used in the disputation. The Archbishop contended, reasonably, that apparel was a thing indifferent; to this the dissentients replied that the surplice, having been consecrated to idolatry, cannot be held a thing indifferent, and asserted the infallibility of Scripture in all matters of church government. Parker was desperate, and took the risk of proceeding against the offenders, and the further risk of issuing the Advertisements without royal authority, and of applying them in the diocese of London and elsewhere. His correspondence reveals how carefully he supervised the sermons at Paul's Cross in the spring of 1566, seeking to ensure the preaching of sound doctrine during a difficult period. Ominous signs of the formation of a party within the church were to be seen. Yet a benign moderation distinguishes Jewel's remarks on the question in a sermon at the Cross in 1569. The vessels were brought out of Jericho, he observed, but not things "meet to furnish and maintain superstition, but such things as ... may serve either directly to serve God, or else for comeliness and good order."

From Jewel to Laud the orthodox contended for "comeliness and good order." What could there be in that to which any minister could object? The answer is: both of its terms. Good order meant to a growing number of the faithful a set of rubrics enforced by ecclesiastical authority and not by the conviction of the individual conscience enlightened by Scripture. Comeliness meant to them popish shows and images. The generation who sat at the feet of Cartwright had no notion of the service of God as a judiciously proportioned observance which sanctified the gestures and apparel of men by informing them with style and order. For them the service was purely functional; its purpose was the repentance of the sinner, and to this discipline of the conscience the resources of preaching, carefully designed to produce the maximum effect or *use* from a given text, were turned with all the devotion with which the devout Anglican was able to irradiate the forms of the Prayer Book. Had the precisians won in the Convocation of 1563, it is just possible that some sort of compromise might have satisfied all parties, though it is doubtful if it could have satisfied the Queen. But they did not win, and were forced back upon issues more central to their existence. They began to frame models of church discipline. The triumph of the Elizabethan Establishment made the Puritans into academic theorists upon discipline, and such they remained until the Commonwealth. Yet the attempt was made to secure by the machinery of Parliament some alteration in the form of church government, and in April 1571 Strickland introduced his bill for the reformation of the Book of Common Prayer.

In the previous year Sandys had entered upon his duties as Bishop of London, and thereupon preached a sermon to the diocese at Paul's Cross. Whether or not he foresaw the stormy time before him, he wept on beholding his Jerusalem, and confessed that he shrank from the great responsibilities of the task. He sought to draw the teeth of the Puritan opposition by an affirmation of the validity of the Church's ceremonies:

God be praised for ever! in our churches of England, to our great comfort, God is served even in such sort as himself by his holy word hath prescribed so that no miscontented person can allege any reason sufficient why to withdraw himself from our assemblies. Our church prayers are the psalms, our lessons the scriptures, our sacraments according to Christ's institution.

The immediate debate, however, was not with those who would withdraw into conventicles, but over the vestments and the question of authority. In 1571, while the bishops were busy in Convocation framing the Articles, and in the three weeks following the introduction of Strickland's bill, Sandys secured the services of Bishops Cox, Jewel, and Horne for the Paul's Cross pulpit. All preached against the precisians, and for the sermons of Jewel and Horne there survive confutations written probably by Thomas White and Thomas Wilcox, who was co-author of the *Admonition*. Jewel argued that the vestments were useful and necessary, that black, round, white, and square are "the good creatures of God." His opponents would have none of this argument. The popish garments are antichristian trifles. "Mr Jeull," they asserted, "in defendinge Christs Church against the open papist, did well . . . but now, being an enemy to syncerity and the truth of Christs gospell, he doth evill." Horne was even more roughly treated. He affirmed that he would cease his actions in enforcing ecclesiastical discipline if it could be shown that they were unlawful. His critics replied that his own conscience should tell him that; in other words, they asked an impossible thing, that an Elizabethan bishop should be guided by the private judgment.

Such "answers" as these probably had a considerable clandestine circulation among the disaffected. A party was forming under the stress of what its members considered the persecution of the bishops, and its principles were being laid down in Cartwright's teaching at Cambridge. But it was a party within the Church of England, and there were many moderates who, in spite of their scruples, were far from despairing of compromise. One of these was Edward Bush, who preached at Paul's Cross three days after the new canons appeared in June 1571. When the Reformation first came to England, he said,

then we drew not out of the booke of God a right plat, neither laid we a sure foundation of right reformation, we did not then utterly abolished [sic] all superstitious vanities, which now by Gods just judgement are prickes in our eies: and thornes in our sides.... It is not a cappe, tippet, or surples only, which are but small matters, and the smallest of many matters, which are to be reformed in the Church of England.

Men's consciences should not be forced in these matters, but persuaded; let the ecclesiastical authorities be gentle with their brethren. Bush was uneasy but conformable.

The *Admonition to the Parliament* of May 1572 was different in tone. This solid, picturesque document, demanding a true and learned ministry, really galled the bishops, though the official answer at the Cross, by Cooper, Bishop of Lincoln, was couched in moderate phrases, so far as one can reconstruct it from the Puritan "answer" to it. He maintained, realistically, that good ministers were not to be had at the beginning of the reign because mutability of religion had caused "many towardly wits to refrain the ministry . . . and to commit their studies to physic, to law, to teaching schools, &c." This statement, which throws light on the barrenness of the Elizabethan pulpit, to which I shall return, his critics received with godly scorn. He commended "above the moon" the Book of Common Prayer, to which the precisians replied flatly that the Genevan discipline, and much preaching, were more in accord with God's word. They were moved to cries of "Blasphemy!" by what seem in retrospect his most telling points, that it is erroneous to base the external government of the Church upon the Scriptures at all points, and that the programme of the disciplinarians would lead to the dissolution of the Universities.

In August 1572, the massacre of St. Bartholomew roused Protestant sympathies to fever heat, and Elizabeth's temporization contributed to the anger of those who were eager to see in the compromise of the Establishment a compromise with popery. Meanwhile the bishops had found a champion in John Whitgift, Master of Trinity, who, aided by them, took up the task of answering the *Admonitions*. His

Answer appeared in February 1573, but in November 1572 he preached at the Cross on Sandys' appointment. It is likely that he there rehearsed his main contentions against the Puritans, and chiefly his main argument, that Puritans were like Catholics in denying to civil magistrates authority in relation to the church. He was to argue in his *Answer* that there is "no one certain and perfect kind of government prescribed or commanded in Scripture to the Church of Christ," consequently the pattern of procedure is "the continual practice of Christian Churches, in the time of Christian magistrates." This is a significant argument. It was the first really effective riposte to the Puritan demands for further reformation; if they called a bishop a "petty pope" who stood in the way of pure doctrine and practice, they were inevitably calling the Queen a "petty pope" and in doing so they stood in danger of treason. But not until Bancroft spoke at Paul's Cross in 1589 did the bishops presume to claim "divine right" for themselves, and then the claim met with a storm of opposition from all quarters. The fact is that the Elizabethan church was not fitted to serve as exemplar for any abstract argument; to defend it was almost as perilous as to attack it.

Whitgift's sermon, because it opened up new vistas of discord, did not silence the opposition; indeed it moved them to further efforts in reprisal. Since the Puritans were anxious to obtain the widest possible circulation for their arguments it was natural that they should storm the Paul's Cross pulpit. The brunt of the attack fell upon the unfortunate Sandys; his letter of complaint to Cecil is well known to historians of Puritanism. Even before the events he records with melancholy candour, Dr. Thomas Bickley, one of the less known Elizabethan bishops, attempted there a defence of the Establishment with little success, if one is to judge by the angry response of a Puritan acquaintance. He spoke of Bickley's sermon as "catchyng and cavilling to defame a brother." It may be that he thought of Bickley as a lost leader, for he had been among the most extreme of the Reformers in the days of Edward, and was supposed to have expressed his horror of the idolatry of the mass by breaking the Host in pieces and trampling it beneath his feet. He was Warden of Merton at this time, and his zeal may have been a little tempered by preferment, but the preachers who troubled Sandys in 1573 were out-and-out supporters of the discipline. Mr. Crick and Mr. Wake, as I have already recorded, caused him great pain; furthermore, he could get his hands on neither of the offenders and, writing to Cecil in August, he was sore disturbed:

Such men must be reformed, if the State shall stand safe. Truly, my Lord, I have dealt as carefully as I can, to keep such fanatical spirits from the Cross: but the deceitful Devil, enemy to religion, hath so poured out the poison of sedition, and so suddenly changed these wavering minds, that it is hard to tell whom a man may trust.[36]

He preached at the Cross himself in November, admitting as Cooper had done that there were "certain maculats" in the ministry, but pointing out that they must be dealt with according to the authority of the government established for the Church, and not by appeal from unconstituted minorities.

This sermon too was "answered." These "answers" or "confessions" upon which one has to depend for the content of some of these sermons point to the habit of note-taking at the Paul's Cross sermons, and with a purpose other than pure edification. One of the most significant aspects of such controversy as that inspired by the *Admonitions* is the development of a habit among the brethren of using a sermon by a member of the opposition as an opportunity for exercise in their favourite technique of testing by proof-texts. The authors of the "answer" to Cooper's sermon warned him that many were not prepared to swallow his doctrines without such a sifting:

There resort to that place [*sc.*, Paul's Cross] such as can try all things, and prove the spirits, whether they be of God or not and, though they lack your countenance and estimation, are able to deal with you, or the best bishop in this church, in any point of Christian religion. Who come not to sleep, as some, or for a show, with other some, or to tangle you (as you unjustly report), but to hear your doctrine, and to search the scripture daily, whether things be so that you speak.[37]

It is not clear whether these are laymen or clergy: one suspects the learned layman is among them. Certainly this was the gift which the "prophesyings" cultivated in the ministry, and there is no doubt that it could be subversive, as the Queen believed. It was the failure of the reforming brethren to secure a hearing in such an influential pulpit as Paul's Cross—apart from some chapters of error—which forced their energies into prophesyings and into the production of a clandestine and vivid literature.

As time went by, the opposition to "ye proude druncken whore of Babylon, the triple crowned Bishop even ye great Antichrist" was expressed, not only in invectives against immediate dangers, such as Jesuit missionaries, or recusants wavering in their allegiance, but also in a continuous formal polemic from Paul's Cross. It is not necessary to assume that the danger from Catholic powers abroad was greater than it actually was, or that a large proportion of the population, especially in the north, remained Catholic in sympathies, to explain the long-continued and violent assaults upon Rome from this and other Elizabethan pulpits. The real reason for these full-scale attacks upon all aspects of the Roman faith was that the *via media* was being defined by this process. Anglicanism was still revolutionary; for all the protestations of the Puritans and sectaries to the contrary, it was a reforming doctrine. Its validity could be assessed by negatives, and the vast apparatus of invective by which the preachers organized their virulent and unceasing assault upon the old faith provided the foundations for the new. At the same time it was obvious that such an approach left room for an attack from the left within the reforming movement; those who insisted upon their status as reformers could easily be accused of not having reformed enough or quickly enough. Like North American liberals in the twentieth century, the apologists of the middle way were embarrassed by their own definitions.

No summary of arguments, no collection of excerpts, can convey the insistence, the overwhelmingly tedious energy of these tirades from the Paul's Cross pulpit. A few typical arguments will serve as index to the whole. John Dyos, a stern gospeller who thought *The Praise of Folly* the fruit of learning ill bestowed, took upon himself to detect "the false Church: or rather malignant rable" in a sermon on July 19, 1579. His text was Luke 5:1-11, and he compared the ship from which Christ taught to the Church militant. It is shaken, he said, by "Turkes, Jewes, Anabaptistes, Libertines, Sectaries, Atheistes, Schismatikes, the Familie of Love, the Romishe rable, and to be short the devill and all his members." He then set forth to prove that Rome is not the true Church; the Pope is Antichrist, Rome is Babylon. Rome urges antiquity, universality and succession, but these make nothing for her. Her "antiquity is iniquity"; Christ is more ancient than all traditions. "For all this," he added, "I will not strike to graunt these men antiquitie even from Nimrod, yea to pleasure them from Cain." He inveighed against the adoration of the Host, pointed out that the word *mass* is not to be found in the Bible, and entered upon a long argument to prove that transubstantiation is false. Romish apologists break the net of the Church militant by the doctrines of justification by works and by purgatory, which has no scriptural warrant but dates only from 1439. They differ among themselves over the location of Purgatory: "It came from Virgill and Plato and other Heathen writers. If a man aske them where it is: Some of them say in Ireland, some in Etna, and some of them say it is in the Iland Thile [Thule?], which is also called Ireland."

Other preachers echoed these commonplaces. Romish doctrines, declared Bishop Curteys, are "mere dreames and devices of the Poets, As Purgatory, in the sixt Book of Virgilles Æneodos, Invocation of Saints in Ovid *de tristibus*, Holy Water in the first book of Ovids *Metamorphoses*: and so forth." "As the heathen in time of warre did invocate Mars & Bellona," said Adam Hill in 1595, "so the Papists doo invocate S. George: the heathen in povertie went to Ceres, the Papists to Saint Anne." Some preachers proceeded more by citation of authorities, as William Gravet on June 25, 1587; indeed so various were his allusions that he was attacked in a later sermon from Paul's Cross for too much reliance on other warrant than the letter of Scripture. Holding the noses of the papists to the grindstone, to use his own phrase, he disputed with them the significance of certain ambiguous phrases of St. Augustine concerning faith and works, and resisted their claim of antiquity. He agreed with John Hudson, harping on the same theme in 1584, that the true Protestant doctrine is only new in the sense that it is *restored*.

Such sermons as these were well described by the lawyer-diarist John Manningham, reporting on a sermon preached at the Cross in December 1602, by "one with a long browne beard, a hanging looke, a gloting eye, and a tossing learing jeasture": "His whole sermon was a strong continued invective against the papistes and jesuites. Not a notable villanous practise committed but a pope, a cardinall, a bishop, or a priest had a hand in it; they were still at the worst end." These efforts were distinguished neither by subtlety of argument nor by variety of attack; what strength they have lies in a colloquial harshness and violence, derived as much as anything from fervent reading in Foxe and Bale, the latter the foulest of all controversialists. Yet, one may suppose, such sermons served a limited purpose. If the higher flights of apologetics and exhortation were left to Hooker and Andrewes, these less gifted parsons had their part in exhibiting the perils of Romish allegiance and Romish missionary work.

From the 1570's to the end of the reign the preachers' invectives against Catholic assault and infiltration sounded as echoes to the fears of the government. Curteys of Chichester warned against "false speeches, false rumours, false surmises, sclaunderous Bookes and infamous Libels"; he had his suspicions also of Romanism in the Universities and the Inns of Court. John Stockwood in 1579 was certain that obstinate papists were roosting in the Inns of Court. In general, the preachers, like Ascham, were justly exercised over the influence of Catholic propaganda upon young "intellectuals," especially those who went on the Grand Tour. Just as dangerous was the private tuition available in some of the houses of the northern recusant magnates. The papists, said Stockwood, full well understand the malleability of young minds, "And therefore have their picked scholemaisters privately to nousel up their children in their houses in the Popes religion. . . . By this meanes are many towarde gentlemen otherwise, utterly marred & spoiled." Some of these schoolmasters are "olde Popishe persecuting Masse Priestes." Against the Jesuit fifth column the preachers fulminated with zeal, and some attempts were made to exhibit the rather mixed nature of the Catholic underground. "Even now," said William Fisher in 1580,

> [the Pope] layes about him in England & strikes more desperately at all estates then ever he did: for al our bold Recusants, al our quondam priests, al our harpers upon a change, all our lookers for a golden daye, all our private whisperers, and subtile surmisers whiche we have in Englande, what els are they but the Popes souldiers.

It is certainly true that the Catholic cause enlisted more than Campion and Gerard; the cause appealed to the unstable as well as to the heroic, to the disreputable adventurer as well as to the cloistered lady of the manor. If such persons could be made to turn Queen's evidence, or to serve as spies, they became pretty strong propaganda instruments on the other side, and were now and again set forth as examples to the multitude. In 1583, for example, one Lawrence Caddy, a man of good family who had entered or had been planted (it is not clear which) in the English College at Rome, performed a not very edifying recantation at Paul's Cross, and in December 1588 two converted seminary priests, William Tedder and Anthony Tyrrell, set out and recanted their errors in the same place.

Dangers, both real and imagined, to the realm and the Queen's person, arising from the efforts of the Catholic underground, were responsible for the repetition and elaboration of the doctrines of obedience according to the Book of Homilies. No subject called forth more eloquence in England's principal pulpit than the defence of the Queen's right to allegiance. Thomas White, in December 1576, affirmed that England had a "ryght braunch" in the royal chair, "not a bastards bramble, as Abimelech was." May the Lord "lengthen hir lyfe longe to raygne over us: And though I maye not saye as the Olyve tree to beare fruite, yet to florishe as the Palme." (Elizabeth's vaunted virginity interfered even with a preacher's metaphors.) The true head of the Church is Christ, who bears rule immediately as he is God and mediately through prince and pastor, the sword and the word. To the end that God's word may be preached and defended the powers that be are ordained of God, and a prince is subject to no one under God. "Both good and bad princes, gracious, and tyrannous, are all of the Lord." Returning appropriately to the same theme in his anniversary discourse in 1589, White enforced the parallel between the Queen and King David:

For Dangers, whether shee resembles David or not? Consider you: He afraide of Saule, and shee of her Sister. And who was worse beset, he, with Saul before, and Absalom behinde; or shee, set between two (Marahs) the one Crowned before hir, the other shrewdlie hastening to hir Crowne.

A more precious parallel was drawn in 1599 by Thomas Holland, regius professor of divinity in Oxford and "mighty in the scriptures." He worked out an elaborate analogy between Elizabeth and the Queen of Sheba, and, since in the mystical sense the queen who came to Solomon prefigures the faithful in Christ, so the Queen of England is the body of the elect incarnate, and her safety a matter of religious care.

Elizabeth told her last Parliament: "This I account the glory of my crown; that I have reigned with your loves." It was true and it was the secret of her amazing success. The preachers who drew these laboured comparisons between their Queen and the paragons of Old Testament story were only expressing in terms of pulpit exhortation what had become an immense, comforting yet exhilarating platitude. Only once or twice does any sign of popular discontent with the Queen appear in the records of Paul's Cross. She almost went too far in straining her subjects' loves in her diplomatic flirting with Anjou in 1579. John Stubbs's publication of his *Discovery of a Gaping Gulf* and the punishment inflicted on him in September of that year are well known. The sullenness of the crowd who watched his agony disturbed the Queen, as well it might, and a preacher was appointed to extol the government and her Protestantism at the Cross, probably in October. His remarks got a mixed reception. It is worth noting that William Fisher, in his sermon the following January, while the negotiations with Anjou were still, as far as the people knew, in progress as before, took it upon him to assure the audience that the Queen would never return to the damnable idolatry of the mass: "No, it hath caused too many conspiracies and rebellions against her most noble person, for her majestie ever to brooke it: even in pollicie." For the length of a phrase, the pleasant fiction of the Queen's single-mindedness was abandoned—"even in pollicie"! Fisher went on to offer a godly and fervent prayer that heavenly wisdom might direct the Queen's proceedings.

Six years later how different was the state of affairs and of public opinion. Catholic plots against Elizabeth, culminating in the Ballard-Babington affair, finished the task of cementing affection between Queen and people. When Sandys preached at the Cross, probably in August 1586, "at what time the main treason was discovered," his pious fear and heart-felt praise found an echo, no doubt, in the minds of most of his auditors. "We see," he said, "that the security of princes doth not rest upon their power; be they never so strongly guarded, but upon their innocency: We see from whence they ought in their troubles to look for succour." After asserting this suitable doctrine, which perhaps gives too little credit to Walsingham, Sandys reviewed the conspiracy of Absalom as it seemed to apply to the present situation, catalogued and condemned civil seditions from the rebellion of Korah down, and ended with a poignant prayer for the Queen's deliverance out of all danger. The preachers, like the poets, were developing a scheme of adulation, a formula of praise. The full range of this is best illustrated in the accession anniversary sermon of John Duport, delivered at the Cross in 1590, which also illustrates what became a major theme in the Paul's Cross sermons of the next half-century, the theme of thankful remembrance.

Duport began by celebrating the virtues of the Queen's noble predecessors: Henry VII, "in whom was united the happie knot of peace betwixt the houses of Lancaster and Yorke, to the utter rooting out of that horrible dissention which wasted as much of our English blood, as woulde safely have quieted the whole state of the lowe Countries, and conquered all Spaine and Italy besides"; Henry VIII, "our worthy Alexander;" Edward VI, a prince of incomparable hope; Mary, "deceived with the witchcraft of Rome." He praised Elizabeth's "singular ripenes in all manner of learning" ("M. Ascham wil tel you"); her Periclean sway over free Englishmen; her moderation. Carried away by his own eloquence, he for a time forgot the course of his sermon, and was swept by patriotic passion to this conclusion:

Beholde (you Englishmen) behold your naturall Prince, the offspring of your . . . kinges, the image of their nature, the peer . . . of their virtue, the onelie reminder of so manie worthies, the flower of all princehoode and royaltie, the miracle of nature, the glorie of womanhoode, the paterne of all godlinesse and vertue, the modile of perfections, the wonder of the world, the Phenix of our time, the honour of England.

Nationalism and Protestant piety found united expression in fulminations against Spain. The war with Spain was a great gift to the preachers, for England was fighting a holy war, and the bloody pennons which waved over the flats of Flanders and the splintered decks of English privateers were the banners of the Church militant. The preachers at Paul's Cross rose to the opportunity with gusto; too long they had had to stifle their thoughts upon foreign affairs; the stern simplicities of war were more suited to their extravagant metaphors than the devious complications of diplomacy which had informed those affairs until 1580. Antichrist had always elevated the Host; his instruments had now raised the sword.

Appropriately, the Spanish menace first appears in a Paul's Cross sermon as a menace from Ireland, in the rebellion of Desmond with some little encouragement from Spain which Grey of Wilton had put down by November 1580. In January 1581, James Bisse, Fellow of Magdalen, preached at the Cross, and in the course of a general invective against the sins of the realm, pointed to the victory in Ireland as earnest of what England could accomplish under a Deborah in the service of God:

By Elizabeth, a woman, the Goates of Italy, the wolves of Spain, the cormorantes of Rome [shall be overcome]. The Irish coltes, and the Foxes of England, that are now in Ireland, and all other her enemies shall bee brought to shame. . . . Goe tell them . . . that those Goates, Wolves, cormorantes, Coltes, Foxes, shalbe so hunted and bayted by an English Grey, that not one of them shalbe left to pisse against a wall.

Bisse was obviously enjoying himself. But greater triumphs were to come. The year '88 was a legend almost as soon as the last crippled galleon reached the coast of Spain, and a legend with power even in 1940. This was *annus mirabilis, mundi climactericus* beyond all reckoning. For generations preachers mentioned it with awe and pride. We have little evidence for what they said in the five sermons of thanksgiving at Paul's Cross from August 20 to November 24; as John Piers stood in that pulpit before the Queen on November 24 and exulted in her glories, one wonders whether he divided the credit for the victory as Drake divided the necessities of preparing for it. "The Lord is on our side," wrote that expert, "but I beseech you to consider powder and shot for our great ordnance."[38]

Just as Elizabeth could be compared to the heroes of Israel, so Philip's prototype might be found among their enemies. Thomas White, preaching in the year after the Armada, saw in him the lineaments of Sennacherib, and announced: "We would not have him to come into our Countrie neither a Friend nor a Foe; for we have tried his comming both wayes to be nought." "Tell it in Spaine," he cried, "and in the Ilands there about, where (perhaps) you may come," that God hath magnified Elizabeth. They did come to the islands. In the three years following the Armada the English sea-dogs preyed upon Spanish communications with indifferent success but magnificent bravado. On February 14, 1590, Roger Hacket, son of a Lord Mayor of London, and "cried up for an eminent preacher," preached a sermon in which the insolence of Naash King of Ammon was compared with that of Philip II, "the great monarch of the west, whose treasures are fed with the gold of Indy . . . , whose navy as a forest hath shadowed our seas." As the men of Israel were recruited by Saul against the evil king of old, so Englishmen, now that God has decreed war with Spain, should fight for the faith.

A more elaborate justification of war was provided in 1598 by the redoubtable Stephen Gosson. Like Hacket, he found a precedent in Old Testament history, in the war of Jehoshaphat against the men of

Moab and Ammon. War, he said, is undertaken on the lawful authority of the prince, which makes it no affair of private revenge. The wars of Spain, in the Indies, in Portugal, in Granada, in the Low Countries and France, are "uncharitable and unjust," uncharitable because they weaken Christendom and strengthen the Turk, unjust because of the "rough regiment of his warriors."

> Looke upon your own warres another while, you shal find them to be very charitable and just . . . , [undertaken] in defence of England and an innocent maiden Queene, whose glorious life hath injuriously and dishonourably been fought and thirsted after these many years.

If there was a pacifist conscience in his auditory, which is doubtful, Gosson probably smothered it.

From these vigorous certitudes, we must turn again to the intestine struggle in the Church of England. Step by step, the quarrel with Puritanism as a platform of church discipline and with the undisciplined supporters thereof may be traced at Paul's Cross in the years following the publication of the *Admonitions*.

Between 1572 and 1588, when the Marprelate tracts stirred up so much contention (and amusement), the energies of the disciplinarians were turned chiefly to the formation of their programme through what are usually known as "prophesyings." These godly exercises, which flourished chiefly in Lancashire and Northamptonshire, were really debating societies, with strict rules and pious formularies; they were very useful to the less learned of the ministry. There is little doubt that out of such sessions often grew unorganized associations imbued with the assurance of their own righteousness and, as customarily happens in programmes of adult education, their own learning. But certainly the educational value of the prophesyings could be and was defended, chiefly through virulent attacks upon the "dumb dogs" who filled many a benefice. John Walsal, sometime tutor to Francis Bacon, in his Paul's Cross sermon of 1598 put up a mild defence of the "dumb dogs":

> The meanest of all our ministers, though unable to preach, are notwithstanding such, as for their true religion, right worshipping of God, zealous affection to the Gospell, prayinge for and with their congregations in a knowen language, onely to the Lord, and their wishing well, and seeking, as they can, to doe good in their charges, &c., may justly be preferred to the learnedest, to the wisest, and devoutest of all that Romish rabble of sacrificing priests.

His case would have been better had he been able to point to a power in that "&c." Generations were to pass before that inclusive and delightful term was to include studies of natural history and old genealogies, or any of the various avocations by which the rectors in little parishes have enriched the cultural heritage of the Church of England.

Although Hooker dared to attack Calvin's theory of the will of God at the Cross in 1581, the issues dealt with there were for the most part not doctrinal but disciplinary. In 1583, Whitgift succeeded to the primacy, and in November of that year, preaching on the accession anniversary upon the familiar theme of obedience, he spoke of the "wayward and conceited persons," and reminded them that Christian liberty frees us from subjection to Satan, but not from subjection. They speak evil of bishops and magistrates, and large numbers at their sermons are no guarantee of right doctrine and behaviour. The same subject, the disturbance of unity by private fancies, was discussed in the next year by John Hudson, canon of Chichester. Everyone, he declared, "hath a revelation, hath an interpretation by himselfe"; let us, he pleaded, put aside these petty quarrels.

Appeals like his went unheeded, for another paper war was brewing. It was in that year 1584 that Dr. Copcot of Cambridge answered in a sermon at the Cross the *Counter-Poyson* of Dudley Fenner, that ubiquitous Puritan pamphleteer who was associated with Cartwright in the Presbyterian pastorship at Middelburg. In that year also the Presbyterian faction brought forth that very important document, *A Brief and Plain Declaration*, usually known as the *Learned Discourse*, in which their whole position was put with great clarity and force. Dr. John Bridges, Dean of Salisbury, preached against this work at the Cross in 1584, and "in an evil hour," as Bishop Frere put it, undertook to expand his arguments into the monumental *Defence of the Government Established*, a line by line refutation of the *Discourse*, tedious, weighty, of 1,409 pages, inviting ridicule. What it invited it received. In the following year the first of the Marprelate tracts began to be surreptitiously circulated. "O, read over D. John Bridges, for it is a worthy work," cried its title-page irreverently. The most mystifying and fascinating chapter in the history of Puritanism was just beginning.

The major riposte by the Establishment was made on February 9, 1589, in a sermon at Paul's Cross by Richard Bancroft. His allusion to the *jure divino* validity of episcopacy is often referred to, but the general line of his attack on the extremists deserves more notice than it has received. False prophets are abroad, he said, spirits of error:

> They had (saie these men) in their synagogs their priests, we must have in every parish our pastors: they their Levites, we our doctors: they their rulers of their synagogs, we our elders: they their leviticall treasurers, we our deacons.

Where such discipline as this is not erected they say God's ordinance is not performed. They affect the places and preferments of their superiors; they are moved by self-love and covetousness:

> For I am fully of this opinion, that the hope which manie men have conceived of the spoile of the Bishops livings, of the subversion of cathedrall churches, and of a havocke to be made of al the churches revenues, is the cheefest and most principall cause of the greatest schismes that we have at this day in our church.

They "wring and wrest the Scriptures" according to their fancy, which has ever been the property of heretics. "One of fower or five and twentye yeeres old, if you anger him, will sweare he knoweth more then all the ancient fathers." In their perfect platform the civil magistrate is quite forgotten; they mention the magistrate "for maners sake," but in such a cold and sparing way that there is not a priest in Wisbeach who would not subscribe to their limited notions of obedience. Consider, he went on, the dire experience of the Scottish king with presbyteries; consider the danger of such books as *Vindiciae contra tyrannos*.

The Puritans are covetous then, and they are seditious. No Church has been planted since the Apostles' time without bishops. Such were Bancroft's arguments. Storms arose to left and right. That earnest Welshman John Penry issued *A Briefe Discovery* of the untruths and slanders he found in the sermon; Sir Francis Knollys, who was sure that what Bancroft had said about government by bishops had put him in a *praemunire*, wrote to the learned Dr. John Rainolds of Oxford to clear his mind on the matter, and Rainolds replied with a *Judgment of Doctor Reynolds* (reprinted in 1641 as a Long Parliament manifesto of the Root-and-Branch party). Meanwhile William James, Dean of Christ Church, formerly chaplain and death-bed confessor of Leicester, repeated Bancroft's arguments at the Cross in November 1589, and added that Martin was enemy of the Universities, that his manners were abominable, inquiring, with a curious lack of humour, how such a one could be filled with the spirit of God.

After this crisis, the quarrel with the disaffected settled into stereotyped appeals for unity in the bond of peace. Thomas White, in his 1589 sermon, proceeded to "warble sweetlie, to cast out the foule spirit of the Faction, with Davids harpe," and Gervase Babington and Richard Lewes, in 1590 and 1591, pleaded for temperance on both sides. Rome is the real enemy, said Roger Hacket; Robert Temple, preaching in 1592, quite properly suggested the answers to Martin and others like him might well be left to professional pamphleteers, and not suffered to disturb the gravity of serious religious exhortation:

[Martin] handleth divinitie with scurrilitie, & scripture with laughter, more pleasant to a sight of gospell libertines, and Church robbers, then meddling at all with the matter in hande, much lesse deciding the controversies by moment and wayght of argument, and therefore better answered alreadie by some merrie mates like himselfe, then to bee vouchsafed so muche as a silable by learned replye.

His "merrie mates" were perhaps Lyly and Nashe.[39]

The direction of attack upon the Puritans was, in fact, changing. The original issue of the discipline, clouded by the libels, receded somewhat, to be succeeded by consideration of the threat involved in an alliance of the Puritan lecturers with the gentry and the common lawyers. This enlivens Adam Hill's attack upon what he calls (generically) "Martin" in a sermon at the Cross in 1593. He asserted that "Martin findeth fault that a Minister should have two benefices, but for a nobleman or Gentleman which hath sixe hee reprehendeth it not.... What is the reason, he reproveth the ministers so sharply, and leaveth the other unreproved?" Five years later the intrepid Gosson was more sweeping in his condemnation of the suspected alliance of the disaffected parsons with a set of laymen. The age is plagued by distorting glasses; "such a glasse is the new Presbyterie couching downe at the gates of great personnes, with her bellie full of barcking libells to disgrace the persons of the best men, and the laboure of the best learned in the Church of England." The gentry and the lawyers persecute the poor ministers; schismatics and "caterpillars" are determined to reduce the Establishment to disgrace and penury.

The Cleargie of Englande may nowe joyne hande in hande in a faire roundelay and sing and record one to another, as little children do in the streets, When shall we eat white bread? when the puttock is dead.... To this purpose it may be you shal perceive some broker belonging to the common law, or some jester hanging upon the Court, or some Lyris Poet and common Rimer hovering about this Cittie, subborned and bolstered to deale in derision of the Church in time of Parliament as Italians do in their plaies. . . . A great part of this mischief being hatched by the presbyterie.

There is a carefully veiled suggestion in this sermon, preached in 1598, that some great persons well enough known, could they be named, were behind the defamers and robbers of the Church. Gosson remarked in his conclusion that he had been reprehended (though not officially "called in question") for a sermon treating of the "Churches quarrel" preached at the Cross in 1596(?), in which he seemed to strike at "some great person." The whole passage is portentous and heavily ambiguous, but it is safe to conjecture that if Gosson had in mind any great person that person was Essex.

In all these attacks upon Puritanism, there is little or nothing of reasoned objection to the religious *ideal* of the opposition party, no analysis of their view of the nature of the worship of God. Yet before the end of the reign one champion of the Establishment arose at the Cross to point out how the Puritan idea of worship was related to that contempt for the physical fabric of the Church which was leading to such spoliation of its effects by the greedy patrons. John Howson had a distinguished career; of Christ Church, Oxford, he was appointed one of the Queen's chaplains in 1598, and in 1602 became Vice-Chancellor of Oxford, where he strove to put down Puritanism with a heavy hand. He won the favour of James by these efforts and by his violence in attacking popery, and in 1619 he was consecrated Bishop of Oxford. Nine years later he was elevated to the see of Durham, and died in that difficult office. But it was in the last decade of Elizabeth's reign that he made his mark, with two sermons at Paul's Cross, the one preached against simony in 1597, the other upon sacrilege and neglect of common prayer in 1598. It is the latter sermon I now consider.

His theme was Christ's casting out of the thieves from the Temple. In our days, he said, the temple is spoiled by "irreligious Julianists" who have made some village churches no better than "pigstyes," and in cities the churches are like "a country hall, faire whitelimed, or a citizens parlour, at the best wainscotted, as though we were rather Platonists than Christians." To contend for seemly furniture in the Church is not superstition but "true Christianitie"; the sin of spoliation will not escape without punishment. The reason why such avarice is sanctioned by some is that they differ from true Christians in their view of the end and use of God's house. Christ said that his Father's house was a house of prayer. That is, of public service, in which prayer is the chief element. In the primitive Church the house of God was called *oratorium*.

> Now we say . . . let the first and chiefe place be given to preaching: and provision is made, that the people be not overwearyed with too much praying. And though the Church of England hath no such constitution, yet the people entertain the practice of it, many of them condemning common prayer, but a greater part neglecting [it], and holding it the only exercise of the service of God to heare a sermon.

This is the ancient error; St. Chrysostom complains of it. Even under the law of nature without benefit of revelation men were moved to the service of God not by instruction, "but only by a naturall and inward motion." This must have been the fruit of prayer, not preaching. "The blessing is not promised to hearing, but to doing."

Such was the complaint of Gardiner against the extreme reformers almost fifty years before:

> These men speak much of preaching, but note well this, they would we should see nothing in remembrance of Christ, and therefore can they not abide images. They would we should smell nothing in remembrance of Christ, and therefore speak they against anointing and holy water. They would we should taste nothing in memory of Christ, and therefore they cannot away with salt and holy bread. . . . Finally, they would have all in talking, they speak so much of preaching, so as all the gates of our senses and ways to man's understanding should be shut up, saving the ear alone.[40]

Here is a clear demonstration of the kinship between the radical Reformers and the later Puritans. Balked of their hopes of the right discipline, the Puritans exercised their immense spiritual virtuosity in the examination of the nature of their religious experience, and found it inward, found it to be the effect of the WORD. The attack upon the vestments was in one sense the real battle, and the establishment of *classes* incidental to the main impulse of the movement, which was to bring the wayfaring Christian to a consciousness—a shattering but renovating consciousness—of the overpowering will of the Almighty. Against this powerful impulse a generation of the orthodox was to tilt in vain.

No connected history of the separatists can be constructed from references in the Paul's Cross sermons. There were times when the danger from those withdrawn from the body of Christ and holding opinions dangerous and wild seemed to be greater than ordinary, and at those times the preachers warned and condemned, and that is all.

Reference has been made above to the recurring fear of the Anabaptists, whose tenets, horrible as well from the political as from the theological point of view, seemed a sort of devilish locus for dangers terrible as those to be feared from the Papists. Four foreign heretics termed Anabaptists were burned in 1575, having in May of that year performed a public recantation at the Cross. The next month, five English members of the Family of Love recanted the heresies of the author of their sect. This sect had been founded by David Georg, an Anabaptist of Delft, who died in 1556. His disciple, the Apostle Paul of the movement, was Henry Nicholas, fifteen of whose works were translated into English by the visionary Christopher Vittels of Southwark and printed at Amsterdam. Vittels promoted one of the conventicles of the sect at Colchester. In 1575 the Family of Love addressed an *Apology* to Parliament professing their innocence of dangerous opinions and their loyalty to the Queen. Answers began to appear to Nicholas's works. John Knewstub's Good Friday sermon against these "monstrous and horrible heresies" at the Cross in 1576 was printed in 1579; Laurence Chaderton condemned them in a sermon of 1578, and John Dyos repeated the attack the next year.

References to the Brownists are confined to the year 1592. A silly mad conspiracy had been mooted to murder the Queen; the utterances of the sectaries could be and were interpreted by the nervous authorities as more seditious than in fact they were, and the rearrest of Greenwood in December paved the way for the execution of him and his fellow-zealot Barrow in 1593. While the last act of the sordid little tragedy was in the making the Paul's Cross preachers took occasion to condemn in general terms the Brownist opinions. Robert Temple, preaching in the month before the arrest of Greenwood, took notice of the Brownists and their assumption of perfection; A. W., at the Cross in the same year, observed their "preposterous and rash disordered zeale."

If the separatists were not a menace sufficient to demand such extended and vigorous counter-attack as that delivered upon papists and Puritans, the so-called atheism of the time sadly shook the security of the good men who exhorted the multitude in Paul's churchyard. It must be made clear that when the preachers condemned atheism they meant one very definitely definable sort of unbelief, or they meant almost anything at all. That is, *atheists* meant those "of whom

God is altogether unapprehended" (Hooker), or it was a general term of denunciation. Both these uses appear in the Paul's Cross sermons, and, except for a brief period in the nineties, the second is the more common one. Thomas White described a sermon preached by him in 1577 as a sermon against "covetous Atheists," by which he obviously meant the covetous in general, and Howson referred to the spoilers of the church as atheists and "Julianists." In sermons dating from the last year of the reign, one finds atheism identified with popery. "A Popish Atheist," said Francis Marbury,

is an hideous mongrell, even a verie Centaur. As to say the very truth, Popery and Atheisme are very coincident, and their differences very obscure.... The Papist is a make-god, and ye Atheist is a mock-god.

Dr. John King came nearer to an analysis of men of unstable opinions when he observed in the same year that

men thinke now a dayes, that arrianisme, Atheisme, Papisme, Libertinisme, may stand together, and like salt, oyle, and meale be put togither in a sacrifice. Their conscience is sett in bonde, like Thamar when she went to play the harlot.... Every religion will serve their turne.

In fact, all who questioned the validity of the Scriptures—deists, agnostics, seditious persons who denied that the king was the vicar of God on earth, or at least in England—all these were atheists by Elizabethan standards, and in consequence the term as used by the preachers is often little more than pejorative. The last phrase of King's indictment suggests, however, that for the pious atheism was more or less equivalent to Machiavellianism, or, to put it more broadly, worldliness in general. This is the suggestion in White's and Howson's use of the term, and their view is amplified in Hooker's treatment of the same subject. Machiavellianism in religion he attributes to contentions in religion:

Nothing pleases them [atheists] better than these manifold oppositions upon the matter of religion.... For a politic use of religion they see there is, and by it they would also gather that religion itself is a mere politic device, forged purposely to serve for that use.[41]

It was between 1592 and 1594 that the fear of atheism reached its height. In 1593, Thomas Nashe warned the preachers:

University men that are called to preache at the Crosse and the Court, arme your selves against nothing but Atheisme, meddle not so much with Sects & forraine opinions, but let Atheisme be the onely string you beate on; for there is no Sect now in England so scattered as Atheisme. In vaine doe you preach, in vayne doe you teach, if the roote that nourisheth all the branches of security be not thorowly digd up from the bottome. You are not halfe so wel acquainted as them that lyve continually about the Court and Citty, how many followers this damnable paradoxe hath: how many high wits it hath bewitcht.[42]

In September of that year Adam Hill in his Paul's Cross sermon called atheism the "sinne of all sinnes," reporting that "our Atheists" deny the divinity of Christ. He made some cloudy and euphuistic allegations concerning the provenance of atheism:

As poison when it entreth into the body, it infecteth first the vains, secondly the blood, thirdly, the members, & last of all the heart: so Atheisme began in the vains of the lighter sort of people, and from thence it hath crept into the blood and generositie of this land, by meanes whereof it is spread into all the members and parts of this realme: God keep it from the heart, that is, from the Court and the Cittie of London.

It is hard to tell what he meant, because it is impossible to guess how much he knew and how much was just general exhortation and inflated style. By the "lighter sort" he possibly meant wits like Marlowe; and by "blood and generositie" members of the gentry—Nashe was almost certainly referring to Ralegh. In a sermon of November 1594 John Dove said flatly that atheists "are in the courts of princes." It is likely that these allusions indicate the interest and disquiet felt over the gossip about Ralegh and his circle, which culminated in the inquiry at Cerne Abbas in 1594.

There remain to be considered the very important events at the Paul's Cross pulpit during the last act of the tragedy of Essex, ending with William Barlow's sermon upon the Earl's confession preached on March 1, 1601, three days after the execution.

The story of the last two years of Essex's life is very complicated, for Robert Devereux was a very complicated man, and the definitive analysis of his character remains still to be made. When it is made, it will necessarily include a close study of his latter-end religiosity, and for that Barlow's sermon, taken with other evidence, is valuable. For the most part, however, the Paul's Cross sermons which contain allusions to Essex or which were preached directly upon his case are chiefly interesting as propaganda. Essex had considerable popular appeal, and this may explain the guarded ambiguity of Gosson's references to a "great person" in 1596 and 1598. Stow says that such and so great was the hearty love and deep affections of the people towards him, by reason of his bounty, liberality, affability, and mild behaviour, that as well scholars, soldiers, citizens, sailors, etc., Protestants, Papists, Sectaries, and atheists, yea, women and children which never saw him, that it was held in them a happiness to follow the worst of his fortunes.[43]

In the collapse of his fortunes he became a rallying point for the disaffected, and for this reason it was necessary both to guard against praise of him at the Cross and to proceed with great care in condemning him from that pulpit. His abrupt return from Ireland and his violent irruption into the Queen's chamber took place in September 1599. During his imprisonment in the Lord Keeper's house, and his serious illness, Cambridge divines who came up to the Cross to preach prayed for him there, to the distress of Cecil and Bancroft, protesting that since he was their Chancellor, they were in duty bound to pray for him. After examination by the Council, Essex was set at liberty and went down to the country to await the Queen's decision on the farm of the sweet wines, upon the renewal of which in his gift all his fortunes depended. In October 1600 the Queen decided to hold this monopoly for the Crown. In December Essex came up to London, and from that day Essex House became a place of resort for reckless young gentlemen, Puritan preachers, and the disaffected generally. Sedition was talked there, and this holding court under the Queen's nose was noted with general uneasiness. To all objections Essex answered that he supposed he might freely entertain his friends, since he was under no inhibition, and as for the preachers, they were for his spiritual comfort. On the afternoon of February 7, 1601, some of the gentlemen of Essex's company attended a performance at the Globe of *Richard II*, having persuaded the Lord Chamberlain's men to revive the play for 40s. and the promise of a well-filled house. The next morning Essex made his abortive attempt at rebellion, was received with mingled affection and fear by the citizens of London, and by night was a prisoner with some of his confederates at Lambeth. The preacher at the Cross that morning was John Boys, Rector of Tilmanstone; as the crowd dispersed after the sermon, followers of Essex were shouting in the cathedral that Essex was to have been murdered by Ralegh, and that they carried arms to defend themselves till the Queen should hear of it. In this crisis the Council acted with dispatch. Suspected persons were rounded up and interrogated, including one John Bargar who used the Paul's Cross sermon as an alibi; a proclamation was issued setting forth the facts of the rebellion and warning against seditious rumours, and directions were issued for the preacher at the Cross the following Sunday. The speaker chosen was John Hayward, Rector of St. Mary Woolchurch. So great was the fear of disorder that the Lord Mayor contemplated keeping five hundred armed men all day in Paul's churchyard. There was no demonstration, however, and Bancroft expressed himself well satisfied with Hayward's performance:

> The auditory was great (though the Lord Mayor and his brethren were absent) and the applause for her Majesty's deliverance from the mischiefs intended exceedingly great, loud and joyous. The traitor is now laid out well in colours to every man's satisfaction that heard the sermon, as I suppose or could judge by men's countenances. The preacher's text was II Sam. 21. 17, in these words: "Then David's men sware unto him, saying, thou shalt go no more out with us to battle lest thou quench the light of Israel," and he handled it exceedingly well, being a most fit text for the present occasion.[44]

Well received the sermon may have been, but in the crisis the Council and its agents went too far and accused Essex publicly of treasons for which he was not arraigned, thus keeping alive a considerable sympathy for him which might otherwise have been dissipated. This error was noted at the time:

> Order was taken ... that the preachers at Paul's cross and other churches in London should deliver the same matters from the pulpit, and decry the Earl as a hypocrite, Papist, and confederate with the Pope and King of Spain, to make him King and bring in idolatry. But as usual in such cases, they, from malice or desire to please, amplified it beyond all probability. On the one side they cry "crucify," on the other there is such a jealousy of light and bad fellows, that it is rumoured the preachers of London will rise and deliver him out of the Tower.[45]

The trial took place on February 19. Essex, condemned, awaiting execution in the Tower, was in a strange mood. He was first visited by Dr. Thomas Dove, Dean of Norwich, who came primed to get a confession from him and failed. Rev. Abdy Ashton, one of Essex's favourite gospellers, was more successful, convicting him of sin against God in rebelling, and prompting him to make a confession to Cecil and Howard. He wrote a full confession, which disgusted his tough and ambitious secretary Henry Cuffe. He received Barlow with a fervent desire to prepare himself for death, being affected, as one biographer (Harrison) asserts, by "acute religious melancholia." After his execution, Barlow, later to achieve prominence as the reporter of the Hampton Court conference, the first Powder Plot preacher, and Bishop of Rochester, was set up to report the confession and its significance to the multitude at the Cross. His instructions from Cecil survive, and deserve reproduction, at least in part:

I leave all things which I have delivered you by my Lords' direction to be carried and applied as you like, only the Lords desire that when you touch the practice and purpose of coming to Court with a power, you move them to consider how perilous a thing it was to have put a Lady, the Queen, in that fright she must have been in. . . .

(The Queen was in no fright. She had her father's nerve, and an "old rusty sword," and wished to go forth and see whether, by God's Son, anyone would dare to lay a hand on her.)

In any wise remember to name the particulars of his obstinate speeches to Mr. Dove, which my Lord of London [Bancroft] can deliver you. Remember also precisely to declare it, as it may be clearly conceived how great suit the Earl made that he might die privately in the Tower, and how much even to yourself he expressed his thankfulness for it, wherein also you may not forget how himself was possessed with an opinion that he should have had of the people a great acclamation. If you can bring it in well, it will be very fit to remember that his purpose of taking the Tower was only to have been a bridle to the city, if happily [haply] the city should have misliked his other attempt.[46]

The sermon got a mixed reception. In his preface to the published sermon, Barlow confessed that he spoke "with much fear and trembling." For three days before, he continued, "I was not one day from the Court, still labouring to informe myself of every thing which I doubted, that I might in these calumnious times, keep my selfe, for anything I would there deliver; from the controlment either of ill tongues, or mine owne conscience." In spite of all his care, "the malignitie of the many" was such that it was given out after the sermon that he was struck with madness, that he was next day committed to the Tower, or at least that he had offended the Queen and Council. (Either the public mind was in a sad state of confusion, or these reports were spread by interested parties.) Some contended that he broke the canons both of religion and of law in revealing a penitent's confession, others that he spoke for spleen, because, although he had proclaimed the victory of Cadiz with praise of Essex at the Cross in 1596, he had received no emolument or advancement for it.

In the sermon proper, he descanted at some length upon the virtue of obedience, and then proceeded to a "short preface personall." Here he observed the necessity of defending his sermon, because the City preachers are described as "time servers & men pleasers, leaving the great man that is dead, and now cleaving to others, and closing with them for preferments." In reply to this gossip, Barlow cited his own experience after the sermon on Cadiz:

> Why should this be imputed to me, who about foure yeares sithence, in this place, uppon like suddayne warning, celebrated the glory of both the generals, the right honourable the Lord Admirall, and the late Earle, the victorie at Caliz: at which time, and long since, he soared in his highest pitch of favour with her Majestie, and yet from that day to this, though it were given out that he wold advance me, I am not either a penny the richer or a steppe the higher for him: and in truth I never moved him, neither did it move my affection from him, which I continued as intire unto him as any follower of his until his open fall.

Always, he continued, he has abhorred flattery of great persons,[47] and popularity with the multitude; but he is a subject, and nature and Scripture bind him to obedience. In this capacity he is appointed to declare what he knows, "and what is fit for you to heare." He promised to deliver nothing upon mere information or report, "but what these eares of mine have heard from his own mouth."

So he began: "Now for the late Earle; dead he is, and his soule, no doubt, with the saints in heaven: you will say, then, that dead men bite not . . . , nor by reason, or religion should be bitten." Solomon notes it as a point of atheism to prefer a living dog before a dead lion, but there is a difference in the faults of men: those who hurt only themselves, let their faults be buried with their bodies; others will annoy, and so must be remembered after death. Would to God the Earl's offence might have been buried with him, "which himselfe confessed to be a leprousie infected farre and neare." Next he proceeded to a generous praise of Essex: "so honourable in office, so gratious with his prince, so witty by nature, so learned by conference and study, so religious in profession, so valiant in warre, so beloved by the commons, so followed and honoured by men of all sortes." But he would be "the onely great man," and so he has fallen, dragging others with him. At this point, Barlow quoted in illustration Plutarch upon Coriolanus, "a gallant young, but a discontented Romane, who might make a fit paralell for the late Earle, if you read his life." (One wonders if Shakespeare was there, and noticed that.) The heinousness of the Earl's crime needs no emphasis: consider the Queen's favours to him, with his disobedience to her and his exhausting her treasury in the fruitless Irish campaign. The night of his apprehension, at Lambeth, he said smilingly to the Archbishop, "that the sinceritie of his conscience, and the goodness of his cause" comforted him. But how is it possible to be patient when one sees God's word alleged against God's ordinance?

Clement the Frier who killed Henry the third the French king, reasoned thus with himselfe to his bloudy murther out of Gods booke, Ehud killed king Eglon, therefore I may kill Henry. Eglon was a king, so is Henry. What then? Eglon signifieth a Calve and Henry is a Calvinist. *Ergo* I may kill him by authoritie of Scripture.

The Earl's complaint from beginning to end was "some things to be reformed," but, though stiff with the Dean of Norwich, he told Barlow: "I am become another man," and ascribed his change to God's spirit working in him through Dr. Ashton. Before his execution he had conference with members of the Council and laid open the whole project, confessed it, and prayed pardon of the Secretary for the unjust calumny he had cast upon him at the trial. He asked to die in the Tower, and set down his confession in writing; "it selfe filled foure sheetes of paper, every worde in his owne hand, and his name at the end, which my selfe have seene, and will shew unto you so much as is fit." In this he confessed that his purpose was to surprise the Court with a power, Blount at the gate, Davies in the hall, a third to seize the halberds, Danvers to possess the privy chamber. What a cause of fear to the Queen! Two of these lieutenants were

stiffe and open Papists, and the fourth, by report, affected that way, what danger to her person, to religion, to the Realme they may gesse, who have reade the libells of Reynolds, Gifforde and others of that church, writing slaunderously of her Majesties person, blasphemously of our religion; and basely of our Realme and policie.

They thought of calling a Parliament, but who in England has authority to do that but the monarch? Bodin is witness upon this point of the English constitution. The Earl himself has said that God was to be thanked that the device was prevented; he admitted that "he knew that the Queene could not be in safetie so long as he lived upon the earth."

His offence and treason [was] the compound of all the famous rebellions eyther in Gods booke, or our owne land . . . consisting of Abners discontentment, of Corahs envie, of Absalons popularity, of Shebas defection, of Abimelechs faction, and banding his familie and allyes, of Hamans pride and ambition: in pretence finall, all one with that of Henrie Duke of Lancaster, against Richard the second, *remooving certaine which misled the king.* In pretence originall, that of Kettes and Tylers for the king, as they in your citty cryed in that insurrection *for the Queen, for the Queene.*

This was shrewd stuff; Barlow was following Cecil carefully. He continued to do so. You may say, he went on, addressing the City representatives, that he loved you well, but the night of his taking, in Lambeth House, he said "that you were a very base people: that he trampled up and downe your city without any resistance: that he would undertake with four hundreth men of his choise to have overrunne your citie." He said further that to trust in the multitude is vain, that your love was but vanity, and that he wished to die in the Tower lest your acclamations "should have hoven him up," and he desired to remain humble in spirit. When he was asked why he proposed to seize the Tower, he said "that it should have been a bridle to your citie."

After this stroke, Barlow summed up, desiring his auditory to "conferre these points together." He then read appropriate passages from the "true copy" of the Earl's confession at the time of his execution, and closed.

I have dwelt long upon this sermon, chiefly because it brings us closer than any other which I have seen to the living moment itself. Cecil's instructions, and especially the sermon itself, the implied hostility and confusion of the London crowd, all convey with great vividness an atmosphere of tension, fear, and wild rumour. This gets us little closer to plucking out the heart of Essex's mystery, but it does teach us not to undervalue the seriousness of this episode.

Diverse indeed are these utterances from the most important Elizabethan pulpit, but one can find a likeness in them all. There is in these sermons a singular preoccupation with what in our time is called *security*, with the theme of unity and the power and happiness which attend unity and justify it. In no other collection of Elizabethan documents does this theme emerge with more intensity and immediacy than in these sermons. England was made by such fervid exhortations as well as by profitable speculation at Antwerp and daring upon the high seas. It was one of Elizabeth's great virtues as queen that she perceived and fostered this aspect of the development of the English consciousness as well as the more romantic.

The clergy who were summoned to the Cross, fresh from the common rooms, from convocation, from the mixed business of the dioceses, were impelled to these affirmations as much by the motive of self-preservation as by the loftier impulses proper to their theoretically indispensable position. They felt engaged to maintain a tradition older than most of them would openly acknowledge, the tradition of the warning voice, hallowed by generations of Dominicans, and hallowed for them by the generation of Reformers upon whom that sometimes dangerous mantle fell. They were all the sons of Latimer, and Latimer was the son of Bromyard. What was Latimer, after all, but a preaching friar with a new theology but an old rhetoric and an old conscience? How should such men as Stockwood and Hill perceive that they were to be supplemented, even supplanted in a century by the political economists, that their divine certitudes were to be replaced by statistics, and their apocalypse by prophecies of progress? They were forever being distracted by crises. They dwelt in the midst of situations the full import of which they could but feebly understand. The foreboding widsom of a Hooker was not in them. Bancroft was supposed to know all the "dangerous positions" of Puritans, but he never really understood the significant power of a clandestine press in the hands of intemperate and frothy spirits; Barlow (and perhaps even those who instructed him) hardly saw that the Essex rising was not a prologue to danger but an irresponsible feudal gesture. To the preacher in the shadow of the cathedral these things were, of course, hidden. Preachers, like spies and lawyers, are instruments of destiny. This much may be said, that the Elizabethan Paul's Cross preacher was still abreast of history, if not enough in advance of it to make it an effective weapon in his armory of exhortation; we shall see how under the Stuarts he became a period piece, and a contributor rather to a heritage than to a programme. He stood still, and the sweep of events washed over him, and left him, dwelling in a dry place, his power surrendered to the thundering brethren before the Commons and Army, and his eloquence out of fashion.

3. Jacobean Interlude

THE CIRCUMSTANCES of James I's accession set the tone for most of the sermons at Paul's Cross during the first seventeen years of his reign. It had been generally supposed, says Bacon, that when the Queen died, "there must follow . . . nothing but confusions, inter-reigns, and perturbations of estate; likely far to exceed the ancient calamities of the civil wars between the Houses of Lancaster and York," but James succeeded quietly, and "it rejoiced all men to see so fair a morning of a Kingdom."[48] This happy state of affairs, disturbed only by one episode of terror (and that mingled with thankfulness) is reflected in the sermons at the Cross. The pulpits, nourished studiously though inconstantly by a pedantic connoisseur of clerical eloquence, reflect the stability and self-gratulation of the times, though in the background one may see the lines of the coming struggle being laid down.

At the beginning of his reign, James was prepared to use his dispensing power to make lenient the execution of the penal laws against recusants, but the bias to toleration, evident in his address to his first Parliament in 1604, did not last. The "Bye Plot" and the "Main Plot" hardened James's heart, and in February 1605 he announced a change of policy to the Council, asserting that he was so far from favouring the religion and practice of the papists that "if he thought his son and heir after him would give any toleration thereto, he would wish him fairly buried before his eyes." The penal laws were enforced accordingly with some severity, and this perhaps contributed to the formation of the Gunpowder Plot.[49]

The Plot is part of English folklore, and the preachers helped to make it so. The first of these, preaching on the Sunday after the Plot was discovered, was William Barlow, again appointed to instruct the Paul's Cross audience at a time of crisis, but on this occasion with a somewhat easier task. Yet he was nervous, for if in 1601 he feared the opinions of the London crowd, in 1605 he was upset because he had had a very bad scare, as the "Preachers Friend" reported in the published sermon. The "censorious reader," he admitted, might find some incoherence in the exegesis, but

> if he will withal, remember the shortnes of the time for the gratulation, the dreadfulnes of the danger, the fresh escape whereof could not but leave an impression

of horror in the Preachers minde (able to have confounded his Memorie,) who should have bin one of the hoisted number . . . , he will perhappes not bee so rigide in his Censure.

Barlow constructed his sermon with the aid of the King's speech to the Parliament, the Lord Chancellor's speech, and "divers circumstances conceived and imparted to him over night, by the Earle of Salisbury." It is a painfully elaborate effort. In the Plot, he said, we are first to note "a cruell Execution, an unhumane crueltie, a brutish immanitie, a develish brutishnesse, & an Hyperbolicall, yea an hyperdiabolicall divelishness." There was "divelish feritie" in the gunpowder which the devil invented as a copy of the fiery massacre from the infernal pit. In this design,

with one blast at one blow, in one twinkling of an eye, should have been crushed together, the Government, the Councell, the wisedom, the Religion, the Learning, the strength, and Justice, of the whole land.

The country would have been laid open to foreign invasion, to domestical usurpation.

But we were delivered; even if the King alone had escaped we would have been delivered, for the lives of the whole nation are contained in the King's person. In fact the King's whole life has been a succession of deliverances:

It seemeth by his Majesties speech yesterday; that his case and race hath bin the same with the Prophet, being preserved *in utero* . . . *Ab utero* . . . *Ex utero*. . . . For no sooner was he conceived in the wombe, but presentlie he was hazarded, no sooner delivered from the wombe, but invironed with danger, and what perils he hath passed ever since he was borne, need not to be related, they are so manifest: dismissed from those parts with a dreadfull farewell of a desperate Treacherie [the Gowrie conspiracy], and entertained among us with a Conspiracie unnatural & as dangerous: there crowned with Thornes, before hee coulde get on the Crowne of Golde.

When fully launched on sycophantic flattery, what little taste and sense Barlow had were likely to desert him. He gave most of the credit for the discovery of the Plot to the King's perspicuity; he read the letter to Mounteagle which revealed the design to the King's sensitive apprehension, making him suspicious of "some fiery engine, perhaps remembering his Fathers case, who was blowne up with powder." A long and florid eulogy of the King follows. The whole sermon set the formula for all the Plot-anniversary sermons to come.

The Parliament which had so narrowly escaped being "hoisted" proceeded to pass severe penal legislation against recusants and missionaries. On November 2, 1606, a stern exhortation was delivered from the Paul's Cross pulpit to magistrates to seek out the papists and impose upon them the full rigours of the law. The preacher was Richard Stock, a Cambridge man and pupil of Whitaker, who had two years before been appointed curate of Allhallows, Bread Street, the elder Milton's church. This angry Puritan observed with scorn the lethargy of those who should execute the laws, "being laid asleep like Sisera with the milke of that harlot." Other preachers echoed the same fear and the same reproach. In the Plot sermon of 1608, Robert Tynley, Archdeacon of Ely, inveighed against the craft of the Jesuits, affirming that the Catholic religion utterly perverts true obedience, and confuted "a Prophane Fugitive" who had written a letter against the "*Apology* for the Oath of Allegiance." Thomas Adams, "the Shakespeare of the Puritan divines," preaching in 1612, coupled the Plot with the massacre of St. Bartholomew, asserted that papists could only take their orders from the Pope and him a usurper and tyrant, and declared that papistry could never be made into Christianity. No truce is possible, said Sampson Price in 1613; toleration is "a Machiavellian pollicie." Thomas Sutton adjured the judges and other officers, in his sermon of 1615, to rise to their duty of protecting the weak against the malicious, hence to punish recusants and Jesuits, and to prosecute their offices against the papists without fear or favour. There is no society with a papist, observed John Hoskins, and William Worship briskly flouted the Jesuits and their converts in 1616 in these terms:

Are these the men so renowned for Artes, Tongues, Reading? Are these the Kil-cowes of the World, for learning? Are these the best Schollers of their Seven-headed Parnassus? Come, come, the Jesuits, the Popes Roaring Boyes, know well enough we have got the start of them, and therefore they make now no Syllogismes, but in FERIO. Yet some of our Gentlemen, that have made a steppe beyond the Alpes, looke as bigge as Bull-beefe, if we offer to compare with them: and tell us with a shrugge, that They, have Scripture, Councels, and the Fathers on their side.

There is less to be feared, then, from the arguments than from the daggers of the enemy. In fact, when Theophilus Higgons recanted his Romish errors at the Cross in 1611, he related that the Dominicans of Rouen had admitted to him the justice of the Oath of Allegiance, saying that the papal assertion of power over Christian princes was "an Italian conceit."

Such were the outbursts in the popular pulpit which succeeded the King's very moderate utterances, first, that the Oath was designed "onely for making of a trew distinction betweene papists of quiet disposition" and others malignant; second, that persecution is a good way to strengthen the persecuted in faith and heroism.[50]

Some might believe with William Worship that the adversary was not well equipped for controversy, but the English divines who crossed pens with Bellarmine were under no such delusion. The formal controversy with Rome, never relinquished at any time, was still echoed at Paul's Cross. For example, on February 14, 1608, the audience listened to the first draft of a treatise by William Crashaw, prominent among English controversialists, ironically remembered as the father of one of the chief English Catholic poets. He exhibited "the XX Wounds found to be in the body of the present Romish religion, in doctrine and manners." Some of these "wounds" are of interest since they illustrate the points upon which what Bishop Frere called the "lower level" of controversy was carried on. For example:

The Pope hath done more then God: for he delivered a soule out of hell.

Frier Francis was like to Christ in all things, and had 5. wounds as Christ, that did bleede on good-Fridaie; yea, he did more then Christ ever did.

Such priests as be continent, and have no whores, yet must pay a yeerely rent, as they that have, because they may have if they will.

A very different preacher carried on the controversy on points of doctrine the next year. Joseph Hall, "the English Seneca," set out a justification of Protestantism as the true faith, and condemned the "strange glosses and ceremonious observances" of the papists, but made his attack the basis for a reminder that a good cause demands purity of life, and strictness of conscience. Doubtless the auditory enjoyed Crashaw more. The preachers whose like were to form the core of opposition to the Laudian reforms sharpened their invective upon what they regarded as the papist compromise with human nature, with the inconstant faculties which do not aid in the true service of God. Such a preacher was John Hoskins, who in his Rehearsal sermon of 1614 cleverly made the occasion itself a point of "Puritan" theology and a point of attack upon Rome. The nature of a preacher's errand, he said, is "no late device starting up upon occasion in the phantasie, but an ancient record long since enrolled in the memorie." After the Gospel, there is no need of further inquisition, all sermons are rehearsal sermons. Only one faculty, then, the "memorative" faculty, is engaged in the formation of a Christian's faith; his belief and acceptance is a mental act; no compromise is to be made with his "humourous appetites." In other words the repetition of the fact of grace is designed to eliminate from the consciousness of the hearer the "green and unseasoned" conceits of his human nature. Upon this basis Hoskins was equipped to attack the truckling of the papists with what he called "imagination": the papists well know how men are transported by phantasms which arise from their base nature:

Therefore have they devised a penance in apparrell, a devotion upon the fingers ends to please imagination, a Transubstantiation like a Metamorphosis, to please imagination; orders of Friars of all colours, like the dreame of a Painters apron, to please imagination; Masses, Elevations, Processions, like Measures, Mummeries, Enterludes, and all to please imagination.

The reader will observe in such arguments as this not only the sort of diagram of religious experience against which Howson had inveighed in 1598, but also the clue to the association of Laud's reforms with papistry, and the possibility of a natural shift in the focus of attack from Rome to Canterbury.

But those issues had not yet appeared. There were more immediate disturbances within the church, uneasy stirrings as of a giant yet in his swaddling clothes, voices lifted in cries of protest at once silenced, stern censure from the pulpits of those who would rend the seamless garment upon a presumption of their unspotted consciences. The Puritan party, complex and diverse in its composition, animated by a single theology and by a thousand motives of legal injury and economic inhibition, was gathering strength for the day of wrath as yet far off.

The barometer of Puritan hopes rose and fell at Hampton Court; after a flurry of deprivations, the Church of England, in theory arbitrarily constituted by the Canons of 1604, became in practice under Abbot almost latitudinarian. The Puritan lecturers expanded their tactics of infiltration, and their opponents, the spokesmen for the Establishment, attacked not so much a programme, as a way of life, an attitude. A typical attack is that of Samuel Collins, delivered at the Cross in 1607. "Though the Papists be troublesome," he warned, "yet the Puritans must not looke to goe uncontrolled." He reviewed the Puritan attack upon the Prayer Book:

> I should defend our Orders, and Hierarchies; which they say are Anti-Christian, we knowe to be Apostolique: our habite and vestments; which, they thinke, are so farre off from the Camels skinne, that they are made of the Dragons taile: the imperfections of our prayer-book; which they have made to stinke in the nostrils of men, as much as ever it smelt sweet in the nostrils of God: our praying for all men; which, they say, is against particular election: for all that travaile by land, or by water; which they say, is for Theeves and Pirats: against lightning and tempests; which, they say, is against sparrow-blasting, unlesse it be at a certaine time of the yeare onely.

They vaunt their virtues, and have made "the pulpits to lose much of their ancient estimation and credit" by unprepared sermons, filled with "the spirit." Addressing the Puritans, he affirmed: "There was none of us ever placed so much Religion in a garment, as you doe in a Booke." A very good point. George Benson vigorously attacked the lecturers in 1609. They are never well, he declared,

> but when they have their sickles in an other mans harvest, as though they would rob all the Ministers about them of their crowne of rejoicing; like Ivie winding about the oke, that it may stand it selfe, but yet sucking the juice out of the oke they flatter so, they winde themselves into favour with great ones, thereby standing themselves in credit.

These "oyly mouthed Absolons speake plausible things, to bring the people out of love with their true Father . . . their David." The metaphor is telling, but Benson's chief complaint was as old as the complaint of the parish priests against the friars: the regular pastors are disgraced while people listen to these wandering souls:

> The people come to heare their own Parson or Vicar, as M. Bilney sayd the people came to heare him, like Malchus, having their right eares cut off: they bring their left only, sinisterly interpreting whatsoever they heare. So the nurses of Schisme do invade the possessions of many painefull labourers.

Robert Johnson reiterated this complaint in the same year:

> A number of the laitie, the roes and hinds of the field, which will start aside at the cracking of a sticke, will refuse their owne parish Churches, and to heare their owne Pastors preach, be they never so learned or well habited in speech, because they wear a Surplisse, and make a crosse upon a childe, and wil runne after and get them a heap of teachers that speake evill of them that are in authoritie.

In the previous year George Downame had addressed a sober exposition of the doctrine of Christian liberty to those afflicted in conscience by kneeling at communion, the surplice, and the cross in baptism. Christian liberty, he declared, includes freedom to impose ordinances which are not repugnant to the word of God. Freedom works both ways, and obedience binds twice also; obedience, said Sibthorpe, is necessary in Church as in commonwealth; how then can the disobedient children in the Church plead exception? "Their pretended pure tender conscience is impurely polluted, and their faith worse than infidelity." And Daniel Donne held up to ridicule those "apish professors, and Mocke-Christians," who are "precise and demure in habit and behaviour." From time to time the preachers hinted darkly at revolutionary sentiments among the discontented; Richard Crakanthorpe, for example, referred to the presbytery as "a Seminary of sedition, and a Sanctuary to every turbulent and seditious Gracchus, both in Church and kingdome."

These are stereotyped observations, thrusts on the left to balance the thrusts on the right. One preacher, however, Parker, precentor of Lincoln, was so ill-advised as to censure the Commons' proceedings upon ecclesiastical questions. Early in May 1606 the Commons sent up to the Lords a bill intended to "restrain the execution of canons ecclesiastical not confirmed by parliament." The Lords rejected this bill, but the Commons gave short shrift to a bill sent down to them by Bancroft, making provision for recovering impropriations by parliamentary subsidy. With the two Houses at such cross purposes, the sermon, which condemned certain members of the Commons for defending Puritan ministers deprived under the canons, could not fail to cause trouble. The House protested, and Parker was committed to custody for his rashness. This isolated incident illustrates clearly how sensitive was the balance in affairs ecclesiastical, and may stand as a symbol of the declining prestige of the Paul's Cross pulpit as an effective direct agent of the Crown.

This decline is partly attributable to the divided counsels in that pulpit. Except when appointees got out of hand, as in 1573, the Elizabethan preachers spoke, on all important matters, with one voice. But now those who constituted what one might call the solid centre of the clergy, conformable but scrupulous, were some of them actively disturbed both by the enforcement of Bancroft's canons and by certain trends in Anglican theology. Anglican thought, under the influence of Andrewes, was being purged of the more rigid elements in its

Calvinist heritage, was becoming more benevolent and rational. The ministers who had learned nothing since the Lambeth Articles were highly suspicious of doctrines and practices which to their tender consciences smacked of popery. Even before the Synod of Dort they called this body of doctrine Arminianism, and they made little distinction between Arminianism and popery. Accordingly one finds in some of the sermons at the Cross during this period protests which one may hesitatingly term "Puritan," though the first of them, by Richard Stock, is at least potentially schismatic. Governors and ministers of a visible Church, he declared, may err in faith, manners, and doctrine; the best know but in part, since the promise of incessant guidance from the Holy Spirit was made only to the Apostles. Every man, then, must labour for the knowledge of the word, to try the doctrines which are delivered from the seats of authority. In the past, persons in positions of ecclesiastical authority have always fallen into error,

so that the sinceritie of religion was upholden, and the truth defended, and maintained, only by some fewe, that were molested, persecuted, traduced, as turbulent and seditious persons, and enimies to the common peace of the Church.... Often times meaner men may sound the depth, and see more then great schollers.

In 1609, William Holbrooke, a godly precisian, deplored the contempt in which the worldly held the righteous:

Is it not a common and knowen tricke amongst you, to vaunt what you have done in vexing the godly, saying . . . O Sirrah wote you well what and where I have bene? I was where a Puritane one of these precise fellows was, that cannot endure an oath, but so I sware, star'd and swaggerd that I rid him out of the house and companie where I was? O miserable and wretched!

Sampson Price, preaching in 1613, listed his pantheon of Anglican apologists: Foxe, Jewel, Whitaker, Humphrey, Perkins, Reynolds, Abbot—a list notable for the exclusion of Hooker, Bancroft, and Andrewes. Thomas Sutton, in 1615, condemning the Laodiceans, called those who would mediate between the Church of God and the "Romish Synagogue" perfect examples of the lukewarm. He delivered a violent exhortation against "Church Papists," and it is clear that he did not mean just recusants who attended church. The lukewarm professor is a continual disturber of the Church, and is it not then most improper for such to condemn the pious and scrupulous?

Which conclusion may serve to stop the stentorious mouths, and pare the Satyricall and bloudy pencils of some men, who in all their learning can finde none that either disquiets or endangers the Church but the strict Precisian, who cannot swallow down some of our Church Ceremonies, and therefore employ their whole strength and spend their whole life, in humbling them who are brought already to the lowest *nadir*, as if they had swept and purified the Church of all her imposthumes: whereas yet our Churches hang full of Romish spiders, who in their Italian cobwebs would strangle our English soules.

He seems to have had in mind the welcome accorded two Italian friars, who professed allegiance to the Church of England: the Archbishop of Spalatro did not come to England until 1616, but when he did he became a centre of adherence for certain of the Arminian party. William Worship, preaching in that year, confessed that he could not abide the "Newtrals" who would mediate between the Church of England and Rome, and Samuel Ward, who was prosecuted for nonconformity in 1635, delivered in 1616 a blast against "Popery and nature, and the old leaven of Pelagius, newly scoured by Arminius," affirming that no minister can keep a good conscience and be given to popery and Arminianism. Roger Ley launched a similar attack upon Arminian theology in 1618.

But these notes of disquiet, striking enough when collected, were lost in the general sound of satisfaction and adulation of the King which swelled from Paul's Cross during the reign of James. A spirit of almost mid-Victorian complacency and enterprise informs sermons preached, chiefly in 1609, in favour of the Virginia enterprise, when the Virginia Company was reorganized in that year. Motives jingoistic, commercial, and pious were lauded to the skies. The general tone of these exhortations is reflected in a contemporary poem of advertisement:

> We hope to plant a nation,
>   Where none before hath stood.
> To glorifie the Lord 'tis done,
>   And to no other end;
> He that would crosse so good a worke,
>   To God can be no friend.[61]

Daniel Price preached on May 28, 1609, a sermon at the Cross against "scandalous and slanderous Detractors" of the enterprise, which had already been commended in a March sermon by Richard Crakanthorpe, who emphasized the planting among the savages of "humanity" and piety. George Benson expressed the hope that the natives would not be treated with Spanish cruelty. Even William Leveson's lottery of 1612 was approved at the Cross, by John Boys.

The nation was at peace and for the most part prosperous, and few preachers were so dour as to neglect these manifestations of God's abundant mercies. Our state is blessed, cried George Benson; witness the failure of the Papists to baptize the realm in blood. For all their plots the late Queen "lived . . . til she was olde and mellowe for the kingdome of God," and when we changed, "we changed almost nothing but the sex." After a David we have a Solomon. If ever March came in like a lion and went out like a lamb, it was in 1603. Let us be thankful for our peace, said Thomas Adams in 1612, a peace they enjoy not in France or in the Low Countries. This peace is a gift of God:

Though nature hath bound up the loins of our kingdom with a girdle of waves, and policy raised another fence of wooden walls, yet God must put about us a third girdle, the circle of his providence, or our strength is weaker than the waters.

We are the wonder of the world, "we are the Lillies and the Rose," we have high and rich prerogatives:

Many and mighty deliverances hath the Lord given us; from furious Amalekites, that came with a navy, as they bragged, able to fetch away our land in turfs; from an angry and raging pestilence, that turned the popular streets of this city into solitude; from a treason wherein men conspired with devils, for hell was brought up to their conjurations, and a whole brewing of that salt sulphur was tunned up in barrels for us to drink.

Our land, said others, is a Colchis. "A mightie Nation we are, whose bulwarke is the Sea, whose confederate Neighbours round about are our Sentinels. . . . The bees may hive themselves in our helmets." I shall have occasion later to comment on the significance of this georgic allusion.

The loyal and sycophantic preachers affirmed that the highest gift of God to England was the King. Upon him they heaped praise without stint. Perhaps the most fulsome exhibition of this order was Barlow's in the Plot sermon of 1605. The King, he said, is

of pregnant wit, of ready apprehension, of sound judgement, of present dispatch, of impregnable memory . . . , an universall Scholler . . . , a perfect Textuar, a sound Expositor, a faithfull Christian, and a constant Professor . . . , a chast husband, of sweete carriage, of humble deportment, of mortified lusts, of sanctified life . . . , a loving father to his subjects, a carefull guardian of his kingdomes, a wise manager of his State, an especiall favourer of this Citty.

So this ecclesiastical Osric, praising a soul of great article. The preachers above all hastened to assure their audiences of James's care for religion. Upon the Gowrie anniversary in 1605, Richard Vaughan, Bishop of London, declared that the King

had made a protestation before God and his angels that he was so constant for the maintenance of the religion publicly in England professed as that he would spend his own dearest blood in the defence thereof rather than that the truth should be overthrown.

Upon the accession day in 1617 Donne called for thanks to God that when the King had come,

he was beholden to no by-religion. The papists could not make him place any hopes upon them, nor the puritans make him entertain any fears from them; but his God and our God; as he brought *via lactea*, by the sweet way of peace, that flows with milk and honey, so he brought him *via regia*, by the direct and plain way, without any deviation or descent into ignoble flatteries, or servile humouring of any persons or factions.

One of the most striking of those sermons in which the audience at the Cross were invited to give thanks for their blessings in such a king was Bishop John King's *Sermon of Publicke Thanksgiving* in April 1619, upon the King's recovery from a grave illness. It is a splendid effort in the "witty" style, upon the themes of death and recovery so enriched by the genius of Donne and Taylor. He descanted elegantly upon the sickness of Hezekiah and upon the bitterness of death:

Death hath ever her arrow in her bow, though in the prime ages of the world she was sometimes nine hundred yeares before she sped, yet now she hitteth quickly; and when God saith, shoote, she shooteth; and so long as God saith, spare, she spareth. For what is thy life? *Breve suspirium*, a short panting.

The story of Hezekiah is a model and pattern of the condition of our gracious King. He has not restored religion, like Hezekiah, but he has maintained it; he has spared not the high places of Antichrist more than Hezekiah; his deliverance from the Plot is like Hezekiah's from Sennacherib. Under him we have enjoyed the blessings of peace for sixteen years. He has been sick unto death, but God has brought comfort out of bitterness in his recovery; the prayers of the King's loving and devoted subjects have reached the throne of grace, "have pierced through the clouds, and knocked at the gate of his mercy at midnight, and given him no rest on behalfe of their king."

How are we to explain this transformation of the monarch into an object of veneration? Certainly James's personal character did not inspire any such reverence, although no doubt he attracted many of the clergy by his genuine interest in theological problems, by his pompous and heavily witty flattery. He was for them in some respects a kindred spirit. To Elizabeth the bishops were agents of the Crown, required to serve; to James they were its ornaments, required to shine. But there are deeper reasons than these. The Church of England, reconstructed by the Canons of 1604, had become more of a coherent organism than was permitted by Elizabeth. It was more efficient but it was also more of a kingdom within a kingdom, existing by virtue of the royal prerogative. That prerogative, already challenged in the reign of Elizabeth, was seriously attacked in the reign of James through rulings of the common law courts and exercises of privilege by the Commons. As the rift widened, it was inevitable that the preachers should turn their energies to the exaltation of their true source of power. When Holland extolled Elizabeth in 1599, he saw in her the type of the faithful, symbol at once of the *nation* and the *congregation*. The Jacobean eulogist was determined to set up the image of the King's *person*. No letter had actually been changed in the constitutions ecclesiastical, but the implications of the prerogative were insisted upon first of all by James in his capacity as mediator at Hampton Court, and when thus emphasized the prerogative changed as a colour changes when it is placed under a strong light. What had been comforting was now blinding.

This does not mean that when a preacher under James set himself, upon the accession anniversary or at another time, to exhort to obedience he drew upon a doctrine different in source or meaning from the Homily of Disobedience and Wilful Rebellion of 1571. In this, as with the eulogy of the royal person, it was a matter of emphasis. Note that when Donne approached the subject at Paul's Cross, he began as it were from the top of the hierarchy. The king is a step below God; kings have no example but God. Such are the fervid pronouncements of John White in his accession sermon in 1615. Kings are God's anointed, though bad servants may come like clouds between a king and his subjects; our King was anointed to reign over us. "All the eminency and distinction of authority" under the king is equally of God's ordinance. It was to be expected that the substitution of *anointed* for *set over*, of *right* for *duty*, made a great difference both in the delivery and in the reception of these doctrines. It is the difference that may be found in the speeches of Elizabeth and James upon the prerogative: Elizabeth was accustomed to remind her subjects that such matters were her *concern*, her *business*; James observed loftily that these things were a *mystery*. Yet in these sermons one finds no such explicit statement of the divine right idea as notoriously appears in Cowell's *Interpreter*. Here is enthusiasm but no instruction. The preachers echo the double voice of James himself, who in one speech proclaimed that kings exercise "a resemblance of Divine power upon earth," and in another that a king is a tyrant "as soon as he leaves off to rule according to his laws." On matters of power, right, and obedience the best Paul's Cross preacher of the reign never preached there; James would have been much happier in that pulpit than in the chair of state. His talents were exactly suited to that office.

In a sermon at the Cross on the anniversary of the Gowrie conspiracy, August 5, 1622, Samuel Purchas made a characteristic itinerary of all these happy sentiments. "The time itself [he began] may be a Text, to quicken our Memorie; Memorie may awaken Consideration; Consideration may excite Admiration; Admiration may incite Thankfulnesse; Thankfulnesse may swell into extaticall Jubilees of joye." The tower of II Samuel 22:51, led him to that familiar manifold analogy most luxuriantly expressed in Spenser's House of Alma. Then, by a natural extension, he went on to speak of "heads," kings. Paying due praise, if perfunctorily, to Elizabeth, he told the tale of James's deliverances, praised his learning, set him forth as "neither the Peoples king, nor the Peeres king, nor the Priests king, nor his owne king, as Absalom; but His, Gods King." He turned then to the blessings of England:

No forren Enemie creeping in at the Irish window as before, or Irish Traytor starting into a Scottish covert; no borderer at the threshold, nor other leaping out of the Northerne back-side for France. Wee need no wall (as of old) against the Picts; the Ocean it selfe is our wall round about to guard us; stretcheth out his lovely armes and creekes, to enrich us; insinuateth his *Sinus*, bayes, bosomes, and harbours, to embrace us; melteth himselfe in liquid loves, & mustereth waves, sands, tides, all his forces, as becommeth the great Ditch of this Towre of salvation for his King, and his Kingdomes.

And, to come nearer home,

Hail London! The Towre of thy King is in the East for thy safetie; the Bowre, and Palace of thy King is in the West, for light and Majestie: in the middest is thy Guildhall, for Justice: besides thee, is Westminster-Hall, that bringeth the whole Kingdome to thee, and maketh thy Termes and Vacations. . . . How many Gentlemen, and Noblemen walk thee into the fields? How many Lawyers sit on thy Skirts and Suburbs? . . . O thy Pulpits, O their Divinitie!

London trades to all the world; to her come diamonds from Soeodanna, bezars from Macassar, civet-cats and aloes from Zocotora, suckets from Surat, great grained pepper from Iambe. Blessed be the Lord!

That was in 1622. Hidden among Purchas's high-piled hyperboles is a gloomy little sentence, to the effect that those who hailed the manna of James's coming once now find it full of worms. There was trouble in Israel, and for the first time in half a century, the Paul's Cross pulpit got out of hand.

When Bishop John King spoke at the Cross on March 26, 1620, before the King and all the notables, appealing for the repair of the "sickly and crazie constitution" of the cathedral, many ironies attended his eloquent exposition of the happy state of the realm and his plea for the re-edification of the temple. The King appointed a commission, which included Francis Bacon and Inigo Jones, to look into the problem, but nothing was accomplished for years because not enough money was raised. Later, the energetic and conscientious Laud took up the problem, persuaded Charles to appoint a new commission, used his influence to get contributions, and by 1632 was successful in getting the "houses" against the nave demolished.[52] These and other cleaning-up operations put an end to the outdoor sermons in the churchyard, as I have noted above. Besides this delay in Bishop King's plans, there is the fact that many of the vast crowd gathered to hear his words came hoping for some official pronouncement on the negotiations with Spain or perhaps a declaration in favour of the Bohemians. Protestant sentiment was much roused.

The negotiations for a treaty-match between Prince Charles and the Infanta of Spain began in 1614. The pedantic and intermittently confident James hoped at first for a major alliance which should turn swords into ploughshares; after the outbreak of hostilities in the

Empire in 1618 he sought to maintain his Bohemian son-in-law by policy since he was by temperament incompetent and in treasure ill-fitted to face the arbitrament of war. For this cause he sacrificed Ralegh; in this cause he tried to protect the pro-Spanish Howards, but failed because of their crimes and incompetence and because of the charms of Villiers. Although in all the complicated negotiations he was acting within the fact as well as within the theory of his prerogative, popular distrust of the royal proceedings became steadily more intense. Gondomar, the Machiavellian Spanish ambassador, was thought to have almost complete ascendancy over the King's mind, and was feared and hated by the multitude. What, men asked themselves, could be the results of this repudiation of the Protestant cause? A Spanish Catholic to be the mother of a line of English kings, Catholics in all the chief positions of state, the end of militant Protestantism. In and out of London the feeling was described by a contemporary as "wth all violence agaynste Catholiques."[53]

In November 1620 Frederick of Bohemia lost the battle of the White Hill. When the bad news reached England popular anger and anxiety reached a high pitch: Gondomar's life was threatened, and in December, in spite of express warnings from the King that the clergy were not to meddle with state matters, a "younge fellow" spoke at the Cross "very freely in general" against the mooted Spanish alliance. James's third Parliament met on January 30, 1621, suspicious of what commitments the King might have made to Gondomar, and determined, in spite of the King's warnings, to make known their stand on foreign affairs. In February the Houses joined in a petition requesting the full enforcement of the penal laws against Catholics, and received what they regarded as an evasive answer. On February 25 John Everard, a Cambridge man and a powerful preacher, who had been in trouble two years before for a sermon at the Cross, preached there against the Spanish match, alleging the "craft and crueltie" of Spain. For this he was committed to the Gatehouse, was released, unrepentantly and stubbornly preached on the same theme in City churches, and was again committed. James, on being appealed to in his behalf, angrily made a characteristically atrocious pun. "What is this Dr. Ever-out?" he inquired. "His name shall be Never-out." The extent of anti-Catholic feeling about this time may be judged from the Commons' treatment of Floyd, a Catholic lawyer who spoke some slighting words about the Elector Palatine and his wife; on him the House laid "the most ferocious series of punishments ever inflicted in England for a political offence."[54] Once this Parliament, after having made the famous protestation which James rent out of the Journals with his own hand, had been dissolved, relaxation of the penal laws proceeded apace as part of the programme to consummate the long drawn out negotiations with Spain. In July, Samuel Buggs, minister of Coventry, made a strong plea at the Cross that Englishmen should respect the distressed condition of the continental Protestants, but his tone was elegiac rather than revolutionary, and a rumour that he was imprisoned for the sermon was untrue. But general distrust of the King's proceedings was so great that lecturers who a few years before would have been received with derision or at least with indifferent calm were now acclaimed as they thundered against the Spanish Antichrist.

The intemperate preachers had to be silenced. On August 25, 1622, Mr. Claydon of Hackney preached at the Cross a scurrilous sermon against the Spanish match, "at which many of his hearers cried out Amen." A week later one Richard Sheldon, self-styled "a Convert from out of Babylon," performed his duty in that pulpit. He had been, like some Paul's Cross preachers before him, a student in the English College in Rome, had returned to England and suffered imprisonment in 1610 under the recusancy laws. Seeing the error of his ways, he published in 1611 a treatise on the lawfulness of the oath of allegiance, and later, having convinced the King of the purity of his convictions, was employed in the controversy against Vorstius and made a royal chaplain. Being, as his sermon shows, an exceedingly dull man, he made the mistake of entering, in his Paul's Cross sermon, upon that hoary controversy over the identity of the Beast of the Apocalypse, deciding, as might be expected, that the Beast is the Antichristian state of the Pope. He condemned with violence the "Neutralizers" who saw any ground of mediation with Rome, and in his closing exhortation dared to suggest what policy should be pursued with those who worship the Beast. He adjured magistrates to lay waste the dwelling of the whore of Babylon; there is, he said, only one ground on which Catholics should be allowed to worship freely in the realm and that is if in their cities a similar privilege should be accorded to Protestants (this was precisely what no amount of negotiation could secure from the Spaniards). The truth of God will prevail, he went on, so long as it is not cut off by censorship; the enemy's chief weapon is censorship, and ours freedom of discussion. In this Sheldon was practically throwing the ministers' glove at the King's feet, though he assured his audience in closing that it was "royally impossible" for the King to be anything but *semper idem* in religion.

Sheldon received a severe reprimand. He had disobeyed the orders sent by the King to the clergy in a letter to Archbishop Abbot of August 4, forbidding the discussion of sermons in matters outside the Articles, of predestination and election, of the royal prerogative, and demanding an end especially to "bitter invectives and undecent railing speeches." In forbidding attacks on Rome, the King, thought the Venetian ambassador, was sowing the seeds of civil war; "the idea of bridling the tongues of the preachers in matters considered to pertain to their faith is like damning torrents."[55] It was left to John Donne, Dean of St. Paul's, to defend the preaching orders and the King's proceedings at Paul's Cross; this he did on September 15. He preached from Judges 5:20, "The stars in their courses fought against Sisera" —which was, as John Chamberlain observed, "somewhat a straunge text for such a business." He spoke of the God of battles, but warned the audience that he was "far from giving fire to them that desire war." God's purposes are not abandoned because they are sometimes slackened—here an obvious reference to the King's designs, which many citizens were not inclined to consider the working out of God's purposes. Chief among the subordinate means of God are princes, and their services in God's cause are not always seen: "Kings cannot always go in the sight of men, and so they lose their thanks." Governors and great officers have their place, so long as they assist in the promotion of the king's will. All callings have their place. The stars fought in order; the stars in their courses are the preachers. They must fight in order "and according to these directions which they, to whom it appertains, shall give them." In a spiritual war there may be no peace between Christ and Belial, but there may be peace between men and men. The preachers preach against Sisera, that is against error, and should preach *manentes in ordine*, for order implies a head, and the head has lately issued an order. Here Donne hid himself in a cloud of citations to prove that the injunctions to preach the substance of the Creed and the Homilies were actually a return to the practice of the primitive Church. The King, he concluded, is grieved that any should think he wishes a restraint of preaching itself or a reduction in the number of sermons. Could so learned a prince be suspected of laying a plot to bring in ignorance?

This is a poor performance, which adds nothing to a great reputation, though there is no need to "correct" one's view of Donne by it. The art of this kind of persuasion had fallen off sadly since the days of Bancroft; there is in this effort embarrassment, preciosity, awkwardness. These failings in what might be called the totality of appeal from the pulpit happen when the king is a theologian, and when the theologians are something like kings. Donne gave "no great satisfaction," said Chamberlain, and indeed seemed somewhat unsatisfied himself. Four years later in a sermon in St. Paul's he recalled the preaching orders and set them in what he was then prepared to pronounce their proper context:

> There was a time but lately, when he who was in his desire and intention, the peacemaker of all the Christian world, as he had a desire to have slumbered all field-drums, so had he also to have slumbered all pulpit-drums, so far, as to pass over all impertinent handling of controversies, merely and professedly as controversies, though never by way of positive maintenance of orthodoxal and fundamental truths; that so there might be no slackening in the defence of the truth of our religion, and yet there might be a discreet and temperate forbearing of personal, and especially of national exasperations. And as this way had piety, and peace in the work itself, so was it then occasionally exalted, by a great necessity; he who was then our hope, and is now the breath of our nostrils, and the anointed of the Lord, being then taken in their pits, and, in that great respect, such exasperations the fitter to be forborne. . . . But things standing now in another state, and all peace, both ecclesiastical and civil, with these men, being by themselves removed . . . , and he whom we feared, returned in all kinds of safety, safe in body and safe in soul too . . . , it becomes us also to return to the brasing and beating of our drums in the pulpits too.[56]

This whole review of the situation, which ties the pulpit to diplomacy in a gross and Erastian way, is surely disingenuous. But in Donne's case, it is very hard to distinguish between disingenuousness and painful getting over a task unsuited to his eloquence.

On the Sunday following the Prince's departure for Spain the preacher was expected to make some official pronouncement about the Spanish match, since it was beginning to be known that Charles had left for Spain, secret though his going had been. But the preacher merely prayed for his prosperous journey and safe return. On March 30, the preacher, a Mr. Wilson, spoke "general words of evil interpretation" in an invective against popery. Perhaps some indication of the lack of enthusiasm for the Crown at this time may be gained from Chamberlain's account of the anniversary accession sermon on March 24, preached by John Richardson of Magdalen. He "performed yt reasonable well" because "he was not long nor immoderate in commendation of the time, but gave Queen Elizabeth her due." In October Charles returned, to be greeted by a great surge of happy welcome and rejoicing, and the whole sorry episode was finished. The virus of the wars of religion had infected the English polity.

In other invectives against Rome from the Paul's Cross pulpit during the last years of James there is little instruction. Two dramatic incidents deserve mention, since one provided the theme for a sermon at the Cross and the other served as epilogue to a sermon. When Bishop John King died the Jesuits circulated a pamphlet containing an account of his alleged conversion to Rome and receiving communion before his death at the hands of the priest Thomas Preston. This scandal the Bishop's son, Henry King, confuted at large in a sermon preached at the Cross on November 25, 1621, an eloquent monument to the poet's learning and ingenuity. He vindicated his father's memory, and exercised his powers of invective upon the Jesuits, "the great Paracelsians of the world, whose practice is Phlebotomy, to let States blood in the Heart-vaine." The other incident occurred on October 26, 1623, twenty days after the return of Charles from Spain, while anti-Rome feeling was still violent among the populace. On that Sunday afternoon some three hundred persons were collected in a large upper room in a house attached to the French embassy in the Blackfriars to hear the Jesuit preacher Father Drury. In the midst of his sermon one of the floor joists gave way and the congregation was carried in a shrieking mass to the floor below. Some ninety-one persons perished in the accident, which the pious hastened to attribute to "God's wisdom permitting." The "fatal vespers" served as a lesson of God's fearful judgments upon papists, especially since the coroner's jury found that there was no weakness in the flooring, "in utter disregard of the fact," as Gardiner observes.[57] That morning Thomas Adams had preached at the Cross on Luke 13:7, the cutting down of the fig tree, mentioning among other sins condemned by the parable the papists' abuse of the doctrine of excommunication and the Jesuits' monarchomachy. In a postscript to the published sermon Adams insinuated himself into the scheme of God's judgments:

It pleased God Almighty to make a fearful comment upon this, his own text, the very same day it was preached by his unworthiest servant. The argument was but audible in the morning, before night it was visible. His holy pen had long since written with ink; now his hand of justice expounded it in the characters of blood.

A year later John Gee, a converted Catholic who had escaped death in the fall of the house, preached at the Cross one of the usual revelations of Jesuit conspiracy, and pointed to the moral of the "fatal vespers."

4. *The Gathering Storm*

CONVERTS FROM ROME had often stood in the pulpit in the churchyard; no convert from Puritanism, enlightened by reading Andrewes, shall we say, or admiring Laud, ever confessed his errors there. Instead, there rose, during the years before the Rebellion, a steady chorus of exhortation to obedience in Church and State, maintained with dignity and even eloquence, but never with that rough-and-tumble effectiveness which had distinguished some Elizabethan defences of the state ecclesiastical. Paul's Cross was no longer a direct voice, only an echo, sometimes fuzzy, always monotonous, of the administration.

Ground bass to this orthodox melody was the ideal of order set forth elegantly by Henry King in 1621. The Word proclaims, he said, that the servant is not greater than his lord. "There is nothing so much sets out the Universe as Order, to see how subordinate causes depend of their Superiours, and this sublunary Globe of the Celestiall." Order brought the creation out of chaos; the elements are subordinate one to another; harmony in music consists in variety of stops higher and lower. Equality in men would breed nothing but confusion; men are not born equal, but each to his appointed station. The host of heaven is so ruled: there are two lights in the heaven, sun and moon, and two on earth, Religion and State, "shining like lampes in the great assembly of Parliament; and a[n] . . . imperiall Starre, whose peacefull influence hath many yeeres blest our Land. May it bee long ere this sunne goe downe, or by his set, leave us in darknesse and mourning." The idea was developed in characteristic fashion by Donne in May 1627. Preaching from Hosea 3:4, "For the children of Israel shall abide many days without a king, and without a prince, and without a sacrifice, and without an image, and without an ephod, and without teraphim," Donne asserted the primacy of the royal power from the order of the words in the text:

Therefore also, in this place, God proposes first the civil state, the temporal government, (what it is, to have a king and a prince) before he proposes the happiness of a church, and a religion; not but that our religion conduces to the greater happiness but that our religion cannot be conserved, except the civil state, and temporal government be conserved too.

This is not strictly an Erastian position, since he did not assert the subordination of the church to the state; Donne was a long way from Selden. But whatever the opinions of Anglican apologists concerning the divinely constituted authority of bishops, the exigencies of current politics as well as the theory of the supremacy made it necessary for them to set first in their exhortations to obedience not just the "civil state" but the rights of the king by prerogative.

The preacher engaged to defend the royal prerogative in matters ecclesiastical found no embarrassment in dealing with the Puritans, whether he set out to condemn their religious practices or their political theories. King paused in his review of the enormities of the papists to comment on the abuse of the good practice of preaching:

No wonder then, if Preaching may breed surfets, that so many Crudities lie in the stomackes of this Citty; that so many Fumes and giddy vapours flie up into the head, to the no small disturbance of the Churches quiet; that so many hot spirits, like Canons overcharged, recoyle against all Discipline, breake into divers factions, and with the splints of those crackt opinions doe more mischiefe than deliberation or Justice can suddenly solve.... This communitie of Preaching hath brought it into such cheape contempt, with many, that, as if the gift of tongues were prostitute to Idiots and Trades, you shall have a set of Lay Mechanicke Presbiters of both sexes ... presume so far upon their acquaintance with the Pulpit, that they will venter upon an Exposition, or undertake to manage a long unweildy prayer conceived on the sudden, though not so suddenly uttered; nay, they are so desperate, they will torment a Text, and in their Conventicles teach as boldly, as if they were as well able to become Journeymen to the Pulpit, as to their owne Trades.

The phrase "Lay Mechanicke Presbiters" is a slander, of course, for the sectaries against whom King cunningly shifted his attack were not "Presbiters," quite the contrary. There was this much justice in his case, however, that *Scrutamini Scriptores* was already beginning to undo the world, as Selden had prophesied. In 1626 H. Valentine made a strong appeal at the Cross for public prayer, and condemned the abuse of preaching, and the next year Stephen Denison, on the occasion of the penance of a Familist, exhibited a list of sectaries breeding in England, which reads like an index to Edwards's *Gangraena*.

Fanatics and splinter parties were convenient objects of attack partly because the Presbyterians and moderate Puritans could be accused through them of guilt by association. Dangerous glosses on Scripture with political implications were more solid and respectable sources of revolution. Such was Paraeus' interpretation of *Institutes* IV, xx, 30, 31, which is a gloss upon "Let every soul be subject unto the higher powers," the indispensable text for the doctrine of obedience. John Knight, fellow of Pembroke, preached at Oxford in 1622 that "yf kings grow unruly and tirannicall they may be corrected and broughte into order by theire subjects" (i.e., by the inferior magistrates), and was of course imprisoned. Paraeus' books were burned at the Cross on June 23, 1622, though the sophisticated Chamberlain observed that it was of little good when the theme of resistance was "current all Christendom over."[58] Another important element in Protestant doctrine, wide and vulnerable in its implications, the doctrine of Christian liberty, was first handled at the Cross in 1624 by Robert Sanderson, then as long afterwards rector of Boothby Pagnell in Lincolnshire, destined to be Bishop of Lincoln and to find a place in Walton's *Lives*.

Sanderson was a Calvinist and a conservative, as a letter describing his opinions, of 1649, makes clear.[59] His sermon, upon I Timothy 4:4, was a solid argument, the sort of exposition one might expect from an able logician and casuist. Let no man, he said, preach disobedience under the colour of Christian liberty:

> Whosoever then shall interpret the determinations of Magistrates in the use of the creatures to be contrary to the Liberty of a Christian, or under that colour shall exempt inferiors from their obedience to such determinations, he must blame St. Paul [e.g., I Tim. 6:1–5], nay he must blame the Holy Ghost, and not us, if he hear from us that he is proud, and knoweth nothing, and doateth about unprofitable questions. . . . Neither let any man cherish his ignorance herein, by conceiting as if there were some difference to be made between Civil and Ecclesiastical things, and Laws, and Persons in this behalf. The truth is, our Liberty is equal to both, the powers of Superiors for restraint equal in both.

He proceeded to justify obedience to superiors on the ground of restraint in respect of charity: "Say what can be said on behalf of a brother: all the same, and more, may be said for a Governor. For a Governor is a brother too, and something more; and duty is charity too." Sanderson willed his opponents to use "common reason" as umpire: they were prepared to invoke the decision of the individual conscience upon "purity of faith," guided by the omnipotent Word. Their notions of duty were different from those of Sanderson, who in this respect stood in the tradition of Aquinas and Hooker. Behind the revolutionary extension of the doctrine of Christian liberty lay an individualism which considered obedience privative rather than positive. Sanderson's "Duty is charity" was becoming as outmoded in the political theory of the gentry as the doctrine of "stewardship" in their economic thinking.

Sanderson's second Paul's Cross sermon on the same theme, preached in 1632 when Laud's efforts to secure conformity had been some time in application in the London diocese, illustrates by shift of emphasis the change in the times. His text upon this occasion was I Peter 2:16, expressing strongly the negative aspect of the exercise of Gospel liberty. He struck the new note in his exordium: "There is not any thing in the world more generally desired than Liberty, nor scarce any thing more generally abused."

God forbid any man of us, possessed with an Anabaptistical spirit, or rather frenzy, should understand either of those passages [Matt. 23:8-10; I Cor. 7:23], or any other of like sound, as if Christ or his Apostle had had any purpose therein to slacken those sinews and ligaments, and to dissolve those joints and contignations, which tye into one body, and clasp into one structure, those many little members and parts whereof all human societies consist: that is to say, to forbid all those mutual relations of superiority and subjection which are in the world, and so to turn all into a vast chaos of anarchy and confusion. . . .

Some inveigh against the Church Governors, as if they lorded it over God's heritage, and against the Church orders and constitutions, as if they were contrary to Christian liberty. . . . Alas that our brethren, who thus accuse them, should suffer themselves to be so far blinded with prejudices and partial affections as not [to] see that themselves, in the mean time, do really exercise a spiritual lordship over their disciples, who depend in a manner upon their judgments, by imposing upon their consciences sundry Magisterial conclusions, for which they have no sound warrant from the written Word of God.

Milton might have written so against the Presbyterians; in fact he did. The objectors to church ceremonial, Sanderson continued, are unconscionably partial,

in laying the accusations against the Ecclesiastical Laws only, whereas their arguments, if they had any strength in them, would as well conclude against the Political Laws in the Civil State. . . . Let them either damn them all, or quit them all,

and he observed in a grimly prophetic passage:

If they were put to speak upon their consciences, whether or not, if power were in their own hands, and Church affairs left to their ordering, they would not forbid those things they now dislike, every way as strictly and with as much imposition of necessity as the Church presently enjoineth them, I doubt not but they would say, Yea; and what equity is there in this dealing, to condemn that in others which they would allow themselves?

The Anglican apologists and the Presbyterians necessarily collided in this line of argument, but the situation changed when the Independents took up some of Sanderson's weapons.

Very different was Donne's defence of the ceremonies. In his sermon of 1627, already referred to, he dwelt on analogies. The ephod prescribed by implication in Hosea 3:4 represents ecclesiastical garments, and the teraphim in the same text represent images, which are not idols if used as aids to instruction, properly conceived as adjuncts to the completion of the Christian life. In November 1629 he was similarly ineffectual as an official voice: speaking at the Cross during the popular commotion which accompanied the imprisonment and before the impending trial of the Commons members who had offended the King during the session of 1629, he limited himself to a pious objurgation against "wilful misinterpreting of other men, especially superiors," and against casting aspersions or imputations upon the Church or the State. Richard Farmer, who preached earlier, in June, was more specific, attacking those "statising" discoursers whose daily pastime it is to rail on those in authority, prophesy alterations in government, and project new forms of commonwealths. Edward Boughen, a Christ Church man and Kentish vicar, was tougher in controversy than these. In April 1630 he preached at the Cross upon I John 4:1–3, that text beloved of the orthodox and the defenders of the status quo. His warnings against extravagant spirits were based upon the King's Declaration concerning religion, issued in 1628 to discourage controversy concerning matters of faith. Between the promulgation of this Declaration and Boughen's sermon the royal prerogative had been assailed in the Parliament of 1629 and in such violent pamphlets as Leighton's *Sion's Plea*. The time is fruitful, Boughen complained, in "saint-seeming Heretickes," in windy sermons full of zeal but no matter. Trust no man who teaches anything contrary to what the Church believes; too many are immoderately wedded to their own conceits. We must not stagger at "every new-broached fancie." Any man can brag of the "spirit"; and now, as in the days of King James, we are in danger from "ungrounded divines." They seek to banish the fear of the King from our hearts, and if they do this they also seek to banish the fear of God.

Banish one, and banish both; for there is but one *Time* belongs to both; *Time Dominum & Regem*. . . . If we feare not the king, wee feare not God.

Now all will be law-givers and law-makers:

Let the King command Divine Service before Preaching; no, not so, wee know not how to submit, to bowe; but wee know how to controule, to command out of a Pulpit. . . . At common prayers we are not, where humility, and feare, and reverence are shewed; there we are *tanquam rari nantes in gurgite vasto*, one in a Pewe, and two in an Ile; and well if so. But at Sermons, where no humility is required, or at least not decried, there we are like gnats in the ayre.

Humility, Boughen added, if I interpret him aright, is induced by the *act* of bowing, by the posture of reverence enjoined in the rubrics; the sermon requires no such act and consequently does not inculcate humility. It is not for every man, he proceeded, to examine doctrine. Calvin himself has affirmed that the Scripture may not be used to settle differences when we are not certain of its meaning, and that no man not skilled in divinity should try the spirits by Scripture. Little do some nowadays heed these warnings:

I know, there be many in the world, that never saluted either University, and have no tongue, but what their mothers taught them, that hold the Scripture every mans profession; and thinke themselves so well seene in the booke of God . . . that they are able to explaine the most difficult Scripture *stantes pede in uno*, with as much ease as to suppe up a messe of broath; because CHRIST hath promised to reveale his will to babes and sucklings.

We are grown to a wonderful pride these days, ready to contradict "the whole current of Interpreters," better at confuting than establishing, "good at the stabbe, bad but at the word: desperate men." The lecturers, he concluded, are fomenters of rebellion, Wat Tylers, Jack Straws. "If a man be but of their faction, Oh, hee is a brave sparke."

Boughen came down into the lists, and took stock of his opponents before he struck. This was not Laud's method, as his accession day sermon at the Cross in 1631 demonstrates. Laud did not argue; he nagged. For him the issue of obedience to the order established was as simple as could be; there was nothing to be conceded, nothing to be debated; debate was dangerous and unnecessary. His adjurations were pointed and precise, his irony heavy, his threats explicit. The age is bad; "they will not endure a good King to be commended, for danger of flattery: I hope I shall offend none by praying for the King." So he exhorted:

Take heed, I heartily beg it of you—I say it again, I heartily beg it of you—that no sin of unthankfulness, no base, detracting, murmuring sin, possess your souls, or whet your tongues, or sour your breasts, against the Lord, or against his anointed.

And threatened:

And here I should take occasion to tell you of the care and devotion of our David in his days, and of his prayers, both for himself and his son; but that the age is so bad, they will not believe he is so good beyond them. And some, for they are but some, are so waspishly set to sting, that nothing can please their ears, unless it sharpen their edge against authority. But take heed: for if this fault be not amended, justice may seize upon them that are guilty, God knows how soon: and the King's judgment that God hath given him, may pull out their stings, that can employ their tongues in nothing but to wound him and his government.

Laud took the Star Chamber with him right into the Paul's Cross pulpit.

Amid the almost universal temper of unyielding assurance and controversial determination, one small voice was heard at the Cross, probably in 1637, imploring moderation in all controversies and the exercise of Christian charity. The preacher was John Hales, a "prettie little man," as Aubrey affectionately called him, and modest rationalist, who at the Synod of Dort "bade John Calvin good-night." He spoke "of dealing with erring Christians." In some things all men agree; even the heathen are to be received when their voice is the universal voice of law. For unity's sake, weak men are to be restrained from doubtful disputations.

For nothing is there that hath more prejudiced the cause of Religion, than this promiscuous and careless admission of all sorts to the hearing and handling of controversies, whether we consider the private ease of every man, or the publick state of the Church.... For what need this great breed of Writers, with which in this age the world doth swarm?

Let there be variety of opinions, comprehended in the larger unity of common truths and aspirations. Mr. Hales went back to Eton, to his books and his violet-coloured dressing gown, and Paul's Cross remained the dwelling-place of wrath.

Laud's asseverations concerning the purity of the King's intentions were reiterated by Henry King in his accession sermon in 1640; the King is just, he stated; the Church of England orthodox, not fallen as some say into popery. In October 1641 Thomas Cheshire contemplated in his Paul's Cross sermon the extravagances of the sectaries and lay preachers, who published pamphlets in defence of new and strange creeds, and deplored the iconoclasm of some London congregations:

In one Church they have pulld downe the Kings Crowne, because it had a Crosse upon it; I would to God brethren, that in stead of pulling downe Antiquities, we did all of us endeavour to pull downe the *old man*, and demolish our owne unsanctified hearts, instead of the memory of the Saints. . . . I shall tell you a thing which would have made the good Primitive Christians to have trembled themselves out of joynt, my selfe was a sad spectatour of it; not many daies since, comming into Saint Sepulchres Church, a little before the hour of prayer, on a week-day, I saw a woman dandling and dancing her child upon the Lords holy Table; when she was gone, I drew neere, and saw a great deale of water upon the Table; I verely thinke they were not teares of devotion, it was well it was no worse.

Ministers are abused: "there (they say) goeth a Jesuit, a Baals priest, an Abbey-lubber, one of Canterburies whelpes, the ordinary language, as we walke the streetes." The sense of good form is abused too. Cheshire quoted the opening of the prayer for rain in the Book of Common Prayer, and set beside it a typical extempore prayer on the same subject:

Lord there have been some semblances, and some overtures Lord of raine, the clouds indeed were gathered together, but they were suddenly dispersed Lord, Lord thou knowest that the kennels of the streets yeeld a most unsavoury smell, &c.

This sort of thing would have delighted Matthew Arnold, had he been there; one may assume that it did not delight the representatives of the City congregations who heard it. Nor would they be convinced by the arguments of Mark Frank in the same year. He preached upon Jeremiah 35:18–19, the commendation of the Rechabites' obedience, observing grimly that the text was not fit for the time, but surely needful, since disobedience has set men apart from one another. God delights in obedience; we delight in disobedience:

I need call nothing else but the dismal experience of these last tumultuous times to witness it, wherein tongues, and pens, and actions have so horribly expressed it.

England abounds in ignorant and malicious teachers, and "riots, riches, pride, and a desire of raising families, have made many of you forget to keep under." How, the preacher asked the City fathers, can you deny the King obedience you demand in your Corporation? You plead laws and customs in your tenures, lands and corporations, may not the Church plead them too?

May not I as lawfully serve my God in a reverent posture, as thou in thy saucy and irreverent garb? Is it superstition in me to stand, because thou sittest or leanest on thy elbow? Is it idolatry in me to kneel, because thou wilt not foul thy clothes, or vex thy knees?

The obedience enjoined by the Church is no heavy burden, nor is obedience to the King, but the King has been evilly used!

Let the affronts at his own palace-gate, the saucy language in every rascal mouth, the rebellious sermons, the seditious libels cast about, his own words, where he is fain to proclaim to the world he is driven from you—let these speak; I say nothing.

Frank saw nothing but ruin and desolation before the kingdom, and upon a like melancholy note, though overlaid with the sweetness of an apparently good temper, did Richard Gardiner, canon of Christ Church, preach on the accession day, March 27, 1642. Charles was in York; in August he raised his standard at Nottingham.

"The drift of the Discourse," wrote Gardiner in his preface to the Earl of Dorset, "is to cement together affectionate obedience in the People, and cheerful protection in the Soveraigne." Our prayers, he told his audience, ought to be multiplied for the King.

It is by him that we move in our proper sphere, and are not justled out of it. . . . Were it not for the binding force of Soveraignty, who durst raise a damme against the Torrent of Corruption? Our meetings would be mutinies, our Pulpits Cockpits, authority would lose its authority, no subordination, no subjection, the honourable would be level'd with the base, the prudent with the childe, all would be amass'd, and hudled up in an unjust parity, and the Land over-runne with inflexible generations.

There is much good constitutional sense in that, shorn of some dated phraseology; much of it reads like a prophecy of the years to come. Gardiner professed that he would not have the King's prerogative enlarged to the prejudice of the laws, but he feared the influence of men's untamed private fancies more; he deplored the adoration of images as much as any man, but would have such "decorements" used in the common wisdom of the Church's management. He praised the refined and sanctified temper of the King, and closed with a fervent prayer for unity.

How many, one wonders, sat or stood in the cathedral that day to hear this, one of the last of the sermons preached on the old foundation, in the old way, for the old purpose?

III SOCIOLOGICAL

THIS IS THE HISTORY of an institution, and institutions, like men, have their ages, their periods, their grand and lesser climacterics. The period between More and Milton, Latimer and Laud, represents the middle and old age of Paul's Cross. During the century before us, we observe the stiffening, the dying, of the institution of the Paul's Cross sermon; that weekly theatre for voluptuous worldlings, for loyal subjects, loses its capacity for drama, its repertoire becomes narrower, its staging worn, its acting stilted and wooden. Sermons which had once been programmes for action become items for albums.

Albums, reminders, little books of remembrance. Let us not undervalue, in our search for the historically significant, these continually repeated "remembrances." Repeat a thing often enough, din it into the ears of the multitude, and it may prove a prolific dragon's tooth—or a most powerful opiate. A highly integrated state, such as the Tudor and Stuart monarchy, needs both.

What, then, did these self-styled "remembrancers" at Paul's Cross invite their audiences to remember, in the old age of that pulpit? First, upon the wreckage which the Reformers had made of the traditional Holy Year, with its recurring saints' days, its calendar of Christendom, they imposed a new "calendar," a new set of festivals to supplement or to supplant the old. The "royal saint" took his place in the continually celebrated pantheon, and it is idle to tax the preachers with vain expense of adulation, for the Church was attached to the monarchy by ties not only statutory but binding in conscience. The anniversaries of the monarch's accession were, as we have seen, celebrated as holy days, and Dr. Holland defended the practice in "an

Apologeticall discourse," in 1599. But the days chiefly to be remembered were not accession days or natal days, but days of deliverance, of the realm's and the sovereign's deliverance, by the immediate providence of God, from danger and death. Such were, for James I, August 5 and November 5; and to these were added, as corollary reminders, the deliverance of '88, Queen Elizabeth's various escapes from plots on her life, and other signal examples of God's mercy to England bestowed. Among the papists, said John Boys in 1613, preaching on the Plot anniversary, which was solemnized by law, Sanders is a saint, he who "lived in plotting and dyed in acting rebellion," and also Garnet, "that lecherous treacherous Arch-priest, Arch-traitor, Arch-divell," but we celebrate the deliverance of God's vicegerent on earth. So the preachers helped to create and mark the red-letter days on what Samuel Garey called, in 1618, "Great Brittans little calendar."

"The deliverance of a king," said Barten Holyday, "is the greatest Epocha in the Chronicle of Gods mercies, and releeves the curiositie of expectation with a gratefull period." "When God delivers a private man," contributed Thomas Adams, "he doth, as it were, repeat his creation; but the deliverance of a king is always a choice piece in the Lord's chronicle.... When the Lord delivered him, what did he else but deliver us all?" Such were the lessons taught from that most dubious, indeed scandalous, affair of August 5, 1600. But the axis upon which all this cycle of remembrance turned was fixed by the main deliverances: from the Armada in 1588, from the Powder Plot in 1605, from water and from fire. Preacher after preacher repeated the platitudes, best illustrated in the title-page of Bishop George Carleton's *A Thankfull Remembrance of Gods Mercie*, which went to four editions between 1624 and 1630.[1] There the true Church, her foot upon Pope and Puritan, sits in the centre. Over her cherubs proclaim: "Glory be to God. Peace be to England." She is flanked by the English Deborah, whose flag exhibits the Armada, and by the English Solomon, whose flag shows a conspirator about to ignite the gunpowder. At the base of the design an ark (*Per aquas*) faces a burning bush (*Per ignem*). The picture is a sermon, a century of sermons, in emblematic form.

God hath put "golden snuffers" into the hands of his preachers, said Robert Wilkinson, to keep your spiritual lights bright. But those lights were not solely the victorious glare of Drake's fire-ships, or the quenched flame of Guy Fawkes's brand. "Remember Lots wife," remember the sins of England. Remember, cried many a preacher, the days of Marian idolatry, remember the *threat* of the Armada, the plague of 1603, the death of Prince Henry. The formula for the Paul's Cross sermon is tri-partite: England's blessings—England's sins—the inevitability of God's judgments. "The dewe of Gods blessing hath onely fallen on our land," said Martin Fotherby in 1607, "when all our neighbour countries have been destitute of it." But we are not thankful, we run into sin and make gods of our bellies, and then God sends the plague to hang over us, "the droppes of Gods displeasure." So John Jones in 1630:

All other countries are in some things defective; but England like a provident parent, doth minister unto us whatsoever is usefull.... The summer burnes us not, nor doeth the winter benumme us.... As in situation, so in felicity, our beloved Isle is wholly disjoyned from all the world. They that have travelled the Belgicke provinces, can witness the miserable footsteps of warre, and the tyrannie of desolation.... Our deare Country, hath stood like the Center, with unmooved firmnesse.

Yet we sin greatly; Anglia swarms with all abominations, and so God's judgments have fallen upon us. God has suffered our enemies to prevail, we are afflicted with the plague; his hand is heavy upon us. So scores of others. William Hull, preaching in 1612, gave the typical sermon a more apocalyptic flavour:

Our good God by the hand of our dread soveraigne hath poured down flouds of peace: peace continued hath brought forth prosperity: prosperity abused hath ingendred carnall security: carnall security hatched epicurisme: epicurisme hath bred contempt of God, his word and sacraments. Impiety seemeth to be at the height. So that (if Gods providence follow common experience) the world will shortly end or amend.

The preacher was the Lord's voice, concerned to proclaim the salvation of the elect and to declare the day of the Lord. Did the day of the Lord and England's day fall together? How did the preacher stand in time? The answer is that he stood near the end of things, but also at their beginnings. In the time of God there is no difficulty, no choice to make; our times are in His hand; his Gospel flourishes and our doom is upon us. But in nature the apocalypse and the growth of the Gospel are set in the linear frame of time, and this paradox had to be applied to the history of reformed England. On the one hand, the preachers espoused a nationalistic type of messianism; the people of England, they said, have come up from Sheol into a land flowing with milk and honey, out of darkness into light. This progressive principle, implying broadening revelation of God's purposes, was often accompanied by a brisk defence of the "moderns," and an anti-intellectual repudiation of the past. "I think," affirmed Robert Temple, "there was never age afore us soe excellent for manye florishing witts both in all kinde of learning, and in Devinitie," and this judgment was echoed by John Stockwood. The Greeks, said John White, "were Barbarians whom Christians must not imitate." Notice the cultural primitivism in this passage from a sermon preached in 1626 by H. Valentine, lecturer at St. Dunstan's in the West:

The Westerne part of the world hath beene oft and much troubled with heresie; but the East never quiet, till the deluge of misery wherin now they are overwhelmed them. And the cause was in the restles wits of the Grecians, evermore proud of their own curious inventions, which once contrived, were made plausible by the great facility of their language. Those grand hereticall impieties which so immediately touched God and the glorious Trinity were all in a manner the Monsters of the East.

But the preachers also brooded upon the twilight close at hand. Humane learning, however by times discountenanced in comparison with clear revelation, gave them some sense of the long reaches of the past and the mutability of all earthly things. So the lesser preachers join the great threnodists of the age, in elegiac meditations over past times. "Where are the glorious and mightie Monarchies, on whom the world it selfe did wait?"

As the grave of Pompey had not so much as an inscription, to distinguish the dust that covered his victorious body from ignoble slaves and cowards, or to shew, Here lyes Pompey; No more have those once glorious dayes, now any difference in our memory or esteeme. They lie promiscuously raked up in the dust of time, without any monument set over them, to tell they once were: no Rubrick, or capitall letter inserted, to distinguish them from the common heape of dayes piled up in the Almanacke.[2]

Most were agreed that the world itself was declining. "Nature beginneth to intermitte her wonted course . . . the celestial spheares be almoste weary of theyr wonted motions and regular volubility . . . tymes and seasons of the yeare do blend themselves with disordered and confused mixture . . . the windes are in a readiness to breath out their laste gaspe . . . and man himselfe whome all these things doo serve, is of lower stature, lesse strength, shorter life than at the first he was."[3] "The world is old and now in her dotage . . . the sun of this world is ready to set, and the night drawing on . . . the world lies bedrid." All things shall soon "vanish with the wind & fal away as the smoke."

Signs and portents were to be seen, not only in the immediate acts of God in plague, famine, meteors, flood, and fire, but in reading of the biblical evidence, and applying it to the times. The prophecies of Daniel concerning the four monarchies were rehearsed and proved what they usually prove; the Antichrist (the Pope) is a sign of the end of things; even the level-headed Sanderson had "a strong suspicion" of the truth of this, and such pedants as John Dove triumphantly proved the point by a *gematria* upon 666. It is horrible presumption, all were agreed, to fix the date of the last hour, but the fatal figure of 6,000 years was in all their minds, and the temptation great to apply it to the chronology of the West.

Few preachers, however, expatiated upon these esoteric matters simply for the intellectual exercise or the delicious shudder of doom. All sought to apply these visions to England in the moment. So Lancelot Dawes spoke for a whole school of thought in 1609, when he reviewed the causes which had been suggested for the periods of commonwealths. The Epicurists attributed the end of nations to fortune, the Stoics to destiny, Pythagoras to numbers, Aristotle to disharmony in the body politic; as for Bodin, "how wittie is he in pleading for numbers"; "Cardanus hangeth all upon the taile of the greater beare"; Copernicus would have it "the conversion & motion of the centure of his imaginarie excentricle circle . . . caused . . . by the earth, which he will have continually wheeled about." But what is the true cause? "The sinnes of the people." In these circumstances, moved by the breath of the Judgment trumpet, by national pride, by moral fervour, and indeed by simple custom, the preacher declared himself the voice of the Lord, the prophet calling the sinful city to repentance. He was the successor of Zephaniah, of Micah, of Jeremiah, of Jonah. The powerful language of the prophets, which described the *city* both literally destroyed and as a symbol of corruption, sank deeply into the preachers' minds and served to blow the coals of their eloquence in their hour in that important pulpit, in the centre of the City, in the heart of England.

Rebuke of sin is "the usuall subject" of discourses at Paul's Cross, remarked William Proctor, preaching *The Watchman Warning* in 1625.

"Much preaching against transgression" here, Roger Ley observed. "Sometimes here doe spring bitter hearbes to cure the corrupt diseases, and to expell the spirituall pestilences out of this citie." The preacher is physician to the body politic; he does not appear, on most occasions, to expel particular sins, but to perform a sort of weekly "check-up," which means that he passes sins in review, exhibiting their ugliness and their pervasiveness, and thus excoriates the consciences of his hearers, purging them of error. He would awake the sleepy organism out of "carnall security," a favourite term—but then the sins of Englishmen have often derived, as Robert Burton suspected, from the wintry humour. Accordingly, one sometimes finds a dirge over virtue, like that of Daniel Price—"I cannot speake of Pietie, for Pietie is sicke, nor of Faith, for Faith is dead, nor of Works, for Works are buried"—but usually a catalogue with commentary, and appropriate exhortation. Such are the great pageants of humours in the sermons of Thomas Adams, with their expert "characters" of usurer, gallant, whoremonger, drunkard, and so forth, out of the Parson's Tale by Timothy Bright. For the most part the catalogues have only the merit of inclusiveness; Adam Hill, for example, dealt with the following in two hours: manifest idolatry of papists, blasphemy, swearing, profanation of the Sabbath, murder, sodomy, whoredom, oppression of the poor, rebellion, atheism, pride in apparel, idleness, Martin Marprelate, sacrilege, drunkenness, corruption of magistrates, seditious talk, simony, covetousness. Each list was directed to the attention, not only of the sinner, but of the magistrates, who were usually present to hear what their duties should be and how they should enforce the laws. "Sermons delivered in that audience," said Roger Ley, "are principally for the governours of this Honourable Cittie." The preacher sought a text which should "speake to all persons," and, conscious of addressing all "estates," spoke to the "judges" of justice, to the "inferiour subjects" of obedience, to all of sin. The familiar theme was God's judgment and mercy. The preacher was the prophet in the temple court, Hosea *redivivus*: "Hear ye this, O priests; and hearken, ye house of Israel; and give ye ear, O house of the King; for judgment is toward you."

The typical Paul's Cross sermon, then, which is a distinct type, like the funeral sermon, the convocation sermon, the assize sermon, is an exhortation addressed to all estates of the realm, entreating of God's judgment and His mercy, balancing the blessings and the sins of

England upon the fulcrum of God's special providence. The preacher is the voice of God speaking to the fallen city; he is the physician to the body politic; he is the servant of the Church of England whose canons he is bound to defend, and in defending them to justify the Church's existence by this audible and visible demonstration of her care for the body politic.

"If we shall be so affected," said John Howson, "that every man for his owne commodity will rob and spoyle another man, the society of mankind, which of all things is most naturall, must needes be dissolved." No other preacher, not even Thomas Adams, put more succinctly the ideal which the preachers set before their audiences in Paul's churchyard, Sunday after Sunday for a century. This was the age of Sir Thomas Gresham and the East India Company, of the expansion of coal-mining and the development of the cloth-trade, of merchant adventuring and the promotion of risk capital, of the shift of financial power from the guild to the stock company, from the old nobility to the new gentry, from the Crown to the Commons. It was also the age when the *Book of Private Prayer*, issued for the devotions of the faithful, contained this prayer for landlords:

We heartily pray thee to send thy holy spirit into the hearts of them that possess the grounds, pastures, and dwelling-places of the earth, that they, remembering themselves to be thy tenants, may not rack and stretch out the rent of their houses and lands, nor yet take unreasonable fines and incomes, after the manner of covetous worldlings . . . , but so behave themselves in letting out their tenements, lands and pastures, that after this life they may be received into everlasting dwelling-places.[4]

The doctrine of the Church of England preachers upon usury and enclosures, upon engrossing and rack-renting, was throughout the period the traditional doctrine, inherited from the middle ages and preached when it seems to us a voice crying in the wilderness. They quoted Aquinas upon the just price; they made no distinction between producers' and consumers' loans in the matter of usury. Their diatribes against economic individualism were based not only upon the pronouncements of the theorists from Raymond de Pennaforte to Thomas Wilson, but upon the observation of dispossessed villagers and rumours of the debts of the nobility. To theory and popular prejudice was added the effect of that intimate relationship between Church and

State, that curious and powerful product of Tudor statesmanship, which made it impossible for the Council to countenance a society in which any group of persons should operate without state regulation, and equally impossible for the preachers to regard such intrusions upon order with anything but a conservative remonstrance. The statutes in any collection of government documents closely parallel the pronouncements from the pulpits and the injunctions in the Homilies. The two arms, ecclesiastical and secular, were joined in purpose; the welfare of the commonwealth was, in ideal, an accomplishment to God's glory, and obedience to the sovereign in all matters economic as well as political, a religious duty. To these reasons for the persistence of the traditional attack upon all forms of progressive individualism must be added, in the case of such Church of England "Puritans" as Thomas Adams or John Stockwood, another factor no less cogent. Whatever ecclesiastical discipline the Puritan spirit might submit to, whether of Canterbury, of Geneva, or of the congregation, there existed in such men a temper which the visible church organization does not adequately describe, a posture of the spirit rigorous and stern, arrogant and humourless, austerely tender to the sinner and pitiless to the sin. It was, I suppose, a sort of "hard primitivism," which found in the primitive Church and in the supposed severities of an earlier age the simplicities of conduct and stability of opinion which it admired. This feeling is present in Latimer's famous apostrophe to his father's yeomanry, and it animates Charles Richardson's fine sermon, sixty-five years later, against oppression and fraudulent dealing. It is a grave mistake, said John Walsal, to think that inflation is Protestant; let us have no vulgar nostalgia for the good old days, when "we lived as we lusted, Priestes were good fellowes, adulterie was borne withall, bread was bigger, ale was stronger, beefe more plentifull, troutes fatter and better, all things cheaper, xxiiij egges for a penie." But on the other hand, can we, asked Lawrence Chaderton, always defend ourselves against the papists' condemnation that in Protestant England charity is cold? The "outwarde workes," as cathedrals and colleges and abbeys where the poor were relieved, were good, "which in deed are such as do stoppe our mouthes, & put us Protestantes to silence." The old days of the papal tyranny were bad, no doubt of that, but somewhere in the past society was ordered better than it is now.

It was *ordered*; it was static. "Happy that State, wherein the Cobler meadles with his Last, the Tradesman with his shop, the Student with his booke, the Counsellor with State, the Prince with the Scepter, and each Creature lives in his own Element."[5] Each in his place. It was a spatial concept, based on the equivalence of power and land, and it was being undermined as the preachers spoke by the new concept of the equivalence of power and time, not God's time (the time of the church bells) but man's time, the period of a loan, the date of a contract. Land binds men together, money separates them.[6] No Christian man is an island:

If any man be so addicted to his private, that he neglect the common, state, he is void of the sense of piety, and wisheth peace and happiness to himself in vain. For, whoever he be, he must live in the body of the Commonwealth and in the body of the Church.[7]

The Christian commonwealth, said Latimer, is as the going of two ploughs: as it is necessary to have the bodily ploughing for "the sustentation of the body," so we must have the spiritual ploughing for the sustentation of the soul. The sin of the times is that "the bodily ploughing is taken in and enclosed through singular commodity"; the spiritual ploughing is hindered by "lording and loitering" among God's ministers. "Both ploughs must still be going . . . and wherefore are magistrates ordained, but that the tranquillity of the commonweal may be confirmed, limiting both ploughs?"

The nature of ownership in the society ordained of God is very different from that determined by economic laws. No man in his calling, said William James, works for himself alone, but for all. Twenty-five years later, John Hoskins affirmed that a man is not the owner of that which he calls his own:

The principall right of all outward things God hath reserved to himselfe . . . , yet hath hee committed to the sonnes of men a right of use and dispensation agreeable unto reason, which asketh that things in nature perfect, should serve creatures of more perfection; whereunto, for the avoyding of disorder, a generall distinction of ownages, was added by the Law of Nations.[8]

Ownership as stewardship is conformable to reason and to natural law, which is God's law. "You that are great in this world," said George Benson, "you do not wind and turn those things which are absolutely your own, you are but feofees in trust with them to the use of Gods Orphanes." Degrees of wealth are also the ordinance of

God; "God would have some rich, some poore, for distinction sake, and the mutuall exercise of liberality and patience." All ranks are in the ideal condition bound together by charity; the end and rule of commercial transactions is the "mutual profit" of buyer and seller, "not the gain of one of them alone." This end is not to be gained by Anabaptistical communism. True it is, said Lever, that the Apostles had all things common, "yea and that christen men, in that they are christen men rather then covetous men, have all thynges comen, even unto this day," but in this sense,

that ryche menne shoulde keep to theym selves no more then they nede, and geve unto the poore so muche as they nede. . . . For so it is mete that christen mens goodes shuld be comen unto every mans nede, and privat to no mans luste. . . . For they that imagyne, covet, or wyshe to have all thynges commune, in suche sorte that everye man myght take what hym luste, wolde have all thynges comen and open unto everye mans luste, and nothynge reserved or kept for any mans nede.[9]

It may then be good to be rich. There is no doubt, argued the preachers, that the desire of money is the root of all evil; there is godliness in great gain only if a man is content with what he has. If riches bring contentment and not ambition or immoderate desire of worldly prosperity they fulfil their function as good gifts of God. For riches being the gifts of God are not evil in themselves: it is the abuse of riches, which is covetousness, that is a hydra-headed monster. A man may be rich and also godly. "There is an inward joy, there is an outward dignity and reverence, that accompanies riches, and the godly, the righteous man is not incapable of these."[10] The inward joy and satisfaction of which Donne speaks here may arise, as Perkins observed, from the contemplation of God's ordinance of inequality in worldly goods; "such as have sundry farms . . . may lawfully enjoy them."[11] The tension of duty and privilege which informed this casuistry was never better expressed than by Richard Bernard:

Riches well used bring grace and estimation before men, for they inable men to shew forth godlinesse, & to passe on their time with more comfort, and to countenance and defend their poore Christian brethren in well-doing. Therefore if grace and goods go together, thou hast great cause to blesse God: for it is a most happy estate, to bee rich towards the world, and to God too, to bee rich body and soule. But although this is a very rare estate, yet we see that they may meete together: and therefore we may not thinke that he which is rich, can not be religious. True it is, that it is hard for a rich man to enter the Kingdome of heaven; but it is not impossible.[12]

I have found no other preacher prepared to cut through the problem of the godly rich man as Stephen Gosson did when he suggested that "God is contented to draw them [the worldly affected] unto him, with promises of worldly prosperitie, that by these steppes they may by little and little ascend to love him for himselfe at last." Rather the preachers insisted that the right use of riches is a matter of conscience, and that concentration on business is likely to leave the conscience asleep. So that sturdy Puritan Samuel Ward addressed those that had "mills of business" in their heads while he was speaking to them, warning them that they had scarce an hour in the day to "confer" with their consciences. Thomas Adams was concerned also to emphasize the burden upon the rich man's conscience: the greater riches, the greater danger of sin. "It is hard to bear the bag, and not to be covetous." As Protestants, argued James Bisse (and his argument is typical), we are freed from the tyranny of the Law upon the conscience, as free we are prone to carnality; since we know that we have no merit by works, we are slack in doing works, "we live to ourselves." Though some clerical "clawbacks" will usually be found to eulogize the rich man in a funeral sermon, observed Charles Richardson, God is not deceived. "There is never a tear, which cruel Tyrants wring from the eyes of the poore, but the Lord putteth it into his bottle." The rich say, we will do some deeds of charity before we die, build a hospital or an alms-house. But this is not a true act of charity, being the deed of a guilty conscience, and what appears to man as an instrument of charity is actually an evidence of the rich man's damnation.

But if the preacher reproved covetousness (or was it industry?) in the rich, he also reproved idleness in all estates. There were no embarrassing distinctions to make in the case of sloth, *accidia*, that traditional target of the righteous homilist. Many cumber the ground, said Adams,

men and women, whose whole employment is to go from their beds to the taphouse, then to the playhouse, where they make a match for the brothel house, and from thence to bed again. To omit those ambulatory Christians, that wear out the pavement of this great temple with their feet, but scarce ever touch the stones of it with their knees; that are never further from God than when they are nearest the church.

Idleness is a cause of frays and bloodsheds, said others; the city is full of "desperate ympes," the Kastrils, the Bobadils of the time, the troops of liveried hangers-on, the discharged gentlemen of companies, fruits of a calm world and a long peace. But what of the idle poor, the "masterless men" and "sturdy beggars" mentioned so frequently in Tudor statutes? Upon this question men as diverse as Andrewes and Adams spoke with a single voice, the voice of the Poor Laws and the Statute of Artificers of 1563. There are two sorts of poor, those "of God's making," and those "of their own making." The first are to be cared for with compassion, the others are to be recovered if possible by correction; laws should be made to make idlers work. The righteous are the industrious, said Adam Hill; and labour in their vocations while it is yet day. Here perhaps the way was open for what Professor Tawney has called "the new medicine for poverty" in the Commonwealth and Restoration administration of the Poor Laws,[13] but the case for the "calling" was usually put with some care. James Bisse, for example, showed how we should labour for the meat of the body, but not *carefully*.

God loves the painful man, but He also loves the poor, and their prayers are swift to reach His ears. There is, then, no possibility of one law for the rich and another for the poor, and the preachers fulminated without ceasing against offence's gilded hand. They liked the old simile of the cobweb, "that the laws are like cobwebs; that they hold fast the silly flies, but the great hornets break through them as oft as they list." For the most part, on this ticklish subject they spoke "in the generall," as one of them put it, though occasionally they ventured upon a more specific protest.[14] The judge is in God's place to minister justice and equity, and he ought not to be a lover of gifts; the good judge is no respecter of persons, and so on.

The law is, after all, God's law; it does not absolutely *belong* to anyone, to buy and sell or withhold. Neither, in the sternest application of the theory of stewardship, does land. It was to be expected that the preachers would denounce the revolution in the concept of landowning, not begun but accelerated by the Henrician auctions, by which landowners "took it for no offence, but said their land is their own."[15] Denounce it they did, but perhaps not to the extent that those economic historians who see the land question as the key to all the economic changes of the period might expect. Perhaps it was because these preachers spoke in London, more to merchants than to the gentry, that one finds, after the flurry from the "commonwealth men" in the reign of Edward VI, so little sustained invective on the question of enclosures. Perhaps the paucity of significant allusions supports the view of some contemporary historians that enclosures caused less damage and were less widespread than some earlier scholars believed. What protests there were at Paul's Cross were eloquent and poignant enough.

You whych have gotten these goodes into your own handes [said Lever], to turne them from evyll to worse, and other goods mo from good unto evyll, be ye sure it is even you that have offended God, begyled the kynge, robbed the ryche, spoyled the poore, and brought a comen wealth into a comen miserye.

The "new" landlords, for whom land is a capitalist investment and not a knightly privilege, "take, kepe, and enjoy the roumes and lyvynges of everye mannes vocation." That is the point; what is the "vocation" of the displaced yeoman? Wandering the roads is not a vocation. Land is now in Mammon's market, and the owners have every man's living but no man's duty. Hospitality, continued other preachers in the same strain, is decayed; the magnates keep sheep instead of men. The preachers lamented continually the decline of the yeomanry, the men who won Agincourt, and the social historian of the future may find interesting parallels between their complaints and the twentieth-century worries over the decay of the English gentry, the decline of the great houses built by the objects of the preachers' wrath into white elephants or property of the National Trust.

"By yeoman's sons," said Latimer, "the faith of Christ is and hath been maintained chiefly." It was in relation to the maintenance of the faith of Christ that the preachers made their chief complaints against the agrarian revolution. The faith could be maintained only by faithful ploughmen of God, ministers steadily performing their duties of preaching and charity in their cures. "They have great labours, and therefore they ought to have good livings, that they may commodiously feed their flock; for the preaching of the word of God unto the people is called meat . . . , not strawberries."[16] The root of the trouble was that there were not enough good livings. There had not been enough before the dissolution of the monasteries; benefices in the gift of the great religious houses had suffered much from appropriations;[17] but when the lands of the religious passed into the hands of greedy and ambitious lay patrons, the situation deteriorated at a terrific rate, especially in the reign of Edward VI. Latimer complained that "we of the clergy had too much, but that is taken away and we have too little." In the reign of Elizabeth, the Queen reserved to herself by statute the right to alienate episcopal revenues, and her example, notably in the sees of Salisbury, Ely, and Winchester, was followed "at a respectful distance" by the gentry in their inroads upon the benefices.[18] Furthermore, depopulation resulting from enclosures caused shifts of population, the dispossessed either living miserably, moving to the towns and especially to London, or settling in the weaving and mining centres. As a result, some parishes with tiny stipends as registered by the ordinary were filled with untaught children of God, fair fields for the Puritan lecturers; others, whatever their value, were left desolate, the spoil of pluralists.

The widespread pillaging of the Church and poverty of livings affected the life of the Church at every point. The preachers' protests were the more poignant because the Reformers had expected so much righteousness to flow from the dissolution. As one of them put it,

>   As I walked alone,
>   and mused on thynges
>   That have in my time
>   bene done by great Kings
>   I bethought me of Abbayes,
>   that sometyme I sawe
>   Whiche are now suppressed
>   all by a lawe.
>   O Lorde (thought I then)
>   what occasion was here
>   To provide for learninge
>   and make povertye chere?
>   The landes and the jewels
>   that hereby were hadde,
>   Would have found godly preachers
>   which might well have ladde
>   The people aright
>   that nowe goe astraye,
>   And have fedde the pore,
>   That famishe everye daye.[19]

Lever who had felt these hopes, observed bitterly:

Covetous officers have so used this matter, that even those goodes whyche dyd serve to the releve of the poore, the mayntenaunce of learning, and to comfortable necessary hospitalitie in ye comen wealth, be now turned to mayntayne worldly wycked covetouse ambition.

Later preachers agreed with Latimer that too much had been succeeded by too little. John Howson, for example, admitted that under popery the riches and endowments of the Church were too great, but now the laity practise the vices of the religious; and John King complained:

> There are in England above 3000 impropriacions, where the minister hath a poore stipend; their bread is broken among strangers, the foxes and the cubbes live in their ruines, the swallowe builds hir nest and the satyres daunce and revel where the Levites were wont to sing, the Church livings are seised upon and possessed by the secular.[20]

The ministers felt themselves underpaid, underprivileged, the playthings of a licentious secularism; all men, they felt, contemned their estate.

> Was there ever any time [said Bishop Sandys], any age, any nation, country, or kingdom, when and where the Lord's messengers were worse entreated, more abused, despised and slandered, than they are here at home, in the time of the gospel, in these our days? We are become in your sight, and used as if we were, the refuse and parings of the world.[21]

Ministers are despised by the very "churlish Nabals" who have denied them "their necessary maintenance." Another preacher defiantly advised the patrons of livings to "grease ever[y] halter that stops our breath that the rope may ride, and make a quick riddance of us al," and still another complained: "You benefice-mongers make the ministers your serving-men, you make them journey men, they have the name, you have the profite, they the straw, but you have the corne, nay you have some straw also."

The benefice-mongers often gave the straw to men of straw. The preachers were forced to admit in anger and embarrassment that ministers were often contemned because they were contemptible. The lay patrons gave the livings to "boys, to serving men, to their own children, seldom to learned pastors"; they gave them to their retainers, to "bakers, butlers, cookes, falconers," to artificers and "the basest sort of people," tinkers, tapsters, fiddlers, and pipers.[22] Preaching "ran very low" in the reign of Elizabeth, to use Fuller's phrase. It is no wonder that the Paul's Cross preachers emulated the Puritan brethren of the "classes" and thundered against "dumb dogs." Nothing but "strawberry preachers" even at Oxford in 1566, said one of them; there are still "Abbey-lubbers" in the church, idle drones that they are, complained another. The Church is full, said the dour Stockwood, of "ydel shepheardes, and able to doe nothing"; some are hirelings, knowing not the first word of their accidence, and could not preach if they would—very unprofitable members. Ministers are called to be *vocales*, "but prove *muti*," for fear of straining their voices, forsooth, or because they have no voices. So the attack proceeded. There was a dearth of learned men. The dissolution and the events which followed it had damaged the Universities seriously, not because the monasteries had contributed to them an irreplaceable body of learned men in the years preceding, but because the Universities, unadaptable institutions, had suffered a series of religious tests as damaging in effect as "loyalty" tests in our time. Many fellows compromised with their consciences from 1536 to 1559 to avoid "eating mice at Zurich," and the result was chaos.[23] The university libraries were ruthlessly plundered by iconoclastic visitors. Worst of all, the new gentry were slow in providing means for poor young scholars to study divinity. "None helpeth the scholar now," said Latimer, and Lever, a loyal son of Cambridge, portrayed at the Cross in 1550 its sad state. The late king's mind was to provide amply for the maintenance of learning, but the disposers of this liberality have caused the decay of learning in Cambridge: two hundred students of divinity "all clene gone, house and manne," and a small number "of poore godly dylygent studentes nowe remaynynge only in Colleges be not able to tary and contyne theyr studye in ye universitye for lacke of exhibition and helpe." In the country many grammar schools founded "of godly entent" are taken away by greedy covetousness, and the youth of the land is drowned in ignorance. Nearly fifty years later John Howson renewed the old complaint: one estate of the commonwealth is busy eating up another, making "barren and like desolate and forsaken widowes the two Universities, the two fruitfull Mothers and full of Children, though now readie to give up the ghost." The poor scholar exists in penury, and has nothing to spur him on but the prospect of a poor living. There is so little exhibition for poor scholars, said Thomas Sutton in 1613, that many "golden wits" cannot follow their calling for lack of maintenance.

Competition for good (or even adequate) livings and for pluralities was keen, and that kind of competition corrupts. One preacher gave elaborate advice on how to get a benefice:

If you cannot come to parle with the patron, then you will undermine him by his wife, and you will not sticke to give her twenty or fortie pounds to buy her a Gown or a Nagge, so that she wil stand your good Mistris, and speake for you: If that will not doe, then betake you yourselves to your young Master; and that he may not be meale-mouth'd you will bestow upon him a couple of Dogges, or a Gelding of tenne pounds: If this will not serve, then you wil lay waite in every corner and place, and therefore will be sure to bestow angels liberally upon his attendants, that they may helpe you forward, and lift you to come in by the Windowes: And if all this will not do, then you have an *Ultimum refugium*, And that is, to enter into bonds with the Patron to pay him an hundred pounds, or some summe of money without mentioning of and in consideration of such a Benefice.[24]

Lever condemned simony with passion:

Yf thou by money or fryndshyp have boughte eyther benefice or office, thou canst not be of Christes institucion, but of the Dyvylles intrusion, not a fayethful disposer, but a thevysh extortioner of Gods gyfts.

But the strongest outcry against these practices from Paul's Cross came in the 1590's. There are fashions in invective, and this seems to have been one of them, though scandals attending the transfer of certain bishoprics during this period probably brought the old evil to a position of prominence. In 1591 John Coldwell was forced to surrender a large part of the manor of Sherborne to Sir Walter Ralegh in order to secure the bishopric of Salisbury, and on his decease Cotton surrendered more manors for the same see. Bishop Day paid £1,000 to Sir Francis Carew for the see of Winchester in 1595; he died after only eight months' possession of his honours, and the see was left vacant for him who was willing to impoverish it most to get it. Thomas Bilson got it in 1597 at the price of a £400 annuity to the Queen.[25] The preachers did not of course mention these transactions, but they spoke pretty vehemently "in the generall." These leases, said one, "will cost you the Fee simple of a better thing"; alas, said another, "that ever the clergy of England should draw . . . into her very bowles the deadly poison of covetousness and contention"; patrons, suggested a third, choose their ministers as Minerva chose the olive tree, because it was fat. John Howson, in a full-scale attack upon simony, appealed to the fathers of the clergy not to fall into this sin, and with admirable irony suggested that perhaps the patrons' retaining of tithes was from religious scruples:

Peradventure you are of opinion (as I understand some are now adaies) that either there is no Priesthood in Christianity; or if there be any, we be all alike Priests . . . , and hereof inferre, that seeing Tythes are due to the Priest onely, and either there are no Priests, or if there be any, we are all alike Priests, either Tythes are not due, or if they be due, they belong to us all.

But was it irony after all? Howson's attack on simony is one with his attack on sacrilege, and though an earlier Reformer like Lever condemned sacrilege because it defeated the end of the Reformation, that all men should hear the Scriptures read to them in their own tongue, a High Churchman like Howson was more concerned to preserve the "comeliness" of God's house, against the depredations of the puritanically inclined (and of course covetous) gentry. Robert Temple called sacrilege "that holie covetousness & both honourable and worshipfull Idoll of Protestants," which is a nice reversal of terms, and Howson, in a second sermon upon the whole theme of simony and sacrilege, denounced the "irreligious Julianists" who were ready to despoil the Church:

> They have now brought their desire to the issue, so that in Countrey Villages . . . the Churches are almost become . . . little better than hogstyes; for the best preparation at any high feast is a little fresh straw under their feete, the ordinary allowance for swine in their stye . . . , and in cities and boroughes they are not like the Palaces of Princes as they were in the primitive church, but like a countrey hall, faire white limed, or a citizens parlour, at the best wainscotted; as though we were rather Platonists then Christians, who would neither have gold nor silver in their churches because it was *invidiosa res*, and gave occasion to sacriledge.[26]

We make but a bare allowance to God, he continued, like "a Stoicks dinner, or Philosophers breakfast," bare walls and a cover to keep us from rain. "Neither is it lawful to add any ornament . . . except perchance a cushion and a wainscot seate, for ones owne ease and credite." There sits the Puritan parvenu, comfortable on his cushion, but pilloried on an angry phrase!

Once he had relieved himself of his wrath at the spoliation of the Church and contempt of its ministers, the Paul's Cross preacher turned with renewed vigour upon the abuses in trade, the sins of the merchants. Beneath the rhetorical exaggerations of the attacks upon abuses in land tenure and upon sacrilege and simony lay a body of specific evidence upon which the preachers could draw with confidence if sometimes with caution. But the dishonest trader was a stock figure. There were, of course, crooked merchants—there always have been—but I suspect that the preachers knew very little about them. Their complaints are stereotyped, repeated by rote: merchants show one thing and sell another; they use false weights and measures; they conceal the faults in their goods, sell "bad and naughty wares." The preachers invoked the dark shop, the impudent tongue, the whole practice of *caveat emptor* almost mechanically; it was the thing to do. Occasionally a more romantic view of the merchant appears. In the many sermons commending the East India enterprise about 1609, for example, the merchant (not the retailer but the adventurer) is lauded to the skies, as in this passage from Daniel Price:

> The merchant is the most diligent, careful, assiduous, industrious, laborious, and indefatigable of al other kinds of life. . . . The marchant is the key of the land, the treasurer of the kingdome, the venter of his soiles surplussadge, the combiner of nations, & the adamantine chain of countries.

Man should not be idle, Price continued, but walk in his vocation; but there is a large difference between the good merchant like Sir Thomas Gresham and evil robbers, pirates, *usurers*.

Usurers indeed. From the Paul's Cross pulpit arose for a century a single voice condemning usury. The preachers agreed with Nicholas Heming that it was "the parte of the preachers to inveigh against all unlawfull and wicked contractes, to reprove usury,"[27] which was unlawful by scriptural prohibition and by proofs out of St. Thomas and Aristotle. The most they would admit was that the times gave them but a cold hearing. There is "small or no hope" of amendment in this, said Thomas White, "and yet we must speake stil against it for all that." If you upbraid the usurer, complained William Fisher, he will plead the profit of the city. Quote Luke 6:34 at him, and he will reply:

> Tush, Tush, Scripture is Scripture, but for all the scripture, a man must live by his owne, and I tell you my money is my Plough.

The preachers might well complain. Lay scepticism of the interference of "simple divines" in matters of credit is beautifully set forth in George Phillips' *Life and Death of the Rich Man and Lazarus* (1600), where the story is told of a self-made man who sent his son to university and upon hearing that his freshly ordained offspring had preached against usury at Paul's Cross observed with calm pride:

> I cannot justly blame my Sonne for that he hath done, for it is as well his profession, to speake against usury, as it is my occupation to follow it, otherwise he might want matter to speake on, and both my selfe and my Son might lacke money to live on: proceed therefore my Sonne, quoth this goldfinder, and see you spare not

to invent damning arguments against such as live by loane, and I hope that in time this will become my trade alone."[28]

Men like that, as John Dove bitterly remarked, could "heare three sermons in a day [and yet] thinke thirty poundes interest in the hundred to be too little."

Damning arguments appear in quantity, but are conventional; he who has read Wilson's *Discourse upon Usury* (1572) knows them all. Usury is a sin against nature, like the sin of Sodom; the usurer binds others to himself by other bonds than those proper ones of charity: "his religion is all religation, a binding of others unto himself, of himself to the devil." Usury is the unlawful usurpation of another's goods; creditors should lend only "according to the nature of a loane (a contract of mere gratuitie), their money according to the nature of money, which is an appointed instrument of exchange uncapable of such monstrous improvement." The usurer has no place in the recognized order of guilds and corporations, "he is free of all Companies." Usury eats up many ancient families, the fat of the land, and it grinds the poor to powder. Many a grim "character" of the usurer is sketched, none better than by Thomas Adams, who in sermon after sermon, with the violence of the Dominican Bromyard and the ruthless eye of Dickens, shows us the usurer who "sits at home in his warm furs, and spends his time in a devilish arithmetic."

All the sins so far reviewed in this summary of social criticism from that pulpit are sins against "distinction of ownages." But good order in the Christian society depends also upon distinction in consumption, especially in the apparel of the outward man. The avowed purpose of the ancient acts for reformation of excessive array was the maintenance of "degree and estate" and of "peace, amity and concord."[29] In our days, observed the preachers, this propriety is sadly defaced. Four shillings for a pair of breeches for a king in the days of William Rufus, noted one, "but I feare shortly it will be a proverbe: five hundred pounds for a payre of pant[o]ples for a subject." In these days men do not wear what is appropriate to their calling, but "light, vain, strange, proud, and monstrous apparel." Excess in apparel among the gentry "eateth up the land": "Amongst us the compendious course is taken of gathering our credit neere unto us in cloathes, which lay scattered in hospitality before, and in attendants." No one likes to go in good old English homespun like his forefathers; all must ruffle it in the mode of "the Gascoigne, the Venitian, the French, the Spanish, the Dutch." "Our ancient, substantiall, fundamental trades belonging unto Clothing go downe, and they that fill our Cities are *Nugi-vendi*, trifle-sellers. . . . The men that are busied, and the charge that is imployed, about these painefull and difficult toyes, would serve for many new Plantations."[30]

These remonstrances, which are echoed in the drama, are now and again flavoured with the same salty animadversions upon the vanity of women's dress as those which brighten the pages of the poor Parson's sermon. I do not find many such passages in Elizabethan sermons; it is just possible that they did not please the Queen. When Sandys quoted St. Paul upon the proper shamefacedness and modesty of women, he hastened to add: "I do not doubt but that Hester and Judith did wear gold, and were gorgeously decked." Indeed such show is well enough for a queen, but in woman "in the generall" it is a crown of pride, as John Hoskins observed. "Daughters of England," he warned, "build not Turrets or Castles on your heads," for they are allurements to the enemy. God has given you one face and you make yourselves another: "Neither may you daughters of England . . . abuse Gods Creation, attempt to control, or correct his workmanship, adding to that face, which Saint James termeth naturall, the borrowed features of a face artificiall." He spoke without prompting, in the ordinary course of his exhortation, but in 1619 sermons against feminine vanities were ordered by the King, and were presumably preached at Paul's Cross as well as in the City churches. Chamberlain wrote in February 1619 that "our pulpits ring continually of the insolence and impudence of women," so that they "can come nowhere but theyre eares tingle."[31] Perhaps the last word on this subject may be left to Nathaniel Cannon. After a brisk review of the sin of vanity displayed in "wide and flaunting garments," he concluded with a sombre understatement: "A greate alteration from figge leaves my brethren."

Excess of the belly is as much to be reprehended as excess upon the back. Gluttony and drunkenness are sins against nature, "which, being moderately refreshed, is satisfied; being stuffed, is hurt, violated, and deformed." It is very doubtful if the "ancient sobriety" which the preachers set up as example was diminished by the importation of foreign wines with the expansion of English trade and by the increase in the alcoholic content of English ale by the importation of hops from Artois;[32] but certainly the preachers turned their thunder upon drunkenness especially. Drunkenness, said Sibthorpe,

is the mother of misdemeanors; the matter that ministers all mischiefe, the root of wretchedness, the vent of vice, the Subverter of the Senses, the Confounder of the Capacity, raysing a storme in the Tongue, Billowes in the Body, and Shippewracke in the soule.

All over the land, complained John White, "the justice of the peace is mild, and the drunkard merry."

When [drunkards] are presented, they answer for themselves some flegmaticke conceit . . . that relishes of the broth; and the Magistrate bids, Do no more so: and so the drunkard in honour of the Justice, makes his image for saving him, and writes upon it, Good-ale never wanted a friend upon the bench.

Thomas Adams, edified by the reading of *Othello*, exclaimed:

Oh that a man should take pleasure in that which makes him no man; that he should let a thief in at his mouth to steal away his wit; that for a little throat-indulgence, he should kill in himself both the first Adam, his reason, and even the second Adam, his regeneration, and so commit two murders at once.

He had a theory to explain the common indulgence in strong drink, which is not quite the circle of economic determinism, since it begins and ends in sin:

Drunkenness makes so quick riddance of the ale that this raiseth the price of malt, and the good sale of malt raiseth the price of barley; thus is the land distressed, and the poor's bread dissolved into the drunkard's cup, the markets are hoised up. If the poor cannot reach the price, the maltmaster will; he can utter it to the taphouse, and the taphouse is sure of her old friend, drunkenness. Thus theft sits close in a drinking-room, and robs all who sail into that coast.

John Hoskins told a story to illustrate the "corporall inconveniences" of the vice:

A Monke of Prage . . . having heard at shrift the confession of drunkards, and pawning his wits to purchase experience of the sinne, stole himself drunke; and after three daies drowsy lothsome languishing vexation, when he came abroad, to all that confessed the same sinne, enjoyned no penance but this, Goe and be drunke againe.

This sin never comes alone, warned the moralists; in its train come mocking, murder, adultery, the "storme in the tongue" (swearing and blasphemy), which is a fearful thing, and known in the court itself—indeed the court is "a school of blasphemy."

Ah, noble Prince HENRY [cried William Worship] (whose very name still makes my heart to bleede afresh) wee may thanke our Court-oathes, as one chiefe cause of thine untimely death.

But worse than this is adultery. Robert Sanderson characteristically explored the nature of the sin itself, which is a mixed crime, partaking of injustice as well as uncleanness:

> Every married person hath *ipso facto* surrendered up the right and interest he had in and over his own body, and put it out of his own into the power of another: what an arrant thief then is the adulterer, that taketh upon him to dispose at his pleasure that which is none of his.

Robert Sibthorpe would have men shun this sin through avoiding idleness, for "Cupid hits few but the slothful"—Burton's opinion. He ventured also to point out the location of some brothels in London, the first, like Rahab's house, upon the town wall; the second, like the vale of Sorek, in a valley by a brookside; the third, like the dwelling of the two harlots who came before Solomon, the houses of a couple of victuallers in the City.

The brothels and the theatres stood closer together in the minds of some preachers than ever they did on the Bankside. From wine to plays to harlots, that is the epicure's course, remarked Adams. But there were other reasons for the preachers' campaign against the theatres. In the Jacobean period, for example, ministers of the Puritan persuasion were aggrieved at lewd representations of their kind upon the stage. Players, said William Crashaw in 1608, grow worse and worse,

> for now they bring religion and holy things upon the stage. . . . Two hypocrites must be brought foorth; and how shall they be described but by these names, Nicholas S. Antlings, Simon S. Maryoveries? Thus hypocrisie a child of hell must beare the names of two Churches of God, and two wherein Gods name is called on publikely every day in the yeare, and in one of them his blessed word preached everie day (an example scarce matchable in the world): yet these two . . . shall be by these miscreants thus dishonoured, and that not on the stage only, but even in print.[33]

And Samuel Ward, in 1616, also alluded to such ridicule, in an apostrophe to the brethren:

> As for the players, and jesters, and rhymers, & all that rabblement, tell them, thou wilt one day be in earnest with them, and though thou suffer them to persecute thee upon their stages, and shew their wit, and break their jests on thee now, thou wilt owe it to them, till they come upon the great stage, before God and all the world.

For strict Sabbatarians the players were chief among those who made the Lord's day a time of ungodly exercises. Something was done by the authorities about playing on Sunday,[34] and it was done as a result of the intense wave of protest against playing that swept pulpit and press in the years 1577 to 1579. This barrage of fulmination is a phenomenon of great interest, and some of the heaviest artillery was sounded off at Paul's Cross. The first blow seems to have been struck by Thomas White in his sermon at the Cross in 1577; in December of that year John Northbrooke's *Treatise* was entered in the Stationers' Register; the next year saw the publication of Thomas Brasbridge's *Poore Mans Jewell*, which repeated White's arguments about the relation of plays and plague; in this year also appeared Stockwood's first Paul's Cross sermon and John Walsal's sermon; in 1579 appeared *Newes from the North*, Robert Spark's sermon at the Cross, Stockwood's second sermon, and Gosson's *Schoole of Abuse*. The preachers' invective ran nearly the whole gamut made familiar to students of the subject through the violent and tedious pages of *Histriomastix*, with some timely additions. White, speaking in time of plague, put his case simply: "The cause of plagues is sinne, if you looke to it well: and the cause of sinne are playes: therefore the cause of plagues are playes." Every man, said Stockwood, cries out against "beastly Playes" from Paul's Cross. How can they be tolerated in a Christian commonwealth? The building of theatres is unprofitable expenditure:

For reckoning with the leaste, the gaine that is reaped of eighte ordinarie places in the Citie whiche I knowe, by playing but once a weeke . . . amounteth to 2000. pounds by the yeare, the suffering of whiche waste muste one daye be answered before God.

It has been suggested that such outbursts were not of the conventional "Puritan" kind altogether, but instigated by influential groups of London citizens, and that Stockwood was their chief spokesman because of his connection with the Company of Skinners, being the master of their grammar school at Tunbridge.[35] The attacks of the late seventies do seem organized, but in general the hostility of the preachers to the players is the expression of an old rivalry, a jealousy no less deeply felt for being conventional—in fact the strongest passions are conventional. "Vaine players have had about this citie . . . farre greater audience, then true preachers." "Wyll not a fylthye playe, with the blast of a Trumpete, sooner call thyther a thousande, than an hours tolling of a Bell bring to the Sermon a hundred?"

The licentious Poet and Player together are growne to such impudencie, as with shamelesse Shemai, they teach Nobilitie, Knighthood, grave Matrons & civill citizens, and like Countrey dogs snatch at everie passengers heeles. Yea, Playes are growne now adaies into such high request (*Horresco referens*) as that some prophane persons affirme, they can learne as much both for example and edifying at a Play, as at a Sermon. *O tempora, O mores.* . . . To compare a lascivious Stage to this sacred Pulpit and oracle of trueth? To compare a silken counterfeit to a Prophet, to Gods Angell, to his Minister, to the distributor of Gods heavenly mysteries? And to compare the idle and scurrile invention of an illiterate bricklayer to the holy, pure, and powerfull word of God, which is the foode of our soules to eternall salvation?[36]

The matter (if not the style) of Zeal-of-the-Land Busy is comparable:

I wil remove Dagon there, I say, that Idoll, that heathenish Idoll, that remaines (as I may say) a beame, a very beame, not a beame of the sunne, nor a beame of the Moone, nor a beame of a ballance, neither a house-beame, nor a Weavers beame, but a beame in the eye, in the eye of the brethren; a very great beame, an exceedingly great beame; such as are your Stage-Players, Rimers, and Morrise-dancers, who have walked hand in hand, in the contempt of the Brethren, and the Cause.[37]

The root of the matter is in that phrase "silken counterfeit," echoed in Busy's "heathenish Idoll." The condemnation of the stage was of a piece with the condemnation of the mass, of the vestments, of "comeliness" in the church service. The Puritans hated the *mime*, the formalized dress and movement of the body in any ritual, secular or profane. They did not see that simplicity and plainness is a costume, or that, unlike either the Bankside fripperies or the embroidered vestments of the priest, their sober black could become something far more dangerous than a costume—it could become a uniform.

But, as I have already said, the Paul's Cross sermon was in itself a rehearsed dramatic performance, even when there were no visible penitents standing before the pulpit. How far then were these condemnations of sin conventional, a pious rigmarole, an iron if not silken counterfeit? There are three ways to answer that question. The first is to speculate upon the sincerity of each preacher, which is impossible—and if it were possible presumptuous. The second is to emphasize that these preachers, Puritan or not, were churchmen first and last. The voice of God was also the voice of a corporation hard hit by inflationary values, by a militant materialism, by a diminution of its legal authority. The best answer is a little more complicated, since it involves some definition of the sermon convention. Preaching against Rome, John Hoskins commented that the papists had devised all manner of devotions "to please imagination." In their way, the Paul's Cross preachers fell back on devices to please imagination, exhibiting in sermon after sermon the familiar rogue's gallery of sinners: the adulterer, the blasphemer, the engrosser, the idle gallant, the atheist, the usurer, the drunkard, the vain woman, the corrupt judge—a whole cabinet of characters, a microcosmography of the state of "carnall security." The technique was inherited from the preaching friars, amplified by the Reformers, and varied to suit the times. It was a form which Latimer could use with passion, Thomas Adams with ingenuity and grim humour, some perfunctorily, some tediously, others perhaps cynically. We might even divide the preachers, on this basis, into three classes: the ardent moralists, the artists, and the Puritan "scientists" of the Christian life. Certainly Latimer, Lever, Adam Hill, and Thomas White fall into the first class; and perhaps it is no slander upon their sincerity to put Stephen Gosson and Thomas Adams into the second. John Hoskins and Stephen Denison may stand as examples of the third, whose *formula* is best set out in Denison's The New Creature, preached at the Cross in 1619. We are to cast away all our sins, he began, sins of infirmity as well as sins of presumption. It is the function of ministers to rebuke sin, of magistrates to root it out by the strict application of the laws. Such sins as swearing, sabbath-breaking, theft, whoredom, drunkenness, idleness, stage-playing, usury are to be rigorously denounced and put away. For without regeneration no flesh can be saved, and the "ordinary instrumentall cause" of regeneration is "the word of God, especially preached." The concomitants of regeneration are universal change, combat between flesh and spirit, fruitfulness, persecution, constancy. To persevere in our election we must be careful of God's public ordinances, especially preaching, we must read the Bible regularly in a carefully organized way, ask our ministers for help with the hard places, and sustain our souls by family prayer.

Such a course of life, true to the kindred points of pulpit and family devotion, is the basis of the "holy community." It was, as Professor Haller and others have shown, a revolutionary ideal; like most revolutionary ideals it was also primitivistic and utopian, and went well with that patriotic messianism which preachers of all colours of theology trumpeted from that pulpit. "God is English," Bishop Aylmer (or his printer) once observed. For some preachers at least, the Paul's Cross pulpit was the instrument not only of the Council and the Church of England but of God's English ministers, his prophets to the fallen city, the architects of a new and holy order.

IV HOMILETIC

THE WITS AND MORALISTS of the age had much to say of sermons and preaching, and well they might, for sermons confronted them on every bookstall—"a sermon at Paul's Cross, a sermon in St. Mary's Oxon., a sermon in Christ Church, or a sermon before the right honourable, right reverend, right worshipful, a sermon in Latin, in English, a sermon with a name, a sermon without, a sermon, a sermon, etc.," as Burton, who, unlike most divines, was "desirous to suppress [his] labours in this kind," sharply observed.[1] A high percentage of the many sermons to be heard and read were, naturally enough, of indifferent quality, and condemnation of them ranged from the striking remark of an anonymous auditor at Kirton about the preaching of Robert Blackwood—"the roaringe of an oxe in the toppe of an ashe tree is better than all the preachinge that he can preache"[2]—to the measured criticism of Owen Felltham:

> The excesse which is in the defect of Preaching, ha's made the Pulpit slighted: I meane, the much bad Oratory we finde it guilty of. Tis a wonder to me, how men can Preach so little, and so long: so long a time, and so little matter: as if they thought to please, by the inculcation of their vaine Tautologies. I see no reason, that so high a Princesse as Divinity is, should bee presented to the People in the sordid rags of the tongue.[3]

Even at Paul's Cross, where it was customary to preserve the fiction that all sermons were alike deserving of rapt devoted attention, a preacher might occasionally admit that much pulpit eloquence was poor stuff. Humphrey Sydenham's rueful comment is typical of such asides:

To traffique here at home with a few modern systeames, is no small sinne of the age onely, but our profession too, if we can flayle the transgressions of the time in some few stolne Postellismes, and peece a sacred line with a worm-eaten Apophthegme, so it be done in a frequent and hasty zeale, we are the Sages and Patriots of the time.[4]

Indeed if the student reads much in the sermon-literature of the period, leaving the great names and leafing through the "grete and thikke ratelers out of textis," as Bishop Pecock called their predecessors, he faces a great maze of repetitious bad rhetoric and must grow inured to a singularly dull humourless pedestrian thought and expression.

Why did they publish? To get ahead, chiefly, like the "bold forward man" whom Earle describes, who

if he be a scholar, . . . has commonly stepped into the pulpit before a degree, yet into that too before he deserved it. He never defers St. Mary's beyond his regency, and his next sermon is at Paul's Cross, and that printed.[5]

Apart from such sermons as were set forth by authority, or marked some special occasion, most were published at "the request of friends," a patron, the "godly," the "learned," and so forth, all these reasons being set forth at large in an epistle dedicatory or a letter to the Christian reader, in the style so delightfully parodied by Swift in *A Tale of a Tub*. Here is a typical effusion:

Howsoever this last and evill age afford manifolde discouragements from preaching, but more from Printing, as first, the great number of good bookes, so as it would require a mans life, but to reade over the inscriptions; besides the infinite number of prophane and fruitlesse Pamphlets, good for nothing but an Ephesian Bonefire. Secondly, because lively voice is much more gracious and acceptable than written words, as having a kind of hidden and persuasive power, which made Aeschines increase the peoples wonder at Demosthenes written Oration, saying "What would ye have thought if ye had heard him pronounce it himselfe." Thirdly, the perverse cavilation of many, who spare not bitterly to backbite, reprochfully to slaunder, undeserved to reprove, and malitiously to defame whatsoever it be, though never so learnedly and godly done by others, it being much easier to mislike than to do the like. Lastly, for that a Printed Sermon is commonly to them that heard it as "Lettice twice sod . . ." Yet having the glory of God, and good of his Church before mine eyes, & being both requested by your Lordship and many others to publish. . . .[6]

"The reasons some alleage for their defence therein," observed Robert Johnson, himself an offender, "are common, and overworne." True enough, but sometimes the friends of the preacher, truly anxious that his words should gain a wider currency even than that afforded by the Paul's Cross pulpit, threatened to publish an "unperfit copie" from notes taken during the sermon.[7] Or the note-takers might not be friends at all, and the notes not intended for publication but merely "scattered abroad in London & elsewhere," giving a very imperfect notion of the sermon, as Robert Wakeman for one complained.[8]

Note-taking at sermons was very common, in either long-hand or "brachygraphy," and served not only for the edification of the godly auditor, but for the enrichment of the "table-books" of other preachers.[9] The prince of note-takers was John Manningham, whose deft and often remarkably full summaries, written down it seems not so much in piety as in general intellectual interest, provide evidence of the breadth of appeal which sermons commanded at that time. There was something in a sermon for everyone, for the devout and the ribald, for the ignorant and the learned, for the dull and the curious. Accordingly the printed texts which have survived, whatever their source, whether derived from the preacher's written text, from his notes elaborated by himself or others, from the sermon as preached "with certein additions," or from pirated copies,[10] are so to speak the apex of an immense pyramid of "sermon-literature," a great heap of commonplaces which were possessed in common by the preachers and their experienced auditors, whether these were Puritan intellectuals come to "trie the spirits," worldly "sermon-tasters" (as they were called in Scotland) like Gabriel Harvey,[11] or just easy solid middle-class people who sat comfortably and appreciatively Sunday after Sunday under menacing clouds of damnation.

I have already observed that the typical Paul's Cross sermon is addressed to all estates, exhorting amendment of life, addressed to the will therefore more than to the understanding, and not primarily apologetical. There are certain obvious exceptions to this customary form, such as sermons preached in controversy with Rome, and many individual performances by distinguished and undistinguished theologians. But the pattern is general, and it is essentially medieval. Such was the sermon that Conscience preached to the field full of folk; such was the most famous sermon ever delivered at Paul's Cross, the "sermon no lesse frutefull then famous" by Richard Wimbledon, preached in 1388, which ran to fifteen editions between 1550 and 1635. While performing this task of review and exhortation, the preacher was free of his own place in the hierarchy, he was the Lord's voice. It is not surprising, therefore, that the Paul's Cross sermon often conforms to the Puritan theory of preaching, in both form and content. Certainly the Marian exiles, fresh from the orgy of sermons in Zurich and elsewhere, found at the Cross one place at least in the realm where there was no Roman ceremonial clutter; they were at home there, even if they bridled at the Book of Common Prayer. And any preacher called to the Cross and full of its (and his own) importance, would subscribe to Richard Baxter's challenge: "It is no small matter to stand up in the face of a congregation, and deliver a message of salvation or damnation, as from the living God, in the name of our Redeemer."[12] For that place at least they would agree with the Puritans that "the highest and supreame office and authorities of the Pastor, is to preach the gospell solemnly and publickly to the Congregation."[13] The outdoor sermon, where all the currents of divine grace are directed through one instrument, the human voice, whether preached on a medieval village green by some Dominican, at Paul's Cross by Lever or Thomas Adams, in the camps of the New Model army by an Independent chaplain, in a harvest field by John Wesley, under a tent by some Middle West evangelist, is the perfect expression of Puritan worship, where the man of God, like one come from Tekoa or Galilee, exhorts with "experimental, saving, applying knowledge." The actual process was described by Miles Mosse at Paul's Cross:

Vox est ictus animi: passing through the eare, and braine, and blood, it smiteth (as it were) and giveth a stroake upon the verie soule, and so with a kind of violence doth deeply affect it. . . . But yet further, besides all the worke of Nature, there is in Preaching a speciall gift of grace: which enableth a man to speak with such evidence of the Spirit, & and with such power to the Conscience, as no pen of man by writing can express: whereof Preaching is the most likely, and effectuall instrument of salvation and so to be respected.[14]

The *form*, besides, of the Paul's Cross exhortation falls naturally in with the scheme of "doctrines" and "uses" by which, in contrast to a more "witty" division of the text, we are accustomed to distinguish the Puritan pulpit eloquence; each sin, and each estate especially guilty of it, is treated easily in this efficient if rather mechanical manner.

But qualifications are necessary. All sorts of sermons were preached at Paul's Cross, as the following pages will testify, and moreover the sermons preached there, though no doubt "effectuall instruments of salvation," and designed "to make men Schollers," as Samuel Hieron put it,[15] were also intended to be instruments of political and ecclesiastical order, and to make men scholars in obedience too. Where Hieron meant by "scholler" one trained in the disciplines of religious *experience* (rather than in formal theological learning), the emphasis in most exhortations from the Cross was upon the reiteration of known duties; nothing revolutionary, little exploratory about that discipline, designed to make subjects, not saints.

The Paul's Cross sermons, then, as one might expect, keep for the most part a middle level; one finds neither heights nor depths, but great variety. There was in fact great variety of opinions about the best form, conveniently summed up for us by John Dyos:

> Some would have long texts: some short textes. Some would have Doctours, Fathers and Councels: some call yt mans doctrine. Some would have it ordered by Logicke: some terme that mans wisdom. Some would have it polished by Rhetoricke: some call yt persuasibleness of wordes. And agayne in Rhetoricke some would have it holy eloquence, liable to the Ebrue & Greeke phrase: Some would have it proper and fittyng to the English capacitie. Some love study and learnyng in Sermons: Some allow onely a sudaine motion of the spirite. Some would have all said by heart: some would have oft recourse made to the booke. Some love gestures: some no gestures. Some love long Sermons: some short Sermons. Some are coy, and can broke no Sermons at all.[16]

Most preachers, when they spoke of their calling, condemned the extremes: the witty and the extempore. Indeed that eloquence for which the Jacobean and Caroline pulpit is famed, that antithetic rhetoric, that "mixing the two severall properties of an Orator and a Poet both in one,"[17] all that baroque and "witty" eloquence which called up the contempt of one age and the nostalgic admiration of another, was rarely heard at the Cross. Playfere, Holyday, Barlow, Francis White, Donne (though his style was subdued when he preached there), John King—in their sermons one may find more than one passage for the anthologists, but that makes up the roll, and such elegances as I have noticed are rather perfunctory; witness this of Bishop King, in the manner of Andrewes:

> It is a strong perswasion that floweth from time: and it is as strongly enforced in my text [Ps. 102:13-4], nayle after nayle, driven home to the head. *Time* and (by apposition) *time* againe, and (at the period and full point) *appointed* time, and time *come*: that is to say, time and season of time, and season of season: or time, and opportunitie, and necessitie of opportunitie, and extremitie of necessitie, and the very dregs and setling of extremetie: the *punctum*, the *nunc*, the moment and indivisibilitie of time. *Tempus faciendi domino*, now or not at all.

Such flights (or perhaps hops is a better word) as these, derived from the Fathers, who were "wanton in their spiritual elegancies," as Donne put it, were not commended by the majority of Paul's Cross preachers. They were for the plain style, though one is hard put to it to discover exactly what they meant by *plain*. As early as 1578, Lawrence Chaderton complained of preachers who "stuffe their sermons with newe devised words, and affected speaches of vanity," and after the turn of the century condemnations of the toys of rhetoric multiplied. "The pulpit," observed William Holbrooke, "is not a place for a man to shewe his wit and reading in," but for "plainnesse, and evidence of the spirit." Another preacher confessed: "I never had any facilitie in teaching Periods to daunce Friskin, and such-like curiosities." Others held up the witty preacher to scorn:

One playeth upon every word, and descanteth upon every letter in his text, as though the Scripture were but a rattle for Children and fooles to make sport withall.

Lord what a deale of bumbasting, garnishing, and packing doe we use now adaies in our sermons.

These condemnations, fragmentary though they are, anticipate the full-scale attack upon extravagance in pulpit eloquence in the Restoration, by South, Eachard, Glanvill, and others, and follow the same line as the contemporary Puritan advocates of simplicity, Perkins and Downame.[18]

Plainness, then, eschews all "quaint, and Historicall flourishes," but is the product of study and good ordering, and certainly not of "a sudaine motion of the spirite" alone. The preachers' condemnation of extempore effusions is a nice blend of aesthetic and religious considerations. "It is a late time of meditation for a Sermon, when the Psalm is singing," remarked Donne, who studied hard; and Henry King wondered at the temerity of "Lay Mechanicke Presbiters" who would "venter upon an Exposition, or undertake to manage a long unweildy prayer conceived on the sudden, though not so suddenly uttered." Some sectaries will not have prepared sermons because "that were to ty the H. Ghost to an inkhorn"; "they onelie turne the cocke and let the water runne." Preaching "by the spiritt" was condemned, but the pleasant colloquial manner and material, clever without excess and spontaneous though contrived, was not. "Homely metaphor," "relentless satire," with other realistic elements which Professor G. R. Owst has found in the friars' preaching,[19] and which he and others have found in Latimer and Thomas Adams, brighten many otherwise intolerable pages. The justification for such material may be found in the "psychology of rhetoric":

Therefore even these aunciaent Preachers, must now and then play the fooles in the pulpit, to serve the tickle eares of their fleting audience, or els they are like sometimes to preach to the bare walles, for though their spirite be apt, and our will prone, yet our flesh is so heavie and humours so overwhelme us, that we cannot without refreshing long abide to heare any one thing.[20]

It is a work of supererogation to quote Latimer in this connection, yet who can resist the easy mocking rhythm of such a passage as this:

It hath been said of me, "Oh, Latimer, nay, as for him, I will never believe him while I live, nor never trust him, for he likened our blessed lady to a saffron-bag."

Or this:

"Burgesses," quoth he, "nay, butterflies." Lord what ado there was for that word.

Latimer's familiarity never descends to the level of scurrility or gross facetiousness; every phrase is clean, well turned and fine-spirited. The same cannot be said for other controversialists, in his day or later; witness the preacher who "named the Lord's table an oyster-board," or he who likened priests to apes, "for they be both balld alyke, but yt the prestes be balld before, the appes behynd." Yet this colloquial strain, often coarse but usually pointed, helped to toughen the web of rhetoric, Euphuistic or Theophrastian, which delights us in the "character style" of Hall and Adams. "Familiar comparisons," observed Adams, "give the quickest touch to both understanding and conscience," and his sermons abound in sketches of sinners more realistically drawn than the portraits of Earle or Overbury. He is familiar, but sophisticated; less accomplished preachers give another kind of pleasure, when at the end of a period they drop with a thump into the common speech, their rhetoric exhausted. So Dr. John Bridges ended his attack upon the false Romish argument concerning the nature of God's will with "this is boepeepe in dede," and William Fisher affirmed that the Protestant doctrine of repentance is "a flat dash to the Papists." There is a touch of Latimer in William Worship's retelling of Christ's encounter with the woman of Canaan; the disciples, he said, entreated Christ to send her away, "because she kept such a bawling." Nothing of Latimer, however, only of the lowbrow, in Samuel Gardiner's classification of Seneca among pagan philosophers: "one of the best of that bunch."

There is some evidence that the Paul's Cross sermon was deliberately pitched at two levels, one for the judicious, one to split the ears of the groundlings. Scholars have never been able to decide how valid Hamlet's distinction was for the Elizabethan theatre, and it is likewise difficult to make out how much a practised, literate sermon-goer, unversed in the tongues or in logic, would follow of an intricate exposition of a text. Martin Fotherby, after opening with an exhaustive commentary on the significance of the word *jubilare* in his text, went on: "Then to come somewhat lower from this seraphicall discourse, wherein I have spoken but onely to a few; and to descend unto more familiar and popular matter . . . ."[21] But explication and application of a text are different in kind anyway, and it is not only in Fotherby's sermon that one finds a double level of discourse.

Fotherby's "seraphicall discourse" was philological, but scriptural. How far a preacher might legitimately draw upon his resources of humane learning was another question, unresolved since Justin and Tertullian,[22] and sharpened by the Revival of Learning. The temptation to empty one's commonplace book into the sermon was very great, and not to be overcome merely by hearkening to the warnings of precisians like Lawrence Chaderton, who objected to "stories collected out of the wrytings of prophane men," and "multitude of humane authorities." Variations in practice were great. In citation of the Fathers and the commentators, where, except for an occasional brush with those who tried the Scriptures by the spirit and the spirit by the Scriptures, the preachers felt free to exercise their learning, they dipped according to their capacity into a set of tags gleaned from "Sainct Augustine Basill Gregorie Nazanzene Hierome Ambrose Crysostome Ciprian Theophylact Erasmus and other good writers works," as recommended in the Durham injunctions of 1559, representing common practice.[23] The more learned might quote from the rather awe-inspiring list of dictionaries, concordances, analytical expositions, annotations, reconciliations of places, catechisms, commonplace books, commentaries of orthodox writers, ecclesiastical historiographers, acts and canons, controversies, suggested for the preacher's library by Richard Bernard.[24] Stuffing the margin was, however, frowned on. A man must move moderately and warily among the heathen. Bernard admitted the use "for Humanity," of "all manner of knowledge," as "so many lights to see into a text by," and Samuel Hieron, affirming that humane learning is the "handmaid" of divinity, said that "a man may tollerably alledge a sentence of a profane writer" now and then.²⁵ My impression is that the preachers settled the question of how much Athens has to do with Jerusalem by the simple answer: As much as I happen to know. Some sermons are severely scriptural, the majority studded sparsely with tags from Cicero and Augustine, and a few draw upon a striking range of references, of which these, from one sermon, may serve as an example: Bernard, Prudentius, Damasus, Augustine, Chrysostom, Lactantius, Thomas Aquinas; Josephus; Calvin; Aristotle, Ausonius, Cicero, Aulus Gellius, Theophrastus; Donne, Sandys' *Travels*, Holinshed, Ralegh's *History*.²⁶

But this kind of learning, said Jewel, is "to be likened to that part of the carpenter's wimble which turneth about, goeth round, and by little and little draweth in the iron or steel bit."²⁷ The bit was the Scripture, for

> preaching is . . . a sound and plainely laying open of holy Scriptures, by a publike Minister before the people, to their understanding and capacity, according to the analogie of faith, with words of exhortation applied to the conscience, both to informe and reforme, and where they be well, to confirme.²⁸

The laying "open of holy Scriptures" implies the choice, explication, division, and application of a text, for there is one assumption which is accepted by all who preach from a text, in whatever period, and that is that the Bible is homogeneous, that all its lights combine, to use George Herbert's phrase, into one great light, that each part of it is a microcosm of the whole. Liberal theologians who preach on a "theme" or subject, or merely take a text as suggesting a theme, tacitly deny this assumption. The "opening" of a text takes, appropriately, the shape of a cross. Horizontally, the text is seen in its context; its "coherence" and "scope" are explored. Vertically, the text is extended by division and application from the heights of divine glory to the heart of the listener, piercing through his understanding to "the verie soule." A text is indeed, as the opponents of the Puritan preachers affirmed, an icon, and can become an idol, and the laying open of Scripture to the exclusion of almost all other forms of worship, a form of superstition.

Now the complicating factor in this process is the "sense" in which the preacher reads his text or any part of it.

> It is not the letter of the Word [said Thomas Goodwin] that ordinarily doth convert, but the spiritual meaning of it, as revealed and expounded. . . . There is the letter,

the husk; and there is the spirit, the kernel; and when we by expounding the word do open the husk, out drops the kernel. And so it is the spiritual meaning of the Word let into the heart which converts it and turns it unto God.[29]

Profitable doctrines, said William Perkins, are to be collected out of "the naturall sense," that is, the ordinary meaning of the text. Between that ordinary meaning and the extraordinary meanings possible through application of the traditional fourfold method, in a crooked way lit by the flickering torches of the commentators, the ordinary preacher walked. Most of the Paul's Cross preachers walked warily. They took the simple course of employing the text as *example* for Christian conduct or straightforward theological precept, understood in the "naturall sense." As I have already noticed, they applied the events and personages of Israel's history to the state of England, and renewed the lamentations and exhortations of the prophets in another Jerusalem, Sodom, or Nineveh. A preacher might clear a text of heretical glosses, indulge in an undisciplined and literal-minded interpretation of the images in the book of Revelation, or turn to the "tongues" to twist a parable out of a biblical name, but most sermons offer nothing either erudite or original to the corpus of biblical interpretation. What Jewel called "allegory," and Holland "the figure of mysticall sense," is the typological method of interpreting the Old Testament, used by many preachers with confidence in its familiarity and its utility. Jewel, for example, equates the manna with Christ's body, the rock and the serpent in the desert with Christ; Foxe and John Hudson find types of Christ in Joseph, Joshua, Samson, Aaron's rod, etc.[30]

For a more striking collocation of places of Scripture one may turn to Bishop King's sermon upon the King's recovery from sickness in 1619, which also illustrates some of the possibilities of "division" of the text. His text was Isaiah 38:17: "Behold, for peace I had great bitterness: but thou hast in love to my soul delivered it from the pit of corruption: for thou hast cast all my sins behind my back." These were the words of a king, of a great king, Hezekiah, and so appropriate. King began with *Ecce*, Behold—a preface:

> It is placed at the gates of my text, and a thousand others in this booke, as Porters at the gates of great mens houses: Strangers & Wanderers, and Passengers, and *Circumforaneos*, idle Companions that stand to gaze, they keepe out; admit none but friends and bidden guests, such as are worthy to come in, and bring their garment with them; so is the office of *Ecce* here.

He then intimated how the text fell into two "Hemispheares," the dark one of sin, the other of comfort and light: the text for him is a microcosm of the Christian life, as it is of the history of the Jews and of the history of England under God's providence and love. In the next stage of his "opening" he discovered three parts in the text, corresponding to the three tabernacles of Matthew 17:4, which Peter would have built for Moses, Christ, and Elias. Thus:

1. "In my peace I had great bitterness": Moses: the ark and the rod;
2. "but thou in love to my soul ... corruption": Elias: the widow's cake (I Kings 17);
3. "for thou hast cast all my sins behind my back": Christ: the Gospel.

Nor is this all. For in the first part he entreated (1) of sickness, "in quality bitterness, in extremity, bitterness," (2) of "the time and advantage, in my peace"; in the second of (1) deliverance, (2) of the motive of God, love; in the third, (1) of the cause: sins, (2) of the remove of the cause. (Notice the interplay of threes and twos in this scheme; was the preacher also conscious of the triple occurrence of "17"?)

Though this division is by no means excessively elaborate some preachers would have called it fantastical, and condemned it, for in this matter also there was a cult of the "plain" style. Not that plainness meant the exclusion of the method, but only its refinement into a particular kind of rhetorical effectiveness. The method itself was a child of the marriage between the standard school method of writing themes and the conventions of preaching inherited from the middle ages. The usual rhetorical training of finding the parts of a theme, and then of "flourishing and adorning" the theme with matter out of collections of commonplaces was the basis of sermon construction, plain or fancy,[31] and the various methods recommended for dividing the theme in medieval tractates on preaching, though not always couched in the language of classical rhetoric, are intended to produce a similar invention and disposition of the parts.[32] The medieval tractates advocated a division into three parts, and Keckermann agreed,[33] but this did not bar, rather encouraged, amplification. The critical point, the point on which preachers and theorists differed, was that moment in composition, when the preacher, having worked out the coherence and scope of his text, and decided how much explication it needed, turned to examine it anew to discover what *kind* it was, and what could be made of it. It might be, said Bernard, a plain proposition, or it might be narration, exhortation, dehortation, commandment, threatening, promise, reprehension, admonition, consolation, petition, supplication, deprecation, confession, protestation, exclamation, vow, execration, salutation, valediction, commendation, discommendation, question, answer, objection, reason, definition, description, comparison, accusation, prohibition, affirmation, counsel, declaration, prediction, gratulation, acclamation, thanksgiving, complaint, expostulation, commemoration, "or some such thing."[34] Or indeed more than one of them. Once the name of the text is found, he added, branch it out "by circumstances," by which he meant following the order of the words. Then collect "doctrines," from the occasion of the words, from the coherence and scope, from the "denomination" of the text (as above), from the manner, the order, the coupling of the words, from the natural and figurative meaning of the words themselves, from the circumstances, from the matter. Doctrines inform the judgment; "uses" or applications, to be collected in order, move the affections, so that the whole man is edified and swayed by the sermon.

This is what Abraham Wright called "the plain easie way of Doctrine and Use,"[35] which is not necessarily Puritan, and which did not please everybody, for others, he added, "are not taken with any sermon, but what is fill'd with depth of Matter, height of Fancie, and good Language." There is no doubt that it was mechanical; witness Wright's own version of "the Presbyterian style," which one finds in a few Paul's Cross sermons, and which is no more than a dismal set of spiritual jerks. But within the plain limits of such a typical "denomination" and division of the text as Bernard recommended, considerable variation was possible, and, in the sermons addressed to a large and varied audience, probable. Variation was possible simply because most of the preachers exercised upon their texts like empirics. William Holbrooke spoke for many when he promised to "lay open the parts [of his text], into which it doth divide it selfe." The natural order, with the senses arising out of the ordinary relationships and analogies, was the best order, to be preferred, many preachers affirmed, to any "curious division." So one spoke of "the plaine naturall dresse of the text," divided John 15:20 into monition ("Remember the word that I said unto you"); principle ("The servant is not greater than his Lord"); and inference ("If they have persecuted me, they will also persecute you"), and applied each to the faith and to the times. Another used a similar method with "I came not to call the righteous, but sinners to repentance": (1) the means—Christ's coming; (2) the parties called—sinners; (3) the end—to repentance. This is, one must admit, rather pathetic than plain. More richness of texture was possible in the division of a "history," where the tendency to abstraction in the denomination of the parts was countered by opportunities for description and analogy. A good example of this development is Richard Crakanthorpe's *Sermon at the solemnizing of the Happie Inauguration* of 1609, in which he applied II Chronicles 9:5-9, the words of the Queen of Sheba to Solomon, to both Jewish and English history, taking in order the commendation of the King's wisdom, the happy estate of his subjects, thanksgiving to God, and the testimony of the Queen's gifts. Moreover, though this "plain easie way" moves by straight lines, it was possible, if one had the patience of the anonymous author of *Englands Warning by Israel and Judah* (1633), to weave of the straight lines a close net to catch a sinner. Preaching from Hosea 5:15, "I will go and return to my place, till they acknowledge their offence, and seek my face: in their affliction they will seek me early," he announced: "In handling of these words . . . , I will strive rather to touch the conscience to the quick by the piercing power of the word of God, then to please itching eares with curious deepnesse, or with a compt style, and filed phrase of speech." Coming "abruptly" to open the words, he distinguished the author: God, through his prophet, his voice to be received with fear and trembling; the persons: clergy, commons, and nobles; the reason: their horrid and abominable sins; the manner of His action: by degrees; the matter: *I will go*; the measure: *till they seek*, and so forth. (Here one observes that method of denomination by alliteration, which is a traditional and presumably legitimate ornament.) Pursuing his criss-cross method, he then reviewed the horrid and abominable sins by the ages of man, by sexes, and by classes; passed in review God's mercies and threats to England; and closed with a plea for repentance. This kind of sermon was indeed, as Wilkins noted, suitable for "populous assemblies," being comprehensive, easy, as well as logical, proceeding from generals to particulars.[36]

Useful, capable of some variation if the text was itself either striking or vague, and indeed plain, but with the plainness of Mr. Chadband, grinder of sentences, which in one sense is not plainness at all but the worst kind of affection. Witness Robert Johnson upon Psalm 119:33, "Teach me, O Lord, the way of thy statutes; and I shall keep it unto the end." An ideal text for the purpose:

    Heere is a request   1. Doce, Teach
                                  2. The Partie, mee
                                  3. The Person, O Lord
                                  4. The Summe, the way of thy Statutes.
    And heere is a promise   1. The person, I will
                                  2. The matter, keepe it
                                  3. The continuancie, unto the end.

Under each heading he explained the words, paraphrased them, collected the doctrines, and applied the uses.[37] No better comment upon this sort of thing has ever been made than that of George Herbert:

> The Parsons Method in handling of a text consists of two parts; first, a plain and evident declaration of the meaning of the text; and secondly, some choyce Observations drawn out of the whole text, as it lyes entire, and unbroken in the Scriptures itself. This he thinks naturall, and sweet, and grave. Whereas the other way of crumbling a text into small parts, as the Person speaking, or spoken to, the subject, and object, and the like, hath neither in it sweetness, nor gravity, nor variety, since the words apart are not Scripture, but a dictionary, and may be considered alike in all the Scriptures.[38]

For Herbert the Bible was one and indivisible, as indeed it was for "witty" preachers like Andrewes, whose assonances and plays of prefixes and other dramatic wrestlings with the Word cast a fresh radiance upon it, and do not abstract word-counters from it, to be "applied" in a theological or ethical scheme which is more or less independent of the Scripture itself. A very different critic, Bishop Wilkins, complained of this sort of "division" that it was "a great occasion for impertinency, and roving from the chief sense," and certainly no reader of a course of such sermons as these gets much sense of the Bible either through his judgment or his affections. The purpose of preaching, to "lay open" the Scriptures, seems to have been lost in a maze of subdivisions.

Yet if this "crumbling" is carried off with some finesse, so that one can feel that the process is more art than formula for the preacher himself, it has an effect not to be despised, especially when one remembers that this tricky part of the division is a rhetorical bridge between the exordium, by which the preacher catches his audience, and his first long flight of doctrine, by which he may hope to get a firm hold on them again. There is a simple pleasure in a fine assonance, like that dramatic one of Samuel Buggs upon II Samuel 24:14, where we are told how David came into this strait, for admonition; how he conceived of it, for instruction; how he bore it, for imitation; and how he got out of it, for consolation. And in the opening of Thomas Adams' *The Gallant's Burden*, the very laying out of the pattern is intense enough to bear comparison with some effects of Andrewes. The text was Isaiah 21:11-12.

> As you travel with me into this country, by the guidance of that enlightening spirit, tie your consideration to two special things:—I The map; II The moral. In the map you shall find—1. An inscription; 2. A description. In the inscription: (1) the name of the country; (2) the nature of the prophecy. The description rests itself on three objects: (1) A mountain; (2) A watchman; (3) An Edomite: where is shadowed, (1) under the mountain, security; (2) under the watchman, vigilance; (3) under the Edomite, scorn. Now if you ask, as did the prophet Ezekiel, what these things meant, the moral directs you, 1. by a question; 2. by an answer. The question would know what was in the night. The answer declares it, (1) by a resolution; (2) by an advice. The resolution, *Venit mane et vespere*,—"The morning comes, and also the night"; the advice, "If you will ask, inquire: return, and come."

But Adams had a fine sense of style, and could make even a table of contents into a cadence. The next best thing to a sense of style, though no real substitute for it, is a bright idea, and many a preacher sought to give the impression of a happy visitation. One thought he saw a syllogism in Micah 6:9, another found in II Corinthians 7:1 a *descent*, in the cleansing from filthiness, and an *ascent*, in the perfecting of holiness, and the whole text "a divine enthymeme"; another found six degrees or "steps" in Revelation 1:5-6, of which the first, that God loved us, is the hardest of all the rest, "for if we can but once get footing in his love, then the ascent is easy." John Eachard's description of this sort of thing is irresistible:

> Before the Text be divided, a Preface is to be made: And it is a great chance if, first of all, the Minister does not make his Text to be like something or other. I believe there are above forty places of Scripture that have been like Rachel and

Leah.... In the next place, he comes to *divide* the Text.... Now come off the Gloves, and the Hands being well chafed, he shrinks up his shoulders, and stretcheth forth himself as if he were going to cleave a Bullock's head, or rive the body of an Oak. But we must observe, that there is a great difference of Texts: For all Texts come not asunder alike; For sometimes the words *naturally fall asunder*; sometimes they *drop* asunder; sometimes they *melt*; sometimes they *untwixt*; and there be some words so willing to be parted, that they *divide themselves*, to the great ease and rejoycing of the Minister. But if they will not easily come to pieces, then he falls to hacking and hewing, as if he would make all fly into shivers."[39]

We seem to have fallen upon a contradiction: namely that the preacher works from a text because he believes that that text is a microcosm of God's word, but that he so chops up the "naturall sense" of the whole text into his own headings, making the words a mere index to his discourse, that his original purpose is lost, and his sermon, far from laying open the Scripture, rather stretches a curtain of fusty rhetoric before it. Indeed it was a lively sense of this contradiction which informed the Restoration attack upon the methods of the old preachers, and their successors. But at least three things may be said in defence, not of the style and taste of these preachers, but of their fulfilment of their intention. First, their conviction of the talismanic quality of the Scriptures extended not only to texts but to individual words; "each word hath his weight, and is not lightly to be passed over," as one put it. The conjunction "therefore" engaged the faculties of Immanuel Bourne for a longer (and more eloquent) period than some of our contemporaries would devote to a whole parable. Second, most of these preachers repudiated witty and curious invention; to God alone belong all excellencies and insights, and it is enough if the preacher *reiterates*, under the headings suggested by his text, the familiar patterns of doctrine and application. The sermon, they thought, is a *rehearsal* of the unchangeable process of sin and redemption, of the history of God's judgments upon kingdoms and estates, and any text whatever is reducible to these terms. Third, the preachers to "populous assemblies" simply wished to cover everything in two hours. The perfect Paul's Cross sermon was as encyclopaedic as possible; no one must leave the churchyard unmentioned and unmoved. The subdivisions were numerous because such an approach demanded a multitude of pigeon-holes in which to stuff the appropriate exhortations. "Preachers," growled Selden, "will bring anything into the text." And they were happy in the anticipation of doing so. Thomas

Sutton, for example, after setting forth a fairly elaborate scheme, announced: "Thus you see into what an Ocean of all variety and choice of matter I am now ready to wade." The due proportion of parts in an oration was forgotten, and while the words of the text sounded periodically in the background, the preacher painfully applied his "divine axioms" to the whole estate of man, unborn, living, and dead.

The most fruitful example of many which have come to my notice is Dr. Thomas Holland's sermon on the anniversary of Elizabeth's accession preached in 1599, upon Matthew 12:42, of the queen of the south and Solomon. The text, he began, is an answer made by Christ to the Pharisees, and shows how stories in the Old Testament serve for the instruction of the Church; God's word is never idle. The person, a queen; of Sheba. Many derivations of that name have been suggested, and Josephus suggests more than one name for the Queen herself. She was a queen; God is no respecter of persons. And a woman; many the women who have glorified God: Martha and Mary, Deborah and Miriam. Many the kings and queens of England of noble memory. The Old Testament may often, as in this case, be interpreted "mystically," typologically. She *came*. Should a woman travel? Much of this in Plutarch and Euripides. Should a king leave his kingdom? Englishmen remember what happened when Richard II went into Ireland. (Here a digression of pilgrimages.) This queen was queen of Ethiopia; here a review of Ethiopian history out of Strabo. What was her justification for coming? She prefigures the Church of the Gentiles, as do Rahab, Ruth, Pharaoh's daughter, and the little sister with no breasts. What moved her? The secret working of the Holy Spirit, and its operations are to be extolled and enrolled in memory. The external cause of her coming was Solomon's great gifts; indeed the trumpet of fame sounds at all times for virtue. Solomon was indeed wise, but his wisdom was nothing to the wisdom of Christ. She took pains in coming, as a needle she followed the loadstone, as a heliotrope followed the sun. She came one thousand miles; such is the computation of the distance from Meroe to Jerusalem. She did not fear to spoil her complexion in the sun, as women do nowadays. She came to Solomon, but the Jews would not come to Christ; recusants and libertines will not come to him now; they prefer plays before preaching. She came with a great train, from which we learn that there is a good and necessary use of ornaments and vestments. She came to hear Solomon's wisdom; indeed travel is part of a good education, though not the unprofitable travel of some of our young gentry to Italy. Seneca has good lessons for us upon the frivolity of the eyes in travel. Merchants, soldiers, godly and grave students are good travellers. She came to hear questions of religion, not idle and foolish questions as in the schoolmen. Solomon's wisdom was not only speculative but practical; we should admire models of good civic government, as in Periclean Athens. Princes should always consider God's glory; our Queen does. Finally, the Queen's action and honour in the life to come: she shall rise in judgment against this generation, when all worldly honours are at an end. Her resurrection is a type of the general resurrection.

This sermon, with its quite elaborate scheme of "types," is not typical of the Paul's Cross sermon in interpretation of Scripture; nor was Holland so precise upon particular sins as some of his fellows, but the method of development through the division, the attempt to put in as much as possible, is typical. Load every rift with ore, and manage it so that almost every word is a rift. The unachievable perfection would have every word of Scripture surrounded by a cloud of glosses, doctrinal and practical; the Scripture bears on everything and everything bears on the Scripture. For these preachers, the Book was sword and targe, ointment and refreshment, code and slogan. Beneath all the variety of experiment in thought and feeling which enriches the culture of this period and place lies this solid, unimaginative, persistent mass of sermon-literature, in which all the affairs of men, all their hopes, affections, inquiries, fears are nailed solemnly to the sacred phrase.

Unimaginative? Not altogether. There were soberly eloquent preachers at the Cross: Joseph Hall, John Hales, Mark Frank, Thomas Aylesbury, and others. There were fantastics: William Barlow, Barten Holyday. And even among the uninspired may be found some striking image, some felicitous turn of phrase, which brightens a plodding paragraph. Not many of these effects are original perhaps, but no preacher at any time should disdain to enrich his discourse with other men's flowers, or to allow his phrase to fall easily into the cadences of the English Bible. Some effects are memorable as howlers, for a preacher "flourishing" his theme is subject to the same strains on his style as a schoolboy writing an examination. One preacher, advising against too much care for the things of this world, enforced the lesson by observing that "Ceres the goddesse of corne and bread: is placed in the lowest roome of the heathen Gods and Goddesses, and her daughter Proserpina, was married to Pluto King of hel." But this is *Ovide immoralisé*. Another exclaimed: How happy is the Christian when his will and God's word "play togither, as Isaack and Rebecka did." But in that case one wonders whether the effect was deliberate. In fact it is very unwise to apply too rigorous a standard of good taste to these productions. What are we to say, for example, to this of John Rawlinson? When Queen Elizabeth died, "our hearts did melt like water. . . . Then did God . . . of his own free bounty, and mercy, turne our water, (our salt water) into wine" with the coming of King James. Such an outburst as this against Father Parsons—"he was a cab of dung, an Asses head sold to the Pope for 80. silverlings, and his friends rose up in a misty morning when a sheepe seemed to them as big as an oxe"—is a balmy sentence in the context of the controversies of the period, and no one would quarrel with "God puts keene mustard upon the breasts of the world, that we may be weaned from it," which is as homely and fervent as Latimer, if it lacks his rhythm.

A preacher's capacity to control an image is hardly tested by the Euphuistic citation of Pliny—the elephant is a type of God's patience; as the swallow rubs the eyes of its young with celandine, so may the Lord rub his holy celandine upon the eyes of the papists—but rather by the amplification of a comparison into an elegant set piece without losing the analogy intended. The "metaphysical" preachers, from Andrewes to Taylor, are the masters in this kind of rhetoric,[40] but there is a lower order of it, in which the preacher clings firmly to a traditional and familiar figure, eschews surprise, and achieves a certain complexity and force. Of this kind is John Stoughton's panegyric upon divine love:

> It is a Macrocosme, a great World of Theologicall vertues, the two Poles are God and Man, the Center Love, the Diameter Love, the Circumference Love, divided into a double Semicircle; the first of contemplation, where Love ascends by knowledge to God, and descends by eloquence to man: the second of operation, where Love descends by liberalitie to man, and ascends by martyrdom to God: it is a Microcosme, a little world of Theologicall vertues, the hands of Love stretched out to touch the two Poles, the right hand embraces God, the left hand embraces our

neighbour; the head touches the point of contemplation, in which it flies up to God by reason, and fals downe to man by speech; the feet touch the point of operation in which it moves downe to man by doing good, and mounts up to God by suffering evill for Christs sake; and all these make the perfect circle of divine learning: as you know the line drawne from the verticall point of the head, by the extremities of the hands & feet stretched out, will make a perfect circle, as the curious observers of the secret proportions in Nature have discovered.

He had an emblematic diagram before him. Samuel Purchas had (as his margin tells us) his *Faerie Queene*, and his own *Pilgrim*, when he developed the image of the tower in II Samuel 22:51:

This bodie is a naturall house to the soule: the armes and legs, as out houses; the bellie, breast, and head, as three courts of this goodly Palace; the bellie, or lower court, as offices; the breast, as the hall, great-chamber, presence chappell, where the heart receives and performes her services; the head or third court is a naturall Tower of this Palace, mounted on a Mount, another Citie in this Citie of Man, a Capitoll at least, a Senate-house, or Councell-Chamber, a Microcosme, of the Microcosme, a Heaven to this litle Earth, and abridgement both of the greater and lesse Worlds.

Others with less precision but more range pursued analogies in the elements. The colours of the rainbow, said John Dove, are two:

A seacolour which betokeneth water, where with [the world] was drowned, the other fiery, betokening the other Element, whereunto the worlde untill the day of judgement is reserved.

William Loe was very thorough in his comparison of the wicked:

first unto the fire in unkinde blastings: so these in their wilfull and wicked blasphemies. Secondly, unto the Aire, when it infecteth: so they by their evill examples and mispersuasions, corrupt and taint all those which are neare unto them. Thirdly, as the water by uncouth and unusual inundations doth runne over the land . . . , so doe these cormorants and wretched worldlings depopulate whole countries by enclosures, & by racking their miserable tenants. Lastly, they are fitly resembled unto the Briers and Thornes of the earth.

This is strained indeed. More successful was James Conyers' comparison of the exaltation of the blessed with the coronation of an English monarch:

Their unction is not oyle, but holy blood. Their Diademe is not 12. stones, but 12. stars. The sword is the word of God. The Scepter is the power of his Spirit. The Globe, the world, all things are theirs. Their Royall Robes . . . Christs Righteousness. Their Princely Pallaces, White-Hall, Gods Sanctuary, and Non-Such the new Jerusalem; the Esquires of their bodies, as heavenly guard, even 10000. of Angels; their dyet is of the best, the inconsumptible body and the blood of Christ; and hee that made them Kings, is the King of Kings.

His touch is sure also in a more "conceited" though traditional comparison. That Christ loved us, is *written*:

The wretched Jewes play'd the Scribes; the pens they used, were thornes, and speares, and nayles; the inke, was purest blood; the Volume wherein they writ (and that on both sides) was the body of all Divinity; the capitall letters, deepe and wide wounds; the testimonies, men and Angells; the Seale set to it, was Christs *consummatum est*, it is finished.

But all these are relatively cautious voyages, steered with the eye upon the card. John Stoughton, like Taylor after him, rose with the lark:

You have seen a Lark upon a sun-shine day, mounting and singing, not to the Sun, as Cardan tells us of strange flowers, that make strange hymnes to the Moon; but as Clemens Alexandrinus speaks of that Quire of Grasshoppers, one of which leapt upon the Musitians harp, and supplyed the want of a string which chanced to crack in the midst of his song, A song of thanksgiving, as it were, to him that gave her the art of singing; and so shee climbs aloft with her prettie note, in which shee hath no Peer, peering and peering, as though she would peer into the secrets of Heaven: but when you have long expected what newes she would bring from thence, you have seen her on a sudden fall silently to the earth again. Mee thinks those pulpit discourses flie like the Lark, and fall like the Lark, which in the contemplative part sing sweetly; but when they descend to the practicall, to application, chop up all in a word.

Almost everything is wrong with this: the comparison is not just, the pun on "peer" is distressing, but above all the passage suffers from that familiar passion to work everything in, to the loss of proportion and good sense. Even Thomas Playfere, whose learning in the more flowery of the Fathers and strong influence upon the "witty" preachers has been justly commended,[41] is capable, in an otherwise fine sermon, of a too painful comparison:

For the world and all worldly delight, is likened to a hedgehogge. A hedgehogge seems to be but a poore silly creature, not likely to doe any great harme, yet indeede it is full of bristles or prickles, whereby it may annoy a man very shrewdly. So worldly delight seems to be little or nothing dangerous at the first, yet afterward as with bristles or pricks, it pearcith through the very conscience with intollerable paines. Therefore we must deale with this delight, as a man would handle a hedgehogge. The safest way to handle a hedgehogge is to take him by the heele. So must we deale with this delight . . . considering not the beginning, but the ending of it.

It is the mark in fact of all these passages, and the measure of their imperfection, that the speaker seems relatively unaffected by his own image, which for him is pattern and formula, τόπος rather than illumination. What might have been passion becomes pedantry. The regular and solemn fall of the clauses in Jewel's Ciceronian eloquence is more moving than these eccentricities, and so are those passages where a preacher, intoxicated by the imagery of the Psalms and the prophets, launches upon a catalogue, like this of the Word compared to: the sun, fire, water, a mirror, a clear fountain, an apothecary's shop of medicines, the pillar of fire, a star of the sea, a heavenly jewel, a precious pearl, a most pleasant garden, a candle, the bread of the soul, a royal and kingly feast, the sword of the spiritual manna, the horn of salvation, the incorruptible seed, a hammer, a key, a sceptre, an arrow, a net, a heavenly trumpet.[42] In such passages the content itself supplies that rhythmical surge and withdrawal, like breakers upon a beach, which the best magniloquent oratory can produce. Most preachers were so harnessed to their "divisions," their "doctrines," "uses," "objections," "answers," "considerations," "matters," that any sense of the paragraph or "theme" which they remembered from their school-days was if not abandoned certainly distorted.

I have reviewed these characteristics of pulpit eloquence gathered from a century of Paul's Cross sermons without much consideration of historical change and development, and the majority of my illustrations have been drawn from sermons preached in the period 1590–1630 simply because the materials from that period are most numerous. It is, however, possible to make a tentative classification of the sermons preached at the Cross from the Reformation to the Rebellion, on a roughly historical basis, if two important qualifications are kept in mind. First, the paucity of printed sermons before *ca.* 1570 makes generalization difficult; second, although I would not contend that there was an exact formula for the Paul's Cross sermons, yet the preachers' obligation to be at once timely and comprehensive did, as I have shown, impose a certain pattern upon their exhortations, and the sermons are therefore not wholly representative of pulpit eloquence in that age.

One may say at once that among preachers of force and distinction, for whom a sermon at Paul's Cross was but an episode, and who are known not only to ecclesiastical historians but to connoisseurs of style, it is possible to trace two complementary traditions of pulpit eloquence: the forceful, often homely and colloquial style of the "city" preacher, certainly not unlearned but not "metaphysical," the style of Latimer, Henry Smith, John White, and Thomas Adams; and the more formal, sober, and gracious eloquence, falling sometimes into excess of wit, the style of Jewel, John Spenser, John King, and Mark Frank. In each tradition one finds a growing sophistication: the material that would provide Latimer with a casual sketch appears as a "character" in Adams; a patristic phrase in Jewel becomes in Frank an elaborate and beautifully controlled image. But neither of these traditions contributed in any large measure to the formation of the styles (if one can call them that) of the Commonwealth preachers of whom, making of course certain exceptions, Mitchell observes that their sermons "only differ in degree of dullness." Of profound interest and importance for the historian of political and ecclesiastical ideas, such sermons offer little inspiration to the student of homiletics; and the same must be said of the sermons of their predecessors, the rank and file of the Paul's Cross preachers. Their forum was the Cross, not the Parliament or the Army, but it was at the Cross which the Puritans demolished that the armory of persuasion was forged which was to thunder in the "rebellious times." For most of these preachers, who made no pretence to literary ability, the sermon was an instrumental not absolute form: in the time of the Reformation an instrument of demagogic propaganda; in the time of Elizabeth, of controversy; in the Jacobean period, mainly of social criticism; in the last days, of controversy once more, in defence of the Laudian establishment against a second "Reformation." A sermon at Paul's Cross was traditionally sermon plus proclamation; in times of trial the sermon was merely prelude to proclamation or propaganda. Such development as there is, then, seems to follow these lines: in the time of the Reformation, the Marian interlude, and the greater part of the age of Elizabeth, the theme of the sermon and its immediate topical application are fairly well separated, so that Bridges and Bancroft, for example, insert the main matter of their discourses into a loose and perfunctory opening of the text; later the extraneous material, whether it was eulogy of the monarch, controversy with Rome or Geneva, adjuration to all estates, or any topic of immediate importance, was pretty thoroughly assimilated into the scheme of doctrine and use, woven more solidly into the texture of the discourse, although on special occasions, like the occasion of a penance or the commemoration of the Plot or the Gowrie conspiracy, the preacher was likely to leave his scheme to rehearse, diffidently or with relish, the familiar set piece.

This connection between sermon and proclamation, or more accurately, between Word and application, leads to another distinction. Elsewhere in these pages I have described the Puritan emphasis on the sermon as a means of grace, and the orthodox attack on that position by Howson and others. There seem to be two theories of the sermon, both deriving ultimately from the tradition of apostolic preaching: the first orthodox, catholic; the second Puritan. The first is not very clearly articulated as a theory; it is rather a comprehensive assumption: preaching is a witness of the Word to the world, whereby the Word is proclaimed, and the doctrines and examples to be collected from it are applied to the state of Christian men. The sermon is primarily, then, a work of instruction, and its relation to Scripture may be expressed, analogically, as the relation between text and marginal gloss, between inscription and translation, between oracle and interpretation. The Puritan theory goes much further than this. For the Puritan, the sermon is not just hinged to Scripture; it quite literally exists *inside* the Word of God; the text is not in the sermon, but the sermon is in the text. The physical opening of the Book on the pulpit symbolizes this, so does the "opening" of the text itself, so does the repetition of the words of the text throughout the sermon, supported by numbers of proof-texts, setting up a palisade of holy sounds around the exhortation. "Denominations," doctrines, and uses do not move from the Word to the world, but lead the world into the Word; that is, the preacher, in every application of his text, actually rehearses the divine judgment. Put summarily, listening to a sermon is being in the Bible, where Job is a neighbour and Mary a sister. But this is the same as saying that then the Bible lives in the hearer: the Word is made flesh—not to sight, as in images; not to taste, as in the bread and wine; not to smell, as in the fumes of incense, but to hearing, and dwells among us. Preaching is a sacrament.

One might expect that in form and content the Paul's Cross sermons would be in accord with the first theory, and, so far as this mass of sermon-literature is homogeneous at all, that is the case. But those sentiments of intense messianism which I have described, so often reiterated by preachers of diverse theological convictions, and the rigorous spiritual exercises performed occasionally there by some precisians reflect the growing power of the Puritan concept of the sermon, in which every act and person is judged and sanctified by the Word of God operating through the engine of the preacher's voice. To the cynic, the *politique*, or the dilettante these efforts, in which the sense of holy mission was physically expressed by highly ritualized gestures, pauses, and extravagant exercises of voice and posture, looked like melodramatic acting, coarse but mightily effective. Much more effective as popular persuasion, one suspects, than the measured and good-mannered appeals of the Laudian preachers who preached on the Paul's Cross foundation in the late thirties and early forties. The Cross sermon was literally, symbolically—and stylistically—half-way between chancel and street; it perished, as all half-way houses do, in civil war.

V CONCLUSION

THE PAUL'S CROSS PULPIT was nothing less than the popular voice of the Church of England during the most turbulent and creative period in her history. And, the unkind might add, nothing more either. It is true that these sermons have long since fallen into the portion of weeds and outworn faces, and in a literary way most of them deserve oblivion. Yet there is some value in a different point of view, and the age commonly observed from the Bankside or Westminster looks different from Paul's Cross, the enemy of one and the sometimes unreliable instrument of the other. For this pulpit stood in the City, not yet a synonym for commercial power, nor even, as it was so soon to become, a decisive party in the politico-ecclesiastical struggle, but simply the centre of the realm, where the paths of kings and apprentices, merchants and bishops, judges and seamen crossed, and where all stopped to hear a sermon. As the parish church is a more potent force for unity than any conventicle, the public sermon, in an age when men never ceased to quarrel about rubrics, was the most inclusive of all rituals. For it was a ritual, as old as a folkmoot, as fresh as a ballad or a news-sheet, as unchanging as a mass. The preachers and even more those who appointed them were very much aware of this. When the Puritans captured the Cross they put a period to that era when England was, even theoretically, one audience listening to one voice.

We have learned not to romanticize this oneness, and have dismissed Merrie England to Christmas cards and tourist literature. Perhaps we have learned too well. We hear a good deal these days of the media of mass communication, of the effects of the press, the radio, television, and so forth, on the public mind. One effect, not often enough emphasized, is that these media induce loneliness; the crowd is, as one clever sociologist has put it, a "lonely crowd." This is not the loneliness of the individualist, but of the statistical unit, sitting in the twilight of sensation and addressed by a "personalized" voice. But these Sunday morning sermons were addressed to "estates," to all who climbed Ludgate Hill from whatever motive to hear them; they were a living testimony to the idea of community. They were pretentious and wordy—but so is a parliamentary debate; they were artificial and often absurd—but so is a parade. At a mediocre but respectable level these preachers combined serious intelligence with self-dramatization as their more illustrious contemporaries did in their easy passage between the library and the tilt-yard. The public sermon, like the editorial page of a great city newspaper (this one, said Carlyle, *The Times*, "edited by Heaven"), was at once an arrangement of commonplaces varied in their application to the events of the day, a forum for the great and the would-be great to express their views, and a collection of remembrances. There was enough art in it to satisfy the dilettante, enough sameness to please the sober citizen who did (and does) not like to be startled by new ideas, enough passion for the zealot, enough theology for the Puritan (and Catholic) intellectuals. This eclectic institution, the last of its kind, was a focus for all manner of powers. Primarily, it was the Bishop of London's "chaire," and the bishop was a landed magnate, the representative of the national Church in a municipality jealous of its ancient privileges, a member of Parliament, an officer of Convocation, a deputy of the Privy Council, often a former University official, often a protem. warden of political and ecclesiastical prisoners, the overseer of various hospitals, almshouses and schools, a royal chaplain, and a priest. His functions placed him on the often disputed boundaries between country and city interests, between gentry and merchants, Church and State, lecturers and incumbents, recusants and the faithful, and it was from the centre of this network of forces and responsibilities that he himself or his appointees spoke at the Cross.

The preachers may be taken as representative of the clergy during the period, from curates to archbishops. In general, they came from that fertile crescent of English Protestantism, from Lincoln to Exeter with London in the centre, and they were solidly middle class. They were almost all university men, more from Cambridge than Oxford, and their worldly success may be measured by masterships, readerships, prebends, and pluralities, though a City minister might have considerable reputation and influence without these evidences of advancement. In the long tradition of the rich and varied avocations of the English clergy, their number included a botanist (William Turner), a translator and playwright (Barten Holyday), an author of popular travel books (Samuel Purchas), and a doctor (John Burgess). Some were sought-after preachers, with a column nowadays in the *Short-Title Catalogue*; some were pamphleteers, like Robert Crowley and Stephen Gosson; some, like Hall and Donne, were men of superior learning and abilities to whom the church offered a career—not the best perhaps, but satisfactory, often drawing upon their talents for controversy and their oratorical powers; some were churchmen, born, it seems, for the episcopal gaiters, like Jewel and Sanderson; some were *politiques*, like Gardiner and Bancroft; some were just clergymen, with no distinction at all, at least in the eyes of the world.

In the early years of the Reformation, in fact until well into the reign of Elizabeth, they hardly constituted a clearly recognizable class. The pattern of an exhibition, a fellowship, a college living, "a sermon at Paul's Cross, and that printed," a prebend, another living, a treatise against Rome, another living, is generally late, Jacobean in fact. (Then it was violently interrupted, to be resumed—with some changes—only after the Restoration.) The Reformers and the Marian exiles, about whom we know so much from the patient labours of historians and the impatient labours of controversial divines, constituted a special body of men, rooted in the medieval Church Catholic, with continental Protestantism grafted upon them. But the next generation is not so clearly defined and at first view is not so impressive. It is hard to find a doctrinaire Protestant of any consequence in England in the first thirty years of the Reformation; fanatics, yes, but not such totalitarian intellectuals as the study of the *Institutes* produced in the young Cambridge dons of the 1570's and 1580's, men as ready to reduce existence to a set of marginal glosses on the Pauline epistles as their spiritual successors the Marxist intellectuals were to cleave all questions with the dialectic. The Paul's Cross pulpit, as we have seen, was never captured, though it was assaulted, by these fiery spirits, who, as C. S. Lewis says, hated bishops not beer. In fact, as one reads the surviving Paul's Cross sermons from the last half of the reign of Elizabeth, one feels that most of the preachers hated beer and loved bishops, a position certainly safe and even virtuous, but hardly of any intellectual consequence. What one finds in these sermons is a sort of residue of the more easily assimilated elements in the Reformers' theology and morality, in other words the substance and often the language of the Homilies of 1547 and 1563. It would not be true to say arbitrarily that there is nothing in what I have elsewhere described as the typical Paul's Cross sermon that is not in the Homilies, but until a more sophisticated, "professional," and formalistic approach to public persuasion was developed in the earlier seventeenth century, this collection, designed to fill the mouths of an unlearned clergy, was the greatest single influence in forming the Anglican attitude and temper, and beneath the rigour or the polish of the Jacobean and Caroline divines it persisted until the Rebellion.

When I finally come to terms with this concept of "Anglicanism," to which this whole large body of evidence has led me, I am conscious of pitfalls everywhere, in every sermon in fact. So long as we can cross this century on the firm stepping-stones of Jewel's *Apology*, Hooker's *Ecclesiastical Polity*, and Laud's *Conference* with Fisher, we are as safe—as the Church of England. But to forsake these positions, or at most to glimpse them afar off, and to seek in the weekly sermons of the clergy—and those preserved by Time, that whimsical archivist —some clear notion of the ordinary assumptions of this heterogeneous group, that is a task full of difficulty.

Since it is clear, as I have suggested, that the Homilies were a trusted guide and ready inspiration for the preachers, an index to most of their commonplaces, what can be discovered there? First, a position purely, even naïvely conservative, in which is assumed the final perfection of the Protestant Reformation as it had been achieved in the reign of Edward VI. Second, in apparent contradiction to this, the steady inculcation of a reforming temper, applied to the conduct of life, and to the continued re-examination of the faith through the Scriptures. The ideal set forth is above all of *order*: there is no encouragement for any revolutionary thought; but that order is not considered a passive formula but a source of lively Christian experience. Now this flexible conservatism, designed in the first place as a comprehensive and simple spiritual food for congregations who, if they were anything, were indifferent Catholics, or "reformers without tarrying for any," persisted through the popular exhortations of Anglican churchmen for a century. It is the basis of the reasonableness of Jewel and Cooper in their encounters with the extremists; it animates the final appeals of the Laudian clergy against the Puritan lecturers and pamphleteers. The "single eye, pure intent, and good mind" which the framers of the Homilies recommended is the spiritual preparation both for Hooker's great intellectual edifice and for the continual appeals from the Paul's Cross pulpit for moderation, reason, and pious good sense.

This attitude, carried firmly through all aspects of life, emphasizes the possibilities, yes even the inspiration, of the *actual*. The Paul's Cross sermon by the very circumstances of its delivery was inevitably topical; indeed any sermon, by definition, is an application of the otherworldly and eternal to the here and now. But if we compare such a Puritan effusion as Isaac Craven's *Gods Tribunall* (1631), a striking exception to the customary form and spirit of these sermons, with such a typical exhortation as John Jones's *Londons Looking Backe to Jerusalem* (1633), the first thing that strikes us is that the Puritan invokes a world in which absolute laws of belief and conduct are ranged like the soldiers of a new model army, like the formulae in a scientific text-book, or as in a utopian constitution, while the other is involved in the ordinary flux of the present world, taking account of all its varieties and approximations. Second, while Craven and his like, with their homiletic slide rules, calculate the spiritual velocity, so to speak, of the individual soul, the others, so loosely prophetic in tone, and so superficially conventional and tame, invite their congregations to contemplate their sins in relation to their neighbours; they extol the virtues of the Christian *citizen*, not of some elect community, but of England, and now.

These conservative yet vigorously constructive elements in the Anglican position may be found implicit in the administrative methods of Matthew Parker and John Whitgift, as well as in the philosophy of Hooker,[1] and of those preachers who expressed its spirit at Paul's Cross, for example, John Howson and John Spenser. From the Puritan point of view this looked like Erastianism or popery; from the Tridentine Catholic point of view it looked like heresy and national schism. Like the English constitutional monarchy and the parliamentary system of later centuries, it was a compromise position, very difficult to explain to strangers or to justify to zealots. And precisely because it was a *via media*, its establishment created by a despot but created in Parliament, its sacraments Protestant in intention but framed, so to speak, in the traditional rubrics, the furniture of its churches running the gamut from Genevan severity to almost Roman richness, its head a governor but not a "petty Pope," its bishops royal appointees but claiming consecration in an unbroken line with their pre-Reformation predecessors, its theology Calvinist but as time went on increasingly tempered with Arminian and rationalist elements, its membership theoretically national but never embracing many powerful and strategically placed subjects—for all these reasons, it was actually the most revolutionary of all the Reformed churches. There had always been heretics in the Western Church, but never heretics like these. The literature of controversy was, accordingly, voluminous and vast; the output of treatises on each side bulky enough to astonish even a generation like ours, smothered in woodpulp.

There were open and crypto-Catholics at home; there were co-religionists from the continent who came to England on business, affairs of state, or otherwise; there was a representation of ambassadors and their servants. For the benefit of these, as well as to reinforce the faith of the faithful, the Paul's Cross preachers, of their own intent or by instruction, carried on the controversy steadily from that pulpit, with that appalling persistency and in those terms of "improperation and scurrility" which I have sadly noted elsewhere in these pages. The violence of the language, the intransigence of opinion, the perverse interpretation of documents, the prominence given and respect paid to converts, should not be incomprehensible to the mid-twentieth century. The little voice of John Hales alone, among sermons I have seen, spoke with the accents of Great Tew. The others affirmed an irreconcilable enmity to the Beast of Rome, carried the conflict beyond reason into the clamour of invective, and reiterated, usually without his sobriety and sense of intellectual emergency, the classic arguments of Bishop Jewel. How far these tirades were inspired by recurring crises in foreign relations, by the bull *Regnans in excelsis* of 1570, by the Spanish menace of the 1580's and 1590's, by the Powder Plot, by the opening of the Thirty Years' War and the Spanish negotiations of the 1620's, I have discussed above; but some account must be taken of the routine aspect of this controversial element in the complex of

Anglican ideas. Here I invoke again Bishop Frere's fastidious distinction between the two levels of controversy: the "higher" conducted by Jewel, Harding, and others in one century and by Andrewes, Bellarmine, and others in the next, and the "lower," open to all comers. The first was academic, though enlivened, as were those illustrious encounters of Milton with Salmasius, by personalities; the second was conventional—and scurrilous, of the sort which Matthew Arnold imagined as brightening evening conversations in Toronto seventy-five years ago, and impressing on the public mind the image, rather over-simplified, of the Roman priesthood (and especially the Jesuits) as a set of whoremongers, spies, and murderers. It may be objected that to call these commonplaces "ideas" is to dignify them out of all conscience. Yet they constituted a militant element in the national church feeling without which its more reflective and constructive ethos could not have flourished. For the keynote of these polemics was, after all, pride in the purity, the gravity, the primitive single-mindedness of the English faith, and these preachers helped to create that respectable, insular, Protestant Englishman who was to astound and amuse the satirists—and innkeepers—of Europe for two centuries.

That English sobriety, at its worst philistine, at its best comely, which stands at the opposite pole of religious experience and expression to the brilliant and passionate achievement of the Counter-Reformation, is reflected in these sermons. There is no other word for it but biblical. The metamorphosis of the Bible into an "English book" was complete, and profound in its effects. The chronicles of Judah were interfoliated with those of Lancaster and York; the psalms mingled with the native songs; the prophets were reformers; the Apocalypse blazed in every comet, every summer storm; the Lord addressed Adam in the language of Coverdale and the Hampton Court committee. "God is English." Not until the visions of "English Blake" does one find again in English writing that prophetic identification of past and present, Israel and England, which animates these sermons and others of their kind. This body of feeling and belief is not necessarily antihumanist, for it could co-exist in an uncritical mind with recognition of humane values and proficiency in profane learning. But it was opposed to, and perhaps in the long run more influential than that happy synthesis of insular Anglican conviction and learned cosmopolitan tolerance which is exemplified in different degrees by Hooker, Browne, Hales, and Taylor.

The "great and publique taske" of the Paul's Cross preachers was, then, a summons to the imperial mission. If the Tudor preachers congratulated Englishmen on their escape (by means of the Word of God and the Statute of Appeals) from corrupt and papistical Europe and especially from the Mediterranean ("Italianate") infection, their Jacobean and Caroline successors envisaged an Atlantic (and Anglican) *imperium*. These sentiments are explicit in the propaganda for the Virginia enterprise in 1609; they are implicit in the proud image of the invincible sea-girt nation which decorates so many of these sermons. Not that the preachers proposed any compromise with those concomitants of enterprise, "good business," and high living; on the contrary, as I have shown, they held firmly to the ideal of an essentially static, hierarchical, plain-living society. They would have their Englishman exemplify at once pastoral or georgic simplicity and heroic splendour, those virtues celebrated by their own poet Spenser, whose English paladin is Georgos,[2] and typified by the young David, shepherd of Bethlehem, king of Judah.

There is nothing mean in this ideal, far from it. In the long run, these preachers escape the sneers of Selden, the anger of Milton, even the carelessness of bibliographers. In the library of St. Paul's Cathedral they keep these Paul's Cross sermons in a modest book-press. There the little quartos stand, bound with antiquarian tenderness and churchly frugality in plain blue and red boards, making no show beside the mountains of calf and vellum which dominate them from the shelves, the fathers, the doctors, the casuists, the canonists, the historians, the controversialists, the interpreters. Yet their authors had read those shelves, and it was no small achievement to reduce the vast apparatus of Christian doctrine and history to the dimensions of popular persuasion, in service of the ideal of a Christian commonwealth. They were *time-servers*, not usually in the sense intended by their Puritan brethren, but literally, serving the time, a harsh and often indifferent master. They served it not as slaves but as stewards, not to be quelled by it but to redeem it, and, as St. Paul told the Ephesians, that is to be "not as fools, but as wise."

NOTES AND REGISTER

ABBREVIATIONS
USED IN NOTES AND REGISTER

APC	*Acts of the Privy Council of England.* New Series, edited by J. R. Dasent, 1542–1627. London, 1890–1938.
Ath. Cantab.	*Athenae Cantabrigienses.* By C. H. Cooper and T. Cooper. Cambridge, 1858–1913.
Ath. Oxon.	*Athenae Oxonienses: An Exact History of all the Writers and Bishops who have had their Education in the University of Oxford.* . . . By Anthony à Wood. Edited by P. Bliss. London, 1813–20.
Burnet-Pocock	Burnet, Gilbert. *The History of the Reformation of the Church of England.* Edited by Nicholas Pocock. New York, 1843.
CSPD Eliz.	
CSPD James I	
CSPD Charles I	*Calendar of State Papers, Domestic.* By Robert Lemon and M. A. E. Green. London, 1856–72.
Chamberlain	*The Letters of John Chamberlain.* Edited by N. E. McClure. Philadelphia, 1939.
EHR	*English Historical Review.*
Foxe-Townshend	*The Acts and Monuments of John Foxe.* Edited by Rev. George Townshend. London, 1843–9.
Grey Friars Chron.	*Chronicle of the Grey Friars of London.* Edited by J. G. Nichols. London, Camden Society, 1852.
HLQ	*Huntington Library Quarterly.*
Holinshed	*Holinshed's Chronicles of England, Scotland, and Ireland.* London, 1808.
L & P Hen. VIII	*Letters and Papers, Foreign and Domestic, of the Reign of Henry VIII, 1509–47.* By J. S. Brewer, James Gairdner, and R. H. Brodie. London, 1862–1910.
Machyn	*The Diary of Henry Machyn, Citizen and Merchant-Taylor of London: From A.D. 1550 to A.D. 1563.* Edited by J. G. Nichols. London, Camden Society, 1848.
Manningham	*The Diary of John Manningham, of the Middle Temple, and of Bradbourne, Kent, Barrister-at-law.* Edited by John Bruce. London, Camden Society, 1868.
Salisbury Papers	Great Britain, Historical Manuscripts Commission. *Calendar of the Manuscripts of the Most Hon. the Marquess of Salisbury, preserved at Hatfield House.* London, 1884–1940.
SP Ven.	*Calendar of State Papers and Manuscripts relating to English Affairs existing in the Archives and Collections of Venice.* Edited by H. F. Brown and A. B. Hind. London, 1900–25.
STC	*A Short-Title Catalogue of Books Printed in England, Scotland, and Ireland and of English Books Printed Abroad, 1475–1640.* Edited by A. W. Pollard and G. R. Redgrave. London, 1926.
Strype, *Annals*	Strype, John. *Annals of the Reformation and Establishment of Religion.* . . . Oxford, 1820–40.
Strype, *EM*	Strype, John. *Ecclesiastical Memorials, relating chiefly to Religion.* . . . Oxford, 1820–40.
UTQ	*University of Toronto Quarterly.*
VCH London	*Victoria History of the Counties of England.* Edited by W. Page, H. A. Doubleday, and others. Westminster, 1900——. *London,* I.
Wrioth. Chron.	Wriothsley, Charles. *A Chronicle of the England during the Reigns of the Tudors, from A.D. 1485 to 1559.* Edited by W. D. Hamilton. London, Camden Society, 1875–77.

NOTES

I ANTIQUARIAN

1. See G. H. Cook, *Old St. Paul's Cathedral* (London, 1955), p. 70; G. M. Trevelyan, *Illustrated English Social History* (London, 1950), II, 164. Farley's *Complaint of Paules to all Christian Soules* was published in 1616.

2. This survey of the history of Paul's Cross during the medieval period is based on W. Paley Baildon, "The Chronicle of Paul's Cross," *Home Counties Magazine*, VIII (1906), IX (1907), X (1908), XI (1909); Margaret E. Cornford, *Paul's Cross: A History* (London, 1910); H. H. Milman, *Annals of St. Paul's Cathedral* (London, 1888).

3. W. Sparrow Simpson, ed., *Documents Illustrating the History of St. Paul's Cathedral* (Camden Society, 1880), p. 7.

4. In 1552. Quoted in Charles Knight, *London* (London, 1841), I, 52.

5. This information is conveniently summarized in Cook, *Old St. Paul's*, pp. 68-70.

6. Bishop Jewel to Peter Martyr, in 1560. *The Zurich Letters*, ed. Hastings Robinson (Parker Society, 1842-5), I, 71.

7. *Narratives of the Days of the Reformation*, ed. J. G. Nichols (Camden Society, 1859), p. 23.

8. John Stow, *The Survey of London* (Everyman, n.d.), p. 151.

9. *Two Sermons* (1615).

10. *VCH London*, I, 322.

11. For notices of these collections see *Wrioth. Chron.*, I, 77; *APC*, XIV, 253; XIX, 225; XXXI, 270.

12. Miles Hogarde, *The displaying of the Protestantes* (1556), sig. Fiv.

13. Ric. Newcourt, *Repertorium ecclesiasticum parochiale Londinense* (London, 1708-10), I, 4-5.

14. *Ibid.*, p. 4. The list of "Benefactors [to be prayed for] at pauls Crosse" appears in B.M. MS. Harl. 417. f. 132.

15. Samuel Collins, *A Sermon preached at Paules-Crosse* (1607), p. 88. Cf. Thomas Jackson, *Londons New-Yeeres Gift* (1609), p. 8, and Thos. Myriell, *The Devout Soules Search* (1610), p. 80. Why Russell was singled out for special mention is not clear; in Newcourt's list he appears as one of four who set aside a yearly rent charge of £10.

16. *The Judicious Marriage of Mr. Hooker* (Cambridge, 1940), pp. 17-44.

17. Quoted in John Sparrow, "John Donne and Contemporary Preachers," *Essays & Studies*, XVI (1931), 154.

18. *CSPD James I*, 1619-23, 187. There seems to have been trouble in 1592 also. Witness a letter from the Privy Council to the Archbishop of Canterbury, dated December 26, 1592: "We have received from the Bishop of London a letter inclosed complayning of the disobedience of suche as are by order from him required from tyme to tyme to preach at the Crosse at Pawles, who for the most parte (as he al-

leagethe) refuse to come and to performe the directions in that behalf given unto them which he desirethe maie be reformed by auctoritie from us. Forasmuch as your Lordship as Archbishop and otherwise as chief of the Commission Ecclesiastical have power sufficient to redresse that disorder, we have thought good to referre the same unto you." (*APC*, n.s., XXIII, 1592, 383.)

19. A. F. Herr, *The Elizabethan Sermon: A Survey and Bibliography* (Philadelphia, 1940), p. 24.

20. Grindal's directions are in David Wilkins, *Concilia magnae Britanniae et Hiberniae* (London, 1737), IV, 298–9. Cf. the instructions for time and place of public penance in B.M. MS. Eg. 2350. See also Register, July 8, 1543 and Nov. 4, 1554.

21. *Narratives of the Reformation*, p. 51.

22. See S. R. Gardiner's comment, *History of England from the Accession of James I to the Outbreak of the Civil War, 1603–1642* (London, 1883–7), VII, 250–2.

23. Milman, *Annals*, p. 354.

24. Cook, *Old St. Paul's*, p. 70; *CSPD Charles I*, 1635–6, 66.

25. *Commons Journals*, II, 1640–2, 768; III, 1642–4, 105. Cf. above, p. 12.

26. William Dugdale, *The History of St. Paul's Cathedral* (1758), p. 173. This is the usual statement, repeated from one historian to another; but in Henry Peachum's "A dialogue between the crosse in Cheap, and Charing Crosse" (1641), it is said that Paul's Cross "is downe and quite taken away, with intent to be built fairer and bigger when the Church shall be finished." See Cornford, *Paul's Cross*, p. 15.

27. W. Paley Baildon, "Notes on the Early History . . . of Paul's Cross," *Proceedings of the Society of Antiquaries of London*, ser. 2, XXX (1917–18), 209.

II HISTORICAL

1. W. Paley Baildon, "The Chronicle of Paul's Cross," *Home Counties Magazine*, VIII (1906), 188, 189, 284, 289; IX (1907), 146.

2. For this view see C. H. McIlwain, *The High Court of Parliament* (New Haven, 1910), p. 114; A. F. Pollard, *The Evolution of Parliament* (London, 1926), pp. 205, 212–13.

3. *English Works of John Fisher* (Early English Text Society, 1876), pp. 311–48.

4. *VCH London*, I, 252.

5. Philip Hughes, *The Reformation in England* (London, 1950–4), I, 148.

6. *Ibid.* See also Charles Sturge, *Cuthbert Tunstall* (London, 1938), p. 133.

7. *VCH London*, I, 259; John Stow, "Historical Memoranda," in *Three Fifteenth Century Chronicles*, ed. James Gairdner (Camden Society, 1880), pp. 89–90.

8. G. Constant, *The Reformation in England*: I, *The English Schism* (London, 1934), p. 68, a partisan but still illuminating view.

9. For this comment, and the whole sermon, see "The sermon against the Holy Maid of Kent," ed. L. E. Whetmore, *EHR*, LVIII (1943), 63–75.

10. See an ambiguous letter of John Rudd, in *L & P Hen VIII*, VII, no. 303.

11. H. H. Milman, *Annals of St. Paul's Cathedral* (London, 1888), p. 194.

12. *Wrioth. Chron.*, I, 104.
13. *Three Chapters of Letters Relating to the Suppression of the Monasteries*, ed. Thomas Wright (Camden Society, 1843), p. 38. A recent biographer questions the accuracy of the reporting at this point. See Allan G. Chester, *Hugh Latimer: Apostle to the English* (Philadelphia, 1954), p. 124.
14. *Original Letters Illustrative of English History*, ed. Sir H. Ellis (ser. 3, London, 1846), II, no. 208; *Wrioth. Chron.*, I, 78–9.
15. *Sermons* (Everyman, 1926), pp. 22–9.
16. Henry Gee & W. G. Hardy, eds., *Documents Illustrative of English Church History* (London, 1910), p. 278.
17. "The History of Henry VIII," in White Kennett, *A Complete History of England*, &c. (London, 1719), II, 215.
18. *Ibid.*, II, 213.
19. *Letters of Stephen Gardiner*, ed. J. A. Muller (Cambridge, 1933), pp. 168–70.
20. *Ibid.*, p. 170.
21. Dr. Crome's case is reviewed sympathetically by Hughes, *The Reformation in England*, II, 64–6. Contemporary sources are cited in the Register under the dates of his various appearances.
22. J. Gairdner, *The English Church . . . from the Accession of Henry VIII to the Death of Mary* (London, 1912), pp. 234–6; *Grey Friars Chron.*, pp. 51–3.
23. Gairdner, *The English Church*, p. 242.
24. John Stow, *The Survey of London* (Everyman, n.d.), p. 130.
25. *Narratives of the Days of the Reformation*, ed. J. G. Nichols (Camden Society, 1859), p. 29. This episode should perhaps be assigned to an earlier date.
26. Text in Gee & Hardy, *Documents*, pp. 322–8.
27. Ridley's testimony is quoted from Foxe-Townshend, VII, 523. An interesting but controversial analysis of Edwardian opinion on the sacrament may be found in C. H. Smyth, *Cranmer and the Reformation under Edward VI* (Cambridge, 1926).
28. Quoted in John Strype, *Memorials of . . . Thomas Cranmer* (Oxford, 1840), II, 874. The reference in the third verse is perhaps to the Spital pulpit in Easter week.
29. Quoted in H. C. White, *Social Criticism in Popular Religious Literature of the Sixteenth Century* (New York, 1944), p. 70.
30. *Ibid.*, p. 122.
31. Latimer, *Sermons*, p. 130; White, *Social Criticism*, p. 121.
32. *Wrioth. Chron.*, II, 97–8.
33. Samuel Clark, *The Marrow of Ecclesiastical History* (1654), p. 512.
34. William Camden, *The History of Elizabeth* (1765), p. 16.
35. See the brilliant discussion of the political implications of the settlement in A. F. Pollard, *The History of England from the Accession of Edward VI to the Death of Elizabeth* (London, 1923), pp. 212–15.
36. Quoted in John Strype, *The Life and Acts of John Whitgift* (Oxford, 1822), III, 32.
37. Quoted in Strype, *Annals*, II (i), 294.
38. Quoted in A. O. Meyer, *England and the Catholic Church under Queen Elizabeth* (London, 1916), p. 314.

39. See William Pierce, *An Historical Introduction to the Marprelate Tracts* (London, 1908), chap. IV and *passim*.
40. Quoted in M. M. Knappen, *Tudor Puritanism* (Chicago, 1939), p. 68.
41. *Laws of Ecclesiastical Polity*, V, ii, 3.
42. In "Christs Teares over Jerusalem," *Works*, ed. R. B. McKerrow (London, 1904–10), II, 121.
43. Quoted in G. B. Harrison, *The Life and Death of Robert Devereux Earl of Essex* (New York, 1937), p. 347.
44. Bancroft to Cecil, *Salisbury Papers*, XI, 55–6.
45. From a letter by Vincent Hussey, quoted in A. F. Herr, *The Elizabethan Sermon: A Survey and Bibliography* (Philadelphia, 1940), p. 52.
46. In Herr, *Elizabethan Sermon*, p. 53.
47. He got bravely over that; witness his praise of James I in his Powder Plot sermon of March 1605. Donne, who detested him, referred to his *Answer to a Catholic Englishman* (1609) as a tissue of "silly ridiculous triflings," and "extreme flatteries." He finds a place in Donne's *Courtier's Library* (ed. E. M. Simpson, 1930), where is listed "An Encomion on Doctor Shaw, Chaplain to Richard III, by Doctor Barlow." Richard Shaw preached a notorious sermon in 1483, at Paul's Cross, justifying Gloucester's claim to the throne by proclaiming the illegitimacy of the offspring of Elizabeth Woodville. Cf. Ridley's sermon at Paul's Cross on July 9, 1553. What is to be learned from this allusion of Donne's own opinions on the Essex case must remain conjecture.
48. In J. R. Tanner, ed., *Constitutional Documents of the Reign of James I* (Cambridge, 1930), p. 4.
49. The reader is referred to Hugh Ross Williamson's vigorous and scholarly *The Gunpowder Plot* (London, 1951).
50. See W. K. Jordan, *The Development of Religious Toleration in England from the Accession of James I to the Convention of the Long Parliament* (Cambridge, Mass., 1936), pp. 33, 82.
51. In Sir Charles Firth, ed., *An American Garland* (Oxford, 1915), p. 9.
52. See G. H. Cook, *Old St. Paul's Cathedral* (London, 1955), p. 81. In the 1630's, Inigo Jones undertook a major repair and re-facing of the cathedral.
53. The intensity of the anti-Spanish, anti-Catholic feeling at the time is shown in the pamphlet *Tom Tell-Troath*, a surreptitiously printed document of considerable historical interest. See W. H. Dunham and S. Pargellis, *Complaint and Reform in England, 1436–1714* (New York, 1938), pp. 481 ff.
54. Tanner, *Documents*, p. 274.
55. Jordan, *Development of Religious Toleration*, p. 101.
56. *Works of John Donne*, ed. Henry Alford (London, 1839), III, 389–90. The preaching orders were issued in August 1622; Charles started for Spain in February 1623, and returned in October.
57. S. R. Gardiner, *History of England from the Accession of James I to the Outbreak of Civil War, 1603–1642* (London, 1883–7), V, 143.
58. Chamberlain, II, 434.
59. *The Works of Robert Sanderson, D.D.*, ed. William Jacobson (Oxford, 1854), VI, 370.

III SOCIOLOGICAL

1. Reproduced in Hugh Ross Williamson, *The Gunpowder Plot* (London, 1951), p. 156. Cf. Samuel Clark, *England's Remembrancer* (1677), and Nehemiah Wallington, *Historical Notices of Events chiefly in the Reign of Charles I* (London, 1869), I, 2-4, 5, 15.
2. Henry King, *A Sermon Preached at Paules Crosse* (1621), sig. C2v.
3. An oft-repeated dirge, based on Hooker, *Ecclesiastical Polity*, I, iii, 2.
4. Quoted by R. H. Tawney, *Religion and the Rise of Capitalism* (Penguin Books, 1948), p. 154.
5. Robert Harris, *Gods Goodnes and Mercie* (1626), p. 8.
6. This theory is nicely developed by Alfred Von Martin, *Sociology of the Renaissance* (New York, 1944).
7. Laud, quoted in Tawney, *Religion*, p. 140.
8. *Two Sermons* (1615), p. 36.
9. *Sermons*, in *English Reprints*, ed. E. Arber (Birmingham, 1870), p. 27.
10. Donne, *Works*, ed. Henry Alford (London, 1839), V, 241.
11. Quoted in M. M. Knappen, *Tudor Puritanism* (Chicago, 1939), p. 413.
12. Quoted in William Haller, *The Rise of Puritanism* (New York, 1938), p. 126.
13. Tawney, *Religion*, p. 251, etc.
14. See Register: March 6, 1586; Jan. 11, 1618.
15. Quoted in E. P. Cheyney, *Social Changes in England in the Sixteenth Century* (University of Pennsylvania Series in Philology, Literature & Archaeology, IV, no. 2, Philadelphia, 1925), p. 53.
16. Latimer, *Sermons* (Everyman, 1926), p. 58.
17. See the description of the process and its results in J. R. H. Moorman, *A History of the Church in England* (London, 1954), pp. 96-7.
18. W. H. Frere, *The English Church in the Reigns of Elizabeth and James I* (London, 1911), pp. 302-3.
19. Robert Crowley, *The Select Works*, ed. J. M. Cowper (EETS, 1872), p. 7.
20. In a sermon of 1602, noted by Manningham, p. 69.
21. *Sermons*, ed. John Ayre (Parker Society, 1841), p. 350.
22. See William Harrison, *Description of England* (New Shakspere Society Publications, ser. 6, no. 8, 1881), p. 26; Geoffrey Baskerville, *English Monks and the Suppression of the Monasteries* (New Haven, 1937), pp. 39-41; the account of the visitation of Lincoln in 1576 in *Lincoln Record Society*, XXIII (1926), 448, 456-7.
23. See Douglas Bush, "Tudor Humanism and Henry VIII," *UTQ*, VII (1937-8), 164-5.
24. William Holbrooke, *Loves Complaint* (1609), sig. D3.
25. For these episodes see Frere, *The English Church*, p. 303.
26. *A Second Sermon Preached at Pauls Crosse the 21. of May, 1598* (1598), sig. D3. See above, p. 76.
27. Quoted in Tawney, *Religion*, p. 161.
28. Quoted in H. C. White, *Social Criticism in Popular Religious Literature of the Sixteenth Century* (New York, 1944), p. 222.
29. The acts of 37 Edw. III, 3 Edw. IV, renewed in 24 Hen. VIII. See W. H.

Dunham and S. Pargellis, *Complaint and Reform in England, 1436–1714* (New York, 1938), pp. 43 ff.
30. John Hoskins, *Sermons* (1615), p. 49.
31. Chamberlain, II, 289.
32. See Richard Lennard, ed., *Englishmen at Rest and Play* (Oxford, 1931), p. 168.
33. *The Sermon preached at the Crosse* (1608), sig. Y2. I have been unable to locate the source of the allusion.
34. Lennard, *Englishmen at Rest and Play*, pp. 84–6.
35. William Ringler, "The First Phase of the Elizabethan Attack on the Stage, 1558–1579," *HLQ*, V (1941–2), 416.
36. Robert Milles, *Abrahams Sute for Sodome* (1612), sig. Dov. The "illiterate bricklayer" is probably Ben Jonson.
37. Ben Jonson, *Bartholomew Fair*, V.

IV HOMILETIC

1. "Democritus Junior to the Reader," *Anatomy of Melancholy*.
2. Quoted in J. S. Purvis, *Tudor Parish Documents of the Diocese of York* (Cambridge, 1948), p. 140.
3. *Resolves* (1634), p. 69.
4. *The Arraignment of the Arrian* (1626), p. 6.
5. *Microcosmographie*, "A bold forward man."
6. Thomas Jackson, "Epistle Dedicatory" to *Londons New-Yeeres Gift* (1609). See E. R. Curtius' description of the topos of "affected modesty," in *European Literature and the Latin Middle Ages* (London, 1953), pp. 83–5.
7. Cf. George Webbe, *Gods Controversie* (1609), sig. A3.
8. *Jonahs Sermon* (1606), sig. 2v. Cf. John Andrews, *The Brazen Serpent* (1621), sig. A3v.
9. See Simonds D'Ewes, *Autobiography* (London, 1845), I, 137–8, and cf. Earle, "A young raw preacher."
10. On these possibilities see W. Fraser Mitchell, *English Pulpit Oratory from Andrewes to Tillotson* (London, 1932), p. 14; A. F. Herr, *The Elizabethan Sermon: A Survey and Bibliography* (Philadelphia, 1940), pp. 75–7.
11. Cf. his comments in *Pierces Supererogation, Elizabethan Critical Essays*, ed. G. G. Smith (Oxford, 1904), II, 281.
12. Quoted in Horton Davies, *The Worship of the English Puritans* (Westminster, 1948), p. 183.
13. *Ibid.*
14. *Justifying and Saving Faith* (1614), sig. gg2.
15. "The Preachers Plea," in *All the Sermons of Samuel Hieron* (Cambridge, 1614), p. 534.
16. *A Sermon preached at Paules Crosse* (1579), sig. F3.
17. Thomas Nashe, commending Andrewes' style, in *Works*, ed. R. B. McKerrow (London, 1904–10), III, 105.

18. See R. F. Jones, "The Attack on Pulpit Eloquence in the Restoration," *The Seventeenth Century: Studies in the History of English Thought and Literature from Bacon to Pope* (Stanford, 1951), pp. 111–42; for Perkins *et al.*, see passages quoted in William Haller, *Rise of Puritanism* (New York, 1938), pp. 130–1.
19. *Literature and Pulpit in Medieval England* (Cambridge, 1933), *passim*.
20. Thomas Wilson, *The Arte of Rhetoricke* (1560), p. 3.
21. *Foure Sermons* (1608), p. 69.
22. See the relevant passages in Henry Bettenson, ed., *Documents of the Christian Church* (Oxford, 1946), pp. 6–9.
23. Purvis, *Tudor Parish Documents*, p. 10.
24. *The Faithfull Shepherd* (1621), p. 156.
25. *All the sermons*, p. 530.
26. John Jones, *Londons Looking Backe to Jerusalem* (1633).
27. *The Works of John Jewel, Bishop of Salisbury* (Parker Society, 1845), II, 983.
28. Bernard, *Faithfull Shepherd*, sig. A5.
29. Quoted in Davies, *Worship of the English Puritans*, p. 188.
30. The standard commentaries are ably analysed by Arnold Williams, *The Common Expositor* (Chapel Hill, 1948); see also Rosemond Tuve, *A Reading of George Herbert* (Chicago, 1952).
31. Mitchell, *English Pulpit Oratory*, pp. 72–4.
32. G. R. Owst, *Preaching in Medieval England* (Cambridge, 1926), pp. 309–30.
33. See Charles Smyth, *The Art of Preaching* (London, 1940), p. 19; Mitchell, p. 96.
34. *Faithfull Shepherd*, p. 166.
35. *Five Sermons in Five several Styles* (1656), sig. A3.
36. John Wilkins, *Ecclesiastes* (1647), p. 7.
37. *Davids Teacher* (1609).
38. "A Priest to the Temple," in *Works*, ed. F. E. Hutchinson (Oxford, 1941), p. 234.
39. *The Grounds & Occasions of the Contempt of the Clergy* (1670), p. 64.
40. See Mitchell, *English Pulpit Oratory*, chap. v.
41. By Mitchell, *ibid.*, pp. 170–3.
42. John Dyos, *A Sermon preached at Pauls Crosse* (1579), sig. C4.

V CONCLUSION

1. Cf. A. S. P. Woodhouse, "Religion and Some Foundations of English Democracy," *Philosophical Review*, LXI (1952), 503–31.
2. *Faerie Queene*, I, x, 66.

A REGISTER OF SERMONS PREACHED AT PAUL'S CROSS, 1534-1642

NOTE

1. Dates are given in New Style; where there is inconsistency in the documents used, dates between January 1 and Lady Day (March 25) have been corrected by collateral evidence and the use of a perpetual calendar.

2. Sermons which cannot be dated within a year are placed at the end of that year.

3. Sermons impossible to assign to a particular year are placed at the end of the reign in which they were preached.

4. Original editions of printed sermons are indicated by an asterisk before the title.

HENRY VIII

1534

JAN. 15   The customary prayer for the Pope was omitted at the Paul's Cross sermon. (Memorandum of Jan. 14, from Cromwell to the Bishop of London. *L & P Hen. VIII*, VII, no. 48 (2).)

FEB.   A sermon on *Omnes peccaverunt et egent gloria Dei*. On the royal divorce. The sermon included arguments against marriage with a brother's widow. (*L & P Hen. VIII*, VII, no. 266.)

ante MARCH 8   John Rudd (probably Fellow of St. John's, Cambridge, afterwards Vicar of Norton, Durham). A defence of the Holy Maid of Kent. (*L & P Hen. VIII*, VII, no. 303.)

EASTER   Cranmer inhibited preaching on "the king's matters" which tended to the slander of Catholic doctrine. Chapuys reported that the preachers against the Pope "acquitted themselves desperately, saying the most outrageous and abominable things in the world." (*L & P Hen. VIII*, VII, nos. 192, 463.)

APRIL 26   John Stokesley, Bishop of London, "a man of great wytte and learnyng, but of lytle discresion and humanitie" (Hall). On the virtue of masses. One Thomas Merial was falsely accused upon a misinterpretation of the sermon. Preached in the Shrouds. (Foxe-Townshend, V, 601.)

MAY 24   A preacher appointed by Cranmer. They communicated through Cranmer's grocer. (*L & P Hen. VIII*, VII, no. 616.)

NOV. 3–DEC. 18 ("Parliament time")   "Every Sunday preached at Paul's Cross a bishop, who declared the Pope not to be the head of the church." (Foxe-Townshend, V, 68.)

Dec. ?	"One from Norwich," a substitute for John Hilsey, Bishop of Rochester. He was appointed "to the entent that he might declare his mind in the King's matters." (*L & P Hen. VIII*, VII, no. 1643.)
——	An abbot. Preaching the King's cause against Katherine, he was interrupted by Father Robinson, a friar of Greenwich, who offered to dispute publicly with him, and indicated his intention to preach at the Cross on the Queen's behalf the following Sunday. The friar was supported by his vicar, who held the same views. (Strype, *EM*, I(1), 257-8; I(2), 193-4.)

1535

July 11	John Stokesley, Bishop of London. "Much of what I said," he reported to Cromwell, "is in the King's book that Mr. "Ampner" [Fox], Dr. Nicholas and I made before my going over sea in embassy." (*L & P Hen. VIII*, VIII, nos. 1043, 1054.)
July 18	[Simon?] Symons. He was appointed in place of Dr. George Browne, a "provincial of the Friars," who, Stokesley feared, might rail forth "some pernicious doctrine," and "excite sedition against [Stokesley] in [his] own church." (*L & P Hen. VIII*, VIII, nos. 1043, 1054.)
Dec.	The monks of the Charterhouse were commanded to attend the sermons at Paul's Cross weekly, "that their hearts may be lightened by knowledge, their bodies escape such pains as they are worthy to suffer, and their souls escape the judgment of God for such demerits as their ignorant hearts have conceived." (Hilsey to Cromwell, *L & P Hen. VIII*, IX, no. 989.)

1536

Jan. 23	John Hilsey, Bishop of Rochester. (*Wrioth. Chron.*, I, 34.)
Jan. 30	Francis Mallet, chaplain to Cranmer. (*L & P Hen. VIII*, X, no. 120.)
Feb. 6	Thomas Cranmer, Archbishop of Canterbury. A defence of the royal supremacy, with a proof that the Pope is Antichrist. "To injure at a blow the Holy See and the Imperial authority, [he] cited one author who said that Antichrist should come when the empire was ruined. This, he said, it was now, because of all the monarchy only a small portion of Germany obeyed the Empire." (Chapuys to Granvelle, *L & P Hen. VIII*, X, no. 283.)
Feb. 13	John Hilsey, Bishop of Rochester. A defence of the supremacy. (Charles Sturge, *Cuthbert Tunstall*, London, 1938, p. 203.)
Feb. 20	John Longland, Bishop of Lincoln. A defence of the supremacy. (*Wrioth. Chron.*, I, 34.)
Feb. 27	Cuthbert Tunstall, Bishop of Durham. Preaching before Cranmer, many lords, and four Charterhouse monks who did penance for refusing to

acknowledge the supremacy, he declared the Pope's usurped authority, his uncharitable behaviour in marrying the King to his brother's wife, "and how everie king hath the highe power under God, and oughte to be the supreme head over all spirituall prelates." (*Wrioth. Chron.*, I, 34–5.)

MARCH 5   Nicholas Shaxton, Bishop of Salisbury. (*Wrioth. Chron.*, I, 35.)

MARCH 12   Hugh Latimer, Bishop of Worcester. "He saide that byshopis, abbatis, prioris, parsonis, canonis resident, pristis, and all, were stronge thevis, ye dukis, lordis, and all." He declared also that one might "eat fleshe and whit mete in Lent, so that it be don without hurtying of weke consciences, and lykewise in Frydays and all dayes." (*Three Chapters of Letters Relating to the Suppression*, ed. Thomas Wright, Camden Society, 1843, p. 38.)

MARCH 19   John Salcot [alias Capon], Bishop of Bangor. The Imperial ambassador thought that the King's object in ordering these episcopal effusions (see above) was to persuade the people there was no purgatory, that he might seize the property of the religious foundations which kept up masses for the dead. See *VCH London*, I, 264. (*Wrioth. Chron.*, I, 35.)

APRIL 2   Robert Singleton. A description of the Roman Church as Ishmael or servitude, and of the true Church as Isaac or freedom. The true Church has but now appeared in England. The sermon includes a vigorous attack upon Roman "superstitions," for example, purgatory, and a timely protest against chantry priests and monastic wealth. (In the Lincoln Cathedral Library copy, the third line of the colophon,

> God preserve his church universall
> And this church of Englande specyall
> And the supreme hed thereof our king
> And graunte us the blysse without ending,

has been crossed out, and a late-sixteenth-century hand has written *stet* five times above it, adding: "He was a traiterly knave that put out the same.") *A Sermon Preached at Paules Crosse* [1536].

JUNE 17   Hugh Latimer, Bishop of Worcester. He "openly purged himself of the false lies surmised by enemies of the truth," notably by one William Blagges, parson of Harvelingham, who said that he had revoked what he had said against confession and worshipping saints. (*L & P Hen. VIII*, X, no. 1201.)

AUG. 6   [Simon?] Symons, chaplain to the King. The sermon was seditious, in the opinion of Cromwell's informant, William Marshall, who said that the Bishop of London permitted "a rabblement of seditious preachers." (*L & P Hen. VIII*, XI, no. 325.)

1537
FEB. 25   A bishop. "He deceived the people with his crafty bowling wit, more fit for the chattering Arches than for the true sincere preaching place."

He opposed the doctrine of faith without works, and upheld the rule of celibacy for the clergy. (*L & P Hen. VIII*, XII (1), no. 530.)

ante JULY 15 Edward Lee, Archbishop of York. "He did right well touching the supremacy, and as touching the condemnation of the rebels [of the Pilgrimage of Grace]." (*L & P Hen. VIII*, XII (2), no. 258.)

AUG. 19 William Sandwich, of Canterbury College, Oxford. He was appointed by Cromwell, "for the honest report of your lernyng in holly letteres, and incorrupte Jugement in the same," and adjured to prepare "with suche pure syncerenes, trewly to open the word of God . . . , as I may therby take occasion, to thinke the report made of yow to be trewe." (R. B. Merriman, *Life and Letters of Thomas Cromwell*, Oxford, 1902, II, letter 197.)

SEPT. 23 Matthew Parker, Dean of Stoke College. He was appointed by Cromwell, "for the honest report of your learning and uncorrupt judgment in the same." (*Correspondence of Matthew Parker*, ed. John Bruce & T. Perowne, Parker Society, 1853, p. 5.)

ante Nov. 28 Robert Richardine. (*L & P Hen. VIII*, XII (2), no. 1138.)

1538

FEB. 24 John Hilsey, Bishop of Rochester. The exposure and breaking up of the Rood of Grace, from Boxley in Kent, with its device of "old wire and rotten sticks" by which the eyes and lips had been made to move. The sermon was intended to prepare the people for a general destruction of such images. (*L & P Hen. VIII*, XIII (1), n. 339; *Wrioth. Chron.*, I, 75–6; *VCH London*, I, 267.)

MAY 12 Hugh Latimer, Bishop of Worcester. The friar John Forest obstinately refused to do penance for denying the royal supremacy. "standing stiff and proud in his malicious mind." The preacher besought the congregation to pray for him. Friar Forest had preached at Paul's Cross, probably in 1533, his sermon being "more lyker barkynge and raylynge then prechinge," speaking of the decay of the realm. He was an intransigent Catholic. He was burned on May 22, 1538, with this verse set over him:

> Forest the friar
>   That obstinate liar
> That wilfully shall be dead,
>   In his contumacy
> The Gospel doth deny
>   The King to be the supreme head.

(*Wrioth Chron.*, I, 78–9; *VCH London*, I, 270. See also *Original Letters Illustrative of English History*, ed. Sir H. Ellis, ser. 3, London, 1846, II, no. 208; III, no. 331.)

post JUNE 21 A Lutheran named Atkinson recanted his heresy of the sacrament of the altar. Cranmer refused a request of Franz Burckhardt, Chancellor of

Saxony and head of the Lutheran "embassy" in England, that he be permitted to do his penance in a parish church, on the ground that this "error" was "so greatly spread abroad in this realm" that he should recant "when most people might be present." (C. H. Smyth, *Cranmer and the Reformation under Edward VI*, Cambridge, 1926, p. 58.)

Nov. 24   John Hilsey, Bishop of Rochester. The exposure of the "Blood of Hailes." Four Anabaptists, three men and a woman, "all Dutchmen," bore faggots during the sermon. (*Wrioth. Chron.*, I, 90; *VCH London*, I, 270.)

Dec. 22   John Harrydaunce, a Whitechapel bricklayer, who had been preaching to large audiences from a tub in his garden, bore a faggot with two other persons, one of them a priest. He had had "great audience of people both spirituall and temporall" at his extemporal declarations of Scripture. (*Wrioth. Chron.*, I, 82; *VCH London*, I, 270.)

1539

March 30   Cuthbert Tunstall, Bishop of Durham. A defence of the supremacy. (F. Le V. Baumer, *The Early Tudor Theory of Kingship*, New Haven, 1940, p. 42.)

July 6   One George, a priest, bore a faggot for saying that "Christ nor any creature had any merit by his Passion," and that "exorcising of holy water or holy bread was execrable and detestable." (*L & P Hen. VIII*, XIV (1), no. 1219.)

July 20   John Byrde, chaplain to the Bishop of Rochester. Stokesley called Byrde to account for this sermon. (*L & P Hen. VIII*, XIV (1), no. 1298.)

July 27   John Hilsey, Bishop of Rochester. He preached, so he said, with "more fear than ever he did in his life." This, and the preceding sermon, were incidents in the quarrel between Hilsey and Stokesley. (*L & P Hen. VIII*, XIV (1), no. 1297.)

1540

Feb. 15   Stephen Gardiner, Bishop of Winchester. The sermon against Lutheranism, in which he compared "those that call them selfe brethren in Englyshe" to the heaven-selling friars of the old dispensation, and which provoked the controversy with Robert Barnes. (*The Letters of Stephen Gardiner*, ed. J. A. Muller, Cambridge, 1933, pp. 168–70.)

Feb. 29   Dr. Robert Barnes. Using Gardiner's text of February 15, he railed upon the bishop with some violence, "raged after such a sort as the lyke hath not ben herde doone in a pulpete." (Gardiner, *Letters*, ed. Muller, p. 170; cf. *L & P Hen. VIII*, XV, no. 312; Burnet-Pocock, I, 475.)

March 7   William Jerome, Vicar of Stepney. He confirmed Barnes's doctrine that "men's constitutions bind not the conscience," and that "we obteyne remission of synnes wtout works." (Burnet-Pocock, I, 475; Foxe-Townshend, V, app. viii.)

MARCH 14   Thomas Gerrard [Garrett]. Another Lutheran sermon. (Burnet-Pocock, I, 475.)

APRIL 4   [Nicholas?] Wilson, Vicar of St. Martin's, Bishopsgate. The rehearsal of the Spital sermons by Barnes, Jerome, and Gerrard, in which they recanted their various errors. (*Wrioth. Chron.*, I, 115.)

APRIL 11   Stephen Gardiner, Bishop of Winchester. There was "a fraye, made between three or fower serving men" during the sermon. (*Wrioth. Chron.*, I, 115.)

MAY   Thomas Cranmer, Archbishop of Canterbury. Bishop Sampson of Chichester, who was supposed to preach, was arrested, and Cranmer preached the opposite of what Gardiner had preached in Lent. (G. Constant, *The Reformation in England*: I, *The English Schism*, London, 1934, pp. 313, 332.)

1541

FEB. 13   Dr. Edward Crome, Rector of St. Mary Aldermary. His first public recantation of his opinions contrary to the Act of Six Articles, commanded because there had been "vanity of opinions and contentions among the people of London" about his sermons. Among other things he declared: "No man syns the Apostles hathe auctorytie to ordeyne any thing as an Artycle of our faythe; notwithstanding every kinge and prince within his Realme hathe auctorytie to ordeyne dyverse things whyche the subjects are bounde to observe and keape obedyentlye." (Foxe-Townshend, V, 835, and app. xvi.)

JULY 17   [Nicholas?] Wilson. Before the sermon began, Robert Wisdom (see below, July 8, 1543), was arrested by the Bishop of London's summoner, and examined that afternoon on suspicion of heresy. (Sherwin Bailey, "Robert Wisdom under Persecution, 1541-1543," *Journal of Ecclesiastical History*, II (1951), 183.)

OCT. 16   Two priests did penance for performing the marriage of the son of Mr. Heringe, a proctor in the Arches, "to a yong gentlewoman without license or asking," she having been contracted before. This was a breach of the statute 32 Hen. VIII, c. 38, regulating pre-contract. (*Wrioth. Chron.*, I, 130.)

NOV. 13   Dr. Richard Smith, first regius professor of divinity at Oxford, and "the greatest pillar of the Roman Catholic cause in his time." An orthodox sermon against the Protestant doctrines. He was attacked by Alexander Seton, "a Scottish man, and worthy preacher" (Foxe), in the church of

St. Antholine's the same afternoon, for his doctrine of works and his interpretation of *reconciliamini Deo*. (Foxe-Townshend, V, 448-50.)

DEC. 18   Mr. Rudd, chantry priest of Barking. The occasion of the recantation of Alexander Seton and of William Tolwyn, parson of St. Antholine's. Tolwyn began: "Good peple so yt is that I . . . have bene lawfully denounced detected and presented . . . that I have bene and am a man vehementlye suspected noted and infamed of heretycall and sedicyouse oppynyons agenst the catholyke faythe of owr holye mother the churche." "Erroneous heretycall and noughtye bokes" found in his house included works by Frith, Melanchthon, and Zwingli, and a Lollard (?) work called "Thorpe and olde castell." (*Wrioth Chron.*, I; Foxe-Townshend, V, 451; Tolwyn's recantation in John Bale, *Yet a course at the Romyshe foxe*, [Zurich, 1543].)

1543

JULY 8   The recantations of Thomas Becon, Robert Wisdom, and Robert Singleton. Becon was a prominent pamphleteer; Wisdom had been curate to Dr. Crome; Singleton was at one time chaplain to Anne Boleyn, one of Cromwell's "clerical spies" (Philip Hughes), and was later hanged for sedition. Becon cut in pieces eleven of his "unlawful" books; Wisdom recanted his heresy in denying free-will and preaching against veneration of saints. Singleton confessed briefly that he was "an unlearned fantastycall foole." (*Wrioth. Chron.*, I, 142; Foxe-Townshend, V, app. xii; *VCH London*, I, 283.)

1544

JULY 6   One John Haywood [Hayward?] recanted his blindly holding to the supremacy of Rome, and concealing and favouring others of that opinion. He declared the King's clemency in not putting him to death as his offence deserved. (*L & P Hen. VIII*, XIX (1), no. 853; Foxe-Townshend, V, 528-9.)

——   The recantation of Robert Warde, who had spoken irreverently of the mass, had kept unlawful books, and, as he put it, " I have dyverse tymes in alehouses and uncomelie and unmeate places taken upon me to bable talke and rangle of the Scriptures whiche I understode not yea and to expounde it after my folyshe fantasie chieflie in those tymes when I have not ben myne owne man but over come with Ale." (Foxe-Townshend, V, app. xi.)

1544(?)   Cuthbert Scott, after Bishop of Chester. (*Ath. Cantab.*, I, 233.)

1545

FEB. 8   A priest of Kent did penance for counterfeiting the blood of Christ at mass, by "cutting of hys fynger and [making] it to blede on the host."

For his penance he wore "a broad stole of linen cloath, couloured with drops like bloud." (*Wrioth. Chron.*, I, 152.)

1546

APRIL 25   A sermon against Dr. Crome. "The v. sarmondes [at the Spital and Paul's Cross] spake all agayne the sayd oppynyons" of the sacrament of the altar. (*Grey Friars Chron.*, p. 50.)

MAY 9   Dr. Edward Crome. He failed satisfactorily to recant his opinions concerning the sacrament of the altar, asserting: "I said, and say again, that the Bishop of Rome hath wrongly applied the sacrifice of the mass making it a satisfaction for sins of the quick and the dead, as he hath done the bloud of martyrs oftentimes." (Strype, *EM*, III (1), 161–4; Foxe-Townshend, V, 835; cf. *L & P Hen. VIII*, XXI (1), nos. 783, 790, 810, 1127.)

JUNE 27   Dr. Edward Crome. His final recantation. The news of his "canting, recanting, decanting, or rather double canting" was that he on this occasion "openly declared the true meaning and right onderstanding" of the Six Articles, "as he shuld have done upon the ijde Sunday after Ester, but that he was letted from his said true intent by the persuasions of certain perverse mynded persons." (*Original Letters*, ed. Ellis, ser. 2, II, no. 177; Foxe-Townshend, V, 836 and app. xvi; cf. *L & P Hen. VIII*, XXI (1), no. 1138.)

AUG. 1   Nicholas Shaxton, formerly Bishop of Salisbury. He recanted his heresy of the sacrament of the altar, i.e. denial of the corporal Presence. He declared his error the result of "hereticall books of English," and "wepte sore and made great lamentacion of hys offens." (*Wrioth. Chron.*, I, 170; *Grey Friars Chron.*, p. 51.)

SEPT. 26   Heretical books were burned in the sermon time, including Tyndale's Testament and Coverdale's Bible. (*Wrioth. Chron.*, I, 175.)

1547

JAN. 16   John Feckenham, chaplain to the Bishop of London. He deplored the advance of German heresy among the younger generation. "Sanctimony of life is put away, with fasting . . . and beads." The Germans, he said, were seditious heretics of 300 sects, with Frederic Duke of Saxony as their first defender. (*L & P Hen. VIII*, XXI (2), no. 710.)

JAN. 30   Nicholas Heath, Bishop of Rochester. He "declared the Kinges gift geaven to the cittie of London for the releeving of the poore people," i.e., the Grey Friars endowment of 500 marks per year. The audience did not know that the King had been dead two days. (*Wrioth. Chron.*, I, 177.)

EDWARD VI

1547

LENT — William Barlow, Bishop of St. David's; Nicholas Ridley, Master of Pembroke Hall, Cambridge; Hugh Glasier, Cranmer's commissary for Calais. All preached against veneration of images, and Glasier said that "Lent was not ordained of God to be fasted . . . but that the same was a politic ordinance of man, and might therefore be broken of men at their pleasure." (A. F. Pollard, *The History of England from the Accession of Edward VI to the Death of Elizabeth*, London, 1923, p. 14; Burnet-Pocock, II, 37; Strype, *EM*, II (1), 40.)

MAY 15 — Dr. Richard Smith, of King's College, Oxford. He recanted his two papistical books, one written in defence of the mass, the other in defence of unwritten verities. (See above, Nov. 13, 1541.) The books were burned in the sermon time. (*Wrioth Chron.*, I, 184; Strype, *EM*, II (1), 52, 61; see *STC* 22822.)

Nov.(?) — Nicholas Ridley. He preached against abuse of the sacrament of the altar by "the unreverend behaviour of certain evil disposed persons." He was misunderstood by some who thought he preached transubstantiation. (Foxe-Townshend, VI, 437; VII, 520, 523.)

Nov. 27 — William Barlow, Bishop of St. David's. He showed and broke two images, one of the Virgin, "which they of Paul's had lapped in cerecloth" and hidden in a corner of the cathedral; and a picture of the Resurrection "made with vices, which putt out his legges of sepulchre and blessed with his hand, and turned his head." After the sermon, "the boys broke the idols in pieces." (*Wrioth. Chron.*, II, 1.)

1548

JAN. 1 — Hugh Latimer. His first sermon in eight years. (John Stow, *Annales*, (1615), p. 595.)

JAN. 8 — Hugh Latimer. A sermon in which he affirmed "that whatsoever the cleargie commanded, ought to be obeyed, but he also declared that the Cleargie are such as sit in Moyses chaire, and breake not their masters commission: adding nothing thereto, nor taking anie thing there from: and such a cleargie must be obeyed of all men, both high and low." (Stow, *Annales*, p. 595.)

JAN. 15 — Hugh Latimer. (Stow, *Annales*, p. 595.)

JAN. 18 — Hugh Latimer. The famous "Sermon of the Ploughers." It was preached in the Shrouds. (*Sermons*, Everyman, 1926, pp. 54–71.)

JAN. 29 — Hugh Latimer. (Stow, *Annales*, p. 595.) It is possible that Latimer preached eight sermons at the Cross in this month; see Allan G. Chester, *Hugh Latimer, Apostle to the English* (Philadelphia, 1954), p. 163.

JUNE 29	Stephen Gardiner, Bishop of Winchester. He had offered to preach at Paul's Cross to clear himself of charges of misbehaviour in his diocese, during his residence there in Lent. Before an immense audience, he defended the royal supremacy and the dissolution of chantries, but in spite of Somerset's prohibition, he upheld the Catholic doctrine of the mass. (G. Constant, *The Reformation in England*: II. *Introduction of the Reformation into England, Edward VI*, London, 1941, pp. 232 ff.)
JULY 8	Richard Cox, the King's Almoner. He spoke of the sermon of June 29, and of Gardiner's obstinacy, exhorting the audience to pray for Gardiner's conversion to the truth, "and not to rejoice of this his troble, which was godlie done." "All thoys preachers that prechyd at Powlles crosse at that time spake moche agayne the bysshope of Wynchester." (*Wrioth. Chron.*, II, 4; *Grey Friars Chron.*, p. 56; Foxe-Townshend, V, 763.)
JULY 22	Matthew Parker, Vice-Chancellor of Cambridge. Somerset ordered him to preach, "not doubting but that you will purely and sincerely set out the holy scriptures, so as God's glory may be advanced, and the people with wholesome doctrine edified." (*Parker Correspondence*, p. 39.)
Nov. 11	Robert Ferrar, Bishop of St. David's. This was the first sermon after the inhibition of preaching by proclamation of September 28. "He dyd not preche in hys abbet [habit] of a byshoppe, but lyke a prest, and he spake agayne all maner of thynges of the churche and the sacrament of the auter, and vestmenttes, coppes, alterres, with all other thynges." (*Grey Friars Chron.*, p. 57; *VCH London*, I, 292.)
1549	
APRIL 28	Miles Coverdale. The Rehearsal sermon. John Champneys, of Stratford on the Bow, recanted his Anabaptist heresies. (*Narratives of the Days of the Reformation*, ed. J. G. Nichols, Camden Society, 1859, p. 295; *Wrioth. Chron.*, II, 10.)
MAY 5	One Putto, a farmer of Colchester, did penance. He had denied the article of the Creed concerning Christ's descent into hell. (*Wrioth. Chron.*, II, 12; Miles Hogarde, *Displaying of Protestants* (1556), sig. B ijv.)
MAY 12	An Anabaptist, a butcher, dwelling by Old Fish Street, bore a faggot. (*Wrioth Chron.*, II, 12.)
MAY 19	Putto did penance again, having stood the first time with his cap on, which was in the people's estimation impenitent. (*Wrioth. Chron.*, II, 13.)
JUNE 10, 11	(Whitsuntide) Miles Coverdale and William Bill, of Cambridge. Both preached at the Lord Mayor's appointment. (*Wrioth. Chron.*, II, 14.)
JULY 21	[John] Joseph, chaplain to Cranmer, after communion celebrated in the cathedral, according to the "King's book." He rehearsed Cranmer's sermon on the evils of sedition showed by the present commotion in the

kingdom, i.e., the risings in Devon and Norfolk. (*Wrioth. Chron.*, II, 18.)

SEPT. 1 Edmund Bonner, Bishop of London. He had been ordered to preach in favour of the new religion, and to set forth the King's prerogative in his minority, but failed to perform the articles satisfactorily. He "did spend most part of his sermon about the gross, carnal, and papistical presence of Christ's body and blood in the sacrament" (Foxe). (*Wrioth. Chron.*, II, 24; *VCH London*, I, 293-4; Foxe-Townshend, V, 745-6.)

SEPT. 22 John Hooper, afterwards Bishop of Gloucester. A sermon against Bonner, preached on Cranmer's orders. (*Grey Friars Chron.*, p. 63.)

SEPT. 29 The sermon was preached in the Shrouds. A man did penance for "conjuring." (Margaret E. Cornford, *Paul's Cross: A History*, London, 1910, p. 92.)

—— Sir Stephen, curate of St. Katherine Cree. An invective against the maypole of St. Andrew Undershaft, which was taken down the same afternoon and sawed in pieces. The preacher also declared himself in favour of altering the (presumably superstitious) names of churches and days of the week, and said that Lent might be kept any time except between Shrovetide and Easter. (John Stow, *The Survey of London*, Everyman, n.d., p. 130.)

1550

FEB. 2 Thomas Lever, Master of St. John's College, Cambridge. A well-known sermon against wilful rebellion and social injustice. (*Sermons*, in *English Reprints*, ed. E. Arber, Birmingham, 1870, pp. 21-51.)

MARCH 30 A sermon of thanksgiving for peace with France, attended by the Lord Mayor and the aldermen in their scarlet. (*Wrioth. Chron.*, II, 35.)

MAY 25 Nicholas Ridley, Bishop of Rochester. (*Grey Friars Chron.*, p. 66.)

MAY 26 John Hooper, named but not consecrated Bishop of Gloucester. (*Wrioth. Chron.*, II, 50.)

MAY 27 Mr. Cottesfurth [Thomas(?) Cottisford]. (*Wrioth. Chron.*, II, 40.)

JUNE 1 [Thomas] Kyrkham. He asserted that in the sacrament "w[as no] substance but brede and wynne." This was now the official view. This sermon was doubtless part of a programme to suppress the old ritual and belief. See Pollard, *History*, p. 53. (*Grey Friars Chron.*, p. 67.)

AUG. 31 Stephen Caston, clerk. He "spake agayne the Lady Mary as moch as he myghte, but he namyd not hare, but sayd ther was a gret woman, within the realme that was a gret supporter . . . of popery and superstycione, and prayed that she myght forsake hare oppynyons, and to follow the kynges prosedynges, as he sayed. And also he sayed that Henry the viij was a papist, with many obprobryous wordes of hym as yt was harde." (*Grey Friars Chron.*, p. 67.)

DEC. 14   Thomas Lever. A brilliant sermon against "Wicked Mammon," with a famous account of the sad case of the universities. (*Sermons*, pp. 91–143.)

1551

MARCH 16   Matthew Parker, appointed by Cranmer on order of the Council. Cranmer exhorted him "purely and sincerely to set forth God's word there and to exhort your audience to their duties, obedience to his Majesty's highness' laws and statutes and to unity and charity among themselves as appertaineth." (*Parker Correspondence*, p. ix, n.)

post JULY 25   Matthew Parker. Ridley commanded him to preach, warning him of the danger of refusal. Parker had apparently, with characteristic diffidence, pleaded off an earlier request. (*Parker Correspondence*, p. 45.)

1552

NOV. 1   Nicholas Ridley, Bishop of London. An afternoon sermon, after a morning service in which the second Book of Common Prayer was introduced. The sermon lasted till five o'clock, so wearying the Lord Mayor and aldermen that they went straight home, and "came not with-in Pawlles . . . as they were wonte to doo." (*Grey Friars Chron.*, p. 76; *Wrioth. Chron.*, II, 78.)

DEC. 11   Hugh Latimer. He drew attention to the unsanitary condition of Paul's churchyard. (*VCH London*, I, 322.)

1553

MAY 21   Nicholas Ridley, Bishop of London. (*Wrioth. Chron.*, II, 84.)

MARY I

JULY 9   Nicholas Ridley, Bishop of London. Preaching in support of Lady Jane, he called Mary and Elizabeth illegitimate, "and so found both by the clargie and actes of Parliament made . . . in Kinge Henry the VIIIts dayes." "All the pepull was sore anoyd with hys worddes, soo uncherytabulle, spokyne in soo opyne ane audiens." He further "press'd the Incommodities and Inconveniences" of Mary's accession, and declared that "she would subvert the True Religion" now established, witnessing her stubbornness when he sought to turn her from Rome. (*Grey Friars Chron.*, p. 78; Foxe-Townshend, VI, 389–90; Peter Heylyn, *Ecclesia restaurata* (1670), I, 162. *Wrioth. Chron.*, II, 88 gives July 16.)

JULY 16   John Rogers, first of the Marian martyrs. A sermon avoiding politics. (Foxe-Townshend, VI, 590; Pollard, *History*, p. 135.)

AUG. 6(?)   John Rogers. "After the queen was come to the Tower of London [Aug 3], he, being orderly called [to the Cross], made a godly and vehement sermon . . . confirming such true doctrine as he and others had there taught in King Edward's days, exhorting the people constantly to remain in the same, and to beware of all pestilent popery, idolatry, and superstition." (Foxe-Townshend, VI, 592.)

AUG. 13   Dr. Gilbert Bourne, chaplain to the Queen. He praised Bonner, was attacked by the crowd, and saved from injury by John Bradford and others. A notorious incident, of which there are many accounts, propagandist and contradictory. (*Wrioth. Chron.*, II, 97-8; Machyn, p. 41; *Grey Friars Chron.*, p. 83.)

AUG. 20   Dr. Thomas Watson, chaplain to the Bishop of Winchester. He was surrounded by 200 of the Queen's guard. He declared "the obedience of subjects," and exhorted the people "not to believe the preacheres, [i.e., Bradford, Veron, Rogers, Becon, etc.] but that ther faith should be firme and sure . . . , to keep the ould faithe, and edifye the ould Temple againe." (Machyn, p. 41; *Wrioth. Chron.*, II, 99-100; *Grey Friars Chron.*, p. 83; Foxe-Townshend, VI, 768.)

AUG. 27   Dr. William Chedsey. (Foxe-Townshend, VI, 538.)

SEPT. 24   John Feckenham. "A godly sarmon as was hard in that place." (Machyn, p. 144.)

OCT. 22   Hugh Weston, Dean of Westminster. He announced a disputation between the men of the old faith and the Protestants at Convocation. At the beginning of his sermon he willed the people to pray for the souls departed. "He named the Lord's table an oyster-board. He said, that the catechism in Latin, lately set out, was abominable heresy, and likened the setters-out of the same catechism to Julian the Apostate, and the book to a dialogue set out by the same Julian . . . , wherein Christ and Pilate were the speakers" (Foxe). (Machyn, p. 46; Foxe-Townshend, VI, 541; VII, 778.)

NOV. 12   James Brooks, Master of Balliol, afterwards Bishop of Gloucester. The daughter of Jairus (Matt. 9:18) considered "in a mistical sence" as the Church of England, dead in schism, her livings bestowed on preachers of erroneous doctrine, her benefices and tithes, even "the best part of the temporalities of Bishoprikes," spoiled by the greedy laity. But God has raised up "a godlie governesse," "suche an Helena, as shoulde be an ernest restorer of the crucifixe of Christ." Protestants censured the sermon, saying that he made himself to be Jairus, England his daughter, and the Queen Christ (*DNB*). **A sermon very notable, fruictefull, and Godlie* (1553).

1554

APRIL 8   Dr. Henry Pendleton, chaplain to Bonner. A cat made like a priest ready to say mass, with a shaven crown, which was hung on the cross in Cheapside, was exhibited at the Cross. A reward of 20 nobles was offered for the apprehension of the guilty person, but "none could or would earn it." (*Wrioth. Chron.*, II, 114; *Grey Friars Chron.*, p. 88; Foxe-Townshend, VI, 548.)

JUNE 10   Dr. Henry Pendleton, chaplain to Bonner. He was shot at during his sermon; the pellet hit the church wall near where the Lord Mayor sat. Search was made vainly in every house in the precinct of Paul's. (Machyn, p. 65; *Wrioth. Chron.*, II, 117; *Grey Friars Chron.*, p. 90.)

JULY 15   Dr. John Wymmesley, Archdeacon of London. The occasion of the public penance of Elizabeth Croft, who had practised a fraud of a "voice in a wall" which spoke various seditious matters concerning the mass and the King of Spain. She "made this exclamation upon them which had procured her to do that feat, saying, Wo be unto you heretikes, phy upon you all, that thus have the Lorde in your mouthes and the divell in your hartes. This present day have I a good cause to crie out unto you, that in this sorte have brought me to offende God and the Quenes majestie." (*Wrioth. Chron.*, II, 117-8; *Grey Friars Chron.*, p. 90; Hogarde, *Displaying of Protestants*, sig. o7v.)

JULY 29   Nicholas Harpsfield, Archdeacon of Canterbury. He prayed "in ys bedes" for the King (Philip II) and the Queen. (Machyn, p. 66.)

SEPT. 23   John Rudd, Vicar of Norton, Durham (deprived). In his sermon "he recantyd and repentyd that he ever was mared [married], and sayd openly that he cold not more by Gods law." (Machyn, p. 69.)

SEPT. 30   Stephen Gardiner, Lord Chancellor. Many of the Council were present, to hear him condemn the preachers of Edward's reign and praise Philip II. (Machyn, p. 69; Foxe-Townshend, VI, 559-60; *The Chronicle of Queen Jane*, ed. J. G. Nichols, Camden Society, 1850, p. 82.)

OCT. 14   Cuthbert Tunstall, Bishop of Durham. (Foxe-Townshend, VI, 561.)

NOV. 4   Nicholas Harpsfield, Archdeacon of Canterbury. Five priests who were content to put away their wives (Foxe), or four priests and "a temprall man" who had two wives (Machyn), did penance in sheets, with tapers, and rods with which the preacher struck them as he "showyd their oppynyons." (Machyn, pp. 73-4; Foxe-Townshend, VI, 561.)

NOV. 11   Dr. Henry Pendleton, chaplain to Bonner. (Machyn, p. 74.)

NOV. 18   John White, Bishop of Lincoln. (Machyn, p. 76.)

NOV. 25 John Feckenham, Dean of St. Paul's. (Machyn, p. 76.)

DEC. 2 Stephen Gardiner, Lord Chancellor. Philip II and Cardinal Pole were present on this notable occasion. Gardiner preached on behalf of the old faith, and published Pole's papal commission to receive England back into the Catholic fold. He "wondered how the people could, without rebelling, bear such injuries, oppressions, and robberies, which they sustained, as he said, in the fall of money, and otherwise, in King Edward's reign." (*Wrioth. Chron.*, II, 124–5; *Chronicle of Queen Jane*, pp. 161–3; Strype, *EM*, III (1), 259.)

DEC. 9 Gilbert Bourne, Bishop of Bath and Wells. He prayed for the Pope and for souls in purgatory. (Machyn, p. 78.)

DEC. 16 George Coates, Bishop of Chester. On the mass. (Machyn, p. 79.)

1555

JAN. 14 William Chedsey, priest of Allhallows, Bread Street. (Machyn, p. 80.)

MAY 19 Nicholas Harpsfield, Archdeacon of Canterbury. Occasion of the penance of two women who confessed to promoting a fraud in connection with a new-born child who was supposed to have spoken and "sayd that the kyngdom of God ys at hand." (*Wrioth. Chron.*, II, 128–9; Machyn, p. 88.)

MAY 26 William Chedsey, priest of Allhallows, Bread Street. Proclamation of procession and prayer for peace with France, and publication of Bonner's orders from the Council for the suppression of heresy in his diocese of London. (Foxe-Townshend, VII, 286; VIII, 451.)

AUG. 25 Hugh Glasier, chaplain to the Queen. An appeal against heresies and schisms, with a refutation of those who would explain the bad weather of the past two years as God's judgment for the return of the "idolatrous" mass. He vigorously attacked those who enjoyed the spoils of the church: "In dede it were a great shame for so many of you to lie in beddes, & set upon quisshins, made of the Churche stuffe, for the whiche ye have payed, either little or nothing at all." **A notable and very fruictefull sermon* (1555).

SEPT. 15 The Pope's bull of plenary remission declared to "as mony as wyll reseyffe ys pardon so to be shryff, and fast iii days in one wyke, and to reseyffe the blessed sacrament the next Sonday after, clen remyssyon of all ther synes *tossyens quossyens* of all that they ever dyd." (*Wrioth. Chron.*, II, 130; Machyn, p. 94.)

NOV. 26 "A stripling" was whipped about the city, and about Paul's Cross, for speaking there against the bishop who had preached there the previous Sunday. (Strype, *EM*, III (1), 363.)

Dec. 15 An old shepherd created a disturbance before the sermon, by speaking "serten thynges and raylyng." He was taken to the Counter. (Machyn, p. 98.)

1556
Feb. 8 William Peryn, Prior of the Dominican house of St. Bartholomew in Smithfield. "At the same sermon was a prest, on ser Thomas Samsun, dyd penance for he had ij wyffes, and a shett abowt hym, and a tapur in ys hand bornyng a-for the precher, and the mayre of London and the altherman and worshipfull men, and many odur." (Machyn, p. 100.)

March 8 "Ther was a man dyd penance with ij pyges rede dythe [dight?] . . . , the [which] he browth them to selle." (Machyn, p. 101.)

June 14 John Feckenham, Dean of St. Paul's. He declared that thirteen heretics condemned to be burned "had as many sundry opinions as they were sundry persons." (Foxe-Townshend, VIII, 154–6.)

Oct. 18 John White, Bishop of Winchester. (Strype, EM, III (1), 503.)

1557
Feb. 14 John Young, Vice-Chancellor of Cambridge. (Ath. Cantab., I, 428.)

Feb. 21 John Young, Vice-Chancellor of Cambridge. (Ath. Cantab., I, 428.)

March(?) Cardinal Pole's instructions for confession and fasting proclaimed. (VCH London, I, 303.)

April 16 Mr. "Murryn" [John Morwen]. "Ther was grett audyens." (Machyn, p. 131.)

May 2 Dr. William Chedsey. He "declared that serten trayturs that was taken at Skarborow castyll, the wyche they fled over the see a-for." Presumably this was a sermon pointing the moral of the fantastic treason of Thomas Stafford, in April. See Pollard, History, p. 164. (Machyn, p. 135.)

June 20 John Feckenham, Abbot of Westminster. He "mad a godly sermon of Dyves and Lazarus, and the crossear [cross-bearer] holdyng the stayffe at ys prechyng; and ther wher gret audyense." (Machyn, pp. 139–40.)

Aug. 15 Nicholas Harpsfield, Archdeacon of Canterbury. The sermon of thanksgiving for St. Quentin, i.e. for the rout of the French relieving army on August 10. He "declared how many wher taken, and what nobull men they were." (Machyn, p. 147.)

Nov. 21 John Feckenham, Abbot of Westminster. (Machyn, p. 158.)

1558
Jan. 30 John White, Bishop of Winchester. (Machyn, p. 164.)

Feb. 6	Cuthbert Scott, Bishop of Chester. There were sixteen bishops, many judges, besides the mayor and aldermen, at the sermon. (Machyn, p. 165.)
Feb. 20	Thomas Watson, Bishop of Lincoln. (Machyn, p. 166.)
March 6	John Feckenham, Abbot of Westminster. (Machyn, p. 168.)

UNDATED SERMONS TEMP. MARY I

A preacher named P——. "1545. The Stewes & publike bordell houses about London & in other places of England, are abolished, & so continue untill the time of Quene Mary; in whose dayes, some of the Clergy made labour to have them restored againe, & were very likely to have obteined their sute if she had lived a while longer; soche trees, soche frute: 'for the stewes,' saith one of them in a sermon made at Paules crosse, 'are so necessary in a comon welth, as a jaxe in a mannes house:' his name I spare, sith it shall suffice that it beginneth with the same letter that papa [Pope] dothe." (Harrison's *Chronologie*, in New Shakspere Society Publications, ser. 6. no. 1, li.)

ELIZABETH I

1558

Nov. 20	Dr. William Bill, the Queen's chaplain and almoner. This sermon was preached by royal order, on Cecil's suggestion in a memorial to Queen Elizabeth. (Machyn, p. 178; Strype, *Annals*, I (1), 50.)
Nov. 27	John Christopherson, Bishop of Chichester. He made a vehement answer to Bill, loudly exclaiming: "Believe not this new doctrine; it is not the gospel, but a new invention of new men and heretics." (*The Zurich Letters*, ed. Hastings Robertson, Parker Society, 1842–5, I, 4; R. W. Dixon, *History of the Church of England*, Oxford, 1902, V, 5.)

1559

Feb. 10	Matthew Parker. He was called to the Cross during the time when he was attempting to escape the archbishopric. (According to Holinshed (1808), IV, 180, there were no sermons at Paul's Cross between Christmas 1558 and April 1559.) (W. H. Frere, *The English Church in the Reigns of Elizabeth and James I*, London, 1911, p. 7.)
April 2	Thomas Sampson (see above, Feb. 8, 1556). The rehearsal sermon. The Spital sermons had been preached by William Bill, Richard Cox, and Robert Horne. The pulpit had been locked during the inhibition of preaching, and when opened it was found in filthy condition. (Machyn, p. 192; *Wrioth. Chron.*, II, 144.)
April 9	Dr. William Bill. He explained the imprisonment of Bishops Watson and White in the Tower, where they were imprisoned for seditious

REGISTER 201

behaviour in the Westminster disputations concerning the supremacy. (Machyn, p. 149; see Pollard, *History*, pp. 205–6.)

MAY 14   Edmund Grindal. Before an audience which included many members of the Council, he proclaimed the restoration of "King Edward's Book." No dignitary of St. Paul's was present; the cathedral still adhered to the Latin service. (Machyn, p. 197; Dixon, *History*, V, 106.)

MAY 21   Robert Horne, Bishop of Winchester.
MAY 28   William Barlow, Bishop of Chichester.
JUNE 11 Edmund Sandys, Bishop of Worcester.
JUNE 18 John Jewel, Bishop of Salisbury.
JUNE 25 Thomas Bentham, Bishop of Coventry and Lichfield.
AUG. 13 John Scory, Bishop of Hereford.

The new bishops (preaching May 21–August 13) appear in the first pulpit of the kingdom. (Machyn, pp. 197–206.)

AUG. 20 Penance of a minister for performing an illegal marriage. (Machyn, p. 207.)

SEPT. 3 "One Makebray, a Skott." John MacBray, formerly pastor of the Church of the White Ladies in Frankfort. (Machyn, p. 208.)

SEPT. 10 Dr. William Turner, botanist, author of *The Huntyng of the Romyshe Wolfe*, and Dean of Wells. (Machyn, p. 210.)

SEPT. 17 John Veron, a Frenchman, ardent Reformer. "And ther he sayd, Wher are the [Marian] bysshopes [and] old prechers? now they byd ther bedes." (Machyn, p. 211.)

SEPT. 24 John Huntington, who had been in exile with John Bale in Germany; "eloquens orator ecclesiasticus cluebat." (Machyn, p. 212; *Ath. Oxon.*, I, 24.)

OCT. 15 Robert Crowley, publisher of *Piers Plowman* (1550), afterwards a power on the Puritan side in the vestiarian controversy. (Machyn, p. 215.)

NOV. 12 Miles Coverdale. (Machyn, p. 218.)

NOV. 19 Thomas Bentham, Bishop of Coventry and Lichfield. (Machyn, p. 218.)

NOV. 26 John Jewel, Bishop of Salisbury. The first statement of the famous challenge to the papists to prove their doctrines by authority, which was repeated in a sermon at court the following March, and at the Cross March 31, 1560. (Machyn, p. 218.)

1560

JAN. 7   Edmund Grindal, Bishop of London. (Machyn, p. 222.)

FEB. 20	Alexander Nowell, Dean of St. Paul's. In the course of his sermon, speaking of the defence legitimately to be used by a Protestant, he said something about his buckler and a papist's face, which caused some stir. The controversialist Dorman afterwards charged him with it in print. A man did penance for bigamy in the sermon time. (Machyn, p. 226; Dixon, *History*, V, 314.)
MARCH 3	Edmund Grindal, Bishop of London. After the sermon the audience sang a psalm. (Machyn, p. 226.)
MARCH 10	John Scory, Bishop of Hereford. (Machyn, p. 227.)
MARCH 17	John Veron, Vicar of St. Martin's in Ludgate. "After the sermon done they songe all, old and yong, a salme in myter, the tune of Genevay ways." (Machyn, p. 228.)
MARCH 20	Thomas Bentham, Bishop of Coventry and Lichfield. (Strype, *Annals*, I (1), 298; a doubtful entry.)
MARCH 24	Edmund Sandys, Bishop of Worcester. (John Nichols, *The Progresses and Public Processions of Queen Elizabeth*, London, 1823, I, 83.)
MARCH 31	John Jewel, Bishop of Salisbury. A repetition of the challenge sermon of November 26, 1559. (*The Works of John Jewel, Bishop of Salisbury*, Parker Society, 1845, I, 3-25.)
APRIL 7	Robert Wisdom. See above, July 8, 1543. (Machyn, p. 230.)
APRIL 21	Thomas Sampson, whe had been offered but refused the bishopric of Norwich. The Rehearsal sermon. (Machyn, p. 231.)
APRIL 28	Miles Coverdale. (Machyn, p. 233.)
MAY 19	Richard Cox, Bishop of Ely. Someone found a wallet during the sermon; Machyn did not find the occasion otherwise memorable. (Machyn, p. 235.)
MAY 26	Edmund Scambler, chaplain to Archbishop Parker, afterwards Bishop of Norwich. "These sermons so well and learnedly performed [in 1560], at which assembled such vast confluence of auditors . . . , reconciled great respect to the new religion, (as it was called) and to the persons of this clergy newly appearing out of their banishment and recesses, shining with clear consciences, and holy zeal for the truth and gospel." (Strype, *Annals*, I (1), 300; Machyn, p. 235.)

1561

JAN.	James Calfhill [Calfield], Canon of Christ Church, Oxford. He lamented the condition of Oxford, still under the papistical yoke. "He published the dissimulations of the papists, and their practice to dissuade young men from the truth, in such sort that he moved a number to tears." He was blessed

	"with an excellent tongue and rhetorical tale which ravished the minds of his hearers." (Strype, *Annals*, I (1), 236–7; Dixon, *History*, V, 314.)
FEB. 9	James Pilkington, Bishop of Durham. Cecil and others of the Council were present. (Machyn, p. 248.)
MARCH 23	A bishop. (Machyn, p. 253.)
APRIL 13	John Jewel, Bishop of Salisbury. (Machyn, p. 255.)
JUNE 8	James Pilkington, Bishop of Durham. Pointing the lesson of the fire which burned the steeple of Paul's, he preached obedience and good order. (Since the Catholics naturally laid the burden of God's wrath on the Reformers, the sermon was answered by an *Addicion*, to which Pilkington replied with *A Confutation of an Addition*.) (*The Works of James Pilkington, D.D.*, Parker Society, 1842, pp. 647–8.)
JUNE 15	Alexander Nowell, Dean of St. Paul's. A sermon exhorting the repair of the cathedral. (Machyn, p. 259; Nichols, *Elizabeth*, I, 90.)
JUNE 22	Ralph Skinner, Dean of Durham. He recanted the opinions in a book which he had published, and which he said was "very heresy." (Machyn, p. 261; Strype, *Annals*, I (1), 402.)
JULY 6	The sermon was preached at Grey Friars because of the weather. (Machyn, p. 262.)
AUG. 10	John Veron, Vicar of St. Martin's, Ludgate. (Machyn, p. 265.)
SEPT. 21	Matthew Hutton, Master of Trinity, Cambridge. (Machyn, p. 267.)
OCT. 12	Robert Crowley, "sum-tyme a boke-prynter." (Machyn, p. 269.)
NOV. 2	A young man did penance for speaking ill of John Veron. (Machyn, p. 271.)
NOV. 23	Michael Renniger, chaplain to the Queen. On this occasion, Henry Machyn, undertaker, assiduous sermon-goer and diarist, did penance himself for slandering Veron "the Frenchman." (He calls the penitent "monser Henry de Machyn," and deceived Strype. See *Annals*, I (1), 407; J. G. Nichols, Introduction to Machyn's *Diary*, p. x.) He had passed along the story that Veron was "taken with a wenche." He "knellyd down fore master Veron and the byshope [Grindal], and yett [they] would not for[give] hym, for alle ys fryndes that he had worshiphulle." (Machyn, pp. 272–3.)
DEC.	Nicholas Robinson, of Queens', Cambridge, after Bishop of Bangor. (*Ath. Cantab.*, I, 504.)

1562

JAN. 4   Alexander Nowell, Dean of St. Paul's. A dumb man did penance. He seems to have counterfeited dumbness, and was discovered by the masters of Bridewell. (Machyn, p. 274.)

MARCH 27   Miles Coverdale, Vicar of St. Magnus Martyr. (Machyn, p. 279.)

APRIL 5   Thomas Sampson. The Rehearsal sermon. Sampson was called on for these difficult performances—see April 2, 1559 and April 21, 1560—"in regard of his excellent elocution and memory" (Strype). (Machyn, p. 280.)

APRIL 19   Alexander Nowell, Dean of St. Pauls. (Machyn, p. 280.)

JUNE 21   "Master dene of Ettun colege be-syd Wyndsor." (Machyn, p. 286.)

OCT. 18   The publication of the Queen's recovery from "some extremity of sickness," with thanks to God for the same. The sermon was ordered by the Council, "because it may happen that some vain bruits may be spread abroad of the matter, especially in London." (John Strype, *The History of the Life and Acts of Edmund Grindal*, Oxford, 1821, pp. 96–7.)

NOV. 1   Edmund Grindal, Bishop of London. On October 28, he wrote to Cecil: "I pray you let me understand whether it may be certainly avouched that the King of Navarre, the second Julian [he had joined and then abandoned the Huguenots] is killed. I intend ... to preach at the cross the next Sunday, and upon occasion offered would peradventure make some mention of God's judgments over him, if the same be true and certain; else not. If there be any other matter which you wish to be uttered there for the present state, I would be pleased to know it in time, if your leisure will serve." (*The Remains of Edmund Grindal, D.D.*, Parker Society, 1843, p. 253.)

1563

FEB. 7   James Pilkington, Bishop of Durham. (Machyn, p. 299.)

MARCH 21   Robert Horne, Bishop of Winchester. (Machyn, p. 302.)

APRIL 18   William Bradley [Bradburn, Bradbridge], Dean of Salisbury. The Rehearsal sermon. One of the Spital sermons, by Horne, Bishop of Winchester, had been a plea for the French Protestants. (Machyn, p. 305; Strype, *Annals*, I (2), 2.)

SEPT.   [William?] Baldwin. He called for the gallows for the Marian bishops (this month released from the Tower to the custody of the bishops), and other papists. "Hymselfe died of ye plague the next weke after." (John Stow, "Historical Memoranda," in *Three Fifteenth Century Chronicles*, ed. James Gairdner, Camden Society, 1880, p. 126.)

1564

JAN. 26   Thomas Cole, Archdeacon of Essex. He rejoiced at the end of the plague, which he attributed to Romish superstition among the citizens. The Roman faith, he said, stood upon four "rotyn postis": images, purgatory, the mass, transubstantiation. The crafts in their liveries were present at this sermon. (Stow, "Memoranda," p. 128.)

APRIL 23   "A notable good sermon" of thanksgiving for peace with France, i.e., the Treaty of Troyes, April 11, 1564. (*Zurich Letters*, I, 133n.)

APRIL 30   Alexander Nowell, Dean of St. Paul's. He answered Harding's *An Answere to Maister Juelles Chalenge* (1564), reading some passages from it and confuting them, "wherein he had good reason, as he said, seeing the Papists who had not read the book, in corners magnified it above the stars." (Strype, *Annals*, I (2), 113.)

Nov. 19   Alexander Nowell, Dean of St. Paul's. A reply to Dormer's *Proufe of Certayne Articles* (1564), a treatise against Jewel's challenge. This sermon was probably a trial flight of the arguments used in Nowell's *Reproof of the Proof* (1565). He said "that ther was not one trew worde in Master Dormers boke latly brought ovar from beyonde ye seas." (Stow, "Memoranda," p. 130.)

1565

LENT   Thomas Sampson, Laurence Humphrey. Though nonconformist in the vestiarian controversy, they preached at the Cross, appointed out of Parker's authority, possibly by Leicester, possibly by the City authorities, possibly by Bishop Grindal. Parker wrote to Cecil suggesting the need of regular licensing of the Paul's Cross preachers. (*Parker Correspondence*, p. 239; Dixon, *History*, VI, 59.)

EASTER   Edmund Guest, Bishop of Rochester. It is not improper to assume that he "answered" Sampson and Humphrey. (*Parker Correspondence*, p. 240.)

MAY 27   John Jewel, Bishop of Salisbury. A criticism of Harding's *A Confutation of a Booke intituled An Apologie of the Church of England* (Louvain, 1565). He ridiculed some of Harding's authorities, notably "Amphilochius," and "mentioned also, it seems, out of that book, with some sport, a tale of Angels singing pricksong to St. Basil's Mass." Harding wrote to Jewel for a copy of the sermon. (Strype, *Annals*, I (2), 176, and app. xxx.)

JULY 8   John Jewel, Bishop of Salisbury. A second sermon criticizing Harding, likely a forerunner of his *A Replie to M. Hardinges Answeare*, published in August. (A. C. Southern, *Elizabethan Recusant Prose, 1555-1582*, London, 1950, p. 65.)

Nov. 11   Thomas Cole, Archdeacon of Essex. He likened priests to apes, "for, sayth he, they be both balld alyke, but yt the prestes be balld before, the appes behynd." Stow lists this, perhaps without irony, as "A Noate of Divinitye." (Stow, "Memoranda," p. 133.)

1566

JAN. 13   John Oxenbridge. On the mean state of Oxford. She was in piteous case, for there were not past "five or six preachers" there, except "strawberry preachers" (this was Latimer's famous description of non-resident churchmen). (*Sermons of Latimer*, ed. John Watkins, London, 1858, I, 58n.)

MARCH   Richard Cox, Bishop of Ely, *or* Edmund Scambler, Bishop of Peterborough. Cecil had submitted a "bill" or list of suitable persons to preach in Lent; Parker removed the name of Dr. Perne, then Master of Peterhouse. (*Parker Correspondence*, pp. 260-1.)

APRIL 7   Thomas Becon, then Vicar of Christ Church, Newgate.
APRIL 12 George Cary [Carew] Dean of Exeter.
APRIL 15 Robert Beaumont, Master of Trinity.
APRIL 16 John Young, after Bishop of Rochester.
APRIL 17 Thomas Becon(?).

These appointments for sermons through Easter week (April 7-17) reflect Parker's care to keep the Cross an official mouthpiece during the difficulties which followed the issue of his "Advertisements" in March. (*Parker Correspondence*, p. 275; M. M. Knappen, *Tudor Puritanism*, Chicago, 1939, p. 208.)

MAY 5   William Overton, Canon of Winchester. (*Ath. Cantab.*, II, 515.)

JUNE 4   Henry Wright, Rector of St. Stephen Walbrook. (*Ath. Cantab.*, II, 448.)

OCT. 6   Matthew Hutton, Master of Pembroke College, Cambridge. (*The Correspondence of Dr. Matthew Hutton*, Surtees Society, 1843, p. 54.)

1567

JUNE 15 John Jewel, Bishop of Salisbury. A protestation of his truthfulness, against Stapleton's *A Returne of Untruthes upon M. Jewels Replie*. (Southern, *Elizabethan Recusant Prose*, p. 65.)

Nov. 17 John Jewel, Bishop of Salisbury. A sermon on "Cursed be he that goeth about to build again the walls of Jericho," i.e., the Catholic faith. This was possibly a protest against the mooted marriage of Elizabeth to the Archduke. (J. E. Neale, *Queen Elizabeth*, London, 1934, p. 153.)

1568

MARCH 31 Alexander Nowell, Dean of St. Paul's. (*Parker Correspondence*, p. 318.)

1570

MARCH 24 (Good Friday)   John Foxe, the martyrologist. He wrote to Grindal urging his incapacity: "Consider also, in fairness . . . , how unequally this will press upon me, when, as I believe, there never yet was ass or mule who was so weighted down and overdone with carrying burthens, as I have long been by literary labours. . . . By these labours I am almost worn out, not to speak of ill health and want of books. Yet, amidst all these labours and defects . . . I am summoned where, like an ape among cardinals [he still declined conformity to the habits], I shall be received with derision, and driven away by the hisses of the auditory." The sermon is a vigorous exposition of the Protestant doctrine of redemption, and contains a characteristically long and thorough attack on the mass. *A Sermon of Christ crucified (1570).

—— Edwin Sandys, Bishop of London, on his entrance into his diocese. Protesting his unfitness for an "office full of peril and danger," wishing rather rest for "his wearish body, full of diseases and . . . almost worn away like a clout," he went on to speak of the necessary diligence and love in a pastor, and ended with an appeal to the citizens to help the poor of the diocese. (*The Sermons of Edwin Sandys, D.D.*, Parker Society, 1841, pp. 331–45.)

1570(?) John Bolton, elder in Richard Fitz's separatist congregation, recanted his heresies. He afterwards hanged himself, in remorse, it was said, for "judging and condemning a part of Christ's church." (Champlin Burrage, *The Early English Dissenters*, Cambridge, 1912, II, 9, 140.)

1571

APRIL 15(?) Richard Cox, Bishop of Ely. Like Jewel and Horne, who followed him, he defended the Establishment. The Parliament was sitting in which Strickland was inhibited, and Convocation was framing the so-called "Canons" of 1571. (John Strype, *The Life and Acts of Matthew Parker*, London, 1711, II, 58, 61.)

APRIL 22(?) John Jewel, Bishop of Salisbury. He defended the vestments, saying that men who had the wheat should not contend about the chaff, that black, white, round, and square are "the good creatures of God," that those who made a point of conscience out of vestments were sectaries. (*The Seconde Parte of a Register*, ed. Albert Peel, Cambridge, 1915, I, 79–80.)

APRIL 29 Robert Horne, Bishop of Winchester. He commended Jewel's sermon of April 22(?), and recommended Christian forbearance, said he would not deal with controversial matters, because the place was not meet nor the hearers fit judges. He wished those cut off that trouble the church. ("An awnser to such Arguments as B. Horne used . . . ," in *Seconde Parte of a Register*, I, 81–2.)

JUNE 3 John Bridges, Fellow of Pembroke College, Cambridge. A vigorous, colloquial and bitter attack upon Rome, in which he defended at great length the doctrine of justification by faith, and assaulted the Catholic faith at all points. *A Sermon preached at Paules Crosse [1571].

JUNE 10	"E. B." (*STC* lists the sermon as by Edward Bush; the Guildhall copy is attributed to Edmund Bunny, Fellow of Merton College, chaplain to Bishop Grindal.) An exhortation to the foolish and the wicked to fear God's judgments, in the course of which he showed his scrupulous temper in hinting that the Reformation in England had not gone far enough, since some "superstitious Vanities" were still kept. He made suit that men's consciences should not be forced in the matter of vestments, and feared the influence of popish priests still ministers in the Church of England. **A sermon preached at Pauls crosse* (1576).
AUG. 6	One Blackal, a clergyman of Exeter, did penance for scandalous life, or rather cried out upon "Northbroke" [John Northbrooke?], who had detected "his horrible vices." Blackal had four wives alive, and had "intruded himself into the ministry for the space of twelve years, and yet was never lawfully called, nor made minister by any bishop. He was a chopper and changer of benefices.... He would run from ... town to town, leading about with him naughty women. As in Gloucestershire he led a naughty strumpet about the country, named Green Apron. He altered his name wheresoever he went; going by these several names, Blackal, Barthal, Dorrel, Barkly, Baker." On August 10 he was set in the pillory in Cheapside for forging a commission to preach from the Archbishop. (Strype, *Annals*, II (1), 144.)

1572

JUNE 27	Thomas Cooper, Bishop of Lincoln. A sermon in answer to *An Admonition to the Parliament*. His sermon was "answered," from which it appears that Cooper, a "liberal churchman" (Frere), admitted the faults in the ministry, but opposed the Puritan "discipline" and defended the Book of Common Prayer and the dignity of bishops. (Strype, *Annals*, II (1), 286 ff.)
NOV. 2	John Whitgift, Master of Trinity College, Cambridge. He probably preached against Cartwright. (John Strype, *The Life and Acts of John Whitgift, D.D.*, Oxford, 1822, I, 96.)
———	Arthur Wake, Canon of Christ Church, Oxford. He "made a good sermon," having apparently not yet fallen under Cartwright's spell. But see August 2, 1573. (*Puritan Manifestoes*, ed. W. H. Frere and C. E. Douglas, London, 1907, p. xviii.)

1573

APRIL 26	Thomas Bickley, Warden of Merton College, Oxford, afterwards Bishop of Chichester. He admitted in his sermon that the Church of England had not "discipline," but was nevertheless accused of "catchyng and cavilling" to defame the Puritans. (*Seconde Parte of a Register*, I, 97, 98.)
ante AUG. 5	Richard Crick, chaplain to the Bishop of Norwich. He "most spitefully inveighed against the ecclesiastical pollicie now by lawe established, con-

firminge Mr. Cartwrights booke on the true platforme of the syncere and Apostolicall Church." (Sandys to Burghley, Aug. 5, 1573, in *Puritan Manifestoes*, p. xviii.)

AUG. 2   Arthur Wake, Canon of Christ Church, Oxford. He affirmed "to be good whatsoever Mr. Cartwright in writinge hath sett downe." He had been warned by Bishop Sandys not to speak sedition, particularly since the Queen was then in progress, far from London. He answered, "Well, well." (Sandys to Burghley, Aug. 5, 1573, in *Puritan Manifestoes*, p. xviii.)

ante Nov. 25   Edwin Sandys, Bishop of London. A sermon in which he admitted that there were "certain maculats" in the ministry, yet they ought to be removed by public authority, not by any private means. (*Seconde Parte of a Register*, I, 113; this may be the sermon in Sandys' *Sermons*, pp. 370–95.)

1574

AUG. 15   The penance of Agnes Bridges and Rachel Pinder, who pretended to possession by spirits. They had deceived many ministers in London, and their deceits had been published in pamphlets, to Archbishop Parker's disgust. There was "no small derision of profane persons when their forgery was discovered." (*Parker Correspondence*, pp. 465–6.)

1575

MAY 15   Four "Anabaptists Dutchmen" bearing faggots recanted their heresies at the Cross. Their conventicle had been discovered on April 3; two were burned at Smithfield on July 22. (A. F. Scott Pearson, *Thomas Cartwright and Elizabethan Puritanism*, Cambridge, 1925, p. 154.)

JUNE 12   Five English members of the Family of Love recanted "the damnable errors and heresies" of H[enry] N[icholas], the "author of that sect." (Holinshed (1808), IV, 328.)

OCT. 2   "Mr. Fairfax," probably Thomas Fairfax, of Queens' College, Cambridge, and preacher to the University. (*Salisbury Papers*, II, 117.)

1576

ante FEB. 8   Dr. Matthews [Tobie Matthew?]. His sermon, which touched on the delicate subject of the succession, gave occasion of offence. He tried to justify himself in a letter to Leicester. (*Hist. MSS. Comm., Fifth Report*, Part I (1876), 363.)

APRIL 20   John Knewstub, of St. John's College, Cambridge. An appeal for justice in the commonwealth, and an attack upon papists and Anabaptists. "Both of them howsoever in other things greatly differing, have this common principle for their foundation and beginning: that the Scriptures beeing but an ABC to Christianitie, the spelling and reading thereof must be drawne from their spirite, as if the Gospel should give place to revelations, and so carie with it the staine of imperfection: or as if the Spirite could be

	divorced from the written woorde, which it was sent to teach and confirme." *A Confutation of Monstrous & Horrible Heresies, taught by HN* (1579).
DEC. 9	Thomas White, Rector of St. Gregory's under St. Paul's. An exhortation to obedience, with praise of the Queen, "a ryght braunch" to reign over the kingdom and the church militant in England. He warned against the danger of conspiracies; we need, he said, Ulysses as well as Achilles. *A sermon Preached at Pawles Crosse* (1578).
1577	
FEB. 2	John Foxe, the martyrologist. The French Ambassador complained to the Queen, alleging that Foxe had said "that the protestants of France had great cause to take arms against their king, for that he admitted their public enemy the Pope." Foxe, summoned before the Bishop of London, said he had been replying to Osorius' charge that the French Protestants rejected lawful sovereignty: let the King of France but rule in his own right, and the Protestants would lay down their arms. (*APC*, ix, 294; J. F. Mozley, *John Foxe and His Book*, London, 1940, p. 93.)
MARCH 4	Richard Curteys, Bishop of Chichester. A description of the true church, and her triumph over the Dragon, with the dangers to her sovereignty and security from precisians and papists. *Two Sermons Preached by the ... Bishop of Chichester* (1576).
APRIL 30	Edwin Sandys, Archbishop of York. A farewell sermon on leaving the diocese of London. He likened himself to St. Paul leaving Corinth, and left them with an exhortation to godliness, brotherly love, and unity. (*Sermons*, pp. 418-30.)
OCT. 27	A sermon against "covetous Atheists." (Thomas White, *A Sermon Preached at Pawles Crosse* (1578), p. 34.)
NOV. 3	Thomas White, Rector of St. Gregory's under St. Paul's, the founder of Sion College. A recital of England's, and especially London's, sins: profanation of the Sabbath, playgoing, covetousness, corrupt magistrates. The plague has been sent as a judgment, he said, and he moved the people to repentance. *A Sermon Preached at Pawles Crosse ... in the time of the Plague* (1578).
1578	
AUG. 24	John Stockwood, Master of Tunbridge Grammar School. A sermon often quoted for its vehement attack on plays and players as immoral, wasteful, and Sabbath-breaking. The stern moralist also dealt with: the plain style in sermons, the errors of the papists, faith *vs.* works, the soldiers' trade, swearing, *cuius regio eius religio*, Machiavellians, ignorant ministers, profane

writers, bawdy books, and other occasions of sin. *A Sermon preached at Paules Crosse on Barthelmew day* [1578].

OCT. 5   John Walsal[l], Rector of Eastling, Kent, and tutor to Francis Bacon. A sermon on the nature and functions of the ministry, including an interesting defence of the "dumb dogs" against whom the Puritan agitators fulminated ceaselessly. Under the necessity of obedience to the Lord's prophets, he inveighed against idolatrous papists, carnal protestants, dancing, players and minstrels, usurers, and oppressors. *A Sermon Preached at Pauls Crosse* [1574].

OCT. 26   Laurence Chaderton, a strong Puritan from Emmanuel College, Cambridge. "A dreadful declaration of the final destruction of counterfeit and hypocrite professors of Gods word." In the process of discovering these hypocrites, he entered upon the Calvinist doctrine of works as confirming the certainty of election, and took occasion to reprehend preachers who depended upon "excellencie of words." He called for a fast to turn away the plague. *An Excellent and godly sermon, most needefull for this time* [1578].

1579

APRIL 29   "Mr. Spark," perhaps Robert Sparke, of King's College, Cambridge, and "an eloquent preacher." He attacked theatres as "the nest of the Divel, and sinke of al sinne." (William Ringler, "The First Phase of the Elizabethan Attack on the Stage, 1558–1579," *HLQ*, V (1941–2), 407.)

MAY 10   John Stockwood, Master of the Tunbridge Grammar School. Upon the Christian ministry. He deplored the scarcity of "faithfull and painfull labourers," extolled the virtue and absolute necessity of preaching, exhorted his audience to attend church instead of filthy plays, which usurp the time of sermons, and declared for the plain style in preaching, without rhetorical tricks and extensive quotation from the Fathers. A long, repetitive and violent effusion. *A very fruitefull Sermon preched at Paule's Crosse* (1579).

JULY 19   John Dyos. Using the ship of Luke 5:1–11 as a type of the Church, he condemned the finicky and worldly professors of the day, and undertook an extensive "proof" that Rome is the false church, not the body of Christ; the Pope is Antichrist and Rome is Babylon. He attacked Roman doctrines of the mass and purgatory. *A Sermon preached at Paules Crosse...: setting forth the excellencye of Gods heavenlye worde* (1579).

AUG.–OCT.   A preacher was put up to extol the Queen's government and to assure the people that she had been bred and brought up in Christ. The audience applauded this statement, but showed disapproval of the preacher's attack upon John Stubbs and his book *The Gaping Gulph* (1579). (Neale, *Elizabeth*, p. 242.)

1580

JAN. 3   William Fisher, afterwards Vicar of St. Martin's-in-the-Fields. His discussion of the qualities of Christ's adversaries in his earthly ministry led him to condemnation of the Catholic Pharisees; upon the words "I will have mercy, and not sacrifice" he reproved "aleknights," excess in apparel, and false gospellers. *A Sermon preached at Paules crosse the firste Sunday after Newyeeres day (1580).

1581

JAN. 8   James Bisse, Fellow of Magdalen College, Oxford. We should labour, he said, for the meat which endureth, yet we hunt after belly cheer, and our zeal is cold. He pointed to signs of God's judgments: a plague at Oxford, a terrible earthquake. But he set forth God's blessings upon England: a Deborah upon the throne, a late victory in Ireland. The foes of England shall be like a "tottering wal." Yet Englishmen have turned the grace of God into wantonness; and he exhorted them by the memory of God's fearful vengeance to repent of their worldly ways. *Two Sermons preached, the one at Paules Crosse (1581).

APRIL 23   Anthony Anderson, Rector of Medbourne, Leicestershire. A sermon upon the theme of the barren fig-tree, with the conventional attack upon the vicious doings of the papists, and an enumeration of the sins of worldly Englishmen. *A Sermon preached at Paules Crosse (1581).

SEPT.(?)   Lawrence Dyos [Deios], chaplain to Bishop Aylmer. He aroused the ire of the City fathers by accusing them of usury and Puritanism. The Mayor complained that he "had publicly defamed them to their faces, and stated that if the appointing of preachers were committed to them, they would appoint such as would defend usury, the family of love, and puritanism." Dyos and some learned men who were present protested that no such meaning could be taken from his words. (Analytical Index to ... the Remembrancia, ed. W. H. and H. C. Overall, London, 1878, p. 366.)

———   Richard Hooker, Fellow of Corpus Christi College, Oxford. A sermon which "seemed to cross a late Opinion of Mr. Calvins," since he developed the doctrine of an antecedent and a consequent will in God. A rationalist critique of Calvin's voluntarism. This was the sermon which, according to Walton, led to Hooker's injudicious marriage. C. J. Sisson (The Judicious Marriage of Mr. Hooker, Cambridge, 1940, p. 25) accepts the date 1581, but explodes the ancient scandal of the daughter of the Shunamite (Izaak Walton, Lives, World's Classics ed., p. 177.)

1583

ca. FEB.(?)   John Aylmer, Bishop of London. A sermon denouncing Richard Harvey's "An Astrologicall Discourse upon the great and notable Conjunction of the Two Superiour Planets, Saturne & Jupiter, which shall happen the

28. day of April, 1583," entered S.R. on January 22, 1582/3, and dedicated to Aylmer. "No more could Dick (with his predictions) compasse anie thing but derision, being publiquely preacht against for it at Pawles Crosse by the Bishop of London . . . who . . . disproov'd the revolutions to be cleane contrarie." Harvey's discourse "seems to have awakened immense interest, and, among the vulgar at least, a good deal of perturbation" (McKerrow). (Thomas Nashe, "Have with You, to Saffron Walden," in *Works*, ed. R. B. McKerrow, London, 1904-10, III, 82-3.)

Nov. 17   John Whitgift, Archbishop of Canterbury. The accession sermon. A sermon of obedience, in which he outlined the classic Protestant theory of submission, indicated how it was menaced by papists, Anabaptists, and "our wayward and conceited persons," defined the royal supremacy as not including the *potestas ordinis*, and rebuked popular preachers who attacked bishops and magistrates. "Where there is no government, there is no order: where many governe, there is sedition: and where no order is, there a gap is opened to all desolation." **A Most godly and Learned Sermon* (1589).

1583(?)   Lawrence Caddy, a spy expelled from the English college in Rome, having renounced the Catholic faith before the Bishop of London, was ordered to accompany the preacher into "the most celebrated pulpit in London," and "declare publicly the things they should suggest against the Pope and the Roman religion. Being a very coarse-looking fellow, he did this with such a bad grace that they were all ashamed of him." Caddy was a gentleman of good family; he afterwards returned to the Catholic faith, and wrote a *Palinodia*. (Catholic Record Society, *Miscellanea*, IV, London, 1907, p. 11; *Ath. Cantab.*, I, 451.)

1584

Feb. 9   John Hudson, Canon of Chichester. Having demonstrated the main theological position of the Epistle to the Hebrews, that the law is abrogated by the new priesthood of Christ, he proceeded to examine the abuse of this doctrine by popish writers, especially Stapleton, and the flaws in Christians' performance of those duties enjoined upon them as inheritors of Christ's redemption. He spoke against dissembling, murmuring, conceit of the private judgment, and desire of novelty. "Our braynes are busied about Pithagoras numbers, and Platos idea, and Aristotles common wealth." **A Sermon preached at Paules Crosse* (1584).

Oct. 18   John Aylmer, Bishop of London. A sermon in which there was some reference to Sir Thomas More. (*Ath. Cantab.*, II, 172.)

Oct. 27   Samuel Harsnett, Fellow of Pembroke College, Cambridge, and author of *A Declaration of Egregious Popish Impostures* (1603). Like Hooker's sermon of 1581 (*q.v.*), a discussion of the difficult question of free-will and predestination. He concluded: "Let us take heed and beware, that we neither (with the Papists) rely upon our free will: nor (with the Pelagian) upon our Nature: nor (with the Puritan) Curse God, and die, laying the burthen of our sins on his shoulders, and the guilt of them at his everlasting doores; but let us all fall downe upon our faces, give glory to God, and say, Unto thee, O Lord, belongeth mercy and forgiveness." *Three Sermons Preached by . . . Dr Richard Stuart . . . , to which is added A fourth Sermon . . . by . . . Samuel Harsnett* (1658).

DEC. 27 The recantation of John Hilton, who in his preaching had denied the divinity of Christ and asserted that the Old and New Testaments were fables. (*Ath. Cantab.*, I, 509.)

1584(?) Dr. Copcot, of Cambridge. An answer to Dudley Fenner's *A Counter-Poyson* (1584), and defence of the Establishment against the disciplinarians. The sermon was answered by *A Defence of the Reasons of the Counter-Poyson* (1586), the author of which "had the whole Sermon in writing." William Pierce (*An Historical Introduction to the Marprelate Tracts*, London, 1908, p. 93) says that the Paul's Cross sermon was in Latin. (Pearson, *Cartwright*, p. 272.)

1584(?) John Bridges, Dean of Sarum. An answer to the *Learned Discourse* (1584), later included in his *Defense of the Government Established* (1587). (Pearson, *Cartwright*, p. 273.)

1586

MARCH 6 George Closse, of Trinity College, Cambridge. He charged the Lord Mayor, Sir Wolston Dixie, with fraud and partiality in the administration of justice. The Lord Mayor was present. Closse himself had been accused of fraud in 1581, in connection with his means of securing the vicarage of Cuckfield. (*APC*, XIV, 60, 150, 188; Holinshed (1808), IV, 888–9; *DNB*, art. "George Closse.")

MARCH 13 A sermon on the dignity of marriage, with condemnation of the sin of adultery. A man did penance for adultery, his quean having been executed for child-murder. (Holinshed (1808), IV, 889–90.)

MARCH 27 Having been enjoined to recant his sermon of March 6, George Closse lewdly defaced and discredited the Lord Mayor once more. Six preachers appointed to certify how he discharged his duty ruled in his favour, however, and he penned a complacent account of the affair for the next edition of Holinshed. (*APC*, XIV, 60, 150, 188; Holinshed (1808), IV, 890.)

MAY 29 John Chardon, after Bishop of Down and Connor. (Robert Watt, *Bibliotheca Britannica*, Edinburgh, 1824.)

JULY 17 A "grave or learned person." He was to declare to the people the misdemeanours of George Closse (March 6, March 27), "so as therby others

REGISTER 215

maie be warned to behave themselves more duetifullie and circumspectlie towards magistrates and not rashlie to defame them before the multitude." Closse was to be on the platform, but not permitted to open his mouth lest he begin his invectives again. (*APC*, XIV, 188-9.)

AUG.-SEPT. Edwin Sandys, Archbishop of York. On the Ballard-Babington conspiracy. He reviewed the rebellion of Absalom and its contemporary application, and set forth the proper duties of each calling in the service of God, all comprehended in obedience. He prayed in closing for the deliverance of the Queen from all conspiracies and treasons: "Thou knowest, O Lord, that she hath not deserved this treachery at their hands, being most mild and merciful, doing good unto all, hurting none." (*Sermons*, pp. 403-17.)

1587

JUNE 25 William Gravet, Vicar of St. Sepulchre's. He declared the true foundation of the faith and peace of the Church in Christ, against the papists, proving it out of the Fathers and adducing the vain jangling of Roman priests who had recently been examined by a commission of which he was a member. He made a plea to the Companies for the continuance of their liberality to Christ's Hospital, praised the civil peace under the Queen's good rule, and distinguished between Christian peace and carnal security. **A Sermon Preached at Paules Crosse . . . intreating of the holy Scriptures* (1587).

"Shortly after" JUNE 25 The preacher "bitterly reproved" William Gravet for alleging the Fathers, especially St. Augustine, in the controversial part of his sermon of June 25. Gravet added to his sermon when published a section defending the practice of citation of patristic authority. (William Gravet, *A Sermon Preached at Paules Crosse* (1587).)

1588

AUG. 20 Alexander Nowell, Dean of St. Paul's. A sermon of thanksgiving for the victory over the Armada. (Strype, *Annals*, III (2), 27.)

SEPT. 8 At the sermon eleven ensigns captured from the Armada were shown. One of them, with a picture of Our Lady with her Son in her arms, was held over the pulpit. These ensigns may have been those sent by Howard to Walsingham in the care of Thomas Cely. (Strype, *Annals*, III (2), 27; *CSPD Eliz.*, 1581-90 [2], 536.)

Nov. 17 Thomas Cooper, Bishop of Winchester. The accession day sermon. A sermon of thanksgiving for the victory over the Armada. (Strype, *Annals*, III, (2), 27.)

Nov. 19 Another sermon of thanksgiving, attended by the crafts in their liveries. (Strype, *Annals*, III (2), 27.)

Nov. 24 John Piers, Bishop of Salisbury. A sermon of thanksgiving, before Queen Elizabeth, the Council, and the French ambassador, for the victory over Spain. This was the only time Elizabeth came to Paul's Cross. It was a notable occasion, and there was a huge crowd. A ballad on the subject was entered in the Stationers' Register two days later. (Nichols, *Elizabeth*, III, 539; see John King, *A Sermon at Paules Crosse* (1620), sig. F1.)

Dec. 1 The recantation of William Tedder, a converted seminary priest. He confessed that he had dwelt long in error because of fear of worldly shame and "the tickling of vaine glorie." He craved forgiveness of God, of the Queen, and of all present. *The Recantations as they were severallie pronounced by William Tedder and Anthony Tyrrell* [1588].

Dec. 8 "Mr. [Israel?] Pownall Preacher." The recantation of Anthony Tyrrell, seminary priest, who confessed to having fallen away a second time after pardon received. Not many months before he had dispersed libellous papers at Paul's Cross. He praised the Queen's clemency, and gave thanks to God for his recovery from Babylon. (See above, Dec. 1.)

1589

Feb. 9 Richard Bancroft, chaplain to Sir Christopher Hatton, and chief "investigator" of the presbyterian organizations. A sermon often cited as the first statement of the *jus divinum* of episcopacy in the Anglican apologetics of the period. A brilliant if not profound attack upon the "discipline," with a shrewd exploration of the motives of Martin Marprelate and the more respectable of the Puritan minority. He held up certain characteristics of Scottish presbyterianism as a horrible example. *A Sermon Preached at Paules Crosse . . . the first Sunday in the Parleament* (1588).

Nov. 9 William James, Dean of Christ Church, Oxford, after Bishop of Durham. His chief purpose was "to assuage contention," and he followed Bancroft's sermon of February 9 very closely, attacking both the evil designs of the Jesuits and the propaganda of the presbyterians, attributing to them the same motives as Bancroft had done. *A Sermon Preached at Paules Crosse* (1590).

Nov. 17 Thomas White, Rector of St. Gregory's under St. Paul's. The accession sermon. He preached reproof, instead of rejoicing, that "we should have a better sight of ourselves." After the conventional condemnation of enclosers and usurers, he took "a Woolfe by the eares," and dealt with discord in the Church, condemning the importunate libels of the Puritans. *A Sermon Preached at Paules Crosse . . . In joyfull remembrance and thanksgiving unto God* (1589).

1589(?) According to Thomas Nashe, Gabriel Harvey incited "the Preacher at Paules Crosse, that lay at the same house in Wood-streete which hee did, to preach manifestly against Master Lilly and [Nashe], with Woe to the Printer, woe to the Seller, woe to the Buyer, woe to the Author." The allusion is to Lyly's and Nashe's contributions to the Marprelate controversy. Harvey wrote a reply to *Pap with a Hatchet*, dated November 5, 1589, and afterwards incorporated into *Pierces Supererogation*. (Nashe, *Works*, ed. McKerrow, III, 96; V, 74.)

1590

OCT. 11 Gervase Babington, Prebendary of Hereford. A sermon on the doctrine of election. He took occasion to disprove the objection that assurance of election eliminates the necessity of good works, and went on to reprove such sins as endanger a lively faith, especially bitterness in church controversy and lack of reverence towards superiors. **A Sermon Preached at Paules Crosse* [1591].

NOV. 17 John Duport, Master of Jesus College, Cambridge. On the "Queenes day." A celebration of God's great mercies to England, and chiefly of the Queen. To praise her properly, he said, he would need "the wit of the divine Plato, and the high eloquence of Cicero, and as many tongues as the cherubins have eies." She is blest in her progenitors, endowed with gifts of fortune, body and mind, a virtuous virgin, no tyrant, a queen not only of Englishmen but of Christians. "O sweete Virgin! O blessed Ladie! O glorious Queene! O noble Elizabeth! (I have almost forgotten where I was.) Beholde (you English men) behold your naturall Prince ... the onelie remainder of so manie worthies, the flower of all princehoods and royaltie, the miracle of nature ... the Phenix of our time." **A Sermon preached at Pauls Crosse on ... the Queenes day* (1591).

1591

FEB. 14 Roger Hacket, Rector of North Crawley, Bucks. He compared Philip II to Naash, King of Ammon (I Sam. 11), and made Saul's calling up of the men of Israel a patriotic summons to Englishmen to defend country and religion. **A Sermon needfull for these times* (1591).

OCT. 31 William Fisher, Master of Ilford Hospital, Essex. A sermon of God's judgment—"we are all in a praemunire"—and His mercies. In God's book of remembrance, he said, are written our good deeds; he exhorted the citizens to add to theirs by contributing to the subsidy for Paul's Cross preachers. **A Godly Sermon preached at Paules Crosse* (1592).

1591(?) George Gifford, minister of Maldon, Essex, a Puritan and a "great enemy to popery." (*Ath. Oxon.*, II, 291.)

1591(?) Thomas Taylor, Fellow of Christ's College, Cambridge. Taylor was a Puritan. (J. B. Mullinger, *The University of Cambridge*, Cambridge, 1873-84, II, 508.)

1592

Oct. 15   The preacher issued a plague proclamation: the feasts at the Guildhall and Halls of Companies to be cancelled, by order of the Council. (G. B. Harrison, *An Elizabethan Journal*, London, 1928, p. 185.)

Nov. 21   Robert Temple, Prebendary of St. Paul's, and Canon of Bristol. A sermon of discretion in matters of religion. He pointed out that in spite of England's wealth in spiritual gifts, many prideful persons abuse her peace: the "murren sect" of Jesuits, the Martinists, the Brownists. Yet he admitted abuses in the Church: insufficiency of ministers, simony, sacrilege, decay of the universities. *A Sermon teaching discretion in matters of religion* (1592).

———   A.W. On the curse of the flying roll (Zech. 5:1-5), which is the book of God's secrets. He took occasion to rebuke the sin of theft, under its various forms, as deceit of merchants, usury, neglect of preachers, spoliation of the Church; also false swearing, and dissembling profession such as that practised by the Puritans. *A Fruitfull and Godly Sermon* [1592].

1593

Easter Term   Thomas Playfere, Fellow of St. John's College, Cambridge. On the delight of the believer in God. A very stylish discourse. *Hearts Delight. A Sermon Preached at Pauls Crosse* (1603).

July 1   Mr. Buckridge, probably John Buckridge, after Bishop of Rochester and of Ely. After the sermon Thomas Clarke, formerly a seminary priest of the English college in Rheims, recanted his popish errors. *The Recantation of Thomas Clarke . . . made at Paules Crosse* (1594).

Sept.   Adam Hill, Prebendary of Salisbury. A cry to repentance. The destruction of Sodom applied to London. He turned his batteries upon the idolatrous papists, the sin of blasphemy, profanation of the Sabbath, oppression of the poor, and especially atheism, which "hath crept into the blood and generositie of this land." He inveighed against Martin Marprelate, foppery in apparel, sedition, and the murmuring of young divines against the bishops. *The Crie of England. A Sermon preached at Paules Crosse* (1595).

1594

Nov. 3   John Dove, of Christ Church, Oxford. A sermon on the second coming of Christ. He confuted atheists and "Philosophers" who deny the end of the world, with the interesting aside that atheists are to be found "in the courts of princes." He also refuted, point by point, a Protestant book on the second coming, and determined that although we may not know the time of the end, we should ever watch and repent of our sins, for the world grows old. *A Sermon preached at Pauls Crosse . . . intreating of the second coming of Christ* [1594].

1595

Nov. 17 — Richard Fletcher, Bishop of London. The accession sermon. (George Clinch, *St. Paul's Cathedral*, London, 1906, p. 108.)

1596

May(?) — Stephen Gosson, parson of Great Wigborough, Essex, and author of *The Schoole of Abuse* (1579). A sermon for which he was told he might be "called in question," since he seemed to have "stricken at some great person." The great person may have been Essex. (Gosson, *The Trumpet of Warre* [1598], sig. G4.)

June 1 — J[ohn] Tanner, probably the Rector of Offwell, Devon. A sermon of penitence, with elaborate division, and equally elaborate rebuke of all estates. *A Sermon preached at Paules Crosse (1596).

Aug. 8 — William Barlow, at this time chaplain to Whitgift. A sermon in praise of Essex's victory at Cadiz. The preacher commended Essex for his noble behaviour, compared him to the greatest of generals, and severely censured those who minimized the victory. When Barlow published Essex's treasons on March 1, 1601, some persons objected that he spoke for spleen, since he had received nothing from the Earl for celebrating his triumph in 1596. Barlow angrily repudiated this suggestion. (G. B. Harrison, *The Life and Death of Robert Devereux Earl of Essex*, New York, 1937, p. 127; Wm. Barlow, *A Sermon preached at Paules Crosse* (1601), sig. A5.)

1597

Feb. 6 — John Dove, of Christ Church, Oxford (see May 10, 1601). He set out to prove, against Lutherans, papists, and atheists, that (1) it is not the will of God that all men should be saved, and (2) God's secret decree predestines some to salvation and others to reprobation, and (3) Christ died not effectually for all. A solid Calvinist argument. *A Sermon preached at Paules Crosse, the sixt of February* (1597).

Lent(?) — Thomas Bilson, Bishop of Winchester. Some City preachers, "conceited and too much addicted to novelties," had been urging that Christ suffered "the verie paines of hell" on the Cross, and Bilson, probably encouraged by Whitgift, "for the better quieting and settling of the minds of the people, who were now run into differences and discords about it," set out the true doctrine of the Creed on this matter. There was an uproar during the sermon, caused by "the frawd or folly of some one auditor." *The effecte of certaine Sermons . . . , Preached at Paules Crosse* (1599).

DEC. 4	John Howson, Prebendary of Hereford and Exeter, after Vice-Chancellor of Oxford. A splendid attack, based on Matthew 21:12-13, on the sin of simony and the spoliation of the Church. In describing the plight of divinity students at Oxford, he set forth the "miseries of scholars" in a bitter passage which caught the attention of a later student of Christ Church (see Robert Burton, *Anatomy of Melancholy*, I, ii, 3.15). *_A Sermon preached at Paules Crosse . . . Wherein is discoursed, that all buying and selling of spirituall promotion is unlawfull_ (1597).

1598

MAY 7	Stephen Gosson, parson of Great Wigborough, Essex, and author of *The Schoole of Abuse* (1579). A sermon justifying war in defence of true religion. He commented disapprovingly on the Spanish conquests of the American natives, but found the wars of England "charitable and just." An exhortation to trust in God's hand led him to consider the enormity of atheism, and the doctrine "beleeve we cannot but by preaching" inspired an invective against the presbyterians, who he thought had been treated too gently: "one dram of *Elleborus* would have purged their humour." *_The Trumpet of Warre. A Sermon preached at Paules Crosse_ [1598].
MAY 21	John Howson, Prebendary of Hereford and Exeter, after Vice-Chancellor of Oxford. The "conclusion" of the sermon of December 4, 1597. In his discussion of the authority of God's word he shows the influence of the *Ecclesiastical Polity*. He returned to the attack upon the spoilers of the Church, and took to task the Puritans for their undue emphasis upon preaching and contempt of common prayer. *_A Second Sermon preached at Paules Crosse . . . : concluding a former Sermon . . . upon the same Text_ (1598).

1599

AUG. 19(?)	"The Lord Generall [Charles Howard, Earl of Nottingham] with all the great officers of the field came in great bravery to Powles Crosse . . . and dined with the Lord Mayor: and then was the alarme at hottest that the Spaniards were at Brest, which was as likely and fell out as true as all the rest [of the rumours of invasion]." (Chamberlain, I, 83.)
NOV. 17	Thomas Holland, Regius Professor of Divinity at Oxford. The accession sermon. An application to Elizabeth of "the peregrination of the Queen of the South" to Solomon. He dwelt upon the Queen's grace to the Church. When the sermon was printed, he affixed to it "An Apologeticall discourse," designed to confute those who traduced the observing of November 17 as a "holy-day." *Πανηγύρις *D. Elizabethae* . . . A

Sermon Preached at Pauls in London . . . the one and fortieth yeare of her Majesties raigne (1601).

ca. Nov. "Dr. Richardson," probably John Richardson, Fellow of Emmanuel College, Cambridge, after Vice-Chancellor of Cambridge and one of the translators of the Authorized Version. A sermon for which he was arrested and interrogated. He was doubtless one of those who "not respecting the Earl of Essex's restraint as they ought to have done . . . in their sermons, also at Paul's Cross, prayed for him by name," saying that they were bound, by "ancient custom of the University," to pray for their Chancellor when they came to the Cross. (*CSPD Eliz.*, 1598-1601, 365.)

1601

FEB. 8 John Boys, Rector of Tilmanstone. One John Bargar, apparently suspected to be an adherent of Essex, used the sermon at the Cross as an alibi. Being examined by Lord Cobham, he said in part: ' Having been at the sermon at Paul's Cross, and coming into the body of the church, I heard a confused noise, crying Murder, Murder, God save the Queen. Men were crying that Essex should have been murdered in his bed by Ralegh and his confederates and that they were defending themselves till the Queen should hear of it." The subject of the day's sermon has not transpired. (*Salisbury Papers*, XI, 30; *DNB*, art. "John Boys.")

FEB. 15 John Hayward, Rector of St. Mary Woolchurch. His sermon dealt with the Essex rising, on instructions from Cecil and Bancroft. Bancroft was pleased: "The traitor is now laid out well in colours to every man's satisfaction that heard the sermon." (*Salisbury Papers*, XI, 55-6.)

FEB. 22 The preacher spoke from written instructions supplied by Bancroft, which the bishop had first submitted to Cecil for approval. It is not hard to guess the subject: Essex was executed on February 25. (*Salisbury Papers*, XI, 76.)

MARCH 1 William Barlow, Rector of St. Dunstan's in the East. (See November 10, 1605.) A none too successful performance of a ticklish task, the explanation to the public of the significance of the Essex rising, and the publication of Essex' confession, making the Earl condemn himself out of his own mouth. The sermon was apparently ill received in some quarters. **A Sermon preached at Paules Crosse . . . With a short discoverie of the late Earle of Essex his confession* (1601).

MAY 10 John Dove, Rector of St. Mary Aldermary. Of divorcement. The sermon was not well received by some, who objected to the stand taken against Beza, whose position on the highly controversial text Matthew 19:9 Dove refuted point by point, affirming that there can be no divorce, and hence no remarriage of either party to a separation. *Of Divorcement. A Sermon Preached at Pauls Crosse* (1601).

1602

MAY 16 — "Mr. Sanders," perhaps Matthew Sanders, after Rector of Barnston, Essex. He reproved the pride of riches, but was careful to eschew the communism of the Anabaptists. "God made some rich, and some poore, that twoe excellent virtues might flourish in the world, charitie in the riche, and patience in the poore." (Manningham, pp. 28-30.)

JUNE 13 — Francis Marbury, after Rector of St. Martin-in-the-Vintry. Ingenious in his interpretation of the Scriptures, he applied the blessing of Japheth to the calling of the Christian, the fruitfulness of the true Church, and the confounding of its enemies, papists and familists. *A Sermon Preached at Paules Crosse* (1602).

JUNE 16 — "Mr. Barker," probably Lawrence Barker, Vicar of St. Botolph's without Aldersgate. He seems to have dealt with Christian perseverance in general, using the mighty figure of the plough, then with the virtue of perseverance in the ministry. "He selected and spake of the Archbishop of Canterbury as the sunne amongst the ministers, and the old Deane of Paules [Nowell] compared to the moone. And Dr. Overall, the newe deane, to the newe moone, gravity and learning and life; the ministers to starres." (Manningham, pp. 34-5.)

JUNE 20 — Robert Wakeman, Fellow of Balliol College, Oxford. On Jonah's sermon and Nineveh's repentance, with obvious applications: the function of the minister, God's patience with sinful England, and a denunciation of God's judgments. His later remarks were cut short by "sodainly unseasonable" weather. (See Manningham, pp. 37-8.) *Jonahs Sermon, and Ninevehs repentance. A Sermon Preached at Pauls Crosse* (1606).

AUG. 15 — John Hayward, Rector of St. Mary Woolchurch. All estates are God's stewards, and all must give account to God. "You must give account how you have ruled, and woe unto tyrants. You must give account how you have obeyed, and woe unto rebels. You must give account how you have used superiour dignitie, and woe unto the proud. And how you have borne your low estate, and woe unto the envious." *A Sermon of the Stewards Danger: Preached at Paules Crosse* (1602).

OCT. 10 — John Spenser, President of Corpus Christi, Oxford. A sermon upon the Lord's vineyard, in which, as was natural in Hooker's literary executor, he drew largely upon the *Ecclesiastical Polity* in his definition of the visible Church. In his discussion of the fruits of the vineyard, i.e. good works, he sought to root out the pestilent weeds of covetousness and self-love, as expressed in the principal impiety of robbing the Church. *A Learned and Gracious Sermon Preached at Paules Crosse* (1615).

Oct. 24 John King, then Rector of St. Andrew's, Holborn. He attacked impropriations, simony, usury, high living, and diminution of zeal. (Manningham, pp. 64–72.)

Oct. 31 [Nicholas?] Dene. Of the vanity of women. He reprehended Egerton and other popular preachers whose auditory was mostly of women. (Manningham, pp. 74–5.)

Nov. 7 Thomas Holland, Regius Professor of Divinity at Oxford. "mighty in the scriptures." He preached against covetousness, "an Hydra with seven heads," each of which he presumably cut off in the course of the sermon. He introduced a familiar argument: "God would have some rich, some poore, for distinction sake, and the mutuall exercise of liberality and patience, whereby the opinion of the Anabaptists is easily confuted, whoe would have all things in common." (Manningham, pp. 138–42.)

Nov. 14 [Ralph?] Dawson, of Trinity College, Cambridge. "All the while he prayed he kept on his velvet night cap untill he came to name the Queene, and then off went that too, when he had spoken both of and to God with it on his head." The notice is fragmentary, but it is clear that he spoke against contempt of ministers and impoverishing the clergy, mentioned the martyrs of Mary's days, "praysed our happy government for peace and religion; and soe ended." (Manningham, pp. 84–5.)

Nov. 21 Roger Fenton, Reader at Gray's Inn, author of *A Treatise of Usurie* (1611). A sermon of salvation by the example of Zaccheus. To the good, he said, riches are sacraments of God's favour, but to get salvation you must stretch your purse-strings. There is no repentance without restitution. (Manningham, pp. 87–91.)

Nov. 28 Mr. Tolson, of Queens' College, Cambridge. Upon direction from the Bishop of London, he "spake some things against the common enimye," i.e., Rome. (Manningham, pp. 93–5.)

Dec. 19 "One with a long browne beard, a hanging looke, a gloting eye, and a tossing learing jeasture." He preached upon the favorite theme of false prophets, and "his whole sermon was a strong continued invective against the papistes and jesuites. Not a notable villanous practise committed, but a pope, a cardinall, a bishop, or a priest had a hand in it; they were still at the worst end." (Manningham, pp. 104–5.)

1603

Jan. 30 Ralph Barlow, a "beardlesse man of Pembroke Hall in Cambridge," after Dean of Christ Church, Dublin. Following an exordium in which he confessed that he spoke with fear and trembling, he launched into a discourse upon the subjection of the creature to vanity and the deliverance of the sons of God. We live, he warned, in prosperity and peace, but times of trouble and persecution may come. (Manningham, pp. 111–13.)

FEB. 13   "A yong man." He attacked the vanity of women, and duelling. (Manningham, pp. 132-3.)

MARCH 13   Richard Stock, lecturer at St. Augustine's, Watling Street (see Nov. 2, 1606). This sermon was offensive to the City, for he made much of certain abuses in the tax rates, "whereby the meaner sort were overburdened." (*Salisbury Papers*, XII, 672.)

UNDATED SERMONS TEMP. ELIZABETH I

1559–70   John Jewel, Bishop of Salisbury. Upon the re-edification of the Church, before fallen from the pure primitive pattern, now "by a most virtuous and noble lady" restored. Many are weak in the task: some call for a general council (though this is useless); some, clinging to the old faith, obstinately oppose the re-building of the Church; some noblemen and gentlemen pillage the Church. There is a "miserable need" of ministers. (*Works*, II, 986–1004.)

1559–70   John Jewel, Bishop of Salisbury. On "knowing the time" both in spiritual and in worldly business. "Honest and moderate forecast and provision" in earthly affairs is not forbidden; but usury is "a most filthy trade." He reviewed the Romish errors of the dark time just past, and exhibited with contempt an Agnus Dei or consecrated charm. God, he concluded, has restored to us the light of the Gospel. (*Works*, II, 1035–46.)

1570–77(?)   Edwin Sandys, Bishop of London. Upon the time of the Judgment. That there shall be a Judgment Day is certain, and the "darkness" prophesied of that time is upon us, for the age is darkened by the false doctrine of Rome and the sun obscured by our corrupt life and conversation. The "ancient virtues" are decayed, there is trouble and perplexity among the nations. Take heed, then, he concluded; watch and pray. (*Sermons*, pp. 346–69.)

1570–77   Edwin Sandys, Bishop of London. Upon the end of the world, and the Second Coming, which is near: "The prophecies of Daniel, of the four monarchies, of the little horn, and of the times, weeks, and days, are manifestly come to pass." Since the end is near we must put on sobriety, and practise charity, that is, hospitality, which "is waxen a stranger, and needeth harbour." (*Sermons*, pp. 386–402.)

1570–77   Edwin Sandys, Bishop of London. The state of the Church figured by a ship tossed upon the waters. The Church has been afflicted by the usurped authority of the "romish strumpet," and now by "the winds of division and contention" within the fold, raised by "clamorous troublers" who desire reformation. (*Sermons*, pp. 370–85.)

ante 1592   Richard Turnbull. Four sermons of exposition of Psalm 15. The first is of pretended religion; the second of righteousness, with a rebuke of oppression and fraud; the third of slander, malice, and fraud in buying and selling; the fourth an invective against usury, an argument "nothing prejudiciall unto the daungerous adventures of lawfull merchants; neither condemneth it tollerable gains in the retailing occupier." *An Exposition upon the xv Psalme, devided into Foure Sermons. . . . As they were . . . preached at Pauls Crosse* (1592).

ante 1593   Henry Smith, the "silver-tongu'd." A trumpet sounding to judgment. "Whilst the theefe stealeth, the hemp groweth, & the hooke is covered within the baite: we sit downe to eat, and rise up to play & and from play to sleepe: and a hundreth yeares is counted little enough to sin in: but . . . how many drammes of delight, so many poundes of dolour: when iniquity hath played her part, vengeance leapes upon the stage: the comedy is short, but the tragedy is longer." (*The Sermons of Maister Henry Smith* (1593).)

1588–94   Richard Lewes, Rector of Kilmarsh, Northants. A sermon upon the blessing of Isaac. Isaac's case reminds us how we may be swayed by blind affection, not by reason. "The government of reason is a *Monarchia*; the rule of the ordered affections representeth *Aristocratia*; the administration of the lowest part is *Democratia*." He condemned sacrilege and simony and deplored the violence of the Marprelate controversy, reproving the "learned and grave Fathers" for their intransigence, and those that "seek reformation" for their "unbrotherlie reproches, unchristian slaunders, unsaverie and unlearned libels, and almost Pharisaicall contempt of their fathers and brethren." *A Sermon Preached at Paules Crosse . . . , concerning Isaac his Testament* (1594).

ca. 1598(?)   Robert Abbot, after Bishop of Salisbury. He received the benefice of Bingham, Notts., in recognition of his powers displayed in a sermon at the Cross. (Thomas Fuller, *Abel Redivivus* (1651), p. 540.)

ante 1599   Henry Price, Rector of Fleet Marston, Bucks. A homily upon Luke 17:37. By the body is meant Christ, by the eagles the elect, by their gathering the resurrection. The eagle is known by his nest, built upon a rock, high and sure; by his eye, to look into the sun, and behold faith afar off; by his flight, to seek heaven; by his foe, the Dragon; by his age, which is renewed; by his discretion in seeking his prey—here Price attacked oppression and sacrilege. *The Eagles Flight. . . . As it was delivered in a most godly and fruitfull Sermon at Paules Crosse* (1599.)

JAMES I

1603

MARCH 27   John Hayward, Rector of St. Mary Woolchurch. Upon the death of Queen Elizabeth. He showed "how when her Almoner rehearsing to her the grounds of the Christian faith, and requiring her assent unto

	them by some sign, she readily gave it with hand and eye." (Strype, *Whitgift*, II, 468.)
APRIL 14	Mr. Hemmings, sometime of Trinity College, Cambridge. A sermon upon the vanities of women. He said: "If a man would marrie, it were 1000 to one but he should light upon a bad one, there were so many naught: and yf he should chance to find a good one, yet he were not sure to hold her soe: for women are like a coule full of snakes amongst which there is one eele, a thousand to one, yf a man happen upon the eele, and yet if he gett it in his hand, all that he hath gotten is but a wet eele by the tayle." (Manningham, pp. 171-2.)

1604

OCT. 7	Richard Jefferay [Geoffrey], of Magdalen College, Oxford. A denunciation of the sins of England and especially London, worse, he said, than any he saw in his travels abroad. **The Sonne of Gods entertainment by the sonnes of men* (1605).
ca. OCT.	The chaplain to Sir Charles Cornwallis, ambassador to Spain. The chaplain was later converted to Catholicism in Spain. (Chamberlain, I, 211.)
ca. 1604	Arthur Lake, then Master of the Hospital of St. Cross, Winchester. An official-sounding discourse on the proper use of the Scriptures, on ceremonies and discipline, on reformation of religion, and contempt of ministers. **Ten Sermons upon Severall Occasions, Preached at Saint Pauls Crosse, and Elsewhere* (1640).

1605

APRIL 28	John Milward, chaplain to the King. In the midst of the sermon "a cuckowe came flienge over the pulpit, (a thing I never saw nor heard of before) and very lewdly called and cried out with open mouth." It was too bad for Dr. Milward, whose involvement in the affair of Agnes Howe had caused much popular mirth. (Chamberlain, I, 206; for the background see C. J. Sisson, *Lost Plays of Shakespeare's Age*, Cambridge, 1936, pp. 12-57.)
JUNE 9	Samuel Gardiner, Rector of Great Dunham, after chaplain to Archbishop Abbot. Of the resurrection of the flesh, proved at large; of the Judgment; of the book of life; and of the uses of these doctrines in our conduct. The proof of the resurrection from the course of nature is a nice bit of prose. **A Sermon Preached at Paules Crosse . . . Upon the 20. of the Revelation the 12. vers.* (1605).
AUG. 5	Richard Vaughan, Bishop of London. On James's care for religion. The sermon on the anniversary of the Gowrie conspiracy. (G. B. Harrison, *A Jacobean Journal*, London, 1941, p. 218.)
NOV. 10	William Barlow, Bishop of Rochester. On the Powder Plot, "this late Tragi-comicall treason." He invited his hearers to consider the "cruell

Execution, an inhumane crueltie, a brutish immanitie, a develishe brutishness, & an Hyperbolicall, yea an hyperdiabolicall divelishness." In enlarging upon the deliverance of the King, he spent much time in praise of James's many virtues, and passed in review the various dangers through which he had passed, being preserved "*in utero, ab utero, ex utero.*" **The Sermon Preached at Paules Crosse . . . the next Sunday after the Discoverie of this late Horrible Treason* (1606.)

1606

MARCH 24   Thomas Ravis, Bishop of Gloucester. The accession sermon. (Chamberlain, I, 223.)

MAY 25   Roger Parker, precentor at Lincoln. "An Invective Oration" against the House of Commons, "very seditious and Slanderous." "His Text was *Quaerite Pacem Civitatis,*" wherein "he dealt as Garnet did in his booke intituled against lying: Of which the whole Treatise was a defence of Equivocation; So was his text for peace, but his discourse nothing but sedition." Parker, when examined by the King, denied some of the charges, and "other Speeches he Cuppleth with words of Mitigation." He was committed prisoner to the Dean of St. Paul's. (*Salisbury Papers*, XVII, 224; *The Parliamentary Diary of Robert Bowyer, 1606–1607*, ed. D. H. Willson, Minneapolis, 1931, pp. 179–82.)

NOV. 2   Richard Stock, curate of Allhallows, Bread Street. He exhorted magistrates to put into execution with more severity the laws against recusants. He spoke boldly against those who permitted papists to buy freedom from the regulations, and against the suspension of the laws, which made for such dangers as that of the Plot. **A Sermon Preached at Paules Crosse* (1609).

1607

AUG. 5   John Milward, chaplain to the King. (See April 28, 1605.) After an eloquent exordium upon the troubles of man—"his entrance is blindnesse, his birth a crying, his progresse labour, and his end dolour"—he analyzed the Gowrie treason: the authors of it, the action and manner of it, and reviewed the other deliverances of the sovereign from treasons, especially "that Salt-Peter Treason, or Peters salt Treason of Rome." "Let us then," he concluded, "that are but legges and hands or other parts, labour to support this Jacob . . . as much as we may free him from troubles." **Jacobs Great Day of Trouble, and Deliverance. A Sermon Preached at Pauls Crosse* (1610).

AUG. 24   Daniel Price, brother to Sampson Price (*q.v.*), and Rector of Wiston, Sussex. A sermon for Bartholomew Fair. Although, he said, there are evil merchants, robbers, pirates, usurers, yet the calling of a merchant is to be praised. "The state of a Christian is not an idle vaine speculation, but must bee a careful, painful, diligent, walking in his vocation," such as good merchants use. *The marchant. A Sermon Preached at Paules Crosse . . . the day before Bartholomew faire* (1608).

OCT. 25 John Pelling, Rector of Trowbridge, Wilts., and chaplain to the Earl of Hertford. A discussion of the manifold doctrine of God's immutable providence, and of the mediate means through which God works, including the King, who is "immediately under God, over the Church and commonwealth." *A Sermon of the Providence of God. Preached at Paules Crosse* (1607).

NOV. 1 Samuel Collins, Rector of Fen Ditton, Cambridgeshire, after Provost of King's College, etc., "an admirable and biting wit." A full-scale attack on the whole Puritan position: their life ("sitting uppermost at belly cheare"), their learning ("the stronger wit the stronger heretike"), their sermons ("the most of them have made Gods offerings to stinke"). The whole faction was "set on foote . . . by some, that thought well of themselves . . . , afterward by others, that had no such desert of their owne to raise them . . . , lending their handes, and their names with the foremost, partlie for companie, and partly for hope of spoile and booty. . . . At last the people carried away with hobubs and imaginations." *A Sermon preached at Paules-Crosse, upon . . . All-Saints Day* (1607).

NOV. 5 Martin Fotherby, Archdeacon of Canterbury, after Bishop of Salisbury. The sermon on the anniversary of the Powder Plot. A contemplation of England's blessings: "the dewe of Gods blessing hath onely fallen on our land, when all our neighbour countries have been destitute of it." And a review of her deliverances, as in 1605 and in 1588, when "all the elements in their courses fought" against the papists. And a condemnation of her sins, for which the plague is the "droppes of Gods displeasure." *Foure Sermons, lately preached . . . The third at Paules Crosse* (1608).

1607(?) Robert Wilkinson, of Pembroke College, Cambridge(?). God hath put "golden snuffers" into the hands of his clergy, to keep men's spiritual lights bright. He descanted upon the "many prettie superfluities, and sinnes of supererogation" of women, and ended with a warning to London by Sodom. All shall pass away: "Where are the glorious and mightie Monarchies, on whom the world itselfe did waite?" *Lots Wife. A Sermon Preached at Paules Crosse* (1607).

1607(?) George Barry, preacher at Alphamston, Essex. A reproof of sin. "Hath not God called early and late unto you (as unto his people the Jews) for an absolute relinquishment of sinne? Hath he not cryed (even out of this place) by the shrillest trumpets that our land had, to magistrates, do justly, to officers, live not by bribes, to citizens, gain not by usury, to country gentlemen, grow not great by your poor neighbours oppression? . . . Iniquity hath the chaire still . . . ; Mammon is the cityzens God; and the mortar, I may not say of al, but of many of your goodly buildings abroad, are tempered with the teares of Orphanes." *The Narrow Way, and The Last Judgement, Delivered in two Sermons; the first at Pauls Crosse (1607).

1608

FEB. 14 William Crashaw, controversialist, preacher at the Inner Temple, and father of the poet. An immense controversial work against Rome, proving "xx wounds found to be in the body of the present Romish religion, in doctrine and in manners." The twentieth point (which really applies to England) deals with "a generall corruption of manners in all estates," and here he glanced at robbers of the Church, "horrible abuse of the Sabbath," and plays. *The Sermon preached at the Crosse . . . Justified by the Authour, both against Papist, and Brownist, to be the truth (1608).

MAY 1 Joseph Hall. On Pharisaism and Christianity. He pointed out how far Englishmen are behind the Pharisees of Rome in some respects, in diligent teaching, in plentiful almsgiving. Then he set forth their hypocrisy and worldliness, and the covetousness and ambition of the Jesuits—but these too are the sins of Londoners. "Your alms are written in church windows, your defraudings in the sand." (Works, ed. Wynter, V, sermon 1.)

SEPT. 25 Thomas Cheaste, of St. Mary Hall, Oxford. An exhortation to awake out of "the dead sleepe of security," and to seek Christ "that heavenly pellicane" and not the Pope "and his shavelings." *The Way to Life. Delivered in a Sermon at Paules Crosse (1609).

NOV. 5 Robert Tynley, Archdeacon of Ely. After painting a vivid picture of the true Church surrounded by enemies, and especially by the craft of the equivocating Jesuits, he proceeded to "answer" at length the "Letter" against the Apology for the Oath of Allegiance. "Who seeth not . . . that this Religion falsely termed Catholike, utterly perverteth the lawful subjection of people to their Sovereignes?" *Two Learned Sermons. The One, of the mischievous subtiltie, and barbarous crueltie, the other of the false Doctrines . . . of the Romish Synagogue (1609).

NOV. 6 George Downame, Prebendary of St. Paul's, after Bishop of Derry. Upon Christian liberty, which frees the conscience from the ordinances of men in things indifferent, but also "priviledgeth Christian lawgivers . . . to ordaine such lawes concerning outward things, as they shall judge expedient." He defended kneeling at communion, the surplice, and the cross in baptism. *A Treatise upon John 8.36 . . . The Chiefe Points Whereof were delivered in a sermon preached at Pauls Cross (1609).

DEC. 4 William Wheatlie, preacher in Banbury. The causes, effects, signs and remedies of covetousness, which is "the dropsie of the mind, an horseleech humour after wealth." He concluded: "You have looked in the glasse of the word, and seene the spots and staines of earthiness discovered, goe home and purge." *A Caveat for the Covetous, or, a Sermon Preached at Paules Crosse (1609).

1609

JAN. 1   Thomas Jackson, Rector of Wye, Kent. On the little foxes. God's "ordinary Huntsmen" are ministers, magistrates, and the common people. If these are negligent, God sends "extraordinary Huntsmen," pestilence, famine, war. The foxes are atheists ("their Moses Machiavel, Divinity Policy: English Italianate, & Dives incarnate"), papists, "extravagant Jesuites," malcontent "Formalists," schismatics, Brownists, hypocrites, and corrupt patrons. *Londons New-Yeeres Gift. Or the Uncouching of the Foxe. A godly Sermon Preached at Pauls Crosse (1609).

MARCH 24   Richard Crakanthorpe, chaplain to the Bishop of London, and "a great canonist." The accession sermon. On the great wisdom of Solomon, and of James, the modern Solomon. A review of the blessings of peace and true religion enjoyed under the King's rule. He attacked the presbytery, "a Seminary of sedition, and a Sanctuary to every turbulent and seditious Gracchus, both in Church and Kingdome." He extolled the organization of the Virginia Company, and commended the project of planting a colony and bringing true religion to the poor and savage natives. He concluded with an exhortation to loyalty and obedience. *A Sermon at the solemnizing of the Happie Inauguration of our most gracious and religious Soveraigne (1609).

APRIL 14   Joseph Hall. The Passion sermon, and a brilliant performance. He made the theme of Christ's atonement the basis for the usual attack upon Rome, which digs up the rotten relics of the abrogated law, and diminishes the finality of the passion by the sufferings of saints. (Works, ed. Wynter, V sermon 2.)

MAY 7   George Benson, Fellow of Queen's, Oxford. A discourse upon the sins of Ephraim, in which he taxed the "wandring Levits" who are never well "but when they have their sickles in another mans harvest, as though they would rob all the Ministers about them of their crown of rejoicing." *A Sermon Preached at Paules Crosse (1609).

MAY 28   Daniel Price, brother of Sampson Price (q.v.), chaplain to Prince Henry. After a tremendous exordium, on the evil state of the world—"a wilderness, a drie, heathy, thornie, bare, barren wildernesse, wherein Sathan the Serpent, Sinne the Satyre, Wrath the Lyon, Lust the Leopard, Zoim and Iim, the Ostrich and the Scritch-owle and the Vulture doe inhabit"—he drew from Acts 9:4 lessons against atheism and apostasy. He spoke against those who opposed an action intended to the glory of God, the Virginia enterprise, which should produce "great profite" and blessing upon those "that turne manie to righteousnesse." *Sauls Prohibition Staide ... Preached in a Sermon Commanded at Pauls Crosse (1609).

JUNE 11   George Webbe, Vicar of Steeple Ashton, Wilts., after Bishop of Limerick. "A Description of the fearfull and lamentable estate" of the land, upon Hosea 4:1-3, God's summons to a process of law for sinners. We live in a time of "huge barnes, little almes." As for swearing, "Court and Countrie, Towne and Citie groaneth with it; lying, "our Land is another Phrygia"; stealing, "what privie prigging, pilling, proling, purloining"; whoring, "how open and common are your suburbe stewes." He exhorted the City magistrates to supress vice in all its forms, under the threat of God's judgment.   *Gods Controversie with England . . . Preached at Pauls Crosse upon Trinitie Sunday (1609).

JUNE 18   William Loe, Prebendary of Gloucester. He celebrated the efficacy of the prayers of Christ, and the joys of those separated from the world by integrity of life, and attacked the sins of simony and sacrilege. "You shall see their houses like pallaces advanced up to heaven pompous—and specious to behold, every smokey chimney overtopping, and overpeering the Lords temple, which happily obscurely stands stooping and drooping beneath like a rude heape of stones, being made the receptacle of Owles and Ostriches, *Zim Ohim, &* dancing Satyres."   *The Joy of Jerusalem: and Woe of the Worldlings. A Sermon preached at Pauls Crosse (1609).

JUNE 25   Lancelot Dawes, Fellow of Queen's College, Oxford. A long attack on the abominations of Rome, and the sins of the English Catholics, "the very scumme and excrements of this land." He reviewed the various causes proposed for the "periods" of commonwealths, ancient and modern, and concluded that the true cause was "the sinnes of the people."   *Gods Mercie and Jerusalems miseries. A Sermon Preached at Pauls Crosse (1609).

SEPT. 3   Robert Johnson, chaplain to the Bishop of Lincoln. The conventional review of the blessings of England, her sins, and God's consequent judgments, as plague, and heavy rains. He followed this by a thorough exploration of the sins of Puritans, those malicious, mouthy and clamorous schismatics, who "wring the Scriptures as a nose of wax," and give their children strange names, as "Reformation, Joy againe, From above, names in our English phrase not verie usuall."   *Davids Teacher. . . . Discovering Errionious Teachers and Seditious Sectuaries. Preached at Paules-Crosse (1609).

SEPT. 17   William Sclater, Vicar of Pitminster. A rather bad-tempered sermon, by one who had been accused of faction, upon non-proficiency in grace and the perils of apostasy. Ignorant preachers, "Abecedaries in divinitie," are to be contemned, for preaching is all. "I cannot yet see, what that great and important businesse of the Ministery should bee, to which it may beseeme Preaching to give place. I am sure not Sacraments. Christ sent me not to baptize (saith the Holy Apostle) but to preach the Gospell."   *A Threefold Preservative. . . . Prescribed in a Sermon at S. Pauls Crosse (1610).

DEC. 3 — William Holbrooke, a fearless champion of the godly. "Is it not," he asked, "a common and knowen tricke amongst you, to vaunt what you have done in vexing the godly, saying ... O Sirrah wote you will what and where I have bene? I was where a Puritane one of those precise fellows was, that cannot endure an oath, but I so swore star'd and swaggerd that I rid him out of the house and companie where I was? O miserable and wretched!" He reviewed grimly the sordid transactions often endured to get a church living, deplored the lack of family worship, and condemned the sale in Cheapside of "the Reliques of Idolatrie, I meane Rings with Crucifixes upon the same, usually sold there." *Loves Complaint, for want of Entertainement. A Sermon preached at Paules Crosse [1609].

1610

JAN. 14 — Thomas Myriell, preacher at Barnet. The strength of love exemplified in the love of the holy women who sought Christ in the sepulchre. "They were not daunted at their owne weaknesse, the stoutest of them being but a woman, *mulier, mollis aer*, a soft and tender breath, *faemina, ferens minus*, least able to endure and hold out." The text is a lesson against false seeking, of money, ambition, revenge. Some seek a false Christ, as the papists. *The Devout Soules Search ... In a Sermon, Preached at Paules Crosse (1610).

1611

JAN. 17 — Samuel Gardiner, Rector of Great Dunham, author of *A booke of Angling* (1606). A dispute with the papists in nine points, concerning the assurance of election, and a confirmation of perseverance in election against certain passages of Scripture misinterpreted, e.g., Romans 11:20 and Hebrews 6:4-6. *The Foundation of the Faythfull. In a Sermon delivered at Paules Crosse (1611).

MARCH 3 — Theophilus Higgons (who once sawed down the maypole at Christ Church), author, under the name of Thomas Forster, of "A first motive to adhere to the Romish Church" (1609), now reconverted. A painful discourse of sin and grace, followed by a recantation of Romish errors, including his published work while at Douai and St. Omer's. "Some persons of quality, & worth" were instrumental in recalling him from Babylon. He took the Oath of Allegiance, the expediency of which was admitted to him by two learned Dominicans at Rouen. "They added further, that this extension of the Papall power over Christian Princes, was *dogma Transalpinum*, an Italian conceit." *A Sermon preached at Pauls Crosse ... In testimony of his heartie reunion with the Church of England (1611).

JUNE 30 — Thomas Cheaste, of St. Mary Hall, Oxford. His "two houres labour in the Lords Harvest" consisted of an exhortation to follow Christ in the narrow way. "Whereas by naturall inclination wee are addicted to imitation, let us follow the best: wisdome would so; partly because we are English men, who are reported, above all other nations, to be famous or infamous in imitating and following every strange and new-found fashion." *The Christian Pathway. Delivered in a Sermon Preached at Pauls Crosse* (1613).

AUG. 25   Robert Milles, preacher at Sutton St. Edmonds, Lincs. The case of Sodom gave him occasion for an invective against pride, and expecially against plays. "Yea, Playes are growne now adaies into such high request . . . as that some prophane persons affirme, they can learne as much both for example and edifying at a Play, as at a Sermon." He attacked also the profanation of the Sabbath "by idle walking in fields, and drinking in obscure corners." *Abrahams Sute for Sodome. A Sermon Preached at Pauls Crosse* (1612).

1612

JAN.   "A younge mignon of Sir Pexall Brockas did penance..., whom he had entertained and abused since she was twelve yeares old." (Chamberlain, I, 334.)

FEB. 9   One Ratcliffe, of Brasenose College, Oxford. The occasion of the penance of Moll Cutpurse, the Roaring Girl, for wearing men's apparel. She was drunk, the preacher did "extreem badly," her confederates picked pockets during the service, and the whole affair was anything but edifying. (Chamberlain, I, 334.)

MARCH 29   Thomas Adams, at this time preacher at Willington, Bedfordshire. The gallant's burden. An eloquent indictment of atheists, epicures, libertines, and common profane persons. The minister is the watchman, but the watchmen of Rome are usurpers, wolves, tyrants; at home the watchmen are scorned. "No jest ends in such laughter as that which is broken on a priest; the proof is plain in every tavern and theatre." (*The Works of Thomas Adams*, ed. Joseph Angus, Edinburgh, 1861-2, I, 294-328.)

AUG. 2   Thomas Draxe, Vicar of Dovercourt-cum-Harwich, Essex. Of the resurrection of the body, with a refutation of Aristotle and the Sadducees, interrupted by the inevitable digression on the enormities of the papists, "whose faith is faction, whose religion is rebellion, and whose badge is blood." The resurrection of the body excludes the blessed angels, devils and reprobates, all beings of equivocal and mixed generation, as "Mules, Wolfe-dogs, Wolfe-bitches, and all monstrous creatures," all creatures bred of putrefaction, as "frogs, flies, wormes, moules, mise, crickets, bats, barnacles," the ocean ("there shall be no more sea"), and hence all creatures therein, all cities, buildings, monuments, inventions and devices of man. *The Earnest of our Inheritance. . . . Preached at Pauls Crosse* (1613).

OCT. 18   William Hull, Prebendary of Canterbury. A dissertation upon the low state of sinful man, the necessity of repentance, and the crooked dealing of precisians and papists. *Repentance not to be repented of. A Sermon preached at Pauls Crosse (1612).

1613

JAN. 3   Thomas Sutton, Fellow of Queen's College, Oxford. An exhortation to ministers not to cease their reproof of sin, and to the people to yield obedience to them. No nation is so blessed by God but sin can cause variance between it and God; our sins are more harmful to our peace than all the machinations of the Jesuits. He reproved ignorance, swearing, and lying, before the hour-glass caught up with him. *Englands First and Second Summons. Two Sermons Preached at Paules Crosse (1616).

FEB. 5   Nathaniel Cannon, preacher at Wokingham. The preacher's task is to cry mercy and judgment. He recited the sins of England—"for sinne is growne to be a Giant": wilful murder, oppression of the poor, fraud, Machiavellianism, atheism, drunkenness, bribery, abomination of women's fashions. He also objected to rhetorical flourishes in sermons. (A precisian, he survived till 1664, "after he had ran with and submitted to all mutations" [Ath. Oxon., III, 674].) *The Cryer. A Sermon Preached at Pauls Crosse (1613).

MARCH 7   Thomas Adams, at this time preacher at Willington, Bedfordshire. One of his most striking efforts, "The White Devil." Upon Judas, thief and hypocrite. The thoroughness and violence of his survey of contemporary thieves, as he called them, is almost unequalled in the rich literature of this kind. He was expecially and characteristically vigorous in his condemnation of the usurer: "This is a man made out of wax: his Paternoster is a pawn; his creed is the condition of this obligation; his religion is all religation, a binding of others unto himself, of himself to the devil: for look how far any of the former thieves have ventured to hell, the usurer goes a foot further by the standard." (Works, II, 221–53.)

MARCH 24   Joseph Hall. A "holy panegyric" upon the accession anniversary. He eulogized the King's learning, mentioned the Apology for the oath of allegiance, the King's piety and mercy. The deliverance from the Plot was by a divination from the lips of the King. All these favours are forfeited by sin, and the death of Prince Henry was a punishment for the people's sins. (Works, ed. Wynter, V, sermon 6.)

MAY 9   Miles Mosse, pastor of Combes, Suffolk, author of the Arraignment of Usury (1595). Of the natures and powers of devils, of the prevalence of atheism among some knights, gentlemen, and scholars, and of the lively saving faith of the elect. *Justifying and saving Faith distinguished from the Faith of the Devils. In a Sermon preached at Pauls Crosse (1614).

UNE 6   Thomas Baughe, of Christ Church, Oxford. Of the last Judgment, the majesty of God, and the misery of sinful man. God will visit the sins of the usurer, "a scarlet sinner," of the "temple-pirate," and the simonist. Let the magistrates and lawyers, the "Gentles and Gallants," take heed, and the "beauteous Ladies" too who come to the Cross "clothed like Salomon in his royaltie." *A Summons to Judgement. Or a Sermon appointed for the Crosse, but delivered upon occasion in the Cathedrall Church of S. Paul* (1614).

OCT. 10 Sampson Price, of Exeter College, Oxford. A condemnation of atheists and papists, of sacrilege and toleration ("a Machiavellian pollicie"). His attacks on the sin of Laodicea included an explanation of the death of Prince Henry: "What could have taken away that sweet Prince, of fresh and bleeding memory, the expectation of all the Christian world, but our lukewarmnesse?" *Londons Warning by Laodicea's Luke-Warmenesse, Or a Sermon preached at Paules-Crosse* (1613).

OCT. 17 William Pemberton, Rector of High Ongar, Essex. "Religion," he said, "is no bawd to covetousness." Earthly blessings are but the "secondary reflexions" of the great gain of godliness. He warned the City magistrates that the profits of their traffic were as nothing unless their hearts were upright. *The Godly Merchant... A Sermon preached at Paules-Crosse* (1613).

Nov. 5 John Boys, after Dean of Canterbury. The anniversary of the Powder Plot gave him occasion to discuss the question of holy days, and also the pretended saints of Rome, such as "the wit-foundred drunkard, Henry Garnet." Such days as November 5 are holy days in the calendar of England's deliverances, and all Englishmen should rejoice, for, had the Plot succeeded, England would have become "a verie shambles of Italian and Ignatian butchers." *An Exposition of the Last Psalme. Delivered in a Sermon Preached at Paules Crosse* (1615).

ante Nov. 25 Books of Suarez the Jesuit burned at the Cross, as derogatory to princes. (*CSPD James I*, 1611–18, 212.)

1614

MARCH 24 John Rawlinson, Rector of Whitchurch, Salop, and chaplain to the King. The accession sermon. *Vivat rex*: two hours, two words, but a "world of matter." James is greater than Saul, yea than Solomon. "What can all those black-tongued Parrets... of Rome detract from his Majestie?" His stock is fruitful: "no sooner is one golden bough [Prince Henry] shed off, but another shoot's out. For, of those two pretious Pearles which yet survive... is not one of them [Elizabeth of Bohemia] since become a timely and teeming Mother?" He dealt delicately with the relation of the King to the law: "A King though he be free from *co-action* to keepe the law, yet must he voluntarily submit his will to the *direction* of the law." *Vivat Rex. A Sermon Preached at Pauls Crosse on the day of his Majestie's happie inauguration* (1619).

MAY 1 John Hoskins, Rector of Ledbury and Prebendary of Hereford. The Rehearsal sermon. Appropriately a brief discourse, after the summaries of "those delightful treatises" the Spital sermons, upon ministers, the "Lords remembrancers," and the attention due them. *Sermons Preached at Pauls Crosse and else-where* (1615).

JUNE 14 Henry Greenwood, Vicar of Great Sampford. A description of the terrors of Tophet, a meditation to "breake our strong hearts in pieces, and strike us into . . . a dismall dump." The fires of hell are corporal: "The Cicilian Ætna, called at this day *Gibillo Monte*, where roarings are heard, and flames of fire are seene: the flashing of Vesuvius; the cracking, as it were, of fire in a furnace in the Marine Rocke of Barry: what doe all these presage, but assure all those that fear the Lord . . . that Tophet is already prepared?" *Tormenting Tophet, Or a Terrible description of hell . . . Preached at Pauls Crosse* (1628).

DEC. 11 Charles Richardson, preacher at "Saint Katherines neere the Tower of London." A sermon against oppression and fraud. "I know as Luther said wittily, it is not safe for a poore hare to preach such doctrine to these Lions, hee shall have much adoe to escape their pawes'. But whatsoever the Lord commandeth me, that must I speak." The Lord had commanded him to condemn alienation of livings, cruel landlords, delay in lawsuits, deceitful merchants, etc. *A Sermon against oppression and fraudulent Dealing: Preached at Paules Crosse* (1615).

1615

FEB. 5 Thomas Sutton, Fellow of Queen's College, Oxford. A sermon on Revelation 3:15-16, the lukewarm. He exhorted magistrates to put a stop to the breaking of the Sabbath, to cut off papists and Jesuits, and incited ministers to be zealous against the "obscene and whorish stages," judges to be severe in prosecuting recusants. He warned against "Church Papists," who would mediate between us and the "Romish Synagogue." *Englands First and Second Summons. Two Sermons Preached at Paules Crosse* (1616).

MARCH 24 John White, brother to Francis White (*q.v.*) and chaplain to the King. The accession sermon. "Not onely the King himselfe is of God, but all the eminency and distinction of authority that is under him . . . are all of God . . . , and it is but a savage and popular humour to backbite or despise this eminency in whomsoever. . . . The practise of Libelling against Magistrates and great persons, at this day . . . cannot be justified. . . . It is true indeed that among the Greekes, *in veteri Comoedia* the persons of men were taxed: but they were Barbarians whom Christians must not imitate." *Two Sermons; The Former Delivered at Pauls Crosse* (1615).

JUNE 18 John Whalley, perhaps of St. John's, Cambridge. An elaborate discussion of those whose worship of God is imperfect; a distinction between true and false zeal; an attack on blasphemers, drunkards (including "vaine Tobaconists"), slanderers, and covetous persons. *Gods Plentie, feeding True Pietie. Openly shewed in a Sermon at Pauls Crosse* [1616].

Sept. 1   Gabriel Price. A sermon on the authority of God's ministers, and the need of due reverence to them. The age is given to sin: "Whoredom with some is good physicke; honestie is but foolerie; knaverie is commoditie; dissembling is discretion, and idleness is gentrie." In superiors is covetousness and carelessness; in inferiors, profanation of the Sabbath, swearing, pride of apparel, contention. *The Laver of the Heart; or Bath of Sanctification. Preached at Pauls Crosse* (1616).

Sept. 10 Anthony Hugget, Rector of Cliffe, Sussex, and chaplain to Lord Howard of Effingham. Of growth in holiness and of the perseverance of the saints, with an attack on the hellish treasons and idolatries of Rome. "Did not these infernall spirits, Antichristian pioners and Romish Moldwarpes, seeke to extinguish this glorious light, and the light of the whole land, *uno tactu, uno ictu, uno nictu*? Oh unspeakable villanie!" *A Divine Enthymeme of True Obedience . . . Preached at Pauls Crosse* (1615).

Dec. 3   Thomas Adams, at this time Vicar of Wingrave, Bucks. "Many and mighty deliverances hath the Lord given us: from furious Amalekites, that came with a navy, as they bragged, able to fetch away our land in turfs; from an angry and raging pestilence, that turned the popular streets of this city into solitude; from a treason wherein men conspired with devils, for hell was brought up to their conjurations." But still, he said, we treat Christ like Agamemnon. (*Works*, I, 114–36.)

1616
Feb. 25   William Jackson, lecturer in Whittington College. A catalogue and denunciation of sins which owes much to the method of Thomas Adams (*q.v.*). He exhibited vividly the vices of adulterers, brokers, dumb dogs, drunkards, engrossers, idolaters, greedy patrons, slanderers, swearers, and usurers. *The Celestial Husbandrie: Or, The Tillage of the Soule. First Handled in a Sermon at Pauls Crosse* (1616).

March 17 Sampson Price, of Exeter College, Oxford. Our sins, he said, are heralds of the Apocalypse. "We have many Professors in mouth, Atheists in life, Protestants in appearance, Papists in heart, zealous in shew, nothing in deed." London's glory is as great as that of Rome, but if she permits roarers, Jezebels, usurers, atheists, blood-thirsty papists to dwell within her gates, then surely God's judgment will come upon her. *Ephesus Warning before her Woe. A Sermon Preached at Pauls Crosse* (1616).

June 2   William Worship, Vicar of Croft, Lincs. All men are dogs without Christ, but there are dogs within the circuit of the Church which annoy her: "pricke-ear'd Curres of Rome," railers on men in authority, licentious livers, "dumb Dogges," and outrageous swearers: "Ah, noble Prince HENRY wee may thanke our Court-oathes, as one chiefe cause of thine untimely death." *The Patterne of an Invincible Faith* (1616).

OCT. 1   Charles Richardson, preacher "at Saint Katherines neere the Tower of London." An exhortation to magistrates to seek out sin and cast off dissolute members from the body politic. Wizards and sorcerers and traitorous papists should be sought out and punished. Great cities are nests of ungodliness and profanation of the Sabbath. *A Sermon concerning the punishing of Malefactors. Preached at Paules Crosse (1616).

OCT. 20   Samuel Ward, preacher of Ipswich. Balm from Gilead to recover conscience. He believed the sermon needful, for "the time is now come upon us wherein men affect and desire good names, estates, wives, houses, good clothes, good everything," but content themselves with mean and vile consciences. He was a good Puritan, and he pleaded for Sabbath observance, and condemned "popery and nature, and the old leaven of Pelagius, newly worse scoured by Arminius." (*Works of Thomas Adams*, III, 92–112.)

1617

JAN. 5   Immanuel Bourne, preacher at St. Christopher's, London. The opening of the true way, he declared, is the knowledge of Christ. "Get ye to the Bible, that most wholesome remedie for the soule. And againe, Hearken not hereunto only in the Church, but also at home, let the husband with the wife, let the father with the childe talke together of these matters, and both to and fro let them enquire, and give their judgments." This sermon, a significant Puritan document, contains a lucid and admirable exposition of the orders of nature and grace. *The True Way of a Christian.... Delivered first in Briefe, in a Sermon Preached at Paules-Crosse (1622).

FEB. 2   Charles Sonnibank, Canon of Windsor. A dogged pursuit of each doctrine that can be extracted from the story of the eunuch's conversion, for example, the eunuch was noble: "nobility may stand with Christianity"; he went to Jerusalem: he was not, like the papists, tied to the superstitions of his forefathers; he read the prophet Isaiah: we should not neglect to search the Scripture; etc. *The Eunuches Conversion (1617).

MARCH 24 John Donne, Reader in Divinity at Lincoln's Inn. The accession sermon, "his Majesty being then gone into Scotland." "A daintie sermon," reported Chamberlain, which was exceedingly well liked generally, "the rather for that he did Quene Elizabeth great right, and held himself close to the text without flattering the time too much." He gave especial note to James's care of religion. "He was beholden to no by-religion. The Papists could not make him place any hopes upon them, nor the puritans make him entertain any fears from them." (*Works of John Donne*, ed. Henry Alford, London, 1839, VI, 99–142.)

APRIL 5   John Drope, of Magdalen College, Oxford. He complained of the King's unjust impositions. "Out of the Proverbs among other things he would prove that Kinges might steale as well as meaner men both by borrowing and not paying, and by laying unreasonable and undue impositions upon their subjects." For this sermon he was, understandably, "called in question." (*CSPD James I*, 1611-18, 464.)

APRIL 6   Charles Richardson, preacher "at Saint Katherines neere the Tower of London." He spoke sharply of the vanity of ambition. "It was a witty question, that one made; Why *Honos*, that signifieth honour, was written with an aspiration, and *Onus* that signifieth a burden, was written without. And it was as wittily answered, because there are none that desire the burthen that accompanieth honour, but all men gape after the honor and preferment." **The Price of our Redemption. A sermon Preached at Paules Crosse* (1617).

JUNE 10   Immanuel Bourne, preacher at St. Christopher's, London. Of the rainbow. Amid this stylish tissue of allegories, he found place for an indictment of the sins of unthankful England: pride in apparel, drunkenness, simony, sacrilege, schism. The high point of the sermon, however, was "a manifold Analogie betweene Christ and the Bowe." **The Rainebow, or, A Sermon Preached at Pauls Crosse* (1617).

JUNE 29   John Burgess. This notable Puritan preached before the Secretary and his lady, and "as great an auditorie as hath ever been seene there." Chamberlain could "discover nothing so extraordinarie in him but opinion." (Chamberlain, II, 86.)

Nov. 5   Henry King, of Christ Church, Oxford. The first sermon of the poet-bishop, at the age of 23. "Yt was thought a bold part of them both [Henry King and his father John King, Bishop of London] that so younge a man shold play his first prises in such a place and such a time, beeing as he professed *primitiae* of his vocation . . . but this world (as they say) is made for the presumptuous: he did reasonablie well but nothing extraordinarie, nor neere his father, beeing rather slow of utterance *orator parum vehemens*." (Chamberlain, II, 114.)

Nov. 29   A sermon of sin and apostasy, with a record of England's sins: children swearing, young men drunk and blasphemous, old men hardened in wickedness. A record of God's threats to England: the days of Mary, the plague of 1603, the Plot, the death of Prince Henry. An appeal to repentance. **Englands Warning by Israel and Judah. Delivered in a Sermon at Pauls-Crosse* (1633).

1618

JAN. 11   John Everard, reader in St. Martin's-in-the-Fields. The sermon contained reproaches against the Court of Orphans, which "if true" were "unfitting to repeat before a popular assembly." He was censured by the Bishop of London, and required to apologize to the Lord Mayor and aldermen. (*CSPD James I*, 1611-18, 519.)

Feb. 15   Robert Sibthorpe, Vicar of St. Sepulchre, Northampton. He took occasion to speak against the Puritans: "Their pretended pure tender conscience is impurely polluted, and their faith worse then infidelity." But he also had a word for the Romanists who creep into great houses to lead captive "simple women laden with sinnes." To "meete with the impiety of the Papist, the prophanenesse of the Atheist, and the errour of the Anabaptist," he developed at large, out of Perkins, the nature of an oath. *A Counter-Plea to an Apostataes Pardon. A Sermon preached at Paules Crosse [1618].

APRIL 26   Walter Balcanquhall, a Scottish divine, afterwards Master of the Savoy and Dean of Rochester. He preached "handsomely." (Chamberlain, II, 161.)

Nov.   The penance, in a white sheet, of Lady Markham, wife of Sir Griffin Markham, for marrying one of her servants, her husband being still alive. (CSPD James I, 1611–18, 516.)

DEC. 13   Michael Wigmore, sometime Fellow of Oriel College, Oxford. A sermon describing and condemning the typical sins of young and old, and showing how one sin leads to a worse, until the sinner is overwhelmed. This sermon was preached in the church, "by reason of a Tempest." *The Way of all Flesh, A Sermon Prepared for Pauls Crosse (1619).

DEC. 20   Roger Ley, curate of St. Leonard's, Shoreditch. Of the last estate of the world, and the establishing of a new world. In his discussion of the divine order and hierarchy, he condemned "our Novelists . . . that . . . have contended to breake the bond of Ecclesiastical jurisdiction." *Two Sermons, One Preached at Paules Crosse (1619).

1619

JAN. 17   Stephen Denison, Rector of St. Katherine Cree. Preaching on a very cold day, this Boanerges set forth firmly the theory and practice of the Puritan life, which rests on the doctrine of regeneration through the Word, and the manifestation of election in Bible-reading, family prayer, daily self-examination, and perseverance in a lawful vocation. *The New Creature. A Sermon preached at Pauls Crosse (1622).

MARCH 7   Francis White, of Magdalen College, Oxford. Since he had to speak of the voice of God crying against iniquity, he expatiated upon the dignity and duties of ministers, reproved "dumb dogs," and the hearers who listen to the minister but do not obey. He reiterated the familiar cry against worldliness, and set before his audience the man of true wisdom: "Hee, like a good Pilgrime-Traveller, because hee would not cumber his soule too much with the trash of this world, which might hinder his expedition in his journey to Heaven, hee wisely sends his treasures to Heaven before him." A powerful sermon. *Londons Warning, By Jerusalem. A Sermon Preached at Pauls Crosse (1619).

MARCH 24   "A poore sermon" upon the accession anniversary. (Chamberlain, II, 229.)

April 11   John King, Bishop of London. A sermon of thanksgiving for the recovery of the King from his serious illness. He paid the usual tributes to James, his care for religion, the peacefulness of his reign, his noble behaviour at death's door. But the body of the sermon was a fine meditation on death, in the grand manner of the age. "All the people of the earth may stand upon the shore of my text [Isa. 38:17], and see the face of their fraile & inconstant condition."   *A Sermon of Publicke Thanks-giving for the happie recoverie of his Majestie (1619).

May 1   "Mr. Shingleton of Oxford" (probably Isaac Singleton, at this time a canon of St. Paul's). He attacked Bacon, the Lord Chancellor, and his court, "finding himself aggreved with some decree of his wherin he thought he had hard measure . . . , and glanced (they say) somewhat scandalously at him and his Catamites as he called them." (Chamberlain, II, 243.)

1620

March 26   John King, Bishop of London. Upon a text set by the King, "a voyce from earth that is next to heaven," he preached on behalf of the repair, long overdue, of the cathedral. He reviewed the history of the building, and spent much time in extolling the King, who was present on this, the only occasion on which he honoured the place with his presence. "After the sermon the King had a banket in the bishops house." (See Chamberlain, II, 299.)   *A Sermon at Paules Crosse, on behalfe of Paules Church (1620).

April 23   Thomas Walkington, Vicar of Fulham. He descanted nicely upon the love of Mary Magdalen for her Lord, and ended with a passionate exhortation to the love of God.   *Rabboni; Mary Magdalens Teares, of Sorrow, Solace . . . Preached at S. Pauls Crosse, after the Rehearsall (1620).

June 5   Michael Wigmore, sometime Fellow of Oriel College, Oxford. A proof of the existence of God, against atheists; God is to be found manifest in nature and history. A further proof of the Trinity, "a heavenly Subtilty," which though a mystery is yet taught us in the book of nature, for example, in the trinity in unity of the soul's faculties; of the root, trunk and branches of the tree; of the sun, moon, and the "light of the Ayre, proceeding from them both." The sermon is dedicated to Francis Bacon.   *The Good Adventure . . . A Sermon preached at Pauls Crosse (1620).

June 11   "Mr. Chaffin, of the Temple." (This is Thomas Chafin, after Rector of Long Newton, Wilts., and "a great delinquent." He proposed, in the 1640's, that the Litany have added to it another petition: "From all lay Puritans and all Parliament men, good Lord, deliver us.") (Michael Wigmore, The Good Adventure (1620), p. 1; Walker Revised ed. A. G. Matthews, Oxford, 1948, p. 371.)

Dec. 17(?)   "A younge fellow" spoke "very freely in general" on the Spanish match, though the Bishop of London had charged all his clergy, on the King's

Dec. 31　John Andrews, preacher at St. James Clerkenwell. "Let it not seem strange to you," he began, "that for a New-Yeeres gift, I should offer to so honourable an assembly such an ominous present, as a Serpent: For . . . the Serpent cast into a circular figure (holding his Tayle in his mouth) hath of old bin made an Hieroglyphique, and mysticall representation of the revolution of the yeere." The serpent in the wilderness is the type; Christ on the cross the antitype. The sermon is a storehouse of the curious analogies suggested to him by this symbolism. *The Brazen Serpent: Or, the Copie of a Sermon Preached at Pauls Crosse* (1621).

1621

Feb. 25　John Everard, reader at St. Martin's-in-the-Fields. He preached against the Spanish match, "discifring the craft and crueltie of the Spaniards in all places where they come specially the West Indies, all or most part of what he said, cited and taken out of theyre owne authors." He was committed to the Gatehouse for this sermon. (Chamberlain, II, 350; see *DNB*, art. "John Everard.")

March 24　Lewis Bayly, Bishop of Bangor. The accession sermon. (Chamberlain, II, 356.)

July 8　Samuel Buggs, minister of Coventry. On the sin of David in numbering the people, with an exhortation to England: "The Christians in Polonia cry out for ayde: The Protestants in Bohemia groane under a heavie and intolerable burden: The Protestants of France send many sighs to heaven for peace or bare security. Happy Britaines, wee sit under our owne vines, and our own Fig-trees." *Davids Strait. A Sermon Preached at Pauls-Crosse* (1622).

Aug. 26　Thomas Bedford, of Queens' College, Cambridge. A disquisition on the mortal sin, the sin against the Holy Spirit, which is "a generall Apostasie, and revolt of a man wilfully fallen from the truth knowne, even to a malicious, persecuting, and blaspheming of the same." *The sinne unto death . . . In a Sermon Preached at Pauls Crosse* (1621).

Sept. 9　Roger Ley, curate of St. Leonard's, Shoreditch. Of the power and diligence of the devil, and the confederacy of his Romish ministers, and of the exceeding power of God to salvation. *The Bruising of the Serpents Head. A Sermon Preached at Pauls Crosse* (1622).

Nov. 25　Henry King, Archdeacon at Colchester. A book called the *Protestants Plea*, a piece of Catholic propaganda, circulated the rumour that Bishop John King had become a convert to Rome on his death-bed, through the agency of one Thomas Preston. The bishop's son here exploded the scandal, rehearsed with some emotion the tale of his father's dying hours, and took occasion to reprove other occasions of evil, as lay preachers, and above all Jesuits, "those only the great Paracelsians of the world, whose practice is Phlebotomy, to let States blood in the Heart-veine." *A Sermon Preached at Pauls Crosse . . . Whereunto is annexed the Examination . . . of Thomas Preston (1621).

1622

MARCH 4 Humphrey Sydenham, Fellow of Wadham College, Oxford. "We are not here," he announced, "to cheat our Auditory with a thin discourse; Mysterie is our Theame and subject, the very Battlement and Pinacle of Divinity." The "Mysterie" was the omnipotency and inscrutability of God's will, affirmed against Arminians. *Jacob and Esau . . . Sermon at Pauls Crosse (1626).

JUNE 2 Thomas Aylesbury, Vicar of Cardworth, Warwickshire. An interpretation of the "parabolicall proverbe" in Luke 17:37 as referring to the last Judgment. *A Sermon Preached at Paules-Crosse (1623).

JUNE 23 George Montaigne [Mountain], Bishop of London. "There was a great assemblie but a small auditorie, for his voyce was so low that I thincke scant the third part was within hearing. The chief points of his sermon were touching the benevolences, wherein he wold prove that what we have is not our owne, and what we gave was but rendering and restoring. Another part was about the repayring of Paules, and the largest in confuting Paraeus opinions touching the peoples authoritie in some cases over unruly and tirannical Princes; for which heresie of state his books were publikely burnt there towards the end of the sermon." (Chamberlain, II, 443.)

JUNE 30 Robert Harris, Vicar of Hanwell, Oxfordshire. This sermon, very elaborately divided, contains a notable exhortation to good order: "Happy that State, wherein the Cobler meddles with his Last, the Tradesman with his shop, the student with his booke, the Counsellor with State, the Prince with the Scepter, and each Creature lives in his owne Element. . . . Woe to that body that will be all head; members misplaced are neither for use nor ease." *Gods Goodnes and Mercie Laid open in a Sermon, Preached at Pauls-Crosse (1626).

AUG. 4 Daniel Donne, of St. John's College, Cambridge. He laid the axe of his text (Luke 3:9) to the root of the tree of sin, rebuking sloth and pharisaical conformity, church-robbing and ungodliness. We are ungrateful for the blessing of peace, he warned, while "other Nations doe ride even up unto their horse bridles in blood." Surely God's vengeance hangs over our heads. The published sermon was dedicated to John Donne. *A Sub-Poena from the Star-Chamber of Heaven. A Sermon Preached at Pauls Crosse (1623).

AUG. 5   Samuel Purchas, Rector of St. Martin's Ludgate, author of *Purchas His Pilgrimage*. On the twenty-second anniversary of the Gowrie conspiracy. "The Time itself may be a Text, to quicken our Memorie; Memorie may awaken Consideration; Consideration may excite Admiration; Admiration might incite Thankfulnesse; Thankfulnesse may swell into extaticall Jubilees of joye." The sermon developed into a rhapsodical catalogue of England's blessings, in so good and wise a King, so large a kingdom, reaching even to "wide and wilde America," so goodly a city as London: "Hail London! The Towre of thy King is in the East for thy safetie; the Bowre, and Palace of thy King is in the West, for light and Majestie." **The Kings Towre, and Triumphant Arch of London. A Sermon Preached at Pauls Crosse* (1623).

AUG. 25 [John?] Claydon, minister of Hackney. He "cited a story out of our Chronicles, of a Spanish sheep, brought into England in Edward the First's time, which infected most of the sheep of England with a murrain, and prayed God no more such sheep might be brought over from thence thither; at which many of his hearers cried out Amen. So much generally did all men fear that Prince Charles should marry the King of Spain's sister, as they ever hated that nation. He lay awhile in prison for his sermon, but was soon after set at liberty by the mediation of . . . the Earl of Holderness, whose chaplain he was." (*SP Ven.*, XVII (1621–3), 462; Simonds D'Ewes, *Autobiography and Correspondence*, ed. J. O. Halliwell, London, 1845, I, 219–20.)

SEPT. 1 Richard Sheldon, "a Convert from out of Babylon." Upon Revelation 14:9–11, of the Beast and his mark. Praying frequently for divine assistance, which he needed, he proved the Beast to be the Church of Rome. It is morally impossible, he assured the audience, for England to return to the Roman fold, this for instruction of such "who trembling and fearing where there is no just cause of feare, do fearefully presage, and feare to themselves, that there may happen (and also that the same is at hand) some generall fall, and change from Religion to Popery, in this renowned State and Kingdom." Sheldon received a severe reprimand for this sermon, which apparently embarrassed James during the Spanish negotiations. (See *DNB*, art. "Richard Sheldon"; *SP Ven.*, XVII (1621–3), 462n.) **A Sermon Preached at Paules Crosse laying open the Beast, and his Marke* (1625).

SEPT. 15 John Donne, Dean of St. Paul's. A defence of the King's orders concerning preaching, and of his "constancie in the true reformed religion, which the people . . . began to suspect; his text was the 20th verse of the 5th chapter of the book of Judges, somwhat a straunge text for such a business, and how he made yt hold together I know not, but he gave no great satisfaction, or as some say spake as yf hymself were not so well satisfied." (*Works*, ed. Alford, VI, 189–222; Chamberlain, II, 451.)

Sept. 29   Elias Petley. Lessons drawn from the life and death of Hezekiah, with a digression on sermons of evil intent, which are not sermons but "Pasquils, Satyrs to vent a private spleene, tampering with God's secrets and matters of state." This passage was likely inspired by the government. *The Royal Receipt: or Hezekiah's Physicke. A Sermon . . . delivered at Pauls-Crosse (1623).

Nov. 5   John Donne, Dean of St. Paul's. On the anniversary of the Powder Plot. "Wherein I was left more to my own liberty [than on September 15]." The sermon was preached in the church because of bad weather. There is one significant passage: "If this breath, that is, this power, be at any time soured in the passage, and contract an ill savour by the pipes that convey it, so as that his [the King's] good intentions are ill executed by inferior ministers, this must not be imputed to him." (Works, ed. Alford, V, 202–32.)

1623

Feb. 2   Thomas Myriell, Rector of St. Stephen's Walbrook. He praised the preaching place: "Here have you the choysest wits, the gravest heads, the sharpest judgements, continually emptying themselves to you." He extolled the purity of the Church of England and the King's grace in maintaining it. *The Christians Comfort. In a Sermon Appointed for the Crosse (1623).

March 24   John Richardson, of Magdalen College, Oxford. The accession sermon. "He performed yt reasonable well, and the better because he was not long nor immoderate in commendation of the time, but gave Queen Elizabeth her due." (Chamberlain, II, 487.)

March 30   [John?] Wilson. The sermon "contained general words full of evil interpretation." He seems to have spoken against popery, which "leads to perjury, breach of faith, &c." The sermon probably treated of matters of state, connected with the negotiations with Spain. (CSPD James I, 1619–23, 551.)

April 6   Richard Holdsworth, a "very proper man." (Chamberlain, II, 489.)

Aug. 5   Barten Holyday, Archdeacon of Oxford. On the Gowrie anniversary. "The deliverance of a King is the greatest Epocha in the Chronicle of Gods mercies," for "Majesty is a deputy-divinity . . . God having proposed to man the visible Godhead of a King, as his own proportionall and lawfull image." He repeated, elaborately and obscurely, the official version of the events of August 5, 1600, and concluded: "Surely we must acknowledge him the friend of God . . . whom he preserved for the uniting of the Britainies, a worke that required no lesse preface than this Miracle!" *A Sermon preached at Pauls Crosse, August the 5. 1623 (1626).

Oct. 26   Thomas Adams, preacher at St. Gregory's under St. Paul's. The barren tree. A review of the sins of "graceless Christians." The three years of his text (Luke 13:7) he applied to the reign of Edward VI, "who purged the gold from the rust and dross of superstition," the reign of Elizabeth, who "did again vindicate this vineyard" and "taught it anew to speak the dialect of the Holy Ghost," and the reign of James, "under whom we know not whether truth or peace be more." On the day the sermon was preached, "it pleased God Almighty to make a fearful comment upon . . . his own text," in the fall of the house in the Blackfriars where about 300 persons were gathered to hear Father Drury preach. (*Works*, II, 166–85.)

1624

APRIL 11 John Lawrence, "Preacher of the Word of God in the Citie of London." He opened with an apology for his youth and lack of understanding, and followed with a review of the sins of the city, and exhortation to the magistrates to seek out evil in all its "windings and turnings." "Iniquity was never so rife, as since frequent preaching of the Gospell." *A Golden Trumpet, to rowse up a drowsie Magistrate . . . As it was sounded at Pauls Crosse (1624).

APRIL 18 William Laud, Bishop of St. David's. (*The History of the Troubles and Tryal of . . . William Laud . . . , wrote by himself* (1694), p. 12.)

JUNE 4 Humphrey Sydenham, Fellow of Wadham College, Oxford. In a discourse pitched deliberately at a high scholarly level, citing authority at every point, he "traversed (though with some blood and difficultie) the errours of primitive Times in their foulest shapes . . . opened the wiles and stratagems of the adversary," Arius, that "vexation of the Fathers." *The Arraignment of the Arrian . . . In a Sermon Preached at Pauls Crosse (1626).

AUG. 5 Thomas Adams, preacher at St. Gregory's under St. Paul's. Of the temple. "This age is sick of such a wanton levity, that we make choice of the temple according to our fancy of the preacher." He attacked popish idolatry, and the idols of vain pleasure, vain honour and riches. He praised James as a defender of the faith. (*Works*, II, 284–309.)

SEPT. 19 R. V., "Preacher of Gods Word." A badly organized and spotty effusion upon Jonah 4:9, containing some animadversions upon the sin of anger and the common fault of litigiousness in Englishmen. *Jonahs Contestation about his Gourd. In a Sermon delivered at Pauls Crosse (1625).

SEPT. 26 William Proctor, perhaps the Rector of Over Boddington, Northants. "Woe to Ariel!" Pride is the "reigning sinne" of London, pride in apparel: "we cannot by your apparell discerne a young Prentice from a young Gallant, a phantasticke Tradesman, from a great landed Gentleman." He concluded with an exhortation to repentance and prayer. *The Watchman Warning. A Sermon preached at Pauls Crosse (1625).

OCT. 24 Robert Bedingfield, student of Christ Church, Oxford. Denied a large auditory by "the violence of a wet season," he began with a curious disquisition upon the Fall, and proceeded to a careful statement of the Protestant doctrine of faith and works: "We affirme that this faith which alone justifieth, is never alone. . . . Faith justifieth without workes, and yet is not the faith which justifieth without workes." *A Sermon Preached at Pauls Crosse (1625).

OCT. 31 John Gee, formerly Rector of Newton, Lancs. An exhortation to constancy in the faith, with himself as awful example, for he had been "in the Snare of the Fowler." He described in detail the machinations of the Jesuits, and spoke with thankfulness of his delivery from the disaster of the Blackfriars, on October 26, 1623. *Hold fast. A Sermon preached at Pauls Crosse (1624).

NOV. 21 Robert Sanderson, Rector of Boothby Pagnell, Lincs. Upon the just extent of Christian liberty in the lawful use of the creatures of God, in which he made this important observation for the times: "Neither let any man cherish his ignorance herein, by conceiting as if there were some difference to be made between Civil and Ecclesiastical things, and Laws, in this behalf. The truth is, our Liberty is equal in both, the power of Superiors for restraint equal in both, and necessity of obedience in Inferiors equal in both." (The Works of Robert Sanderson, D.D., Oxford, 1854, III, 145-211.)

1625

ante MARCH 23 Sir Robert Howard was excommunicated publicly at the Cross for contempt of the Court of High Commission, which in 1624 had begun proceedings against Lady Purbeck, with whom Howard was living in adultery. (CSPD James I, 1623-5, 507.)

MARCH 24 Barten Holyday, Archdeacon of Oxford. The accession sermon, upon Ezekiel 37:22, and a stylish performance. "The union of Cities into a kingdome, tries the goodnesse of a king: but the union of kingdomes tries his wisdome: the simplicitie of justice beeing enough to manage one kingdome, but two will require the mysterie of wisdome." England and Scotland are united even in religion: "A Prelate and an Organ are now no newes; but the one is everywhere more sacred than a father: the other as cheerfull as a Psalme." *A Sermon preached at Pauls Crosse March the 24. 1624 (1626).

UNDATED SERMONS TEMP. JAMES I

ante 1610 Robert Bolton, Rector of Broughton, Northants. This sermon was "the very first fruites" of his ministry. Most of his time was spent in "decyphering the state of formall hypocrisie," but he also denounced atheism, popery, lukewarmness, and included a vigorous attack on "prophane and obscene Playes," the "Grand empoysoners of grace, ingenuousness, and all manly resolution." *A Discourse about the State of True Happiness: Delivered in Certaine Sermons in Oxford and at Pauls Crosse* (1614).

ante 1611 John Denison, Vicar of St. Mary's, Reading. Of the sin against the Holy Ghost, which is apostasy from the Gospel. **The Sinne against the Holy Ghost Plainely described* (1620).

1605–15 John Hoskins, Prebendary of Hereford and chaplain to the King. "Woe to the Crowne of pride," to the perverse and inordinate desire of one's own excellence! He attacked feminine finery: "The men that are busied, and the charge that is employed, about these painfull and difficult toyes, would serve for many new Plantations. . . . Kingdomes might be conquered, whilest Ruffes are spinning." He also fulminated against drunkenness, and warned that England's long peace and prosperity might breed carnal security. **Sermons Preached at Pauls Crosse and else-where* (1615).

1605–15 John Hoskins, Prebendary of Hereford and chaplain to the King. Upon Zechariah 5:4, the sovereignty of the divine justice. He opposed usury with the traditional argument of man's stewardship: "The principal right of all outward things God hath reserved to himselfe . . . , yet hath hee committed to the sonnes of men a right of use and dispensation agreeable unto reason, which asketh that things in nature perfect, should serve creatures of more perfection." In the church is sacrilege and simony, in government oppression and tyranny, in justice corruption and bribery. Let every man look to the foundations of his house, especially tradesmen, for "it is hard to keepe sin out of trading." **Sermons Preached at Pauls Crosse and else-where* (1615).

ante 1618 Thomas Thompson, Rector of Montgomery. Of the Antichrist, proved to be the Pope, "both by artificiall demonstration, and by testimonie of Ancient Fathers, and of later Writers, digested into a panelled Jurie." **Antichrist Arraigned: In a Sermon at Pauls Crosse* (1618).

CHARLES I

1625
APRIL 16 A bishop. A stately and eloquent description of the sufferings and fruits of the Passion, with this clever application: "And is he not crucified in his members between two Thieves still: the poor Client, he is crucified between the Judge and the Lawyer . . . , the sick patient, he is crucified between the Physitian and the Apothecary . . . , the Protestant is crucified between the Papist and the Puritan . . . , the Gentleman is crucified between the Usurer and Scrivener, and virtue itself was ever tormented between . . . the excess and the defect." **A Sermon Preached at St. Paul's Cross . . . By a late Reverend Bishop of the Church of England* (1653).

1626

APRIL 7 Thomas Aylesbury, Rector of Berwick St. Leon, Wilts. The Passion sermon. The story of the Passion retold, prefaced by a discourse upon the ignorance of the Jews, and a proof out of Aquinas of the necessity of the suffering of Christ. *The Passion Sermon at Pauls-Crosse (1626).

MAY 21 Antony Fawkner, of Jesus College, Oxford. His first sermon before "so generall an audience." An exhortation to compassion, without which man is unnatural. "A man had as good be a stocke, as a man without a neighbour. Wee are better than beasts only in discourse. so that our perfection depends upon a fellow." *Comfort to the Afflicted. Delivered in a Sermon preached at Pauls-Crosse (1626).

MAY 30 Matthew Brookes, Rector of Sudborne-with-Orford, Suffolk. A judgment upon heretics and schismatics, i.e., papists, Anabaptists, Brownists, Familists, etc. He spoke of the monuments of Roman Catholicism in England: "It is true, that their end is their belly, yet doe their outward actions, beare such a shew of holinesse and charitie, that . . . to the sight of the world they exceed us farre. And hence it is that so many Churches, Temples, Oratories, Colledges, Schooles of learning, Hospitalls, Almeshouses, and other monuments of all sorts, which our eyes daily doe behold, have been erected even in the days of blindenesse: to say the truth, we scarce repaire and uphold those most necessary buildings of all sorts, which our Progenitors, in the time that they dranke of the waters of Babylon, have erected to our hands." *A Sermon Preached at Pauls-Crosse . . . Wherein may be seene whom we are to repute Hereticks (1626).

JULY 23 William Hampton, chaplain to the Earl of Nottingham. God has tried by famine and pestilence to bring England to repentance, but in vain. Next will come the sword, the sword of the cruel Spaniard, whose atrocities in the Indies he rehearsed. A plea for money for national defence. *A Proclamation of Warre from the Lord of Hosts. . . . Delivered in a Sermon at Pauls Crosse (1627).

DEC. 24 Matthew Brookes, Rector of Sudborne-with-Orford, Suffolk. Upon the true Church, "the company of Gods Elect and chosen: that Peter was not head of it, but a stone of the building: that Christ is the sure foundation, and that whosoever is builded on him, shall never be broken downe." *The House of God. . . . In a Sermon preached at Pauls Crosse (1627).

DEC. 31 Henry Valentine, lecturer at St. Dunstan's in the West. The peace of the Church is menaced by false prophets and schismatics who balk at ceremonies, yet the Church is never in danger but when she is out of danger; God tries his Church to wean her from the world, he "feeds us with onions and garlike in the Egypt of this world, that we might desire our Exodus." He made an eloquent appeal for public prayer, which is like "a consort of Musique . . . more sweet and melodious than any one instrument." Let us not, he concluded, "shrink up all religion into preaching." *Noahs Dove: or a Prayer for the Peace of Jerusalem. Delivered in a Sermon at Pauls Crosse (1627).

1627

FEB. 11 Stephen Denison, Rector of St. Katherine Cree. A discourse upon false prophets, with particular reference to the Familists, accompanied by the public penance of John Hetherington, a box-maker, who had recently been punished by the High Commission for keeping a conventicle and preaching Familism. Denison concluded with a list of "the severall kinds of Mysticall Wolves breeding in ENGLAND": popish wolves, Arminian wolves, Anabaptist wolves, "Rosey-crosse wolves, Familisticall wolves," including "Gringletonian Familists in the North," and Familists "in the Mountains." *The White Wolfe or, A Sermon Preached at Pauls Crosse . . . . Wherein faction is unmasked (1627).

MARCH 18 John Gumbledon, preacher at Longworth, Berks. Of the misery of man and the great mercy of God. A conventional effusion. *Gods Great Mercy to Mankinde in Jesus Christ: A Sermon Preached at Pauls Crosse (1628).

APRIL 15 Robert Sanderson, Rector of Boothby Pagnell, Lincs., after Bishop of Lincoln. A subtle discourse from a distinguished casuist, upon the sin of Abimelech, treating of how far ignorance excuses sin, and of the nature of God's mercy in restraint of sin. (Works, III, 212-69.)

MAY 6 John Donne, Dean of St. Pauls. He proved the dependence of the ecclesiastical state upon the civil, opposing both papists and presbyterians. He defended ecclesiastical vestments, and the use of church ornaments, not as idols, but as aids to instruction. (Works, ed. Alford, V, 159-79.)

NOV. 28 William Waller, sometime Rector of Chiswick. A sermon against sacrilege. He spoke bitterly of those who, in the reign of Henry VIII, feared popish idolatry so much that they took the ornaments of the Church into their own houses. He proceeded to show how the best families had come to a bad end for such sacrilege. (Sir Henry Spelman, The History and Fate of Sacrilege, London, 1853, p. 81.)

1629

MAY 17 Two libels against the king, blaming him for the loss of Rochelle, were found before the sermon. One Vernon Ferrar, servant to John Locke, said under examination that he was holding a place for his master and saw a "young youth" pick up a sealed letter; the youth opened it, and said it was "for the king." The "old man that belongs to the cross" took the papers away from the youth. (CSPD Charles I, 1628-9, 550, 552.)

JUNE 28 Richard Farmer, Rector of Charwelton, Northants. Overmuch reproof of others leads to schism. "The religion of a great many, consists in nothing so much, as in statising discourses. . . . When they should be at home about their owne affairs, their eyes are in the corners, or in the ends of the earth: the theame of their talke is no lesse then the affaires of all Christendome: their relations all forraine intelligences: their providence is nothing but prophecies of prodigious imminent alterations: their conferences in shops, in private houses, nothing but projects of new formes of government, and elections of new governours: their daily pastime nothing so much as an ignorant, and an uncharitable censuring and traducing of others, especially their superiours: deploring the times, crying out for reformation of all save themselves." *A Sermon preached at Pauls Crosse* (1629).

Nov. 22 John Donne, Dean of St. Paul's. An exhortation to good works, opposing the Protestant to the Catholic doctrine of works. Good works, he said, constitute the reclamation from offence in Christ (Matt. 11:6), and offence may arise from a propensity to misinterpret the words and actions of others. "God bless me from myself, that I lead not myself into temptation, by a wilful misinterpreting of other men, especially my superiors; that I cast not aspersions or imputations upon the church, or the state, by my mistakings." (*Works*, ed. Alford, V, 232-55.)

1630

April 18 Edward Boughen, Rector of Woodchurch, Kent. An invective against false prophets. He spoke in defence and publication of the King's declaration that no one should make changes in the interpretation of the Articles, and declared: "What hath beene once defined by the Church, ought not to be subject to the censure of particular persons." The disciplinarians (he said) are wolves in the midst of lambs; they know not how to submit, but they "know how to controule, to command out of a Pulpit." It is not for every man to examine doctrine, nor are all doctrines to be examined. *Two Sermons .... The Second, Preached at Saint Paul's Crosse* (1635).

May 30 Charles I "went into a roome and heard the sermon at Paules Crosse." (Sir William Dugdale, *The History of St. Paul's Cathedral*, London, 1818, p. 90.)

Aug. 7 John Jones, curate of St. Michael's Bassishaw. England is specially blessed of God: "All other countries are in some things defective; but England ... doth minister unto us whatsoever is usefull .... The summer burnes us not, nor doth the winter benumme us .... Though God hath tossed our neighbour nations ... , yet this Iland ... , our deare Country, hath stood like the Center." Yet England is full of sin, and God has punished us with plague, and with defeat in war. *Londons Looking Backe to Jerusalem ... Preached at Pauls Crosse* (1633).

Sept. 5 Isaac Craven, Vicar of Felmersham, Bedfordshire. A thorough census of the hidden sins of men, which shall be revealed at the last day. "If here thou wouldst often blush for shame, had thy breast but a Momus his grate before it, for men to be prying into thy thoughts: if here thou wouldst loath and abhore thy selfe in case of a sudden surprision as thou actest thy secret folly; how then shall it abash thee, when after so long concealment . . . the very heart of thy heart shall be plainly unfolded, and the darknesse of thy clanculary delights irradiated with the glorious beames of justice in the face of God?" *Gods Tribunall and Mans Tryall* (1631).

1631

MARCH 27   William Laud, Bishop of London. The accession sermon. He began: "The age is so bad, they will not endure a good King to be commended, for danger of flattery: I hope I shall offend none by praying for the King." A king should pray, he continued, and our King is daily at his prayers, but the people should pray too, and not sin in murmuring against the King. If this fault be not amended, the King's "judgment" which God has given him may pull out the stings of these waspish persons "that can employ their tongues in nothing but to wound him and his government." "Kings are ordained of God for the good of the people." (*The Works of . . . William Laud, D.D.*, Oxford, 1860, I, 185-212.)

MAY   Public penance of Sir Giles Alington for marriage with his cousin, by sentence of the High Commission court. (*CSPD Charles I, 1631-3*, 42.)

SEPT. 11   John Robinson, of King's College, Cambridge. An "alarme from the Trumpet of God" to fight the good fight of faith. "Whereas the fight of the world is one man against another: this of a Christian is of one the same man against himselfe." *Vox Ducis: Or, An Alarme from the Trumpet of God . . . In A Sermon at Pauls Crosse* (1631).

1632

MAY 6   Robert Sanderson, Rector of Boothby Pagnell, Lincs., after Bishop of Lincoln. "Concerning the right use of Christian liberty." Preached by appointment of Laud, "to the suppressing of Novelties and the preservation of Order and Peace." He made the necessary distinction between Christian liberty and dishonest license, and answered point by point the objections of the Puritans who contended that the ecclesiastical ordinances set bounds to Christian liberty. He noted the "partiality of the Objectors . . . in laying the accusation against the Ecclesiastical Laws only, whereas their arguments, if they had any strength in them, would as well conclude against the Political Laws in the Civil State, and against domesticall orders in Private Families." (*Works*, III, 270-325.)

1633(?)

MAY 27   John Gore, Rector of Wenden-lofts, Essex. True prosperity must be based on religion and piety; but goods and grace are not incompatible. "It is a great blessing to have the wealth of the world and to prosper outwardly; but it is a greater blessing to have the grace of the Spirit and to prosper inwardly." "Except Christ be with a man in his Shop ...there's no good to be done in any trade." *The Way to prosper. A Sermon Preached at St. Pauls Crosse* (1636).

1634

May 26 John Gore, Rector of Wenden-lofts, Essex. A gracious discourse on the true contentment of "the sifted Christian." Grace and godliness are the ballast of the human ship; yet we are frail creatures: "It is an easie matter to swim in a warme bath, every weakling, every impotent body can do that; but he that can hold up his head in a dangerous sea . . . , that is the triall of a mans strength and life." *The Way to be Content. A Sermon Appointed for the Crosse* (1635).

Aug. 31 Gyles Fleming, preacher at Waddingworth, Lincs. An eloquent plea for the repair and restoration of St. Paul's. "Magnificence, and splendor, hath always beene the fittest way in those places, to express the brightnesse of his glory that is served in them: yet is it now deemed a disgrace and dishonour to him, to be served with any decency at all." *Magnificence Exemplified . . . In a Sermon appointed to be Preached at St. Pauls-Crosse* (1634).

1635

Aug. 23 James Conyers, minister of Stratford-Bow, Middlesex. Upon the power of Christ's sacrifice, and the magnitude of God's love to us, while our love to Him is cold, in its expression through our prayers and our purses. He ventured, none too successfully, upon certain analogies from natural history, to show the "innative virtue" of redemption by blood. *Christs Love, and Saints Sacrifice. Preached in a Sermon at St. Pauls Crosse* (1635).

Dec. 20 John Gore, Rector of Wenden-lofts, Essex. An Advent sermon, on the meaning, author, efficacy, and application of God's grace. "Witt and wisdome, knowledge and Learning, all these are the candles of the Lord, and are purposely given us to light us up heavenward; but if wee take Gods candles and hold them downward, turne them the wrong way, and apply and abuse them to sinne: it is much to bee feared, the light of God will goe out." *The Oracle of God. A Sermon appointed for the Crosse* (1636).

1636

July 17 Thomas Drant, of Shaston, Dorset. Upon the unblemished purity and fairness, the unfailing virtue, and the ubiquity of the Divine presence, with comment by the way upon the evils of the times. "We had rather be Rabbies than Saints"; there are many who would rend the peace of the Church and "warre for the aerie projections of their giddied heads." *The Divine Lanthorne: or, A Sermon preached in S. Pauls Church appointed for the Cross* (1637).

1637

JAN. 8   [Obadiah?] Whitbie, perhaps the Rector of St. Nicholas Olaves. (*STC* lists the sermon as by G. *Whittbie*; St. Paul's Cathedral Library copy has on title-page, O. W., expanded *Obadiah Whitbie*). A sermon preached on the cessation of the plague, with a sharp reproof of those who would lead true Christians into schism, for example, "the seditious man, who sowed his tares by night, his Pamphlet in your streets [the margin informs us that "The newes Carryer of Ipswich" is meant]." As God has punished us for our oaths and our imperfect faith, so by our repentance we may turn away his wrath from us again. To this end, the preacher found in his text "a pebble, to throw against the brow of the Gyant Despaire."
Londons Returne, After the decrease of the Sicknes (1637).

EASTER WEEK   John Lynch, Rector of Harrietsham, Kent. (*Ath. Oxon.*, II, 384.)

MAY 21   William Watts, Rector of St. Alban's Woodstreet. In a discourse plentifully studded with patristic references, he commended true penitence for sin, and cried out upon the pursy times. Anxious that his hearers should be "mortified" at any price, he concluded: "If this Sermon of mine hath mortified the Auditory: it is the properer for the Theme. Perhaps it hath done that by tediousnesse: which it could not do by persuasion."   *Mortification Apostolicall. Delivered in a Sermon in Saint Pauls Church, upon Summons received for the Crosse* (1637).

1638

SEPT. 23   John Gore, preacher at St. Peter's Cornhill. Of the fear and reverence due to God. Devotion should be doubled in time of plague, and now in England is "scarce an house where there is not one sicke." The Lord is "that gracious Master of Requests" who never puts off any supplicant.
The God of Heaven. A Sermon appointed for the Crosse (1638).

1640

MARCH 27   Henry King, Dean of Rochester. The accession sermon. Princes receive their sceptres from God, not from pope or people. Monarchy is "the Archetype, the first and best patterne of all others." Presbytery and popery alike diminish the power of kings. The King is just; the Church of England orthodox, and not fallen to popery; the Prayer Book is essentially that approved by Calvin himself. The King is virtuous and temperate, and a great builder: witness the Royal Navy and the repairs to St. Paul's.   *A Sermon preached at St. Pauls March 27, 1640* (1640).

1641

OCT. 10   Thomas Cheshire, curate at Yarmouth, "an orthodox minister." He brooded sadly over the fantastic and irregular sectaries then flourishing. "Coblers and Weavers, and Felt-mongers . . . take upon them to interpret Gods Word." "A fellow" in a gray suit goes up and down London preaching that the Old Testament is no more use than an old almanac. "In one Church they have pulled downe the Kings Crowne, because it had a Crosse upon it." And, "not many daies since, comming in Saint Sepulchres Church . . . , I saw a woman dandling and dancing her child upon the Lords Holy Table; when she was gone, I . . . saw a greate deale of water upon the Table; I verely think they were not teares of devotion, it was well it was no worse." These things must needs provoke God's heavy displeasure. *A True Copy of that Sermon Which was preached at St. Paul's the tenth day of October last (1641).

—— Mark Frank, Fellow of Pembroke, Cambridge. His text (Jer. 35:18-19) a text of obedience, never more needed. "A little of that, well practised, would make us understand one another, set us all together again." "Authority used to be a logical argument to guide cur reason: and have we lost our logic too, as well as our obedience? The consent of wise, grave, learned fathers . . . with any man not too high in his own conceit, is certainly of a value somewhat above his private imagination." You have hearkened, he warned his audience, to "ignorant and malicious teachers, who have exercised more tyranny upon your consciences, than the most clamorous can prove ever bishop did." (Sermons, Oxford, 1848, II, 413-44.)

1642

MARCH 27 Richard Gardiner, Canon of Christ Church, Oxford. The accession sermon. "The Drift of the Discourse," he said, "is to cement together affectionate obedience in the People, and cheerefull protection in the Soveraigne." It is by the king that we move in our prcper sphere; otherwise we should be all "hudled up in an unjust parity, and the Land over-runne with inflexible generations." The king's prerogative should not be immoderately extended, however, and the king must not be exempt from the rule of law. As for images in churches, they are merely "Historicall Commemorations." He closed with a fervent prayer for unity. *A Sermon Appointed for Saint Paules Crosse (1642).

UNDATED SERMONS TEMP. CHARLES I

1620's John Grent, Vicar of Ashton, Warwickshire. We live in the time of God's mercies, but should not forget his judgments. London may see her face in "Tyres looking glasse." "Dreame not of secure possessing the Fortunate Islands, nor of being begirt with the Sea, and hemmd in with watry walles from all danger; Think not by heaping togeather thicke clay, and therewith building your nest on high; you shall escape wrath and judgement to come." He attacked usury and "church-robbing," though he admitted that "buying and selling are the nerves and sinewes of a kingdome, exercises not misbeseeming the Saints of God." *The Burthen of Tyre. A Sermon Preach'd at Paul's Crosse (1627).

ca. 1637　John Hales, of Eton. An easy and graceful discourse, commending tolerance of erring Christians. The Christian must be gentle with the weak and querulous, though compassion should be bounded by discretion. "Nothing there is that hath more prejudiced the cause of Religion, then this promiscuous and careless admission of all sorts to the hearing and handling of Controversies." He extolled the moderation of the Church of England, even in her relations with Rome. "Had they not been stickling in our state business, and meddling with our Princes Crown, there had not a drop of their bloud fallen to the ground." (*Golden Remains of . . . Mr. John Hales* (1673), pp. 24-55.)

ante 1640　Arthur Lake, Bishop of Bath and Wells. Our faith rests upon God's word, which we receive from the church. "It is too true, that many take too great liberty against those sober bounds which are set them by our Church; every Parish Church almost having their private Catechisme of private draught, not of ecclesiastical prescript." *Ten Sermons upon Severall Occasions* (1640).

ante 1640　John Stoughton, Rector of St. Mary Aldermanbury. A sermon memorable for a panegyric upon divine love, "this Royall Affection, the Soule of Learning, the Grace of Liberalitie," macrocosm and microcosm of theological virtues, to be discovered in "the secret proportions in Nature." *XV. Choice Sermons, Preached upon Selected Occasions* (1640).

ante 1643　Richard Stuart, Dean of St. Paul's and Provost of Eton. A sober defence of the Church established, against recusants and separatists, who give offence to their brethren. "Our Christian liberty consists rather in that we know, then in what we do. If we be firmly resolved, that such things are indifferent, our Freedome remaines untoucht, although for our outward act, we be either ruled by Decency, or else awed by Scandall." *Three Sermons Preached By the Reverend, and Learned, Dr. Richard Stuart* (1658).

INDEX OF NAMES

Notices in the Register of sermons preached at Paul's Cross are indicated by figures in italic type.

ABBOT, GEORGE, 92, 104
Abbot, Robert, 225
Adams, Thomas, 90, 97, 106–7, 117, 121–3, 126–7, 135, 137, 138, 141, 145, 148, 156, 164, 233, 234, 237, 245, 246
Alington, Sir Giles, 17–18, 252
Anderson, Anthony, 212
Andrews, John, 242
Andrewes, Lancelot, 67, 94, 107, 127, 146, 155, 160, 173
Ascham, Roger, 67, 70
Ashton, Abdy, 82, 85
Askew, Anne, 37–8
Aylesbury, Thomas, 243, 249
Aylmer, John, 11–12, 13, 141, 212–13

BABINGTON, GERVASE, 75, 217
Bacon, Francis, 15, 72, 88, 101, 211, 241
Balcanquhall, Walter, 240
Baldwin, [William?], 204
Bale, John, 35, 66
Bancroft, Richard, 14, 63, 73–4, 81–3, 87, 94, 105, 164, 169, 216, 221
Barker, Lawrence, 222
Barlow, Ralph, 223
Barlow, William, Bp. of Rochester, 10, 14, 80, 83–6, 88–9, 97–8, 146, 180, 219, 221, 226–7
Barlow, William, Bp. of St. David's, 40, 192, 201
Barnes, Robert, 23, 32–3, 36, 188, 189
Barry, George, 228–9
Barton, Elizabeth, 24–5, 51
Baughe, Thomas, 234–5
Baxter, Richard, 145
Bayly, Lewis, 242
Beaumont, Robert, 206
Becon, Thomas, 18, 35–6, 190, 206
Bedford, Thomas, 242
Bedingfield, Robert, 247
Benson, George, 8, 93, 97, 124, 230
Bentham, Thomas, 201, 202
Bernard, Richard, 125, 149, 153
Bickley, Thomas, 63, 208
Bill, William, 55, 56, 193, 200
Bilson, Thomas, 132, 219
Bisse, James, 70–1, 126, 127, 212

Blackal, ——, 208
Blackwood, Robert, 142
Boleyn, Anne, 24, 28, 190
Bolton, John, 207
Bolton, Robert, 247–8
Bonner, Edmund, 38, 44, 49, 52, 194, 196, 197
Boughen, Edward, 111–12, 251
Bourne, Gilbert, 8, 49–50, 196, 198
Bourne, Immanuel, 157, 238, 239
Boys, John, 81, 97, 117, 221, 235
Bradford, John, 8, 49–50, 196
Bradley, William, 204
Bridges, John, 51, 59, 73, 148, 164, 207, 214
Bromyard, John, 87, 135
Brooks, James, 51, 196
Brookes, Matthew, 249
Browne, George, 24, 26, 185
Buckridge, Thomas, 218
Buggs, Samuel, 103, 156, 242
Burgess, John, 169, 239
Burleigh, Lord, see Cecil, William, Lord Burleigh
Burton, Robert, 121, 138, 142
B[ush], E[dward], 62, 208
Byrde, John, 188

CADDY, LAWRENCE, 67, 213
Calfield, James, 202
Calvin, John, 12, 33, 73
Cannon, Nathaniel, 136, 234
Cartwright, Thomas, 12, 60, 62, 73, 208, 209
Cary, George, 206
Caston, Stephen, 46, 194
Cecil, Robert, Earl of Salisbury, 14, 81–6, 89, 221
Cecil, William, Lord Burleigh, 14, 46, 48–9, 55–6, 63–4, 200, 204, 205, 206
Chaderton, Lawrence, 78, 123, 147, 149, 211
Chafin, Thomas, 241
Chamberlain, John, 104–5, 106, 109, 136
Champneys, John, 48, 193
Chapman, Thomas, 13
Chardon, John, 214
Charles I, 101–6, 111–15, passim
Cheaste, Thomas, 229, 232–3
Chedsey, William, 53, 196, 198, 199
Cheshire, Thomas, 114, 254–5

258   INDEX

Christopherson, John, 55, *200*
Clarke, Thomas, 218
Claydon, [John?], 103, *244*
Closse, George, *214-15*
Clough, William, 15
Coates, George, *198*
Cole, Thomas, 205
Collins, Samuel, 92-3, *228*
Conyers, James, 161-2, *253*
Cooper, Thomas, 62, 64, *208*, *215*
Copcot, John, 73, *214*
Courtenay, William, 6
Cottisford, [Thomas?], *194*
Coverdale, Miles, 23, 173, 191, *193*, *201*, *202*, *204*
Cox, Richard, 44, 61, *193*, 200, *202*, *206*, *207*
Crakanthorpe, Richard, 94, 96, 154, *230*
Cranmer, Thomas, 14, 25, 34, 38, 42, 44, 54, 57, 184, *185*, 187, *189*, 193, 194, 195
Crashaw, William, 91, 138, *229*
Craven, Isaac, 171, *251-2*
Crick, Richard, 14, 63-4, *208*
Croft, Elizabeth, 51-2, 197
Crome, Edward, 35, 36-7, 39, 179, *189*, *191*
Cromwell, Thomas, 14, 26, 27, 28, 30, 32, 184, 185, 186, 187
Crowley, Robert, 56, 169, *201*, *203*
Cuffe, Henry, 82
Curteys, Richard, 66, 67, *210*

DAWES, LANCELOT, 120, *231*
Dawson, [Ralph?], *223*
Dene, [Nicholas?], *223*
Denison, John, *248*
Denison, Stephen, 16, 108, 141, *240*, *250*
Devereux, Robert, Earl of Essex, 10, 14, 76, 80-6, 180, 219, 221
Donne, Daniel, 94, *243*
Donne, John, 98, 99, 104-5, 107-8, 111, 125, 146-7, 169, 180, *238*, *244*, *245*, *250*, *251*
Dove, John, 8, 80, 120, 135, 161, *218*, *219*, *221-2*
Dove, Thomas, 82, 83, 85
Downame, George, 93-4, *229*
Drant, Thomas, 18, *253*
Draxe, Thomas, *233*
Drope, John, 14-15, *238-9*
Dudley, John, Duke of Northumberland, 46
Dudley, Robert, Earl of Leicester, 59, 74, 205
Duport, John, 69-70, *217*
Dyos, John, 65-6, 78, 146, *211*
Dyos, Lawrence, 11-12, *212*

EACHARD, JOHN, 147, 156-7
Earle, John, 143, 148

Elizabeth I, 54-87 *passim*
Essex, Earl of, *see* Devereux, Robert, Earl of Essex
Everard, John, 102, *239*, *242*

FAIRFAX, THOMAS, *209*
Farley, Henry, 3, 177
Farmer, Richard, 111, *250-1*
Fawkner, Antony, *249*
Feckenham, John, 38, 40, *191*, *196*, *198*, *199*, *200*
Felltham, Owen, 142
Fenner, Dudley, 73, *214*
Fenton, Roger, *223*
Ferrar, Robert, *193*
Fish, Simon, 23
Fisher, John, 22-3, 24, 26
Fisher, William, 12, 67, 69, 134, 148, *212*, *217*
Fitzralph, Richard, 5
Fleming, Gyles, *253*
Fletcher, Richard, *219*
Ford, William, 42
Forest, Friar, 28, 187
Fotherby, Martin, 118, 149, *228*
Foxe, John, 22, 33, 35, 44, 50, 52, 58-9, 66, 151, *206-7*, *210*
Frank, Mark, 114-15, 164, *255*
Frith, Mary ("Moll Cutpurse"), 17, 233
Fuller, Thomas, 15, 50, 130

GARDINER, RICHARD, 18, 115, *255*
Gardiner, Samuel, 148, *226*, *232*
Gardiner, Stephen, 7, 10, 32-3, 38, 43-4, 46, 52-3, 77, 169, *188*, *189*, *193*, *197*, *198*
Garret, Thomas, 34, 36, *189*
Gee, John, 107, *247*
Geoffrey, Richard, *226*
Gifford, George, *217*
Glasier, Hugh, 40, *192*, *198*
Goodwin, Thomas, 150-1
Gore, John, *252*, *253*, *254*
Gosson, Stephen, 71-2, 75-6, 80, 126, 139, 141, 169, *219*, *220*
Gravet, William, 66, *215*
Greenwood, Henry, *236*
Grent, John, *255*
Grindal, Edmund, 16, 56, 58, *201*, *202*, *204*, *205*
Guest, Edmund, 59, *205*
Gumbledon, John, *250*

HACKET, ROGER, 71, 75, *217*
Hales, John, 8, 113, 172, 174, *256*
Hall, Joseph, 91, 148, 169, *229*, *230*, *234*
Hampton, William, *249*

Harding, Thomas, 58, 173, 205
Harpsfield, Nicholas, 52, *197, 198, 199*
Harris, Robert, *243*
Harrydaunce, John, 35, *188*
Harsnett, Samuel, *213–14*
Harvey, Gabriel, 144, 216–17
Harvey, Richard, 212–13
Hayward, John, 82, *221, 222, 225–6*
Haywood(?), John, *190*
Heath, Nicholas, *191*
Hemmings, ———, *226*
Henry VIII, 20–39 passim
Henry, Prince of Wales, 118, 137, 234, 235, 237
Herbert, Lord Edward, 30–1
Herbert, George, 150, 155
Hetherington, John, 16, *250*
Hieron, Samuel, 145–6, 149–50
Higgons, Theophilus, 90–1, *232*
Hill, Adam, 66, 75, 80, 87, 121, 127, 141, *218*
Hilsey, John, 26, 30–1, 35, *185, 187, 188*
Hilton, John, *214*
Holbrooke, William, 95, 147, 153, *232*
Holdsworth, Richard, *245*
Holland, Thomas, 68, 99, 116–17, 151, 158–9, *220–1, 223*
Holyday, Barten, 117, 146, 169, *245, 247*
Hooker, Richard, 12, 55, 57, 67, 73, 79, 87, 110, 170, 171, 174, *212*
Hooper, John, 44, *194*
Horne, Robert, 17, 61, 200, *201, 204, 207*
Hoskins, John, 9, 90, 91–2, 124, 136, 137, 140, 141, *235–6, 248*
Howard, Sir Robert, 17, *247*
Howson, John, 76–7, 79, 92, 122, 130–1, 132–3, 165, 171, *220*
Hudson, John, 66, 73, 151, *213*
Hugget, Anthony, *237*
Hull, William, 118, *233–4*
Humphrey, Laurence, 59, *205*
Huntington, John, *201*
Hutton, Matthew, *203, 206*

JACKSON, THOMAS, *230*
Jackson, William, *237*
James I, 88–106 passim
James, William, 74, 124, *216*
Jerome, William, 33–4, 36, *188*
Jewel, John, 57, 58–9, 60–1, 150–1, 163, 169, 170, 172–3, *201, 202, 203, 205, 206, 207, 224*
Johnson, Robert, 93, 143, 155, *231*
Jones, Inigo, 101
Jones, John, 118, 171, *251*
Jonson, Ben, 140, 182
Joseph, [John], *193*

KEMPE, THOMAS, 4, 6
King, Henry, 106, 107, 108, 114, 147, *239, 242–3, 254*
King, John, 3, 4, 7, 79, 98–9, 101, 106, 130, 146–7, 151–2, *223, 241*
Knewstub, John, 78, *209*
Knight, John, 109
Knollys, Sir Francis, 74
Kyrkham, [Thomas], 43, *194*

LAKE, ARTHUR, *226, 256*
Latimer, Hugh, 6, 26–7, 29, 31, 36, 39–40, 44, 48, 87, 123, 124, 128–9, 131, 141, 148, 160, 164, *186, 187, 192, 195*
Laud, William, 13, 18, 60, 92, 101, 107, 110, 112–13, 114, 170, *246, 252*
Lawrence, John, *246*
Lee, Edward, 29, *187*
Lee, Rowland, 28, 39
Leicester, Earl of, *see* Dudley, Robert, Earl of Leicester
Lever, Thomas, 40, 44–5, 125, 128, 129, 131, 141, 145, *194, 195*
Lewes, Richard, 75, *225*
Ley, Roger, 96, 121, *240, 242*
Loe, William, 161, *231*
Longland, John, *185*
Louthe, John, 7
Luther, Martin, 21, 22–3, 33, 42
Lyly, John, 75, 217
Lynch, John, *254*

MACBRAY, JOHN, 56, *201*
Machyn, Henry, 7, 17, 50, 56–7, 202, 203
Mallet, Francis, *185*
Manningham, John, 66, 144
Marbury, Francis, 8, 79, *222*
Marlowe, Christopher, 80
Mary I, 45–6, 49–54 passim
Matthews, ———, *209*
Milles, Robert, *233*
Milton, John, 110, 117, 173, 174
Milward, John, *226, 227*
"Moll Cutpurse", *see* Frith, Mary
Montaigne, George, 8, 13, 18, *243*
Morwen, John, *199*
Mosse, Miles, 13–14, 145, *234*
Myriell, Thomas, *232, 245*

NASHE, THOMAS, 75, 79–80, 213, 216–17
Northburgh, Michael de, 5
Northumberland, Duke of, *see* Dudley, John, Duke of Northumberland
Nowell, Alexander, 57, *202, 203, 204, 205, 206, 215*

OLDCASTLE, SIR JOHN, 20, 190
Overton, William, 206
Oxenbridge, John, 206

PARAEUS, DAVID, 18, 109, 243
Parker, Matthew, 14, 39, 55, 59–60, 171, *187*, *193*, *195*, *200*, 205, 206
Parker, Roger, 94, *227*
Pelling, John, 14, *228*
Pemberton, William, *235*
Pendleton, Henry, 51, 197
Penry, John, 74
Perkins, William, 125, 147, 151
Peryn, William, *199*
Petley, Elias, *245*
Philip II, 10, 51, 52–3, 71, 198
Piers, John, 71, *216*
Pilkington, James, 58, *203*, *204*
Playfere, Thomas, 146, 162, *218*
Pole, Reginald, Cardinal, 52–3, 198, 199
Pownall, [Israel?], *216*
Price, Daniel, 96, 121, 134, *227–8*, *230*
Price, Gabriel, *237*
Price, Henry, *225*
Price, Sampson, 90, 95, *235*, *237*
Proctor, William, 120, *246*
Purchas, Samuel, 100–1, 161, 169, *244*

RAINOLDS, JOHN, 74
Ralegh, Sir Walter, 80, 102, 132
Ratcliffe, ("de Grayes Inn"), 12
Ratcliffe, ——, *233*
Ravis, Thomas, *227*
Rawlinson, John, 160, *235*
Renham, William de, 5
Renniger, Michael, *203*
Richardine, Robert, *187*
Richardson, Charles, 123, 126, *236*, *238*, *239*
Richardson, John, Vice-Chancellor of Cambridge, 106, 221
Richardson, John (of Magdalen College, Oxford), *245*
Ridley, Nicholas, 40, 43, 46, *192*, *194*, *195*
Robinson, John, *252*
Robinson, Nicholas, *203*
Rogers, John, *195*, *196*
Rudd, John, 178, *184*, *197*
Russell, Thomas, 12, 177

SALCOT, JOHN, 24, *186*
Salisbury, Earl of, *see* Cecil, Robert, Earl of Salisbury
Sampson, Thomas, 9, 56, 59, 199, *200*, *202*, *204*, *205*
Sanders, Matthew, *222*

Sanderson, Robert, 109–11, 120, 138, 169, *247*, *250*, *252*
Sandwich, William, 39, *187*
Sandys, Edwin, 14, 61, 63–4, 69, 130, 136, *201*, *202*, *207*, *209*, *210*, *215*, *224*
Scambler, Edmund, *202*, *206*
Sclater, William, *231*
Scory, John, *201*, *202*
Scott, Cuthbert, *190*, *200*
Selden, John, 33, 108, 157, 174
Seton, Alexander, 34, *189*, *190*
Seymour, Edward, Duke of Somerset, 7, 43–4, 46, 53, 193
Shakespeare, William, 84
Shaxton, Nicholas, 26, 31, 38, *186*, *191*
Sheldon, Richard, 103–4, *244*
Sibthorpe, Robert, 8, 94, 137, 138, *239–40*
Singleton, Isaac, 15, *241*
Singleton, Robert, 36, *186*, *190*
Skinner, Ralph, *203*
Smith, Henry, 164, *225*
Smith, Richard, 34, 43, *189*, *192*
Somerset, Duke of, *see* Seymour, Edward, Duke of Somerset
Sonnibank, Charles, *238*
Spark, Robert, 139, *211*
Spenser, Edmund, 4, 100, 174
Spenser, John, 164, 171, *222*
"Stephen, Sir", 41, *194*
Stock, Richard, 90, 95, *224*, *227*
Stockwood, John, 7, 67, 87, 119, 123, 130, 139, *210–11*
Stokesley, John, 23, 25–6, *184*, *185*
Stoughton, John, 160–1, 162, *256*
Stow, John, 9, 41, 206
Stuart, Richard, *256*
Stubbs, John, 69, *211*
Sutton, Thomas, 90, 95–6, 130, 158, *234*, *236*
Sydenham, Humphrey, 142–3, *243*, *246*
Symons, [Simon?], *185*, *186*

TANNER, JOHN, *219*
Taylor, Jeremy, 98, 160, 162, 174
Taylor, Thomas, *217*
Tedder, William, 68, *216*
Temple, Robert, 75, 78, 119, 133, *218*
Thompson, Thomas, *248*
Tolson, ——, *223*
Tolwyn, William, 34, 190
Tunstall, Cuthbert, 21, 23, 26, 27, *185*, *188*, *197*
Turnbull, Richard, *224–5*
Turner, William, 169, *201*
Tyndale, William, 22, 23, 191
Tynley, Robert, 90, *229*
Tyrrell, Anthony, 68, *216*

V., R., *246*
Valentine, Henry, 108, 119, *249-50*
Vaughan, Richard, 98, *226*
Veron, John, 17, 56, 57, *201*, *202*, *203*
Vittels, Christopher, 48, 78

W., A., 12, 78, *218*
Wake, Arthur, 14, 63-4, *208*, *209*
Wakeman, Robert, 144, *222*
Walkington, Thomas, *241*
Waller, William, *250*
Walsal, John, 72-3, 123, 139, *211*
Walton, Izaak, 12, *212*
Ward, Samuel, 96, 126, 138, *238*
Warde, Robert, 16, 35, 190
Warham, William, 24
Watson, Thomas, 50, 56, *196*, *200*
Watts, William, *254*
Webbe, George, *231*
Weston, Hugh, 51, *196*
Whalley, John, *236*
Wheatlie, William, *229-30*
Whitbie, [Obadiah?], *254*

White, Francis, 146, *240*
White, John, Bp. of Winchester, 56, *197*, *199*, 200
White, John, chaplain to James I, 99-100, 119, 137, 164, *236*
White, Thomas, 68, 71, 75, 79, 134, 139, 141, *210*, *216*
Whitgift, John, 62-3, 73, 171, *208*, *213*
Wigmore, Michael, *240*, *241*
Wilkins, John, 154-5
Wilkinson, Robert, 117, *228*
Wilson, [John?], 15, 105-6, *245*
Wilson, [Nicholas?], 34, *189*
Wimbledon, Richard, 144
Wisdom, Robert, 35-6, 189, 190, *202*
Wolsey, Thomas, Cardinal, 22
Worship, William, 90, 91, 96, 137, 148, *237*
Wright, Abraham, 153
Wright, Henry, *206*
Wymmesley, John, 52, *197*

YOUNG, JOHN, Vice-Chancellor of Cambridge, *199*
Young, John, Bp. of Rochester, *206*

www.ingramcontent.com/pod-product-compliance
Lightning Source LLC
Chambersburg PA
CBHW071153070526
44584CB00019B/2768